HOME PLANNERS'

Style Portfolio

335 HOME PLANS YOU CAN BUILD

HOME PLANNERS, INC.
3275 WEST INA ROAD, SUITE 110, TUCSON, ARIZONA 85741

Table of Contents

Published by Home Planners, Inc., 3275 West Ina Road, Suite 110, Tucson, AZ 85741. All designs and illustrative material
Copyright © MCMLXXXIX by Home Planners, Inc. All rights reserved. Reproduction in any manner or form not
permitted. Printed in the United States of America. International Standard Book Number (ISBN): 0-918894-79-4.

Style Guide

The Right Stuff on Housing Styles

Like many of us, people in the housing industry sometime have trouble with names. When they're describing exterior appearance, the same two experts may well describe the same house in wildly different ways. What gives?

Housing *type* usually isn't a problem. Even journalists can tell the difference between a one-story, 1½-story, two-story, and split-level or split-entry home. *Style* is the nemesis, the term nearly everybody has trouble putting a name to, including many otherwise knowledgeable individuals.

The general definition is easy enough. Style refers to the exterior arrangement of structural features and architectural details. Unfortunately, few pros agree on what to call individual designs, and, worse, when a name isn't handy (and hundreds are available), many people just make one up. Real estate agents, most of

whom couldn't tell a Cape Cod from Cape Canaveral, are especially good at this, but so are architects, developers, and builders. Architectural historians are another matter. They're very precise and categorical, two big advantages in the academic world. However, many don't know when to quit. They pepper their work with such terms as Neo and Eclectic and Revival so frequently that your basic Tudor ends up sounding more like an ivory tower than a house and home.

We've got another idea. The guide beginning on the next page defines eight popular present-day styles: Tudor, Cape Cod, Spanish, Georgian, French, Early Colonial, Contemporary, and Victorian. Some aren't names college professors would use, and some are late 20th-century adaptations of designs that are hundreds of years old. Yet each describes a style: a set of structural characteristics and decorative details that adds up to an immediately recognizable look.

Design T172971 is gloriously Victorian. See page 313.

Cape Cod Style: Small Houses with Big Impact

MULTIPLE ADDITIONS

Cape Cod Style lives in America's heart. It evokes memories—some of them mythic—of gentler, less complicated times when simple means and simple, cheery houses were the norm.

But Capes wouldn't live on as a popular style if they didn't cater to everyday needs. From the viewpoint of countless families on the grow, Cape Cods were and are small homes with lots of promise—flexible and easily expandable. The house shown here, for instance, would seem enormous to 17th-century New Englanders, but they'd recognize it as a cousin to the tiniest one-room colonial dwelling. Minus the garage and shorter sections to the left and right of the middle, this is a classic Cape Cod facade, with central entrance and two double-hung windows on either side.

The ancient boxy shape has proved over the years to be an outstanding architectural building block. Just as colonists put up rooms, or "bays," to the left and right, so have 20th-century homeowners, adding extra bedrooms, master bedrooms, family rooms, and garages, all as need required and pocketbook allowed. Similarly, the half story above, traditionally unfinished, was inexpensive found space, the right spot for another bedroom and bath.

See Design T172615, page 30.

Small is beautiful and has been for centuries. The delightful Cape Cod cottage, cute and quaint, started life as a down-to-earth shelter for the Pilgrims and became, over the years, an American synonym for starting out, for the promise of a full future. Young families moved into their bright white suburban Capes, added to them, remodeled them, then moved up and out, replaced by other young families with similar plans. Easy to build and maintain, inexpensive to heat, and just right for remodeling, the Cape Cod was America's most popular housing style during the first half of the 20th century. In fact, it came to represent the typical 1½-story home and today remains an attractive starter style, second home, and retirement retreat.

Style points

The Cape Cod Americans have grown to know and love has several identifiable characteristics.

● Basic box. Like other housing styles that date to the colonial era, Cape Cods are very straightforward. The one shown here is a simple box with a large kitchen to the rear (see floor plans on page 32). Their very simplicity, however, makes them splendid candidates for additions and full-scale remodeling projects (see accompanying story).

● One and a half stories. The earliest Capes were one-story houses but quickly developed into the definitive 1½-story type. Traditionally, bedrooms were on the first floor, with the half story representing found space for growing families in need of an extra bedroom and bath. Modern Capes generally have at least one bed and bath up.

● Steeply pitched, side-gabled roof. Gables are triangular parts of a wall formed by the intersection of two pitched roof planes. (In the illustration shown here, the visible gable end contains a double-hung window and a rectangular gable vent.) Like this one, most Cape Cods have gables facing the side, fairly steep roofs, and undecorated eaves that link them to their colonial forebears. However, un-

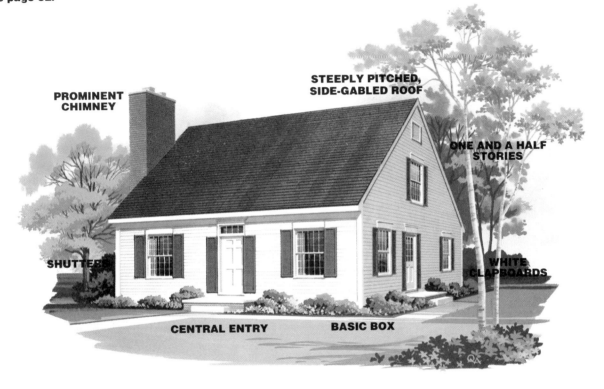

Design T172852 is a fresh-faced Cape with a large country kitchen. See page 32.

PROMINENT CHIMNEY

STEEPLY PITCHED, SIDE-GABLED ROOF

ONE AND A HALF STORIES

SHUTTERS

WHITE CLAPBOARDS

CENTRAL ENTRY

BASIC BOX

like this house, many Capes also display two or more front-facing dormers set into the roof.
● Central entry. Plenty of Capes don't have central entries, but most of the

---

For years, the Cape has been an ideal style—handsome, homey, and eminently adaptable.

---

smaller examples do. Contemporary Cape Cods often borrow details from Georgian-style doors (see page 9). This one, for instance, boasts six-panel wood construction and transom lights (panes of glass above the door).

● White clapboards. Horizontal clapboards are a solid part of the colonial tradition, and white boards, shingles, or brick typified Capes built during the '40s and '50s. Today, builders use a variety of materials and colors.
● Shutters. Exterior shutters weren't part of 17th-century Capes, but by the end of the 18th century, they had become regular additions and have remained so to this day. Cape Cod shutters always match the length of the window, which is typically a double-hung.
● Prominent chimney. Original New England Cape Cods faced the world with a low-slung central chimney that connected to a large heat-giving fireplace within. Some present-day versions do the same, but they're just as likely to show off end chimneys similar to this eye-catching red-brick stack.

"Many Cape Cods were ingeniously constructed so they could be partially built, then expanded when the family grew larger. The half Cape Cod was the 'honey moon cottage.' The three-quarter Cape Cod was the answer when children arrived, and the full Cape Cod was used for the large family. . ."

Source: "American Shelter," The Overlook Press.

5

Tudor Style: Houses with an English Accent

The reassuring face of Tudor style has been a familiar part of American housing for nearly a century. Ironically, though it carries the name, Tudor style bears little architectural relationship to English homes built during the Tudor monarchy (late 15th and early 16th centuries). Instead, Tudor style draws on a number of medieval English models, ranging from small country cottages to expansive manor houses.

The first Tudor residences in the United States were landmark estates designed for the monied class. With the development of masonry veneering after World War I, however, the style became wildly popular. Even the humblest suburban homes began to show off the steep gables, masonry exteriors, and decorative half-timbering so characteristic of Tudor design.

Though its original popularity had waned by the late '30s, Tudor style has made a big comeback in the '70s and '80s. Contemporary adaptations, now among the most sought after of new homes, continue to borrow from old English precedents, while echoing American Tudors built earlier in the century.

Style points

Tudor may be today's most readily identifiable housing style. Even beginning home planners can pick out a few of its benchmark features.
● Side-gabled roof. Mimicking medieval houses, many early Tudor homes had steeply pitched side-gabled roofs.

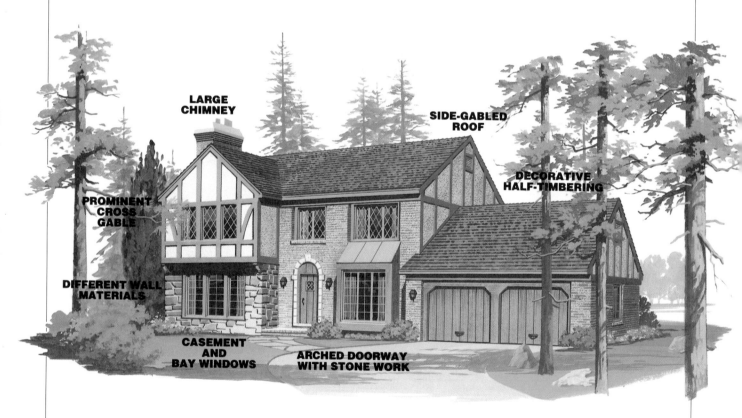

LARGE CHIMNEY

SIDE-GABLED ROOF

DECORATIVE HALF-TIMBERING

PROMINENT CROSS GABLE

DIFFERENT WALL MATERIALS

CASEMENT AND BAY WINDOWS

ARCHED DOORWAY WITH STONE WORK

Economical to build, this Tudor displays the form's fine high style. See page 57, Design T172800.

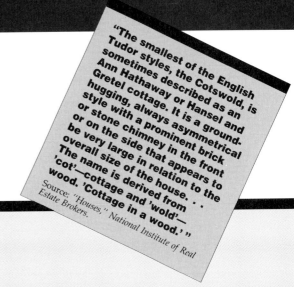
side-gabled roofs. (Gables are the triangular wall parts formed by the intersection of two roof surfaces. The house shown here has a vent near the top of one side-facing gable.) Tudor adaptations employ less steeply pitched gables; a few rely on hipped roofs instead.

• Prominent cross gable. This design features a large front-facing gable "crossing" the side-gabled roof. Most Tudors have at least one cross gable, and many have two or three. Noticeable overhangs also help to identify the style.

• Large chimney. Mammoth, highly decorated chimneys were common

---

The name doesn't say it all, but the recognizable face of Tudor housing certainly does.

---

sights on early Tudor houses, and designs in the '80s often include a sizable chimney made of patterned brick or stone work and topped off by a chimney pot or two (see accompanying story).

• Different wall materials. Various combinations of stone, brick, and stucco are signal traits of Tudor style.

• Casement and bay windows. Generally, Tudors have casement windows, some tall and narrow and grouped in strings of three or more; double-hungs and diamond-shaped panes are also typical. Bay windows, like the one shown here, frequently grace the front facade.

• Arched doorway with stone work. The semi-circular doorway was so common on early Tudor houses that it came to be known as the "Tudor arch." Though it still makes an occasional appearance, it's less prevalent on contemporary Tudors, as are tabs of stone cut into the surrounding brick work.

• Decorative half-timbering. Probably the most widely recognized feature of Tudor style, decorative, or false, half-timbering is found on most modern adaptations (see accompanying story).

TRUE MARKS OF DISTINCTION

Two features go a long way toward defining today's Tudor style: a large, frequently elaborated chimney and decorative half-timbering.

As they did earlier in the century, Tudor chimneys stand out. The one illustrated here is a good example. It has four clear elements of the style: great height, prominent location, sculpted brick and stone work, and multiple chimney pots, each representing a flue inside.

Oddly enough, the truest sign of contemporary Tudor style is actually a false signal. Early colonial houses, like their medieval predecessors, had massive hewn-and-pegged frames made of large timbers. Artisans filled the spaces between timbers with brick nogging or wattle (bound-up twigs) and daub (clay). English yeomen left it at that, creating the effect known as half-timbering, but in America's harsher climate, colonists in New England sheathed the structure in clapboards. Early in the 20th century, architects, designers, and builders included half-timbering in the new Tudor style, filling in with stucco, brick, or both. This time, though, the timbers were decorative only (as they are in the 1980s), set between the masonry exterior panels of a modern balloon or platform frame.

See Design T172356, page 59.

Georgian Style: the Handsome Presence of America's Past

First popular nearly 300 years ago, Georgian style is a survivor, the serene architecture of a confident people. Introduced to the American colonies during the fateful reigns of the four King Georges (hence, the name), Georgian style was a glorious testament to the new-found prosperity of a growing middle class. It was a disciplined, highly symmetrical, geometrically precise design—the essence of architectural order. Today's Georgian adaptations retain the same simple self-assured soul: dignified balance and pleasant proportions.

Style points

What makes a Georgian Georgian?
• Symmetrical facade. This is the hallmark of Georgian style: a neat, precise alignment—the architectural term is "ranking"—of windows and entry door. Traditionally, five-ranked designs were most common, and windows never appeared directly next to each other (as they often do in modern Colonial-style adaptations).

• Massive chimney or chimneys. In one respect, fireplaces were to colonial America what furnaces are to life in the late 20th century. They warmed things up. Most original Georgians had at least one mammoth fireplace and chimney; many had more. Paired end chimneys were common features.
• Dentils. To professionals, cornices are decorative moldings that project from the top of an interior or exterior wall. Characteristically, Georgian cornices featured design elements called dentils, toothy decorations at the juncture of roof and wall. Contemporary adaptations often display the same look.
• Belt course. Early Georgian houses in New England were often post-and-beam structures covered with clapboard siding, but many later Georgians throughout the colonies had solid brick walls; today exterior brick is a veneer only, covering sheathing, insulation, and a wooden frame. On the other hand, brick versions both past and present often look alike in at least one noticeable

"Mirroring the civilizing changes in American society since the first breaching of the wilderness, the new [Georgian] dwellings were well proportioned, composed for formal effect, and embellished with robust ornament . . . Most significantly, the spread and success of the new style were clear signals that America would no longer be satisfied with second-class status."

Source: "A Field Guide to American Architecture," New American Library.

MASSIVE CHIMNEYS

PEDIMENTED DORMERS

MULTI-PANE, DOUBLE-HUNG WINDOWS

DENTILS

SHUTTERS

BELT COURSE

SYMMETRICAL FACADE

LINTELS AND WINDOWSILLS

Boasting more than 3,400 square feet of living space, elegant Design T172192 appears on page 97.

way. Colonial artisans frequently added a pronounced change in the masonry pattern (belt course) where first floor met second, cinching the middle in the process. Today's architects follow their lead.

• Pedimented dormers. Pediments are decorative crowns that sit firmly atop doors and windows. Dormers are vertically set windows placed on a sloping roof. Unbroken triangular pediments like the ones shown here are common signatures of Georgian style.

• Multi-pane, double-hung windows. These are also telltale indicators. Nine panes, or lights, of glass in both

---

The best Georgian design is a synonym for architectural symmetry.

---

upper and lower sashes were routine configurations during the colonial era, as were six-over-nine, eight-over-twelve, and nine-over-six.

• Lintels and windowsills. Masonry elaborations over and under windows—lintels and sills, respectively— appear on many Georgian houses, where they're typically straightforward and uncomplicated. Simple changes in the direction of brickwork are the norm.

• Shutters. The popular perception is that exterior shutters were part of every colonial dwelling, but the reality was different. Most Georgian houses didn't include them, though builders incorporated shutters with increasing frequency during the early days of the American republic, a time when Federal-style architecture dominated new construction in the United States.

• Doors. For most of the 17th century, colonial doors were little more than boards arranged vertically and nailed together. Georgian doors were another story altogether. They became legitimate entryways, often paneled and typically decorated with pilasters, crowns, and a combination of small windows in, alongside, and above the door (see accompanying story).

GRAND OPENING STATEMENTS

Seventeenth-century colonists—the settlers of Jamestown, Plymouth, Williamsburg, and Boston—were down-to-earth people. To survive in an alien land, they had to be. Their houses were small, unadorned boxes, and the doors leading into them weren't stylistic statements' they were practical matters: thick boards held together with horizontal strips called battens (board-and-batten) and hung in simple frames.

In a sense, Georgian doors were America's coming-out party. They were symbols of progress, of a prospering people who were making their way and were here to stay. They were the face of a changing land.

Of course, they were also just doors, and today's Georgian adaptations have many of the same restrained, tasteful features. Paneled wood, elaborate crowns, and decorative pilasters (flattened columns) are characteristic of Georgian styling, as are small rectangular panes, or lights, of glass placed in the door or displayed in a transom above (transom lights). Broken and unbroken triangular pediments, sidelights, fanlights, and entry porches are also common features of contemporary Georgian architecture.

Spanish Style: Outside Has Always Been In

> "The close to 100-year usuage of the Spanish idiom has remained to this day as a remarkably alive architectural language. . . Over the decades, the Hispanic theme of tile, stucco walls, and arches has effectively evoked that human quality labeled 'charm,' a quality that has seldom been realized in the many images of the modern in this century."
>
> Source: "Home Sweet Home," Rizzoli International Publications.

Sun-drenched design. Design T172143 has two patios, three balconies, and an entrance courtyard. See page 142.

This style has a sunny disposition. Long popular in parts of California, Florida, and the Southwest, Spanish designs are an attractive amalgamation of traditional Mediterranean characteristics, architectural effects that blossomed on Spanish-style houses during the 1920s and '30s, and contemporary adaptations. Nearly all share an earthy, robust look and feel, complete with low-slung, asymmetrical facades; arches and archways; white stucco walls; red roofs; and wood windows and doors. What's more, Spanish style features a bonanza of outdoor living areas, including patios, courtyards, balconies, and terraces.

Style points

Spanish-style houses have an informal, easy-to-like familiarity.

● Low-pitched roof. No single roof shape typifies Spanish housing. Gabled, hipped, and flat roofs are all common; many homes feature combinations, like the hipped-and-gabled version shown here. (Gabled roofs always have two connecting surfaces; hipped roofs, four.) On the other hand, among the hipped, gabled, and combination varieties, low-pitched roofs predominate.

● Asymmetrical facade. Traditionally, Spanish houses were one story, but today, multi-level and two-story homes are not unusual. Regardless of type, unbalanced facades characterize the style.

● Red tile roof. Almost a visual benchmark, today it's more likely to be made of light composition materials, rather than heavy clay. Tiles come in two basic shapes: Mis-

DECORATIVE CHIMNEY TOPS

RED TILE ROOF

LOW-PITCHED ROOF

WOOD-PANELED DOORS

BALCONIES

STUCCO WALLS

WINDOW GRILLES

OUTDOOR LIVING AREAS

WROUGHT IRON

ASYMMETRICAL FACADE

ARCHES

sion (half cylinders) and Spanish (S-curves).

• Stucco walls. Another mark of distinction, they're ordinarily white or, less often, pale buff or rose.

• Arches. Nearly as ubiquitous as white stucco and red tile, arches and archways frequently appear on Spanish-style houses. Arcades—multiple arches supported by columns or piers—often surround outdoor living areas. The one illustrated here encloses a large entrance courtyard.

Bringing indoors and out together is Spanish style's brightest feature.

• Wrought iron and window grilles. Two more indicators of high-style Spanish design. Made of either black wrought iron or wood, window grilles come in a wide variety of shapes. Wrought-iron archways like these are also common.

• Heavy, wood-paneled doors. Spanish villas built for moguls earlier in the century featured wonderfully dramatic entryways—magnificently carved doors elaborated with spiral columns, pilasters (flattened columns), decorative stone work, or patterned tiles. Contemporary entries are less complicated but usually retain the massive wood-paneled door or doors so typical of Spanish architecture.

• Decorative chimney tops. Like their traditional English-style cousins, Spanish chimneys are prime spots for decorations. To magnify the effect, some are even topped with small tile roofs.

• Balconies. They come in a range of shapes, sizes, and materials. Like the two shown here, many have wood balustrades.

• Outdoor living areas. Signal features of Spanish style, patios, court yards, terraces, and arcaded walkways are prime parts of many contemporary designs (see accompanying story).

WHERE OUTDOOR LIVING IS EASY

An ancient amalgam of Spanish style, outdoor living space is a prized feature today. Few designs integrate indoors and outdoors so efficiently and effortlessly. And few provide so many variations. Patios, courtyards, arcades, terraces, fountains, gardens, and balconies—both interior and exterior—have long complemented high-style Spanish homes.

The one-story design illustrated here is a prime example. Side steps lead to an expansive arcaded entrance court, highlighted by a central fountain. To the rear of the house are three additional outdoor spaces, each connected to one or more key rooms inside. A long, narrow covered porch reminiscent of ranch houses in the Southwest links family room, dining room, and living room. A second covered porch leads to one of four bedrooms; two more bedrooms, along with a second bath, look out on the front courtyard (as do kitchen, breakfast nook, and laundry room). Best of all, the master bedroom and bath snuggle comfortably next to their own private terrace out back.

See Design T172335, page 131.

Early Colonial Style: the First Word in Housing

Definition of early colonial life: hard winters, bloodthirsty savages, and log cabins. Does this tell it like it was? Not quite. Snow and cold may have been a problem, but native Americans weren't all that menacing, and settlers in Massachusetts and Virginia certainly didn't live in log cabins, which belonged to the *next* generation of pioneers. When they arrived, colonists relied on familiar building techniques, carried over from England and modified to meet the demands of the New World. Supported by post-and-beam construction, houses were small boxes, either one or two stories high and usually just a single room deep. They had steeply pitched gable or gambrel roofs covered by wood shingles, mammoth central or end chimneys, tiny windows with diamond-shaped panes, board-and-batten doors, and either wood or brick exterior walls. Contemporary recreations of Early Colonial style are, of course, much larger than their cramped predecessors, and most are supported by platform frames, rather than posts and beams. Nevertheless, carefully crafted renditions retain at least some of the exterior features.

Style points

The best examples are attractively simple.

● Basic box. The house illustrated here is palatial by colonial standards, but its floor plans (see page 186) echo 17th-century design: simple rectangles, kitchen centered and to the rear (see accompanying story). The attached garage is a distinctly 20th-century feature.

● Large chimney with decorative top. Most Early Colonial adaptations faithfully employ one or more oversized chimneys. To colonists, immense fireplaces were the only way to keep warm and cook food, and they topped their brick or stone chimney stacks with a multitude of decorative effects. To conserve heat during the harsh winters, central chimneys dominated construction in northern colonies. Conversely, to dissipate the heat of summertime cooking fires, end chimneys were characteristic of houses in the South.

● Overhanging upper story. As they

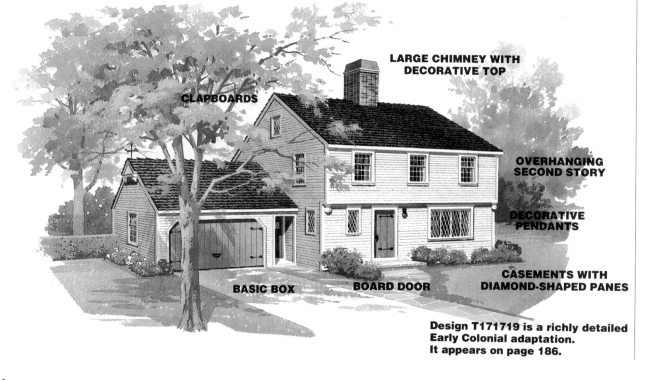

CLAPBOARDS

LARGE CHIMNEY WITH DECORATIVE TOP

OVERHANGING SECOND STORY

DECORATIVE PENDANTS

BASIC BOX

BOARD DOOR

CASEMENTS WITH DIAMOND-SHAPED PANES

Design T171719 is a richly detailed Early Colonial adaptation. It appears on page 186.

did with many other features, 17th-century colonists borrowed an overhang, or jetty, from medieval English building traditions, which often called for an upper floor that projected over the street. Today's real estate agents frequently dub the resulting style a "garrison house," though any colonist would have used the term more precisely to describe a true frontier outpost.

• Clapboards. In New England, wood shingles and boards—clapboards, or weatherboards—covered a massive frame made of timbers. The earliest houses featured vertical boards linked by strips called battens (board-and-batten cladding). However, horizontal clapboards, similar to the ones in the illustration, quickly became the rule in New England. (Solid brick houses were more common in the southern colonies.)

• Casements with diamond-shaped panes. The earliest windows ("wind holes," to provide ventilation) were small rectangles, either fixed or casement versions comprised of tiny diamond-shaped panes held together by lead strips called muntins.

Early Colonial style is a straightforward, immensely appealing design.

Double-hung windows with larger panes of glass, like those shown on the second floor here, were later architectural developments.

• Board door. Throughout most of the 17th century, doors were rigidly utilitarian—heavy planks set vertically in a simple surround and joined by wood battens. Minus its connecting hardware, the front door here is a reasonably good rendition.

• Decorative pendants. Early colonists had little opportunity or motivation to elaborate the exteriors of their homes. High-style jettied examples, though, frequently showed off decorative elaborations at the corners, where jetty and first floor connected. Colonists called them "corner drops," or "pendills."

"Whatever their limitations, and by today's standards there were many, such houses were built by time-tested, widely understood methods, raised by communal effort, and completed with what seems to us an instinctive good sense of proportion and fitness, and unstudied and decided appreciation of form—an understanding of simple beauty that was a by-product of knowing and sound craftsmanship."

Source: "The American Heritage History of Notable American Houses," American Heritage Publishing Co.

THE EARLIEST REMODELING PROJECT

The space race actually started in the 17th century.

Like 20th-century families looking for new room in old homes, early colonists quickly outgrew the first American housing style: a small basic box, one room deep. And like practical do-it-yourselfers in the 1980s, they found and easy and efficient way to gain space: build out back, in this case by constructing a simple lean-to across the rear of the lower story. Presto! Extra room, used initially as storage, then transformed into a full-fledged kitchen.

Later, builders incorporated the change into newly constructed houses, giving them the long, sloping look of a colonial saltbox and providing the characteristic name. Southern colonists, borrowing an old English term, often substituted a wonderfully descriptive alternative—catslide.

By the end of the 17th century, the kitchen was firmly anchored in the newfound space and became, as it is today, the home's center of attention. A huge cooking fireplace, constantly burning, kept the kitchen invitingly warm and helped to create the country's first multi-purpose area: snug dining room, workroom, and gathering point. Today's saltbox styles, like this one, often echo colonial precedents by centering the kitchen, locating it to the rear, and sweeping rooms around it.

See Design T172623, page 159.

Contemporary Style: Simply Magnificent

". . .A nature lover, Wright believed a house should blend with its natural environment. More than that, it should look as though it grows from the ground it is built on. Wright did not speak of architecture so much as he spoke of organic, or living, architecture . . .Wright's houses, even very early ones, have an earth-hugging appearance, with horizontal lines carrying out the lines of the flat prairies."

Source: "American Houses," J.B. Lippincott Co.

By the 1950s, architects began to shape houses that were noticeable departures from traditional American forms. Instead of the usual elaboration and abundance of architectural detail, the results had sleeker lines and fewer exterior features. Most often, they were one-story types. Relying on the pioneering work of Frank Lloyd Wright, Louis Sullivan, Charles and Henry Greene, and other innovative architects earlier in the century, they were designed to blend into the landscape, transforming outdoor spaces into visual and practical extensions of inside rooms.

Dubbed Contemporary style, today's examples come in all types, including one-stories, 1½-stories, two-stories and multi-levels. Flat-roofed and Shed-style Contemporaries (see accompanying story) abound, but the most popular Contemporary is the side-gabled one-story house.

Style points

The best Contemporaries have a distinctive, no-frills flair.

● Low-pitched, side-gabled roof with cross gables. Gables are triangular wall parts formed by the intersection of two roof surfaces. Like the one illustrated here, many Contemporary houses are side gabled, meaning that gables beneath the main roof face to the side. Contemporaries often display one or more gables that run perpendicular to, or "cross," the home's principal gable roof. This house has a single cross gable on the front facade, with another broken gable projecting from it. In addition, unlike the majority of traditional

The clean-lined one-story Contemporary is now an American classic.

styles, most Contemporary homes have low- to moderately-pitched roofs.

● Lack of traditional details. Architecturally detailed windows, doors, roof lines, chimneys, vents, and other

SHED STYLE: GEOMETRY CLASS

Traditionally, staying up on roofs hasn't been a tough job; shapes has remained essentially the same over the years. Gable roofs and hipped roofs have dominated American residential architecture, with flat versions making an occasional appearance. Even the majority of Contemporary houses, which in other ways are so different from traditional styles, typically have gable or flat roofs.

Shed-style Contemporaries, however, represent a clear break from the architectural past. Most rely on multi-directional shed roofs, often combined with one or more gable forms. (A shed roof is a single surface angling downward. The term is short for "watershed.") At first glance, the effect, first popularized in the 1960s by architects like Charles Moore and Robert Venturi, is of massive geometric shapes crashing into each other—visual anarchy. In the hands of skillful designers, though, the look is highly appealing. The house shown here has two shed roofs— one to the left, one in the center over the entryway—linked to two gable roofs on the right. In addition, it displays a pair of details common to Shed-style homes: vertical board siding and smooth, undercorated eaves and cornices.

See Design T172781, page 254.

A spacious one story, Design T172915 has a large kitchen, clutter room, and media room. See page 232.

CROSS GABLE

OVERHANGING EAVES

LOW-PITCHED, SIDE-GABLED ROOF

exterior features were the rule on American residences in the 18th and 19th centuries. Many current styles rely on similar flourishes. Contemporary houses frequently eschew traditional detailing in favor of a less ornamental look.

● Overhanging eaves. Ground-breaking styles developed early in the 20th century by architects like Frank Lloyd Wright typically relied on wide overhanging eaves, which until then had rarely been a part of the residential landscape in the United States. Contemporary designers have used the feature extensively.

● Exposed roof beams. These are common complements drawn from the work of influential architects Charles and Henry Greene, brothers who conceived the so-called Craftsman-style house during the first decade of the 20th century. On some homes, the beams are both decorative and structural; on others, purely decorative.

● Combination of wall materials. Many other styles display more than one exterior cladding, and Contemporary houses are no exception. Various combinations of wood, brick, and stone are typical.

● Integration of indoor and outdoor space. Just as Wright created his Prairie-style houses to link design and landscape, architects of Contemporary homes have long tried to diminish the difference between indoors and out by incorporating large windows, sliding glass doors, skylights, patios, decks, terraces, and the like. The success of this Contemporary thinking, transferred to a variety of other styles as well, has helped transform the ways in which Americans live.

EXPOSED ROOF BEAMS

COMBINATION OF WALL MATERIALS

French Style:
Made for the U.S.A.

THEY'VE GOT HIGH SLOPES

Hipped roofs have been top-of-the-line French features for hundreds of years. The mansard roof, a two-pitched hipped version with a steep lower slope, was the creation of 17th-century French architect Francois Mansart. It became a key part of the ornate, sophisticated Second Empire style that flourished during the middle of the 19th century in France, England, and the United States. ("Second Empire" refers to the French Second Empire of Napoleon III, during whose reign the style first gained prominence.)

After decades of disuse, mansard roofs reappeared on American houses during the early 1960s, rose to new popularity in the '70s, and still appear in the 1980s. There's good reason. Covering them with shingles and other decorative materials, builders have learned that mansards are relatively inexpensive ways to produce dramatic visual effects. More practically, mansard roofs, outfitted with light-giving dormers like those shown here, provide maximum head room for living space in the upper story.

See Design T172249, page 288.

Among the most varied of housing styles, French design has a long and noble history in the United States, incorporating elements from 18th-century frontier settlements, 19th-century Parisian residences, and French-style homes that made graceful appearances in many suburbs during the 1920s and '30s. Out of fashion for a time, French style surged back in the 1970s and is still going strong today. Although they remain architecturally diverse, contemporary French houses typically share several key features, including hipped roofs; brick exteriors; curved windows, doors, and dormers; wings attached to the main house; and a combinations of Georgian-inspired details.

Style points

French style can be explained in easy-to-understand language.
● Hipped roof. Common signatures of French design, hipped roofs (those with four sloping surfaces) have dominated the style for nearly three centuries. Today's versions range from moderately pitched roofs, like the one shown here, to the steeply pitched varieties characteristic of French-style housing in the '20s and '30s.
● Symmetrical facade. Plenty of French homes have unbalanced fronts, and asymmetrical design has been a notable style point for years. Nevertheless, like their early 20th-century antecedents and contem-

Like a fine wine, the French style has aged magnificently.

porary Georgian counterparts, many French-style adaptations display beautiful proportions and fine formal balance.
● Brick exterior. Masonry walls have long been prominent parts of French design. Colonial houses usually had stucco exteriors; brick, stone, or

stucco appeared during the '20s and '30s. Today, brick is the material of choice.

● Quoins. Stone or brick sections used to accentuate the corner of a house, quoins are favorite French details, a treatment also borrowed from Georgian design.

● Arched windows, dormers, and vents. Semi-circular architectural features are another clue to French style. Like the upper two shown here, circle-head windows frequently break through the cornice (the point where roof and wall meet).

● Casement windows, balustrade, and entries. Dual front entries, delicate metal balustrade on the side wall, and full-length casement windows flanking the main entrance all have roots in the earliest French Colonial design. Similar style points are often part of contemporary French houses.

● Dentils. Toothy decorations along the cornice, dentils are another typical refinement. They, too, are reminiscent of 18th-century Georgian style.

"By the late 1960s, the fashions of domestic architecture were shifting back toward styles based on traditional, rather than modern, architectural shapes and detailing. . .The Neo-French style appeared about 1970 and by the early '80s was among the most fashionable throughout the country, reaching a level of popularity never achieved by its pre- 1940. . .forebears."

Source: "A Field Guide to American Houses," Alfred A. Knopf.

Exquisite form marks this 4,000-square-foot French beauty. It is Design T172543 on page 285.

ARCHED ARCHITECTURAL FEATURES

HIPPED ROOF

QUOINS

DENTILS

BALUSTRADE

BRICK EXTERIOR

SYMMETRICAL FACADE

DUAL FRONT ENTRIES

CASEMENT WINDOWS

Victorian Style: New Look For a Great Old Style

Victorian architecture is actually an array of related styles, most characterized by asymmetrical shapes, multiple projections (overhangs, bay windows, wall insets, cantilevers), contrasting materials, and exuberant details. Contemporary adaptations usually rely on a particular style that was immensely popular during the last two decades of the 19th century. Called Queen Anne (after the early 18th-century English monarch), it actually had little to do with the formal, restrained architecture common during her reign. Instead, Victorian Queen Anne houses were an appealing, eclectic mix of architectural features and details. Transported by national magazines and transcontinental railroads, the style enchanted late 19th-century home builders. Today's

versions, among the hottest designs around, retain much of the attractively quirky look and down-home feel of their historical predecessors.

Style points

Details, details, details. Victorian houses are monuments to architectural detail.

● Asymmetrical, two-story facade. Classic Queen Annes were two-story houses that had marvelously diverse, detailed, unbalanced facades. Roof shapes varied considerably. The house illustrated here has a steeply pitched side-gabled roof with a prominent cross gable, a common Victorian type. (Gables are triangular wall sections formed by the intersection of two roof surfaces.)

● Large chimney. Like early English-style houses, Queen Annes often had

"Victorian buildings are perfect symbols of an era which was not given to understatement. They are in complete harmony with the heavy meals, strong drink, elaborate clothes, ornate furnishings, flamboyant art, melodramatic plays, loud music, flowery speeches, and thundering sermons of mid-19th century America."

Source: "The Gingerbread Age," Greenwich House.

FINIAL

LARGE CHIMNEY

GABLE DETAILING

SPINDLEWORK

ONE-STORY PORCH

CONTRASTING WALL MATERIALS

ASYMMETRICAL, TWO-STORY FACADE

Vivaciously Victorian, Design T172970 has over 3,000 square feet of living space. See page 319.

one or more big chimneys, though they were usually tall, rather than massive. Today's adaptations frequently include at least one sizable chimney stack.

• Contrasting wall materials. Colorful, dramatic combinations of different materials and textures were signature traits of 19th-century Queen Annes, and contemporary Victorians often echo the effect. This one has horizontal clapboards and plain shingles.

The fine lines of Victorian architecture are adding a lively look to late-'80s style.

• One-story porch. Spacious porches, always including the entrance and often covering much or all of the front facade, were gracious characteristics of Queen Anne style (see accompanying story). Porches have rebounded in popularity during the '80s, and they've become an endearing feature of contemporary Victorian houses.

• Spindlework. More than half the original Queen Anne homes built in the United States displayed lacy, ornamental, delicately created spindlework (turned wooden elements), similar to the effects created here. Also called "gingerbread," it typically appears in porch balustrades and friezes, in gables, and under wall overhangs left by cutaway bays.

• Windows. Many windows, often with simple surrounds and set in groups of twos and threes, are commonplace on contemporary Victorians.

• Gable detailing. Victorian designers decorated gables with a profusion of architectural effects, including patterned shingles, half-timbers, and sculpted masonry. Decorative trusses like those shown here were also frequent elaborations.

• Finial. Victorians' crowning glory, finials are small ornaments placed at the top of a spire, pinnacle, or, in this case, gable. Echoing the earlier style, they often appear on today's Victorian adaptations. ■

PORCHES AND TOWERS: HIGH VISIBILITY

Porches were the Victorian calling card, the most visible sign of a vibrant style. Dressed in gorgeous spindlework, they appeared in a variety of versions. Full, partial, and entry porches were common, but the elaborate wraparound porch, similar to the seemingly endless one on this contemporary adaptation, was most typical. Second-story porches and pedimented entries also enhanced the Victorian facade.

Round or polygonal towers made of wood frequently graced Queen Anne originals. Some stretched from the ground up to a point above the roof line. Others were cantilevered out at the second floor. Many houses, but especially the high-style examples, had more than one, often topped by finials. Like the one shown here, Queen Anne towers typically appeared at a corner of the front facade, clear signs to passersby of the design's dramatic architectural power.

See Design T172953, page 315.

A Chronology of Colonial Architecture

The chart below represents regions of early America (vertical divisions) and the predominant styles that were found in these regions (horizontal divisions). This period of American architecture clearly reflects climate variables, available building materials, and building technologies of the various regions. However, the inherent charm of these houses is evident in their tendency to echo the ethnic traditions of those who built and lived in them.

It should be noted that while definitive terms are applied to styles and periods, architecture knows no stringent boundaries of time or form. Characteristics of certain styles overlap and repeat in thousands of variations and often adaptations occur, taking the finest points of earlier styles. Much cherished styles can also appear in several time periods. For instance, it is not unusual to find Georgian style homes that were built during what is generally referred to as the Federal period.

A fine modern collection of historic and heritage adaptations can be found in the Portfolio of Homes beginning on page 25.

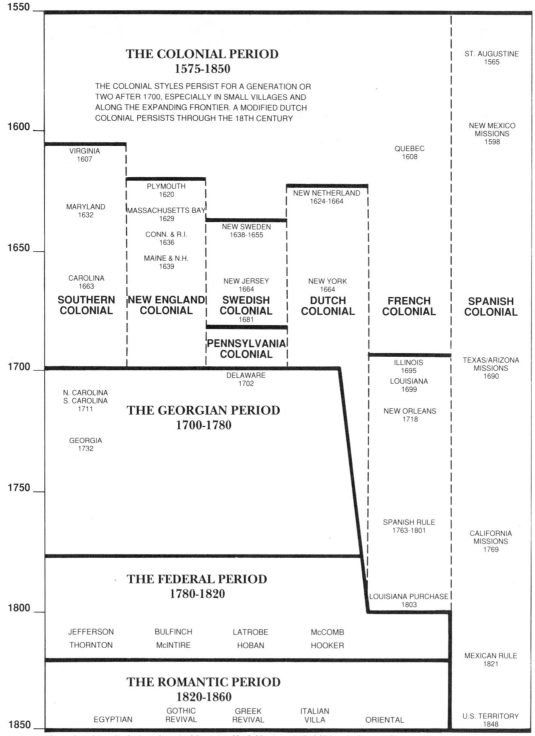

Chart adapted from Early American Architecture, *Hugh Morrison, Oxford University Press, 1952, page 20.*

17th Century Houses

The colonial houses of the 17th Century are noted for an unpretentious simplicity of design. Evolving from Medieval roots, these houses combine clean, vertical lines, simple fenestration (often with dormer windows), steeply pitched or gambrel roofs, massive chimneys, and sometimes an overhung second story.

1640 – Micum McIntyre House
Scotland, ME

1645 – John Clark House
Farmington, CT pg. 181

1652 – Thomas Rolfe House
Jamestown, VA

1660 – George Hyland House
Guilford, CT

1663 – John Quincy Adams House
Quincy, MA

1675 – Jonathan Corwin House
Salem, MA pg. 163

1676 – Paul Revere House
Boston, MA

1682 – Parson Capen House
Topsfield, MA pg. 162

1690 – Shield House
Yorktown, VA pg. 117

The Cape Cod House

can be found in three recognizable types: The half house with two windows to one side of the front door; the three-quarter Cape with two windows to one side of the door and one to the other side; the full Cape with a center door flanked by two windows on each side.

Half House

Three-Quarter Cape

Full Cape

18th Century Houses

Georgian homes, which characterize the 18th Century, are representations of a newly emerging wealth in American society. Perfect symmetry and ornate details are joined by such features as hipped and gambrel roofs, central porticos with elaborate columns, Palladian windows, huge chimneys (often in flanking pairs), and decorative items such as dentils and quoins.

1706 – West House
Yorktown, VA pg. 105

1715 – Anne Bradstreet House
Andover, MA pg. 168

1717 – Brush-Everard House
Williamsburg, VA pg. 184

18th Century Houses (cont'd)

1730 – John Paul Jones House
Portsmouth, NH pg. 183

1730 – Phillip Lightfoot House
Williamsburg, VA

1739 – Mission House
Stockbridge, MA pg. 164

1743 – Mount Vernon
Mount Vernon, VA pg. 100

1745 – Tulip Hill
Anne Arundel County, MD pg. 94

1748 – Thomas Bannister House
Podunk, MA pg. 169

1750 – Nathaniel Hawthorne House
Salem, MA

1750 – Single House
Charleston, SC pg. 97

1750 - Robert Nicolson House
Williamsburg, VA

1752 – Pottsgrove
Pottstown, PA pg. 172

1752 – Joseph Atwood House
Chatham, MA

1752 – Joseph Webb House
Wethersfield, CT

1755 – Gunston Hall
Lorton, VA pg. 116

1755 – Old Poole Cottage
Rockport, MA pg. 28

1758 – Valley Forge
Valley Forge, PA

1760 – Lady Pepperrell House
Kittery Pointe, ME pg. 109

1763 – John Allen House
Nantucket, MA pg. 46

1765 – Whitehall
Anne Arundel County, MD pg. 95

18th Century Houses (cont'd)

1770 – Nathaniel Greene House
Anthony, RI pg. 165

1776 – Pieter Lefferts House
Brooklyn, NY pg. 175

1780 – James Semple House
Williamsburg, VA pg. 119

1781 – Solomon Cowles House
Farmington, CT pg. 98

1790 – Roberts-Vaughan House
Murfreesboro, NC pg. 102

1790 – Julia Wood House
Falmouth, MA pg. 99

1791 – George Read II House
New Castle, DE pg. 106

1794 – Alexander Field House
Longmeadow, MA pg. 118

1799 – William Gibbes House
Charleston, SC pg. 108

19th Century Houses
By the late 1770's, new architectural styles began to emerge. The Federals were the essence of sophistication and dignity, borrowing much from the detailing of Georgian styles. One important introduction was the "Federal doorway" — featuring sidelights and a fanlight. The Romantic styles were highlighted by large porticos and usually featured a classic temple form with stately columns.

1800 – Rose Hill
Lexington, KY pg. 112

1800 – John Jay House
Katonah, NY pg. 161

1805 – Jacob Martin House
Lancaster, PA pg. 173

1807 – Dean Barstow House
Massachusetts pg. 179

1810 – Shotgun House
New Orleans, LA

1818 – Richard Vreeland House
Nordhoff, NJ

1820 – Belle Mina
Belle Mina, AL

1820 – Alexander Bunker House
Nantucket, MA pg. 47

1835 – Asphodel
Jackson, LA pg. 104

Glossary of Architectural Terms

Arcade A row of arches supported by columns.

Arch Curving structure comprised of wedge-shaped blocks, supported at the sides. Examples of types of arches include: semicircular, elliptical, trefoil, and four-centered Tudor.

Baluster A small column or pillar which supports a rail.

Balustrade A series of balusters joined by a rail used for porches and balconies.

Bay Window A projecting window of various shapes, though usually at least three sided.

Beam Ceiling A ceiling that has exposed beams, either real or ornamental.

Belt Course Horizontal band on the outside walls of a building which usually defines interior floor levels.

Casement Window Popular window type with sashes that swing out from the structure.

Clerestory Windows Upper story, usually multi-paned windows.

Cornice A moulded projection that topsoff the part to which it is attached.

Cupola A small domed roof or turret usually built upon the main roof.

Dentil A series of rectangular blocks arranged in a row like a set of teeth.

Dormer A projecting window set in the sloping plane of a roof.

Double Hung Window A window having two sashes which may be opened from the top, the bottom, or both.

Double Portico A two-story porch usually with columns and a pediment.

Dutch Door A door that has two halves — upper and lower — that swing independently of one another.

Eaves The lower edge of the part of the roof which overhangs a wall.

Facade The face of a building.

Fanlight A semicircular window usually found above a door or large set of multi-paned windows.

Fenestration The way in which windows are arranged in a wall.

Finial An ornament fixed to the top of a spire, gable, pediment, roof, or other structure.

French Doors Doors that have large areas of glass, usually multi-paned.

Gable The triangle-shaped part at the edge of a ridged roof.

Gable Roof A roof that slopes on only two sides.

Gambrel A ridged roof having two slopes on each side with the lower slope having the steeper pitch.

Georgian A style that borrows from houses typically found during the reigns of the four King Georges of England.

Glass Sliding Doors Doors with one stationary and one moving panel, both of glass.

Half House Small Cape Cod-style house, characterized by two windows to one side of the front door.

Half-Timbering Ornamentation on walls in which spaces between timber framing have been filled with masonry or other material.

Hearth The floor directly in front of a fireplace and the floor of a fireplace where the fire is built.

Hipped Roof A roof that has four sides, each uniformly pitched.

Lintel The horizontal piece spanning the top of an opening such as a door or window.

Mansard Roof A roof which has two slopes on all four sides.

Masonry Material for building consisting of stone, brick, tile, adobe, or concrete.

Mouldings Bands used as ornamentation for a wall or other surface.

Norman Architecture which derives its style from houses of Eleventh and Twelfth Century England.

Palladian Window Window with a large arched center and rectangular flanking pieces.

Pediment A triangular gable piece which finishes the ends of a sloping roof.

Pent Roof A small roof ledge located between the first and second floors of a house.

Pilaster A rectangular column that projects outward from a wall.

Quoin Decorative pieces of stone or brick at the corners of buildings.

Saltbox Style of house which has a gabled roof with the rear slope much longer than the front.

Three-Quarter House A Cape Cod-style house with two windows on one side of the door and one window on the other.

Transom A small window over a door.

Turret A small round or polygonal tower.

Veranda An open porch with a roof.

Wainscot Paneling in general, or more specifically, paneling which reaches only part way up a wall.

Cape Cod Houses

These delightful 1½-story structures can be found in three easily recognizable types. The half-house features two windows to one side of the door; the three-quarter house has two windows to one side of the door and one window to the other; the full Cape Cod has a centered door flanked by two windows on each side. The following pages show examples and variations of each type.

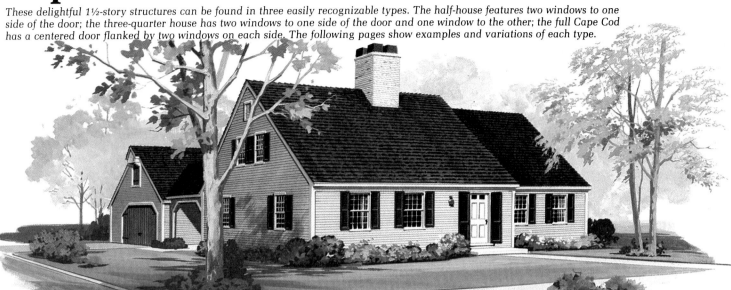

Design T172145 1,182 Sq. Ft. - First Floor
708 Sq. Ft. - Second Floor; 28,303 Cu. Ft.

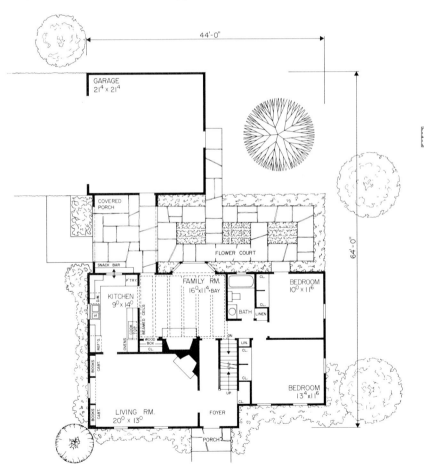

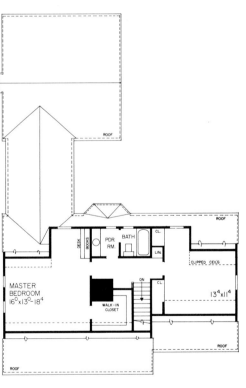

● This authentic adaptation, historically referred to as a "half house", has its roots in the heritage of New England. One of the many features of this house is that it can be developed in stages. Seeing that there are two bedrooms and a full bath on the first floor, the second floor can be developed at a later date for an additional two bedrooms and another full bath. This would double your sleeping capacity. Notice that the overall width of this design is only 44 feet. And, because of its configuration, it is ideal for a corner lot. Observe the covered porch which leads to the garage and the flower court. An in-line version of this plan is Design T172146. It, of course, requires a wider and more spacious piece of property. And, it too, has two fireplaces, one in each living area.

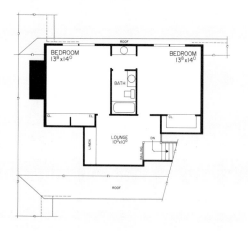

Design T172921 3,215 Sq. Ft. - First Floor
711 Sq. Ft. - Second Floor; 69,991 Cu. Ft.

● This popular traditionally styled house features bay windows, shutters, a fanlight and a cupola on the roof. Interior planning was designed for "empty-nesters," whose children are grown and moved out on their own. Open planning is geared for entertaining and relaxing rather than child-rearing. The major focal point of the interior will be the country kitchen. It has a work island with cook-top and snack bar and a spacious dining area with numerous built-ins. A sun room, 296 sq. ft. and 3,789 cu. ft. not included in the totals above, is in the rear corner of the house, adjacent to the kitchen. Its sloped ceiling and glass walls open this room to the outdoors. Also adjacent to the kitchen, there is a "clutter room". It includes a workshop, laundry, pantry and washroom.

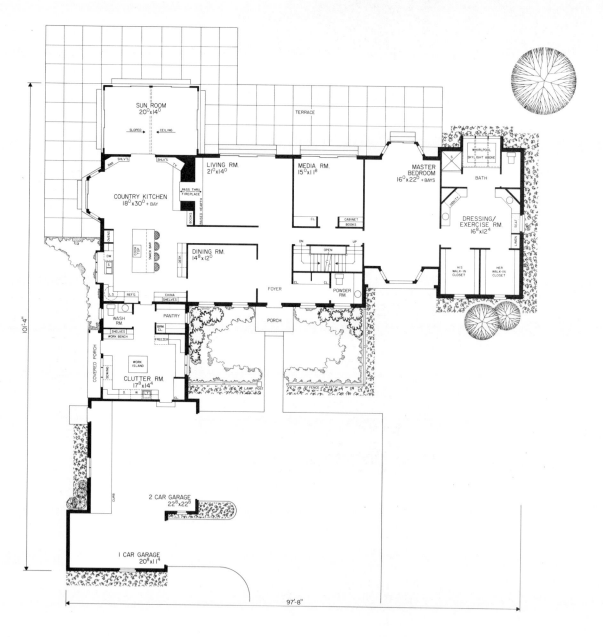

A Trend House for "Empty Nesters"

Design T172661 1,020 Sq. Ft. - First Floor
777 Sq. Ft. - Second Floor; 30,745 Cu. Ft.

● This compact starter house or retirement home houses a very livable plan. An outstanding feature is the large country kitchen. Its fine attractions include a beamed ceiling, raised hearth fireplace, built-in window seat and a door leading to the outdoors. A living room is in the front of the plan and has another fireplace. The second floor houses the sleeping and bath facilities.

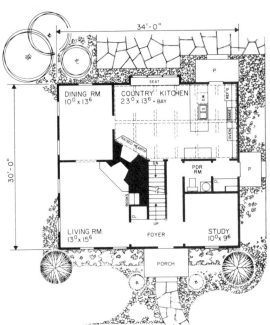

Design T172655 893 Sq. Ft. - First Floor
652 Sq. Ft. - Second Floor; 22,555 Cu. Ft.

● Wonderful things can be enclosed in small packages. This one-and-a-half story design is one of those cases. The total area is a mere 1,545 square feet yet its features are many, indeed. Its exterior appeal is very eye-pleasing with horizontal lines and two second story dormers. Livability will be enjoyed in this plan. The study is ideal for a quiet escape. A powder room is convenient to the kitchen and breakfast room. Two bedrooms and two baths are on the second floor.

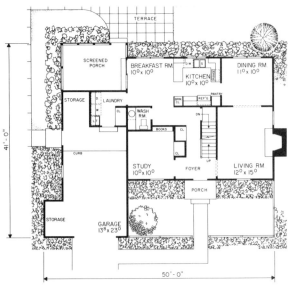

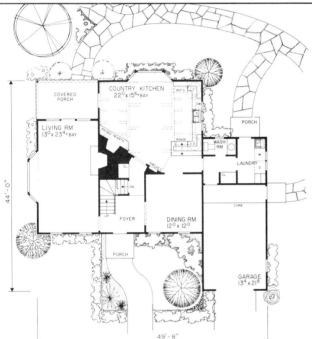

Design T172657
1,217 Sq. Ft. - First Floor
868 Sq. Ft. - Second Floor
33,260 Cu. Ft.

● Deriving its design from the traditional Cape Cod style, this facade features clapboard siding, small-paned windows and a transom-lit entrance flanked by carriage lamps. A central chimney services two fireplaces, one in the country-kitchen and the other in the formal living room. The master suite is to the left of the upstairs landing. A full bathroom services two additional bedrooms.

Design T172615 *2,563 Sq. Ft. - First Floor*
552 Sq. Ft. - Second Floor; 59,513 Cu. Ft.

● The exterior detailing of this design recalls 18th-Century New England architecture. The narrow clapboards and shuttered, multi-paned windows help its detail. Arched entryways forming covered porches lead to the master bedroom and the other to the service entrance. Enter by way of the centered front door and you are greeted into the foyer. Directly to the right is the study or optional bedroom or to the left is the living room. This large formal room features a fireplace and sliding glass doors to the sun-drenched solarium. The beauty of the solarium will be appreciated from two other rooms besides the living room; the master bedroom and the dining room. All of these rooms have sliding glass doors for easy access. The work center will function efficiently. When it comes time for informal living, this design's family room is outstanding. Beamed ceiling and fireplace are only two of its many features. In addition to the first floor master bedroom, there are two bedrooms and a bath upstairs. The detailing that this design offers will be appreciated for a lifetime by every member of the family.

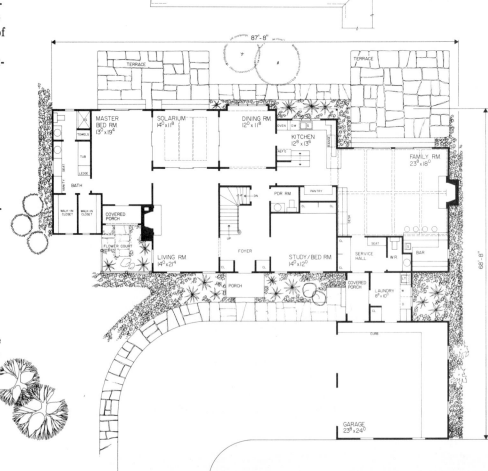

Design T172596 1,489 Sq. Ft. - First Floor
982 Sq. Ft. - Second Floor; 38,800 Cu. Ft.

● Captivating as a New England village! From the weather-vane atop the garage to the covered side entry and paned windows, this home is perfectly detailed. It has lots of living space inside, too. There is an exceptionally large family room which is more than 29' x 13', including the dining area. A raised hearth fireplace and double doors leading to the terrace are in this area. The adjoining kitchen features an island cook-top plus cabinets, a built-in oven and lots of counter space. Attractive and efficient! Steps away is a first floor laundry. Formal rooms, too! The living and dining rooms are both in the front of the plan. Between them is a powder room. It will serve all of the first floor areas. All of the sleeping facilities are on the second floor.

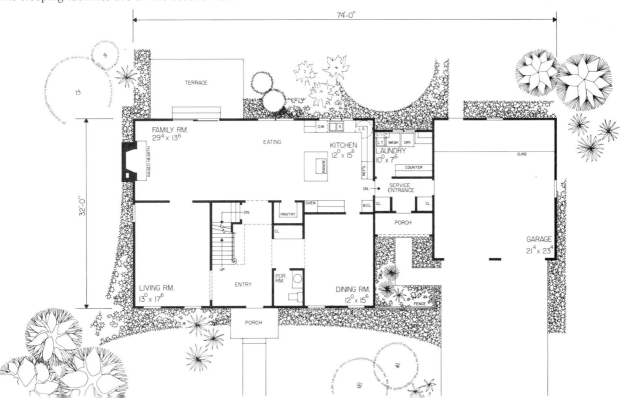

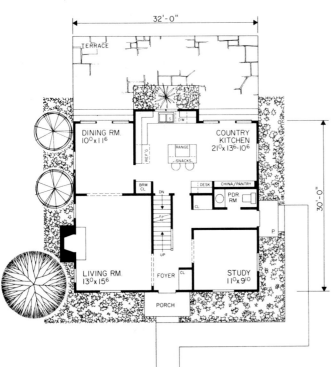

Design T172852 919 Sq. Ft. - First Floor; 535 Sq. Ft. - Second Floor; 24,450 Cu. Ft.

● This charming house will make an excellent first home or retirement retreat. Inside this compact frame is a very livable plan. One of the most outstanding features is the spacious country kitchen. Notice the work island with snack bar and range, desk, and china/pantry storage. Access to the rear terrace can be obtained through the kitchen and dining room doors. Adjacent to the dining room is a large living room. Take note of the fireplace that will bring many hours of pleasure on cold winter evenings. Also, a nice sized study and powder room are on the first floor. Two full baths and two bedrooms are on the second floor of this quaint one-and-a-half story design.

Design T172658

1,218 Sq. Ft. - First Floor
764 Sq. Ft. - Second Floor; 29,690 Cu. Ft.

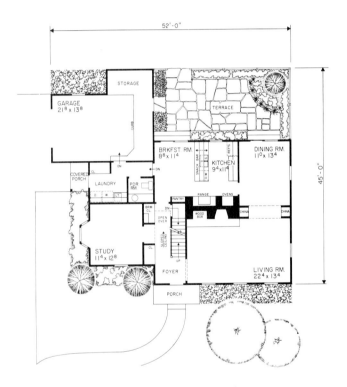

● Traditional charm of yesteryear is exemplified delightfully in this one-and-a-half story home. The garage has been conveniently tucked away in the rear of the house which makes this design ideal for a corner lot. Interior livability has been planned for efficient living. The front living room is large and features a fireplace with wood box. The laundry area is accessible by way of both the garage and a side covered porch. Enter the rear terrace from both eating areas, the formal dining room and the informal breakfast room.

Expanding the Half-House

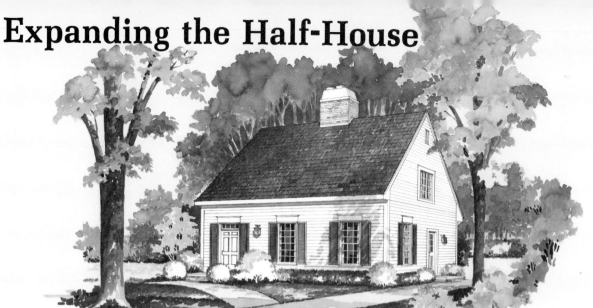

Design T172682 976 Sq. Ft. - First Floor (Basic Plan)
1,230 Sq. Ft. - First Floor (Expanded Plan); 744 Sq. Ft. - Second Floor (Both Plans)
29,355 Cu. Ft. Basic Plan; 35,084 Cu. Ft. Expanded Plan

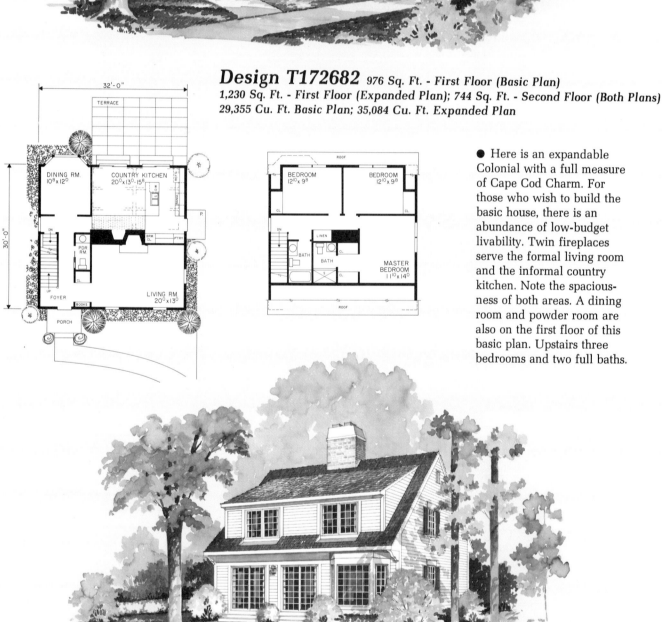

● Here is an expandable Colonial with a full measure of Cape Cod Charm. For those who wish to build the basic house, there is an abundance of low-budget livability. Twin fireplaces serve the formal living room and the informal country kitchen. Note the spaciousness of both areas. A dining room and powder room are also on the first floor of this basic plan. Upstairs three bedrooms and two full baths.

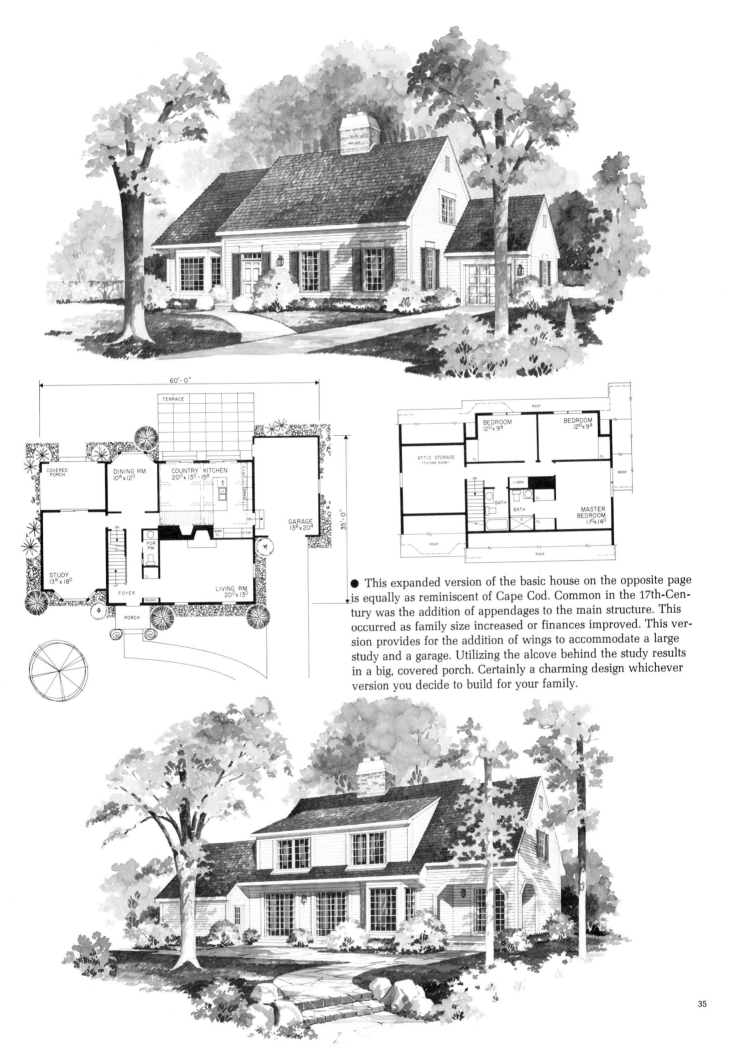

TERRACE

60'-0"

COVERED PORCH

DINING RM
10⁸ x 12⁰

COUNTRY KITCHEN
20⁰ x 13⁰ - 15⁸

GARAGE
13⁸ x 20⁴

35'-0"

STUDY
13⁶ x 18⁰

PDR RM

FOYER

UP

DN

LIVING RM
20⁰ x 13⁰

BOOKS

PORCH

ROOF

BEDROOM
12¹⁰ x 9⁸

BEDROOM
12¹⁰ x 9⁸

ATTIC STORAGE
(FUTURE ROOM)

LINEN

DN

BATH

BATH

MASTER BEDROOM
11⁰ x 14⁰

ROOF

ROOF

ROOF

● This expanded version of the basic house on the opposite page is equally as reminiscent of Cape Cod. Common in the 17th-Century was the addition of appendages to the main structure. This occurred as family size increased or finances improved. This version provides for the addition of wings to accommodate a large study and a garage. Utilizing the alcove behind the study results in a big, covered porch. Certainly a charming design whichever version you decide to build for your family.

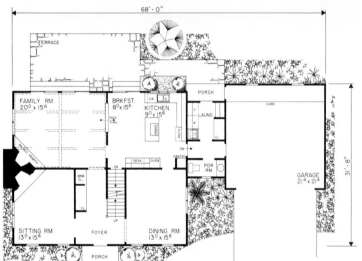

Design T172644
1,349 Sq. Ft. - First Floor
836 Sq. Ft. - Second Floor
36,510 Cu. Ft.

● What a delightful, compact two-story this is! This design has many fine features tucked within its framework. The bowed roofline of this house stems from late 17th-Century architecture.

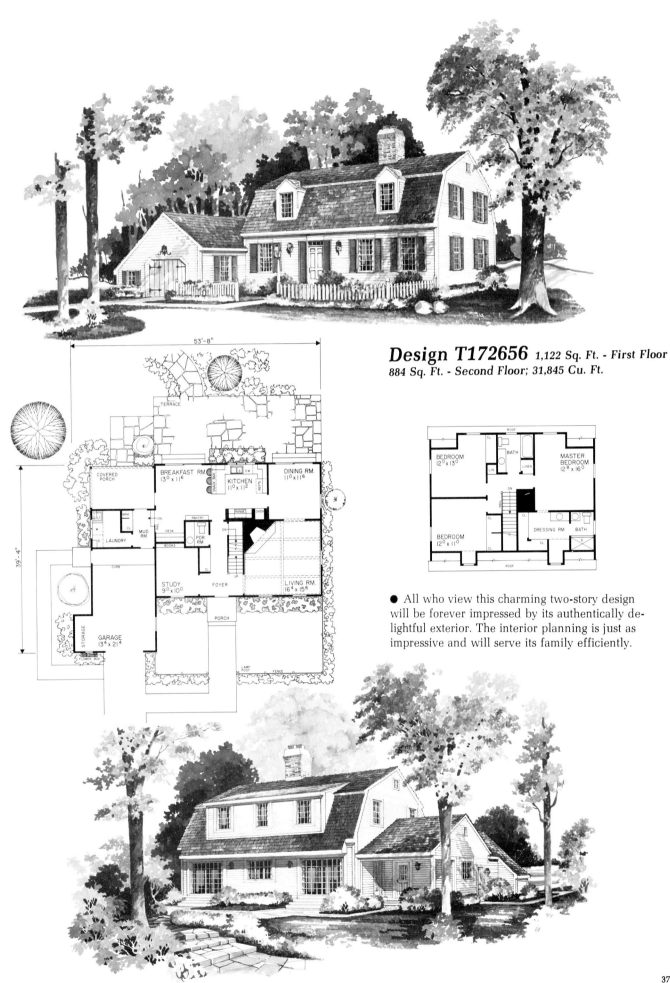

Design T172656 1,122 Sq. Ft. - First Floor
884 Sq. Ft. - Second Floor; 31,845 Cu. Ft.

● All who view this charming two-story design will be forever impressed by its authentically delightful exterior. The interior planning is just as impressive and will serve its family efficiently.

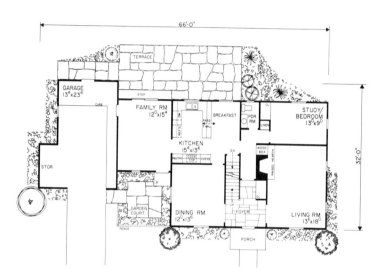

● Colonial charm could hardly be more appealingly captured than it is by this winsome design. List the features and study the living patterns.

Design T171901
1,200 Sq. Ft. - First Floor
744 Sq. Ft. - Second Floor; 27,822 Cu. Ft.

Design T171104
1,396 Sq. Ft. - First Floor
574 Sq. Ft. - Second Floor; 31,554 Cu. Ft.

● Here is a home whose front elevation makes one think of early New England. The frame exterior is highlighted by authentic double-hung windows with charming shutters. The attractive front entrance detail, flanked by the traditional side lites, and the projecting two-car garage with its appealing double doors are more exterior features.

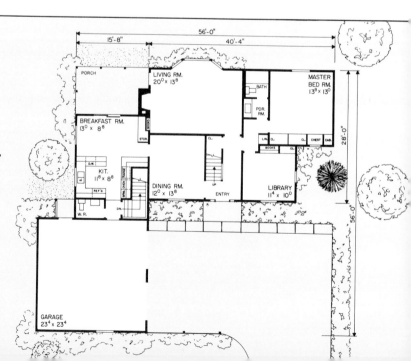

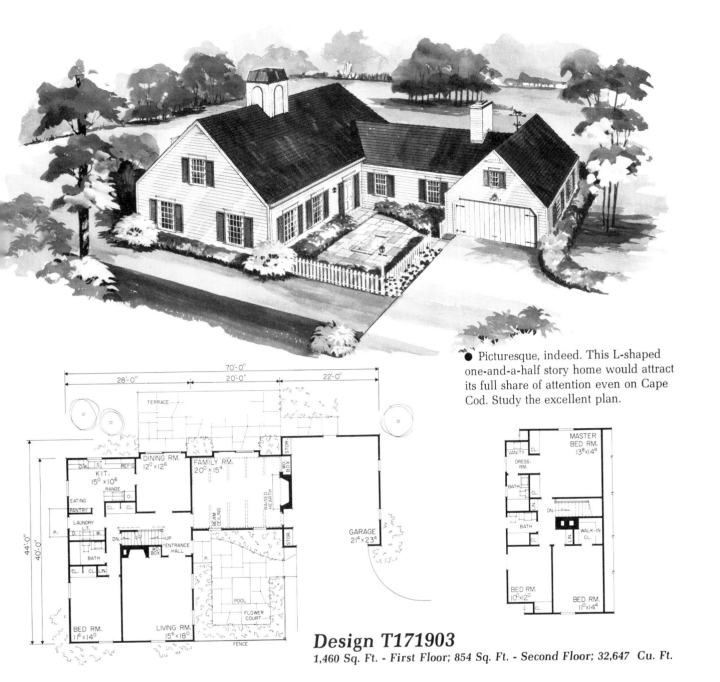

● Picturesque, indeed. This L-shaped one-and-a-half story home would attract its full share of attention even on Cape Cod. Study the excellent plan.

Design T171903

1,460 Sq. Ft. - First Floor; 854 Sq. Ft. - Second Floor; 32,647 Cu. Ft.

Design T172631

1,634 Sq. Ft. - First Floor
1,011 Sq. Ft. - Second Floor; 33,720 Cu. Ft.

● Two fireplaces and much more! Notice how all the rooms are accessible from the main hall. That keeps traffic in each room to a minimum, saving you work by preserving your furnishings. There's more. A large family room featuring a beamed ceiling, a fireplace with built-in wood box and double doors onto the terrace. An exceptional U-shaped kitchen is ready to serve you. It has an adjacent breakfast nook. Built-ins, too . . a desk, storage pantry, oven and range. Plus a first floor laundry close at hand.

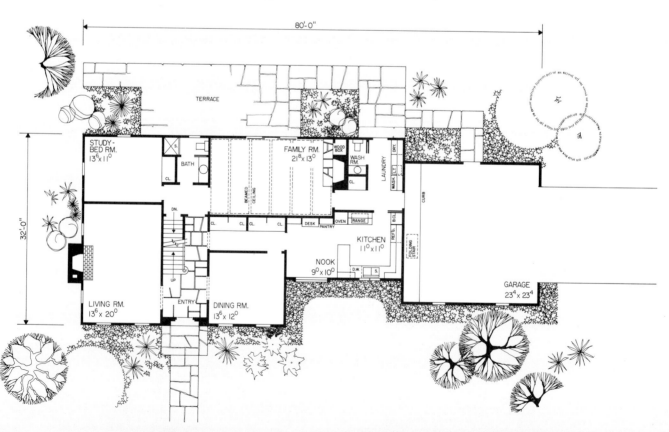

Design T171970
1,664 Sq. Ft. - First Floor
1,116 Sq. Ft. - Second Floor
41,912 Cu. Ft.

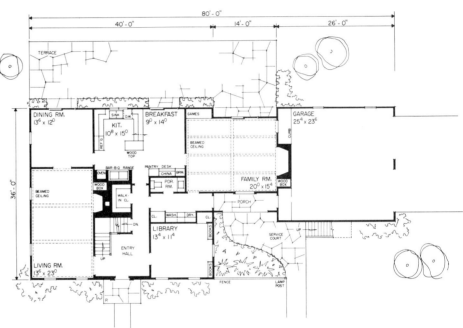

● The prototype of this Colonial house was an integral part of the 18th-Century New England landscape; the updated version is a welcome addition to any suburban scene. The main entry wing, patterned after a classic Cape Cod cottage design, is two stories high but has a pleasing groundhugging look. The steeply pitched roof, triple dormers, and a massive central chimney anchor the house firmly to its site. Entry elevation is symmetrically balanced; doorway, middle dormer, and chimney are in perfect alignment. The one story wing between the main house and the garage is a spacious, beam-ceilinged family room with splay-walled entry porch at the front elevation and sliding glass windows at the rear opening to terrace, which is the full length of the house.

Design T172395

1,481 Sq. Ft. - First Floor
861 Sq. Ft. - Second Floor; 34,487 Cu. Ft.

● You'll have all kinds of fun deciding just how your family will function in this dramatically expanded half-house. There is a lot of attic storage, too. Observe the three-car garage.

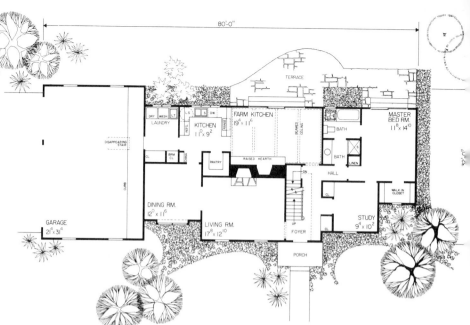

Design T172563

1,500 Sq. Ft. - First Floor
690 Sq. Ft. - Second Floor; 38,243 Cu. Ft.

● New England revisited. The appeal of this type of home is ageless. As for its livability, it will serve its occupants admirably for generations to come. With two bedrooms downstairs, you may want to finish off the second floor at a later date.

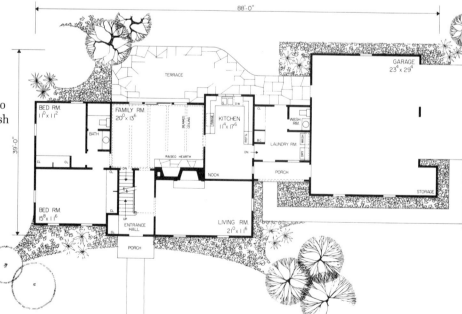

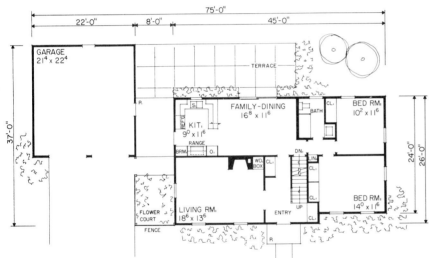

Design T173126 1,141 Sq. Ft. - First Floor
630 Sq. Ft. - Second Floor; 25,533 Cu. Ft.

● This New England adaptation has a lot to offer. There is the U-shaped kitchen, family-dining room, four bedrooms, two full baths, fireplace, covered porch and two-car garage. A delightful addition to any neighborhood.

Design T171718

2,012 Sq. Ft - First Floor
589 Sq. Ft - Second Floor
45,405 Cu. Ft.

MASTER BED RM. $14^0 \times 16^0$

STUDY-LOUNGE $14^0 \times 11^6$

BOOKS

CL. CL.

DRESS. RM.

STORAGE

BATH

DN.

WALK-IN CL.

STORAGE

STOR.

100'-0"

26'-0"   52'-0"   22'-0"

GARAGE $25^4 \times 23^4$

TERRACE

W.R.

CL.   EATING

S.

FAMILY RM. $20^0 \times 13^6$

BATH

BED RM. $14^8 \times 11^6$

D.   W.

LAUNDRY

CL.

KITCHEN $13^6 \times 20^0$

REF.   DW   G.

RAISED HEARTH

BEAMED CEILING

CL.

CL.

LIN.

BRM DESK   P'TRY

CL.   CHINA

RANGE

O.

DN.

CL.

STUDY-BED RM. $10^0 \times 10^0$

P.

DINING RM. $11^8 \times 13^6$

UP

BED RM. $11^4 \times 13^6$

CL.

26'-0"   32'-0"

FENCE

LIVING RM. $20^0 \times 15^0$

ENTRY

P.

● This house has everything - an
extremely attractive exterior and
a fine working, convenient floor
plan. Don't miss upstairs suite.

Design T171902 1,312 Sq. Ft. - First Floor
850 Sq. Ft. - Second Floor; 31,375 Cu. Ft.

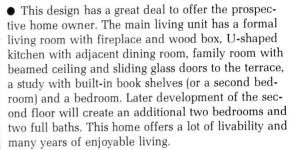

● This design has a great deal to offer the prospective home owner. The main living unit has a formal living room with fireplace and wood box, U-shaped kitchen with adjacent dining room, family room with beamed ceiling and sliding glass doors to the terrace, a study with built-in book shelves (or a second bedroom) and a bedroom. Later development of the second floor will create an additional two bedrooms and two full baths. This home offers a lot of livability and many years of enjoyable living.

Design T171987
1,632 Sq. Ft. - First Floor
980 Sq. Ft. - Second Floor
35,712 Cu. Ft.

● The comforts of home will be endless and enduring when experienced and enjoyed in this Colonial adaptation. What's your favorite feature?

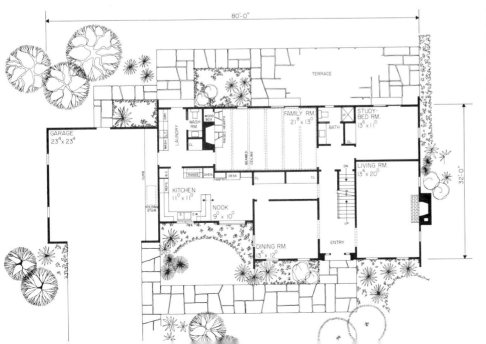

45

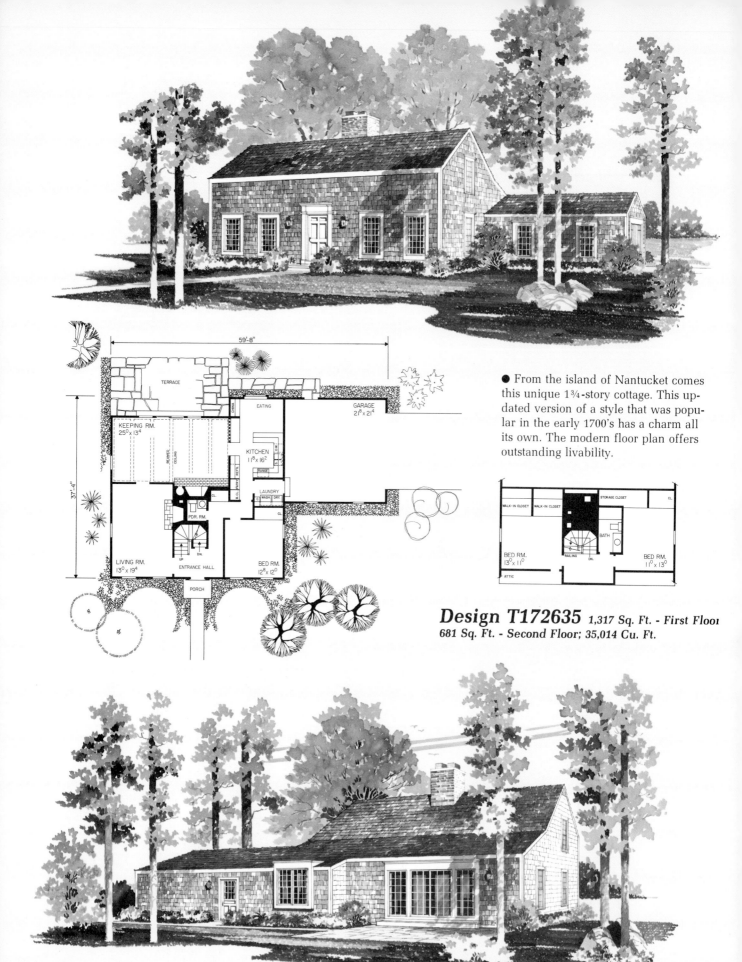

Design labels within floor plans:

59'-8"

TERRACE

EATING

GARAGE
21⁸ x 21⁴

KEEPING RM.
25⁰ x 13⁴

KITCHEN
11⁸ x 16²

RANGE

LAUNDRY
WASH DRY

37'-4"

PDR. RM.

LIVING RM.
13⁰ x 19⁴

BED RM.
12⁸ x 12⁰

ENTRANCE HALL

UP   DN.

PORCH

● From the island of Nantucket comes this unique 1¾-story cottage. This updated version of a style that was popular in the early 1700's has a charm all its own. The modern floor plan offers outstanding livability.

WALK-IN CLOSET   WALK-IN CLOSET   STORAGE CLOSET   CL.

BATH

BED RM.
13⁰ x 11⁰

RAILING   DN.

BED RM.
11⁰ x 13⁰

ATTIC

Design T172635 1,317 Sq. Ft. - First Floor
681 Sq. Ft. - Second Floor; 35,014 Cu. Ft.

● Another 1¾-story home - a type of house favored by many of Cape Cod's early whalers. The compact floor plan will be economical to build and surely an energy saver. An excellent house to finish-off in stages.

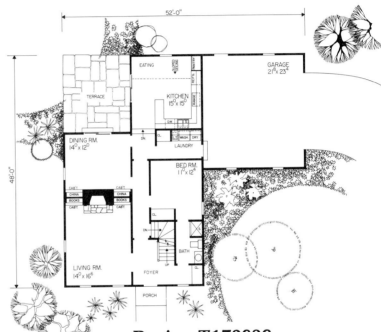

Design T172636 1,211 Sq. Ft. - First Floor
747 Sq. Ft. - Second Floor; 28,681 Cu. Ft.

Design T172569
1,102 Sq. Ft. - First Floor
764 Sq. Ft. - Second Floor; 29,600 Cu. Ft.

● What an enchanting updated version of the popular Cape Cod cottage. There are facilities for both formal and informal living pursuits. Note the spacious family area, the formal dining/living room, the first floor laundry and the efficient kitchen. The second floor houses the three bedrooms and two economically located baths.

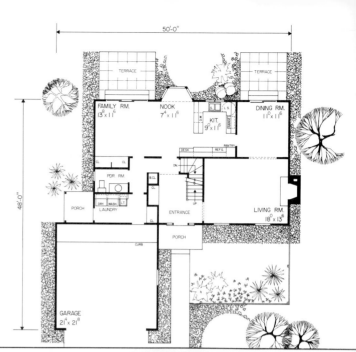

Design T172559
1,388 Sq. Ft. - First Floor
809 Sq. Ft. - Second Floor; 36,400 Cu. Ft.

● Imagine, a 26 foot living room with fireplace, a quiet study with built-in bookshelves and excellent dining facilities. All of this, plus much more, is within an appealing, traditional exterior. Study the rest of this plan and list its numerous features.

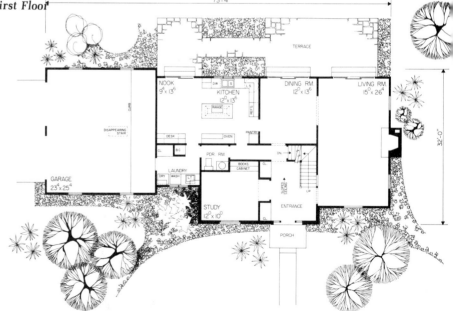

Design T171365 975 Sq. Ft. - First Floor
583 Sq. Ft. - Second Floor; 20,922 Cu. Ft.

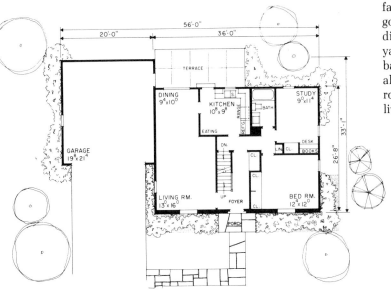

● This cozy, story-and-a-half home will suit a small family nicely. Upon entering this home, you will find a good sized living room. A few steps away is the formal dining area which has an excellent view of the backyard. Adjacent is the nice sized kitchen. A bedroom, bath and a study with a built-in desk and bookshelves also will be found on this floor. There are two bedrooms upstairs and a full bath. This home is big on livability; light on your building budget.

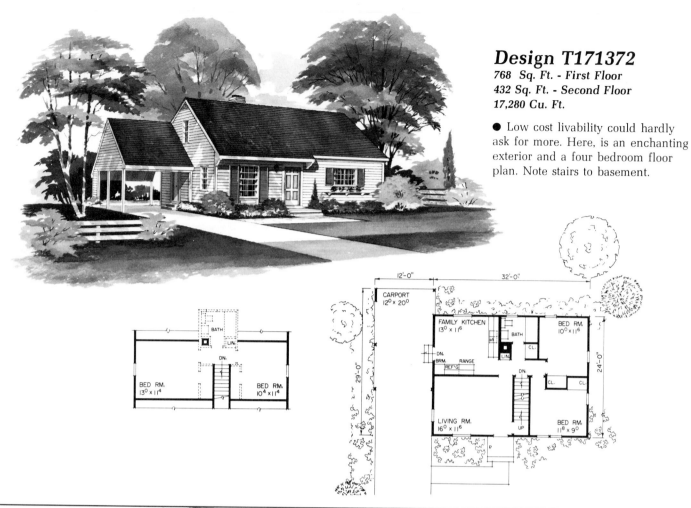

Design T171372
768 Sq. Ft. - First Floor
432 Sq. Ft. - Second Floor
17,280 Cu. Ft.

● Low cost livability could hardly ask for more. Here, is an enchanting exterior and a four bedroom floor plan. Note stairs to basement.

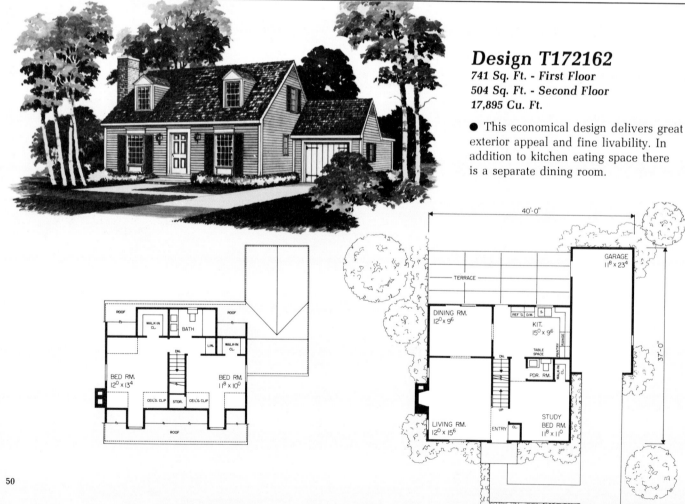

Design T172162
741 Sq. Ft. - First Floor
504 Sq. Ft. - Second Floor
17,895 Cu. Ft.

● This economical design delivers great exterior appeal and fine livability. In addition to kitchen eating space there is a separate dining room.

Design T171394

832 Sq. Ft. - First Floor
512 Sq. Ft. - Second Floor
19,385 Cu. Ft.

● The growing family with a restricted building budget will find this a great investment - a convenient living floor plan inside an attractive facade.

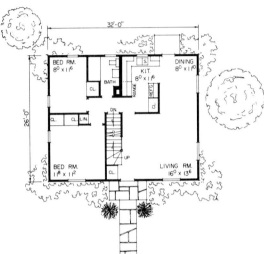

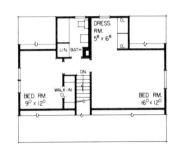

Design T172510

1,191 Sq. Ft. - First Floor
533 Sq. Ft. - Second Floor
27,500 Cu. Ft.

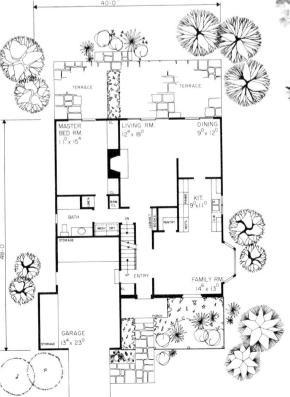

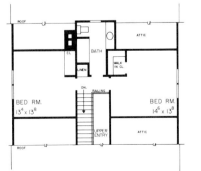

● The pleasant in-line kitchen is flanked by a separate dining room and a family room. The master bedroom is on the first floor with two more bedrooms upstairs.

Design T172571 *1,137 Sq. Ft. - First Floor*
795 Sq. Ft. - Second Floor; 28,097 Cu. Ft.

● Cost-efficient space! That's the bonus with this attractive Cape Cod. Start in the living room. It is spacious and inviting with full-length paned windows. In the formal dining room, a bay window adds the appropriate touch. For more living space, a delightfully appointed family room. The efficient kitchen has a snack bar for casual meals. Three bedrooms are on the second floor.

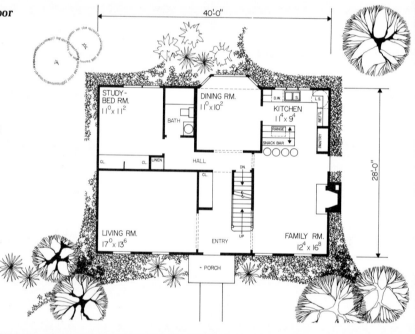

Design T173189 *884 Sq. Ft. - First Floor*
598 Sq. Ft. - Second Floor; 18,746 Cu. Ft.

● A large kitchen/dining area and living room are the living areas of this design. Four bedrooms, two up and two down, compose the sleeping zone. Each floor also has a full bath. A full basement and an attached garage will provide plenty of storage areas.

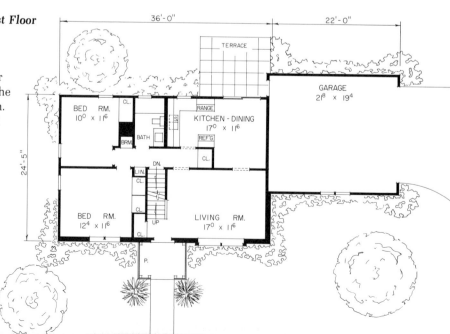

Design T172699 2,188 Sq. Ft. - First Floor
858 Sq. Ft. - Second Floor; 58,141 Cu. Ft.

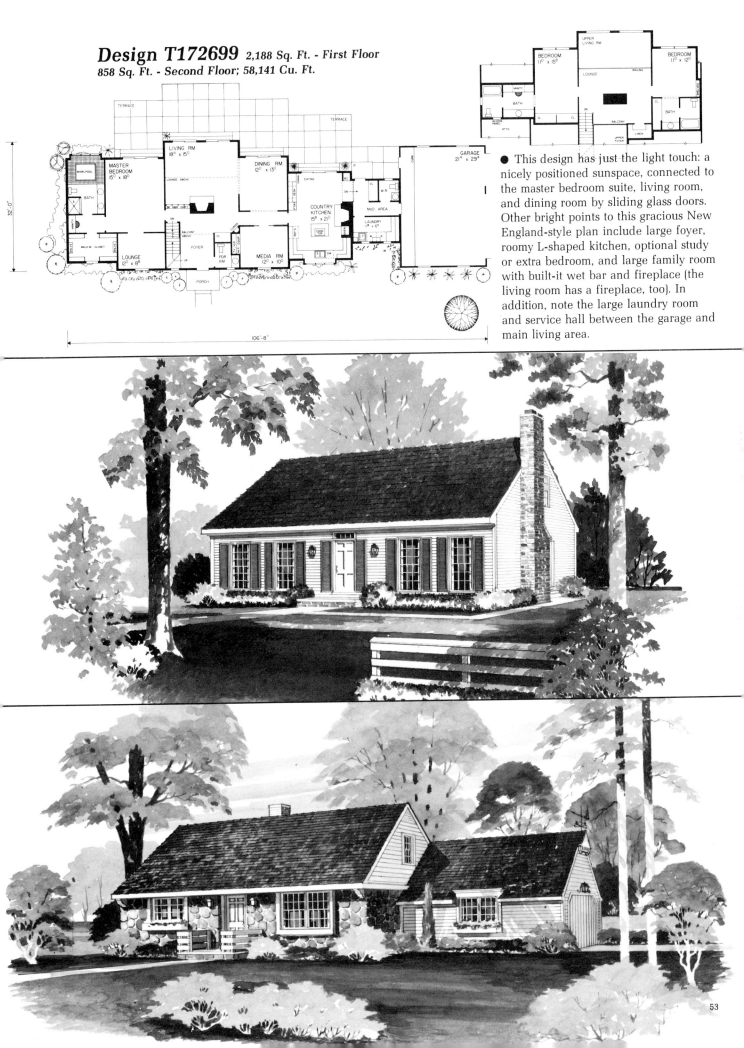

First Floor Plan labels:
TERRACE
TERRACE
LIVING RM 18⁴ x 15⁰
DINING RM 12⁰ x 13⁰
GARAGE 21⁴ x 29⁴
MASTER BEDROOM 15⁰ x 18⁰
WHIRL POOL
BATH
EATING
COUNTRY KITCHEN 15⁸ x 21⁰
MUD AREA
COOK TOP
LAUNDRY 11⁴ x 6⁰
VANITY
WALK IN CLOSET
LOUNGE 12⁰ x 8⁸
BALCONY ABOVE
FOYER
PDR RM
MEDIA RM 12⁰ x 10⁰
PORCH
LOUNGE ABOVE

32'-0"
106'-8"

Second Floor Plan labels:
UPPER LIVING RM
BEDROOM 11⁰ x 15⁸
BEDROOM 11⁰ x 12⁰
LOUNGE
RAILING
VANITY
BATH
BATH
ATTIC
ACCESS PANEL
BALCONY
LINEN
UPPER FOYER

● This design has just the light touch: a nicely positioned sunspace, connected to the master bedroom suite, living room, and dining room by sliding glass doors. Other bright points to this gracious New England-style plan include large foyer, roomy L-shaped kitchen, optional study or extra bedroom, and large family room with built-it wet bar and fireplace (the living room has a fireplace, too). In addition, note the large laundry room and service hall between the garage and main living area.

Design T171791

1,157 Sq. Ft. - First Floor
875 Sq. Ft. - Second Floor; 27,790 Cu. Ft.

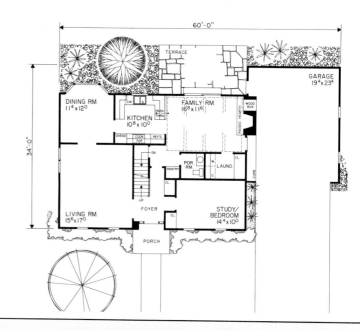

● Wherever you build this moderately sized house an aura of Cape Cod is sure to unfold. The symmetry is pleasing, indeed. The authentic center entrance seems to project a beckoning call.

Design T171870

1,136 Sq. Ft. - First Floor
936 Sq. Ft. - Second Floor; 26,312 Cu. Ft.

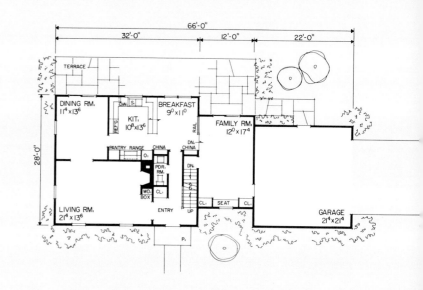

● Besides an enchanting exterior, this home has formal dining and living rooms, plus informal family and breakfast rooms. Built-ins are located in both of these informal rooms. U-shaped, the kitchen will efficiently service both of the dining areas. Study the sleeping facilities of the second floor.

Design T172396

1,616 Sq. Ft. - First Floor
993 Sq. Ft. - Second Floor; 30,583 Cu. Ft.

● Another picturesque facade right from the pages of our Colonial heritage. The authentic features are many. Don't miss the stairs to area over the garage.

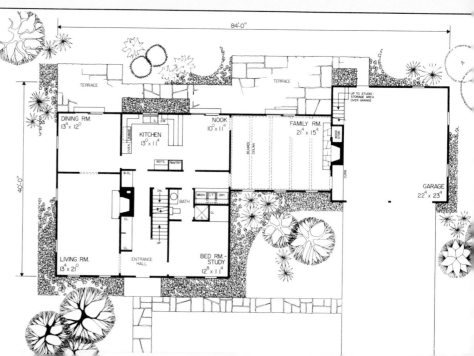

Design T171787

2,656 Sq. Ft. - First Floor
744 Sq. Ft. - Second Floor
51,164 Cu. Ft.

● Can't you picture this dramatic home sitting on your property? The curving front drive is impressive as it passes the walks to the front door and the service entrance. The roof masses, the centered masonry chimney, the window symmetry and the 108 foot expanse across the front are among the features that make this a distinctive home. Of interest are the living and family rooms — both similar in size and each having its own fireplace.

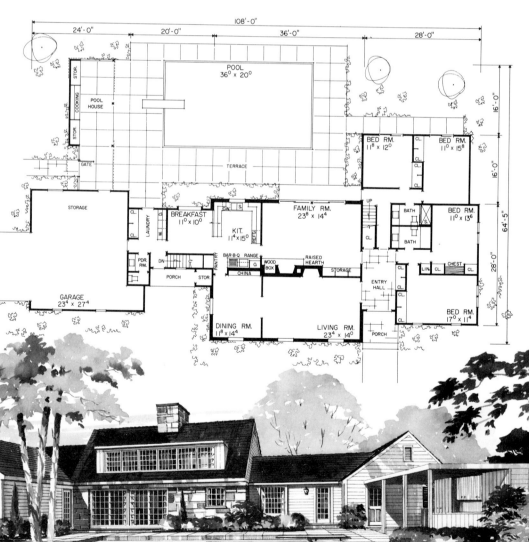

STUDY - LOUNGE
16⁴ x 12⁴

BOOKS

DN.

LIN.

STORAGE

MASTER
BED RM.
15⁰ x 21⁶

DRESSING RM.

BATH

CL.

CL.

108'-0"

24'-0" 20'-0" 36'-0" 28'-0"

POOL
36⁰ x 20⁰

STOR.

COOKING

POOL HOUSE

STOR.

GATE

TERRACE

BED RM.
11⁸ x 12⁰

CL.

BED RM.
11⁰ x 15⁸

CL.

16'-0"

16'-0"

STORAGE

CL.

LAUNDRY

W. D.

BREAKFAST
11⁰ x 10⁰

DW. S.

KIT.
11⁴ x 15⁰

FAMILY RM.
23⁸ x 14⁴

UP

BATH

BATH

BED RM.
11⁰ x 13⁶

64'-5"

28'-0"

PDR. RM.

DN.

PANTRY

BAR-B-Q RANGE
O.
WOOD BOX

RAISED HEARTH

STORAGE

CL.

LIN. CL. CHEST

CL.

PORCH

STOR.

CHINA

ENTRY HALL

CL.

GARAGE
23⁴ x 27⁴

DINING RM.
11⁸ x 14⁴

LIVING RM.
23⁴ x 14⁰

PORCH

BED RM.
17⁰ x 11⁴

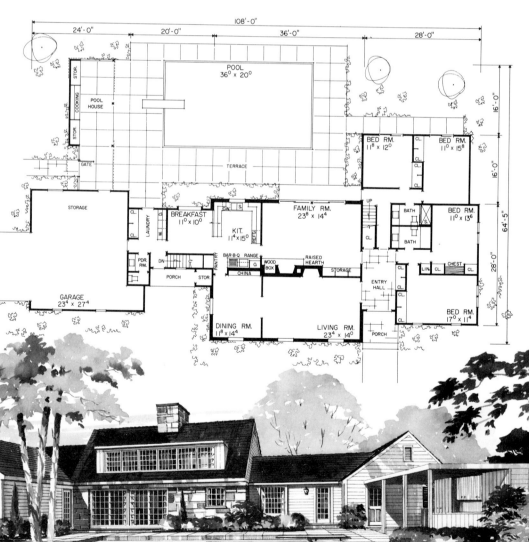

Tudor Houses

This selection of Tudor Houses is extremely varied. Reflected here are the many distinctive architectural features discussed on pages 6 and 7 adapted to differing house types. As you study these pleasing exteriors, notice how they adapt to the one- and 1½-story houses and multi-levels, as well as the ubiquitous two-story. Observe, too, how this style adapts well for all budgets.

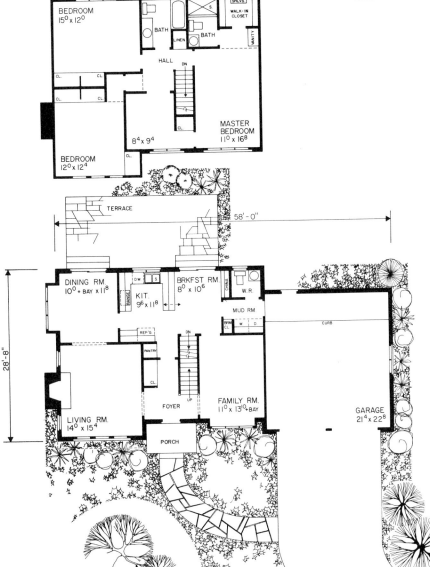

Design T172800

999 Sq. Ft. - First Floor
997 Sq. Ft. - Second Floor
31,390 Cu. Ft.

● This Tudor design has many fine features to make its mark. The exterior is enhanced by a front and side bay window in the family and dining rooms. Along with an outstanding exterior, it also contains a modern and efficient floor plan within its modest proportions. Flanking the entrance foyer is a comfortable living room which houses a fireplace. The U-shaped kitchen is conveniently located between the formal dining room and the breakfast room which has a built-in china cabinet. Both of these eating areas have sliding glass doors to the rear terrace. Even though this design has a basement, the laundry facilities are still located on the first floor. Two bedrooms, bath and master bedroom with bath, vanity, walk-in closet and adjoining study/nursery are conveniently located on the second floor.

Design T172794

1,680 Sq. Ft. - First Floor
1,165 Sq. Ft. - Second Floor
867 Sq. Ft. - Apartment
55,900 Cu. Ft.

● This exceptionally pleasing Tudor design has a great deal of interior livability to offer its occupants. Use the main entrance, enter into the foyer and begin your journey throughout this design. To the left of the foyer is the study, to the right, the formal living room. The living room leads to the rear, formal dining room. This room has access to the outdoors and is conveniently located adjacent to the kitchen. A snack bar divides the kitchen from the family room which also has access to outdoors plus it has a fireplace as does the living room. The second floor houses the family's four bedrooms. Down six steps from the mud room is the laundry and entrance to the garage, up six steps from this area is a complete apartment. This is an excellent room for a live-in relative. It is completely private by gaining access from the outdoor balcony.

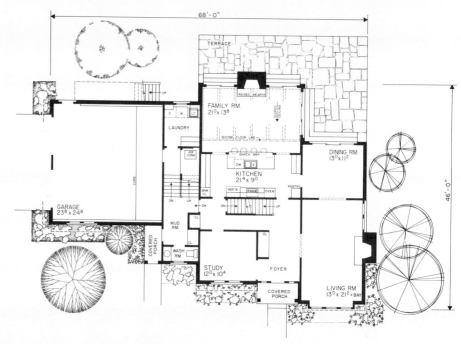

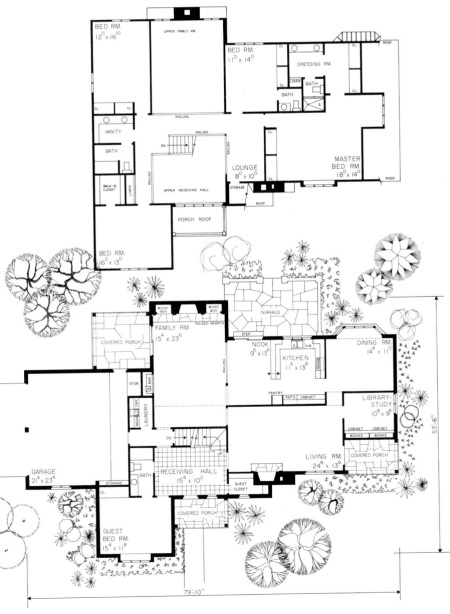

First Floor plan labels:
BED RM. 12⁰ x 16¹⁰
UPPER FAMILY RM.
BED RM. 11⁰ x 14⁰
DRESSING RM.
LINEN
BATH
BATH
CL
VANITY
BATH
RAILING
DN.
LOUNGE 8⁰ x 10⁰
MASTER BED RM. 18⁰ x 14⁰
WALK IN CLOSET
LINEN
UPPER RECEIVING HALL
STORAGE
ROOF
PORCH ROOF
ROOF
BED RM. 16² x 13⁰

TERRACE
WOOD BOX
WOOD BOX
FAMILY RM. 15⁴ x 23⁶
RAISED HEARTH
COVERED PORCH
STEP
NOOK 9⁶ x 13⁶
KITCHEN 11⁶ x 13⁶
DINING RM. 14⁴ x 11⁰
STOR.
BAR
PANTRY
REF'G
CABINET
LIBRARY-STUDY 10⁸ x 9⁰
LAUNDRY
WASH
DRY
CABINET BOOKS
CABINET BOOKS
DN
UP
BATH
RECEIVING HALL 15⁴ x 10⁰
GUEST CLOSET
LIVING RM. 24⁸ x 13⁶
COVERED PORCH
GARAGE 21⁴ x 23⁴
STORAGE
CL
COVERED PORCH
GUEST BED RM. 15⁴ x 11⁸
79'-10"
53'-6"

Design T172356

1,969 Sq. Ft. - First Floor
1,702 Sq. Ft. - Second Floor
55,105 Cu. Ft.

● Here is truly an exquisite Tudor adaptation. The exterior, with its interesting roof lines, window treatment, stately chimney and its appealing use of brick and stucco, could hardly be more dramatic. Inside, the drama really begins to unfold as one envisions his family's living patterns. The delightfully large receiving hall has a two story ceiling and controls the flexible traffic patterns. The living and dining rooms, with the library nearby, will cater to the formal living pursuits. The guest room offers another haven for the enjoyment of peace and quiet. Observe the adjacent full bath. Just inside the entrance from the garage is the laundry room. For the family's informal activities there are the interactions of the family room - covered porch - nook - kitchen zone. Notice the raised hearth fireplace, the wood boxes, the sliding glass doors, built-in bar and the kitchen pass-thru. Adding to the charm of the family room is its high ceiling. From the second floor hall one can look down and observe the activities below.

Design T171991 1,262 Sq. Ft. - First Floor
1,108 Sq. Ft. - Second Floor; 31,073 Cu. Ft.

● Put yourself and your family in this English cottage adaptation and you'll all rejoice over your new home for many a year. The pride of owning and living in a home that is distinctive will be a constant source of satisfaction. Count the features that will serve your family. Three bedrooms upstairs; formal and informal living and dining plus the work centers on first floor.

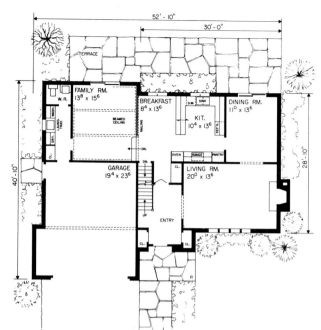

● This is a most interesting home; both inside and out. Its L-shape with covered porch and diamond lite windows is appealing. Its floor plan with extra bedroom, lounge and storage room is exceptional.

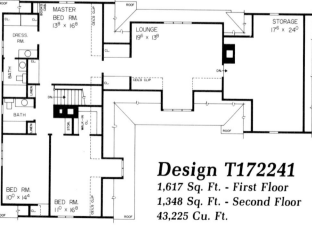

Design T172241
1,617 Sq. Ft. - First Floor
1,348 Sq. Ft. - Second Floor
43,225 Cu. Ft.

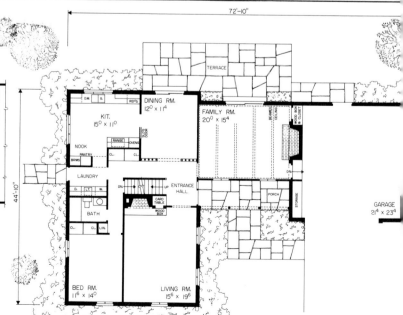

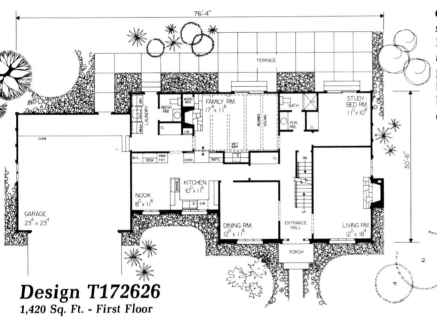

● This charming, one-and-a-half-story home surely elicits thoughts of an English country side. It has a beckoning warmth that seems to foretell a friendly welcome. The exterior features are appealing, indeed. The window treatment, the stylish chimneys, the varying roof planes and the brick veneer and stucco exterior, are among the distinguishing characteristics.

Design T172626
1,420 Sq. Ft. - First Floor
859 Sq. Ft. - Second Floor; 34,974 Cu. Ft.

Design T172170 1,646 Sq. Ft.; 22,034 Cu. Ft.

● An L-shaped home with an enchanting Olde English styling. The wavy-edged siding, the simulated beams, the diamond lite windows, the unusual brick pattern, and the interesting roof lines all are elements which set the character of authenticity. The center entry routes traffic directly to the formal living and sleeping zones of the house. Between the kitchen-family room area and the attached two-car garage is the mud room. Here is the washer and dryer with the extra powder room nearby. The family room is highlighted by the beamed ceilings, the raised hearth fireplace, and sliding glass doors to the rear terrace. The work center with its abundance of cupboard space will be fun in which to function. Note four bedrooms, two full baths, and good closet space.

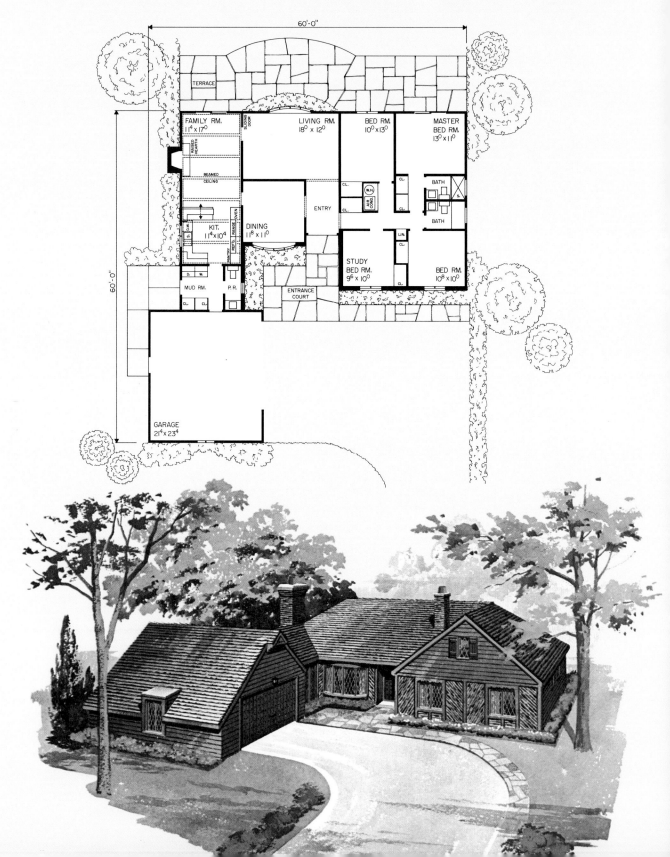

Design T171989 *2,282 Sq. Ft.; 41,831 Cu. Ft.*

● This is high style reminiscent of Old England with a plan as contemporary as today and tomorrow. There is, indeed, a feeling of coziness that emanates from the ground-hugging qualities of this picturesque home. Inside, there is livability galore which will be enjoyed by all family members. There's the bedroom, two bath sleeping wing with a dressing room as a bonus. There's the sunken living room and the separate dining room to function as the family's formal living area. Then, overlooking the rear yard, there's the informal living area. This area features a family room and a wonderful kitchen with an adjacent breakfast room. As a positive plus to outstanding livability, there's the handy first floor laundry with its wash room. Don't miss the storage room.

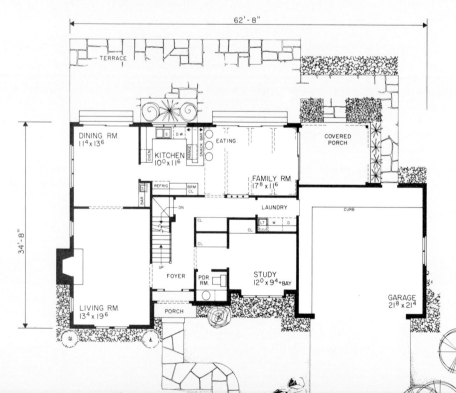

First floor:

TERRACE

DINING RM.
11⁴ x 13⁶

KITCHEN
10⁰ x 11⁶

OVEN
RANGE
DW
SNACK BAR

EATING

COVERED PORCH

BAR
REFRIG
BRM CL

FAMILY RM.
17⁸ x 11⁶

DN

LAUNDRY

CURB

LT W D
CL
CL

CL

UP
FOYER

PDR RM.

STUDY
12⁰ x 9⁴ + BAY

GARAGE
21⁸ x 21⁴

LIVING RM.
13⁴ x 19⁶

PORCH

62'-8"

34'-8"

Second floor:

ROOF
ROOF

CL CL CL

DRESSING RM.

LOUNGE/ NURSERY
10⁰ x 9⁰

CL

BEDROOM
12⁰ x 10⁰

LIN

DN

TUB
CL

MASTER BEDROOM
13⁴ x 15⁴

BATH

BEDROOM
10⁰ x 11⁰

BATH
S

ROOF
ROOF
ROOF

Design T172854
1,261 Sq. Ft. - First Floor
950 Sq. Ft. - Second Floor
36,820 Cu. Ft.

● The flair of old England
has been captured in this
outstanding one-and-a-half
story design. Interior livability will efficiently serve the
various needs of all family
members. The first floor
offers both formal and informal areas, along with the
work centers. Note some of
the various features which
include a wet-bar in the dining room, the kitchen's snack
bar, first floor laundry and
rear covered porch to mention a few. Accommodations
for sleeping will be found on
the second floor. There are
two family bedrooms and
the master bedroom suite.
Don't miss the uniqueness of
the lounge/nursery area
which is attached to the
master bedroom.

Design T172855
1,372 Sq. Ft. - First Floor
1,245 Sq. Ft. - Second Floor
44,495 Cu. Ft.

● This elegant Tudor house is perfect for the family who wants to move-up in living area, style and luxury. As you enter this home you will find a large living room with a fire-place on your right. Adjacent, the formal dining room has easy access to both the living room and the kitchen. The kitchen/breakfast room has an open plan and access to the rear terrace. Sunken a few steps, the spacious family room is highlighted with a fireplace and access to the rear, covered porch. Note the optional planning of the garage storage area. Plan this area according to the needs of your family. Upstairs, your family will enjoy three bedrooms and a full bath, along with a spacious master bedroom suite. Truly a house that will bring many years of pleasure to your family.

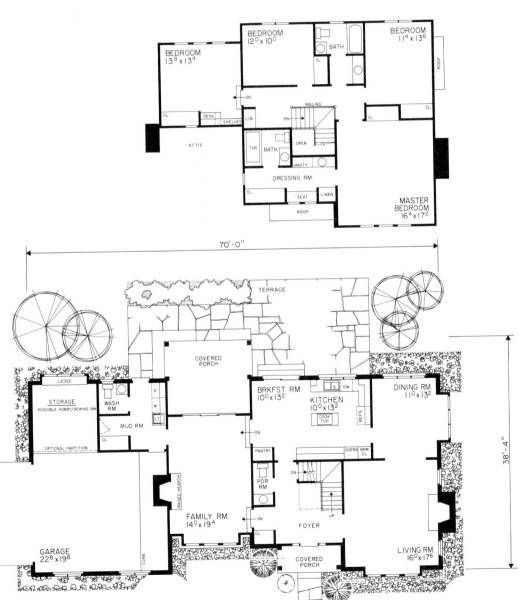

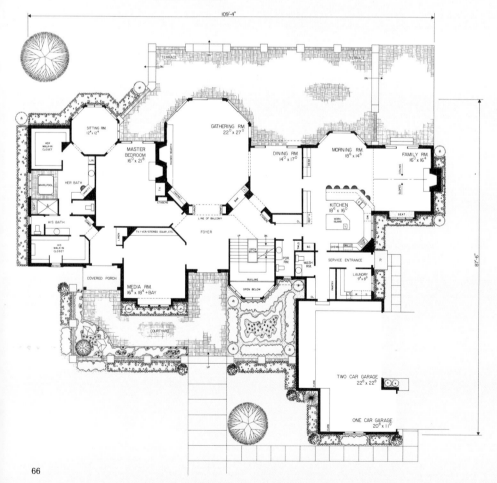

Design T172951

4,195 Sq. Ft. - First Floor
2,094 Sq. Ft. - Second Floor
138,230 Cu. Ft.

● A single prominent turret with two-story divided windows draws attention to this stately Tudor home. The open foyer allows an uninterrupted view into the impressive, two-story great room with wet bar, where a fireplace with raised hearth runs the entire length of one wall. The expansive kitchen, conveniently located near the service entrance, has a U-shaped work area and a snack bar that opens to the morning room. The adjacent sloped-ceiling family room has an additional fireplace and a comfortable window seat. A Victorian-inspired, octagon-shaped sitting room is tucked into the corner of the unique master bedroom. His and Hers baths and walk-in closets complete the impressive first-floor suite. Two bedrooms, a study, and a guest suite with private sitting room are located on the second floor. A magnificent second-floor bridge overlooks foyer and gathering room and provides extraordinary views to guests on the way to their bedroom.

● Cross gables, decorative half-timbers, and three massive chimneys mark the exterior of this magnificent baronial Tudor. A circular staircase housed in the turret makes an impressive opening statement in the two-story foyer. A powder room and telephone center are located off the foyer for easy use by guests. Two steps down lead to the elegant living room with music alcove or the sumptuous library with wet bar. The kitchen is a chef's delight with large work island, full cooking counter, snack bar, and a butler's pantry leading to a formal dining room with bow window. The second floor features four bedrooms, two with fireplaces, and each with private bath and abundant closet space. The master suite has an additional fireplace, His and Hers walk-in closets, whirlpool bath and separate shower, and a private sitting room in a windowed alcove. Adjacent to the master suite is a nursery that would also make an ideal exercise room.

Design T172955 4,274 Sq. Ft. - First Floor
3,008 Sq. Ft. - Second Floor; 136,834 Cu. Ft.

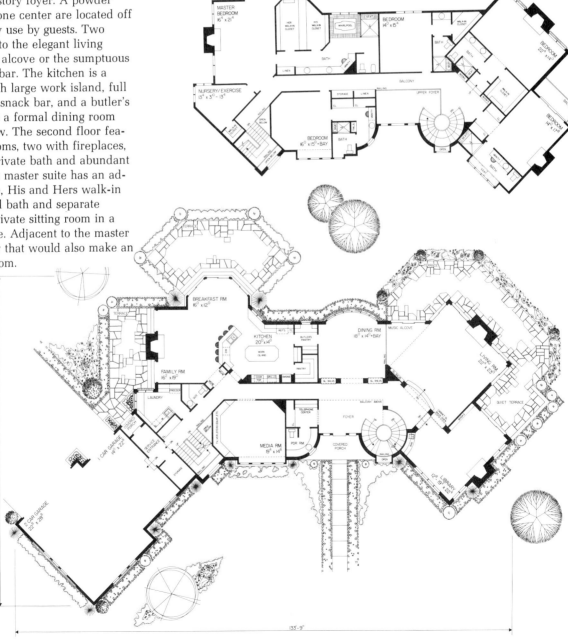

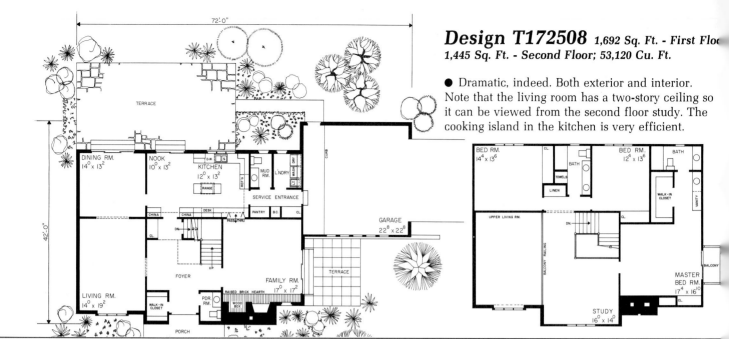

Design T172508 1,692 Sq. Ft. - First Floor
1,445 Sq. Ft. - Second Floor; 53,120 Cu. Ft.

● Dramatic, indeed. Both exterior and interior. Note that the living room has a two-story ceiling so it can be viewed from the second floor study. The cooking island in the kitchen is very efficient.

Design T172128 1,152 Sq. Ft. - First Floor
896 Sq. Ft. - Second Floor; 30,707 Cu. Ft.

● Here is proof that your restricted building budget can return to you wonderfully pleasing design and loads of livability. This is an English Tudor adaptation that will surely become your subdivision's favorite facade. Its mark of individuality is obvious to all.

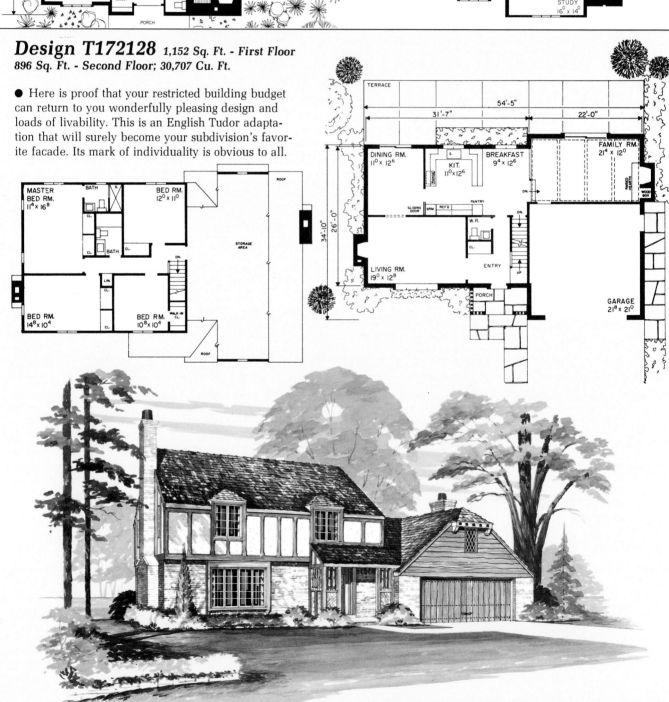

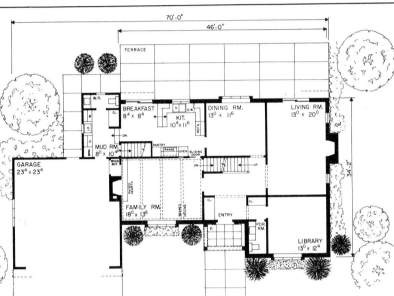

● Imagine, six bedrooms on the second floor.
The first floor houses the living areas: family
room, living room, dining areas plus a library.
Not much more livability could be packed into
this spaciously designed home.

Design T172141 1,490 Sq. Ft. - First Floor
1,474 Sq. Ft. - Second Floor; 50,711 Cu. Ft.

Design T172171

795 Sq. Ft. - Main Level
912 Sq. Ft. - Upper Level
335 Sq. Ft. - Lower Level; 33,243 Cu. Ft.

● This English Tudor, split-level adaptation has much to recommend it. Perhaps, its most significant feature is that it can be built economically on a relatively small site. The width of the house is just over 52 feet. But its size does not inhibit its livability. There are many fine qualities. Observe the living room fireplace in addition to the one in the family room with a wood box. The breakfast room overlooks the lower level family room. It also has a pass-thru to the kitchen. Don't miss the balcony off the master bedroom. Also worthy of note, a short flight of stairs leads to the huge attic storage area.

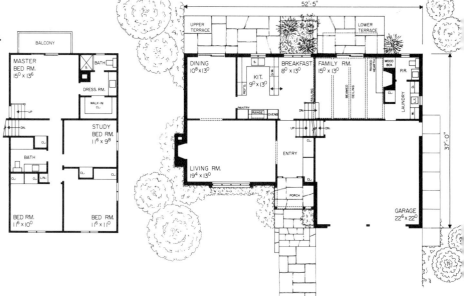

Design T172137

987 Sq. Ft. - Main Level
1,043 Sq. Ft. - Upper Level
463 Sq. Ft. - Lower Level; 29,382 Cu. Ft.

● Tudor design adapts to split-level living. The result is a unique charm for all to remember. As for the livability, the happy occupants of this tri-level home will experience wonderful living patterns. A covered porch protects the front entry. The center hall routes traffic conveniently to the spacious formal living and dining area; the informal breakfast room and kitchen zone; the upper level bedrooms and the lower level all-purpose family room. List the numerous features that contribute to fine living.

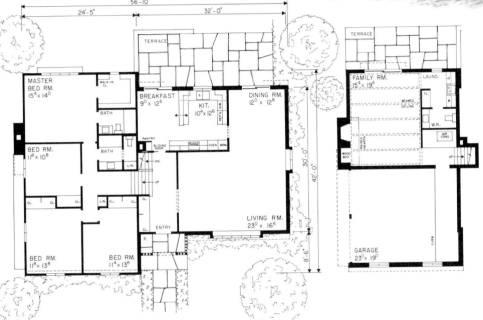

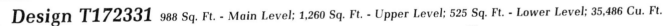

Design T172331 *988 Sq. Ft. - Main Level; 1,260 Sq. Ft. - Upper Level; 525 Sq. Ft. - Lower Level; 35,486 Cu. Ft.*

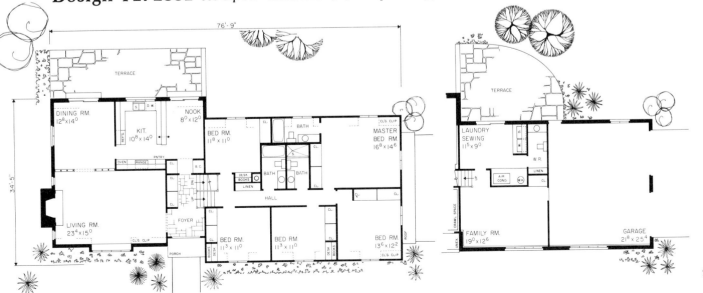

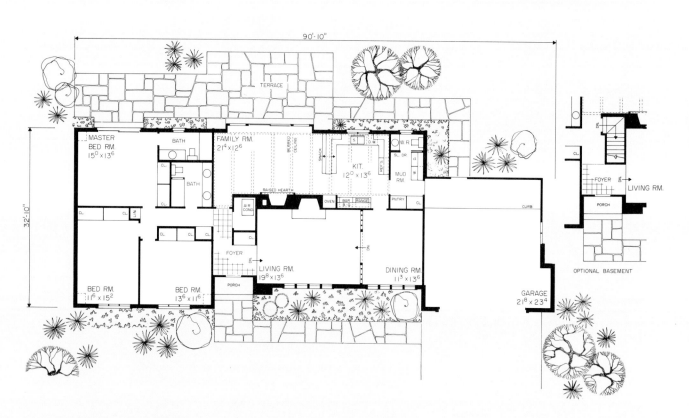

Design T172318 *2,029 Sq. Ft.; 31,021 Cu. Ft.*

● Warmth and charm are characteristics of Tudor adaptations. This modest sized home with its twin front-facing gabled roofs represents a great investment. While it will be an exciting and refreshing addition to any neighborhood, its appeal will never grow old.

The covered, front entrance opens to the center foyer. Traffic patterns flow in an orderly and efficient manner to the three main zones — the formal dining zone, the sleeping zone and the informal living zone. The sunken living room with its fireplace is separated from the dining room by an attractive trellis divider. A second fireplace, along with beamed ceiling and sliding glass doors, highlights the family room. Note snack bar, mud room, cooking facilities, two full baths and optional basement.

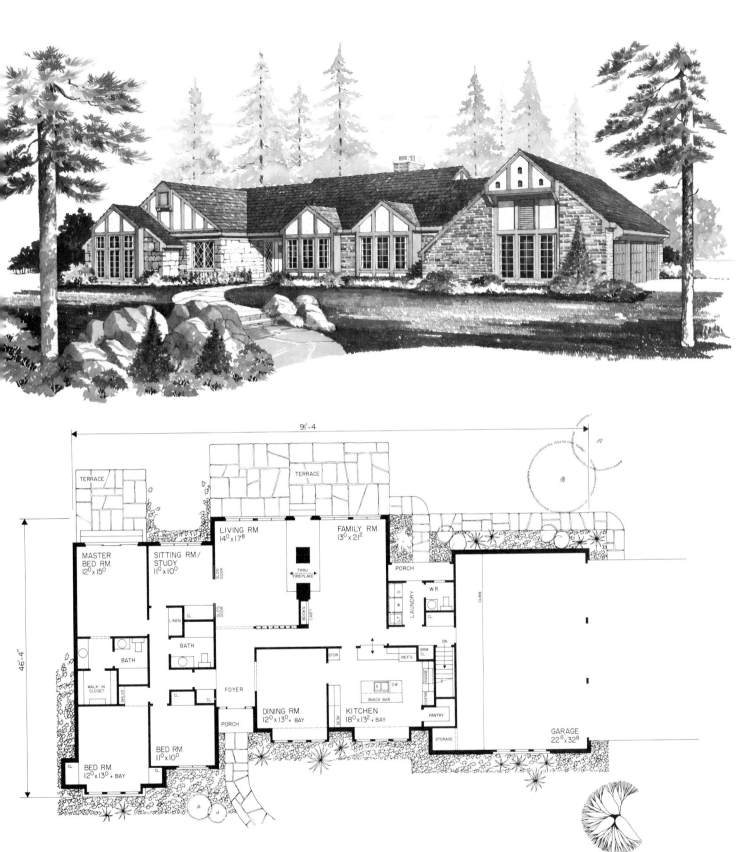

Design T172785 2,375 Sq. Ft.; 47,805 Cu. Ft.

● Exceptional Tudor design! Passersby will take a second glance at this fine home wherever it may be located. And the interior is just as pleasing. As one enters the foyer and looks around, the plan will speak for itself in the areas of convenience and efficiency.

Cross room traffic will be avoided. There is a hall leading to each of the three bedrooms and study of the sleeping wing and another leading to the living room, family room, kitchen and laundry with washroom. The formal dining room can be entered from both

the foyer and the kitchen. Efficiency will be the by-word when describing the kitchen. Note the fine features: a built-in desk, pantry, island snack bar with sink and pass-thru to the family room. The fireplace will be enjoyed in the living and family rooms.

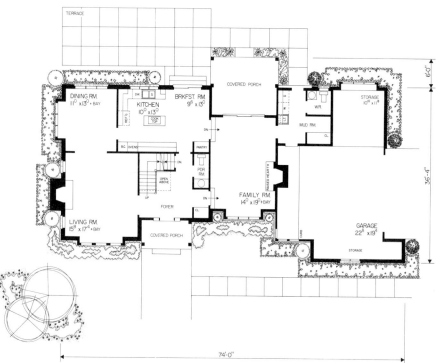

Design T172960

1,372 Sq. Ft. - First Floor
1,245 Sq. Ft. - Second Floor
44,557 Cu. Ft.

● The swooping roof of the projecting front gable results in a sheltered entrance to the foyer of this unique design. It would be difficult to imagine more appealing roof lines than this Tudor has to offer. Roof, exterior wall, and window treatment all blend together to present a harmonious facade. The two chimneys with their massive caps add their appeal, too. Once inside your guests will be impressed again. They will delight to find two such large living areas - one for formal and another for informal living. They will enthuse further over the eating facilities - a formal dining room and an informal breakfast room. The L-shaped kitchen will be a charm in which to work. It has an island cooking station, plenty of cupboard and counter space and a pantry nearby. The homemaker will love the strategic location of the mud room. It is just inside the entrance from the garage and is directly accessible from the rear yard. The covered porch is a nice feature. And don't miss the two fireplaces - one with a raised hearth. Upstairs there are four bedrooms, two baths and good storage facilities.

Design T172959

1,003 Sq. Ft. - First Floor
1,056 Sq. Ft. - Second Floor; 32,891 Cu. Ft.

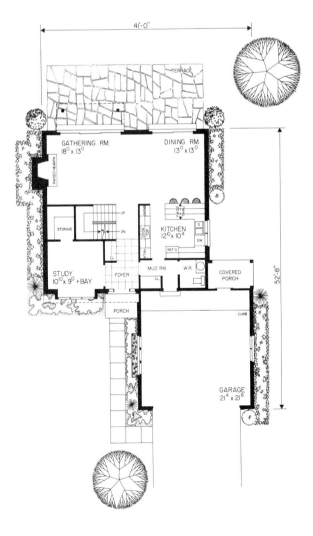

● Here the stateliness of Tudor styling is captured in a design suited for a narrow building site. This relatively low-budget two-story delivers all the livability found in many much larger homes. Imagine, a 31 foot living-dining area that stretches across the entire rear of the house and functions with the big terrace. Then, there is the efficient U-shaped kitchen with built-in cooking facilities and a pass-thru to the snack bar. Just inside the entrance from the garage is the mud room with its adjacent wash room. Enhancing first floor livability is the study with its big walk-in closet. An open staircase leads to the basement recreation area. Upstairs, three bedrooms, two baths and an outdoor balcony.

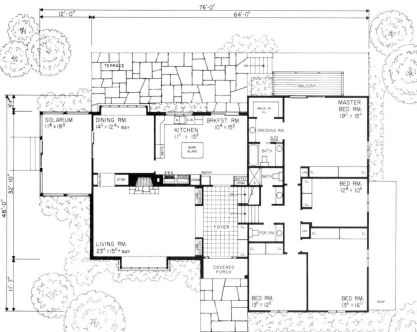

Design T172254

1,220 Sq. Ft. - Main Level
1,344 Sq. Ft. - Upper Level
659 Sq. Ft. - Lower Level
56,706 Cu. Ft.

● Tudor charm is deftly exemplified by this outstanding four level design. The window treatment, the heavy timber work and the chimney pots help set the character of this home. Contributing an extra measure of appeal is the detailing of the delightful solarium. The garden view of this home is equally appealing. The upper level balcony looks down onto the two terraces. The covered front entry leads to the spacious formal entrance hall with its slate floor. . .

Design T172243

1,274 Sq. Ft. - Main Level; 960 Sq. Ft. - Upper Level
936 Sq. Ft. - Lower Level; 42,478 Cu. Ft.

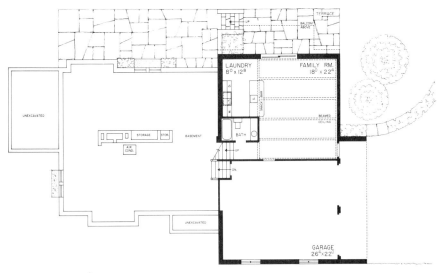

. . . Straight ahead is the kitchen and nook. The open planning of this area results in a fine feeling of spaciousness. Both living and dining rooms are wonderfully large. Each room highlights a big bay window. Notice the built-in units. Upstairs there are four bedrooms, two full baths and a powder room. Count the closets. The lower level is reserved for the all-purpose room, the separate laundry and a third full bath. The garage is adjacent. A fourth level is a basement with an abundance of space for storage and hobbies.

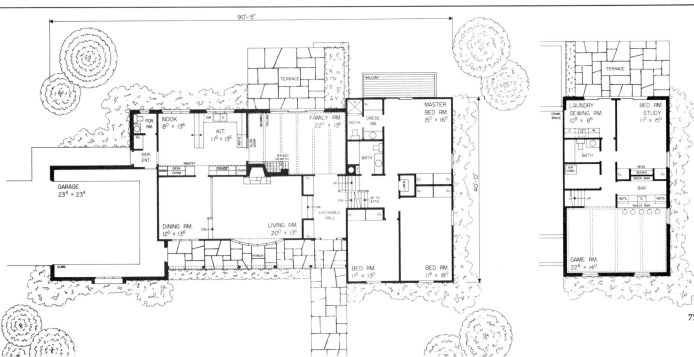

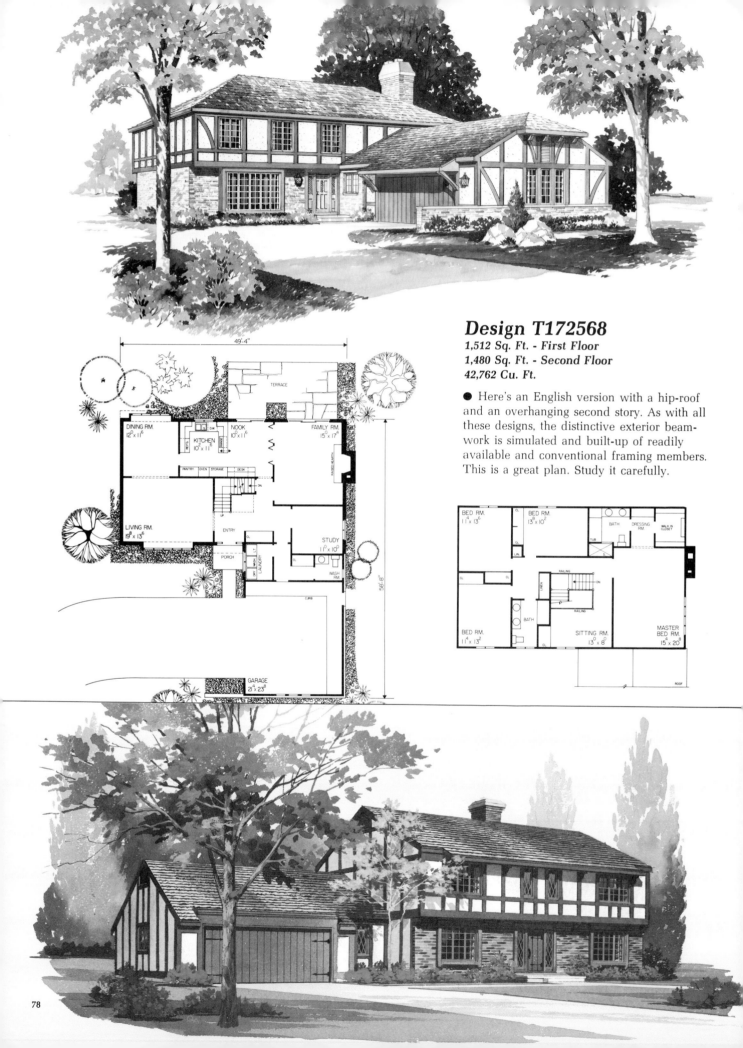

Design T172568

1,512 Sq. Ft. - First Floor
1,480 Sq. Ft. - Second Floor
42,762 Cu. Ft.

● Here's an English version with a hip-roof and an overhanging second story. As with all these designs, the distinctive exterior beamwork is simulated and built-up of readily available and conventional framing members. This is a great plan. Study it carefully.

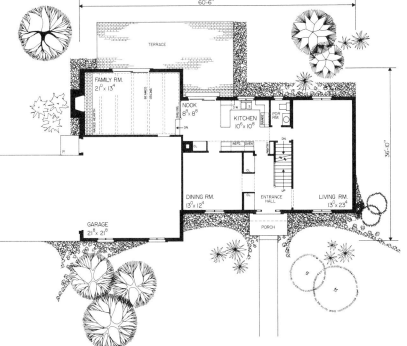

Design T172618
1,269 Sq. Ft. - First Floor
1,064 Sq. Ft. - Second Floor
33,079 Cu. Ft.

● This four bedroom Tudor design is the object of an outstanding investment for a lifetime of proud ownership and fine, family living facilities. Note that the family room is sunken and it, along with the nook, has sliding glass doors.

Design T172637
1,308 Sq. Ft. - First Floor
1,063 Sq. Ft. - Second Floor; 34,250 Cu. Ft.

● A generous, centered entrance hall routes traffic efficiently to all areas. And what wonderfully spacious areas they are. Note living, dining, sleeping and bath facilities. Don't miss first floor laundry.

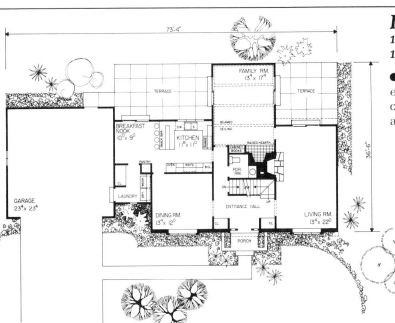

Design T172586

984 Sq. Ft. - First Floor
1,003 Sq. Ft. - Second Floor; 30,080 Cu. Ft.

● A stately Tudor! With four large bedrooms.
And lots of living space . . . formal living and
dining rooms, a family room with a traditional
fireplace, a spacious kitchen with nook.

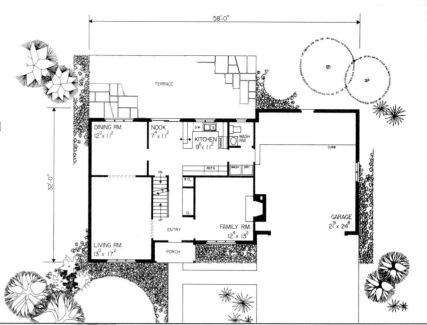

Design T172732

1,071 Sq. Ft. - First Floor
1,022 Sq. Ft. - Second Floor; 34,210 Cu. Ft.

● The two-story front entry hall will be dramatic indeed. Note the efficient kitchen adjacent
to informal family room, formal dining room.
Upstairs, three big bedrooms, two baths.

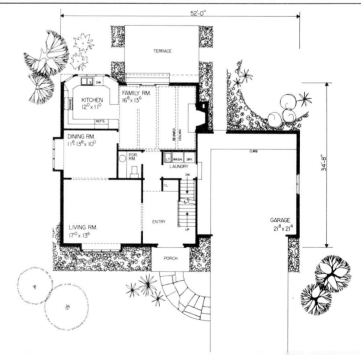

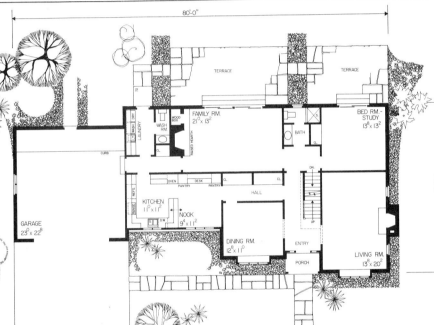

Design T172577

1,718 Sq. Ft. - First Floor
1,147 Sq. Ft. - Second Floor; 42,843 Cu. Ft.

● The exterior of this Tudor has interesting roof planes, delightful window treatment and recessed front entrance. The master suite with sitting room is one of the highlights of the interior.

Design T172758

1,143 Sq. Ft. - Main Level
792 Sq. Ft. - Upper Level
770 Sq. Ft. - Lower Level
43,085 Cu. Ft.

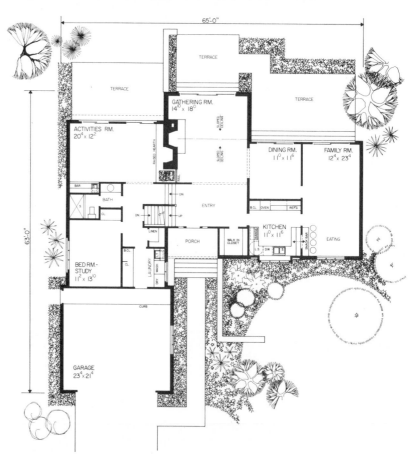

● An outstanding Tudor with three levels of exceptional livability, plus a basement. A careful study of the exterior reveals many delightful architectural details which give this home a character of its own. Notice the appealing recessed front entrance. Observe the overhanging roof with the exposed rafters. Don't miss the window treatment, the use of stucco and simulated beams, the masses of brick and the stylish chimney. Inside, the living potential is unsurpassed. Imagine, there are three living areas - the gathering, family and activities rooms. Having a snack bar, informal eating area and dining room, eating patterns can be flexible. In addition to the three bedrooms, two-bath upper level, there is a fourth bedroom with adjacent bath on the lower level.

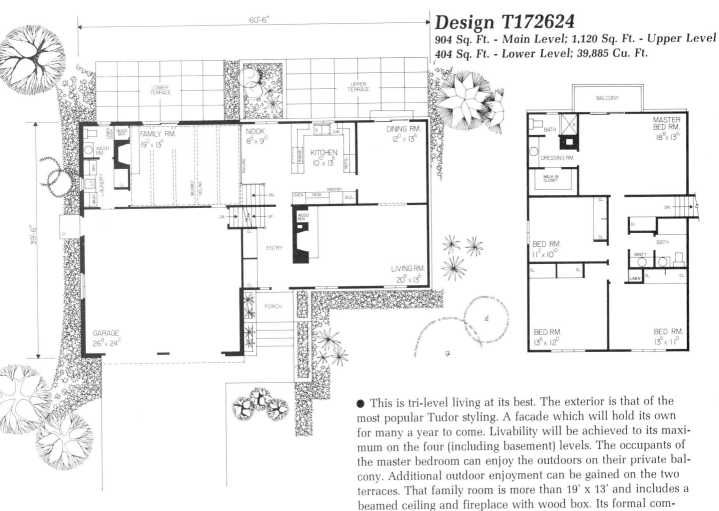

Design T172624

904 Sq. Ft. - Main Level; 1,120 Sq. Ft. - Upper Level
404 Sq. Ft. - Lower Level; 39,885 Cu. Ft.

60'-6"

39'-6"

LOWER TERRACE

UPPER TERRACE

FAMILY RM. 19' x 13⁶

WOOD BOX

WASH RM.

LAUNDRY

NOOK 8⁶ x 9⁰

BEAMED CEILING

RAILING

DN.

DN.

UP

KITCHEN 10⁰ x 13

RANGE

D.W.

REFG.

DINING RM. 12⁰ x 13⁶

OVEN

DESK

PANTRY

B.CL.

WOOD BOX

ENTRY

LIVING RM. 20⁶ x 13⁶

PORCH

GARAGE. 26⁸ x 24²

BALCONY

BATH

DRESSING RM.

WALK-IN CLOSET

MASTER BED RM. 18⁸ x 13⁶

DN.

BATH

VANITY

LINEN

BED RM. 11² x 10⁰

BED RM. 13⁶ x 12⁰

BED RM. 13⁶ x 11⁰

● This is tri-level living at its best. The exterior is that of the most popular Tudor styling. A facade which will hold its own for many a year to come. Livability will be achieved to its maximum on the four (including basement) levels. The occupants of the master bedroom can enjoy the outdoors on their private balcony. Additional outdoor enjoyment can be gained on the two terraces. That family room is more than 19' x 13' and includes a beamed ceiling and fireplace with wood box. Its formal companion, the living room, is similar in size and also will have the added warmth of a fireplace.

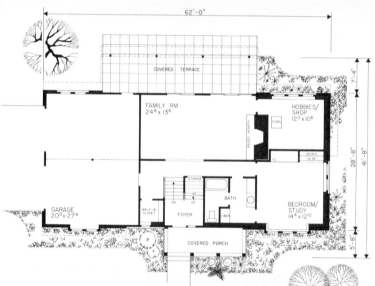

Design T172844 1,882 Sq. Ft. - Upper Level
1,168 Sq. Ft. - Lower Level; 37,860 Cu. Ft.

● Bi-level living will be enjoyed to the fullest in this Tudor design. The split-foyer type design will be very efficient for the active family. Three bedrooms are on the upper level, a fourth on the lower level.

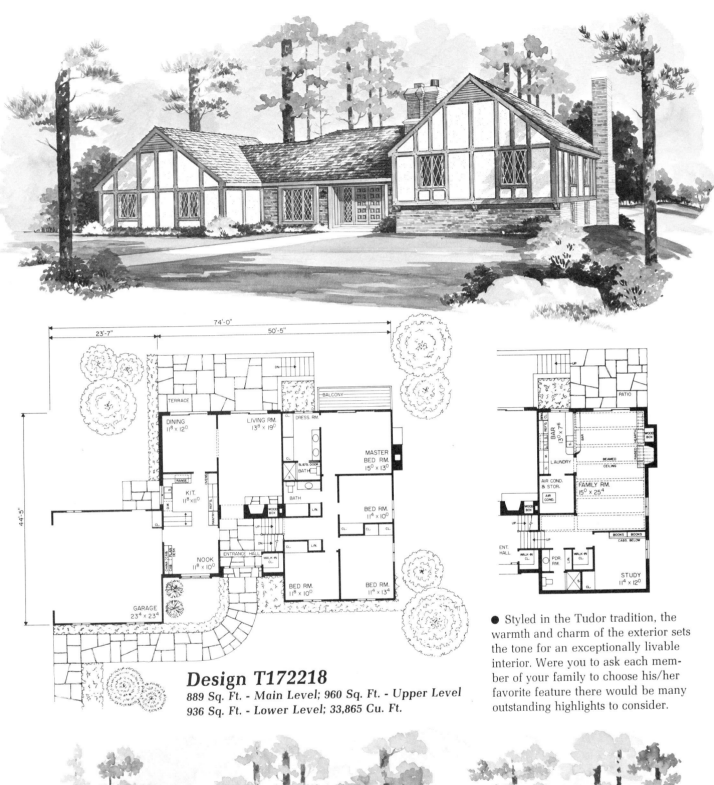

74'-0"

23'-7"   **50'-5"**

44'-5"

TERRACE

DINING
$11^8 \times 12^0$

LIVING RM.
$13^8 \times 19^0$

DRESS. RM.

BALCONY

MASTER
BED RM.
$15^0 \times 13^0$

SLID'G. DOOR

BATH

RANGE

OVENS

KIT.
$11^8 \times 11^0$

PANTRY

REFG.

WOOD
BOX

BATH

LIN

CL.

BED RM.
$11^4 \times 10^0$

CHINA CL.

CAB.

PLANT DESK

NOOK
$11^8 \times 10^0$

ENTRANCE HALL

WALK-IN
CL.

LIN

BED RM.
$11^8 \times 10^0$

BED RM.
$11^4 \times 13^0$

GARAGE
$23^4 \times 23^4$

UP

BAR
$13^0 \times 7^6$

PATIO

LAUNDRY

BEAMED
CEILING

WOOD
BOX

AIR COND.
& STOR.

AIR
COND.

FAMILY RM.
$15^0 \times 25^4$

RAISED HEARTH

WOOD
BOX

BOOKS

BOOKS

CABS. BELOW

ENT.
HALL

WALK-IN
CL.

PDR.
RM.

WALK-IN
CL.

STUDY
$11^4 \times 12^0$

Design T172218

889 Sq. Ft. - Main Level; 960 Sq. Ft. - Upper Level
936 Sq. Ft. - Lower Level; 33,865 Cu. Ft.

● Styled in the Tudor tradition, the warmth and charm of the exterior sets the tone for an exceptionally livable interior. Were you to ask each member of your family to choose his/her favorite feature there would be many outstanding highlights to consider.

Design T172605
1,775 Sq. Ft.; 34,738 Cu. Ft.

● Here are three modified L-shaped Tudor designs with tremendous exterior appeal and efficient floor plans. While each plan features three bedrooms and 2½ baths, the square footage differences are interesting. Note that each design may be built with or without a basement. This appealing exterior is highlighted by a variety of roof planes, patterned brick, wavy-edged siding and a massive chimney. The garage is oversized and has good storage potential. In addition to the entrance court, there are two covered porches and two terraces for outdoor living. Most definitely a home to be enjoyed by all family members.

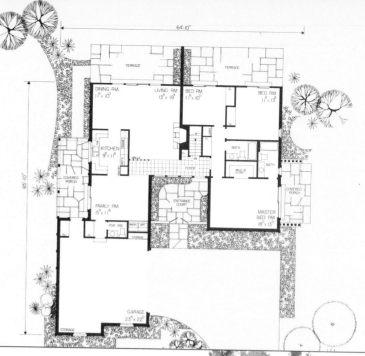

Design T172206
1,769 Sq. Ft.; 25,363 Cu. Ft.

● The charm of Tudor adaptations has become increasingly popular in recent years. And little wonder. Its freshness of character adds a unique touch to any neighborhood. This interesting one-story home will be a standout wherever you choose to have it built. The covered front porch leads to the formal front entry-the foyer. From this point traffic flows freely to the living and sleeping areas. The outstanding plan features a separate dining room, a beamed ceiling living room, an efficient kitchen and an informal family room.

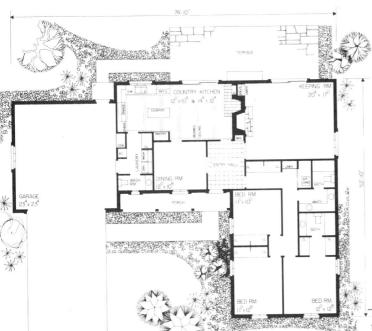

Design T172604
1,956 Sq. Ft.; 28,212 Cu. Ft.

● A feature that will set the whole wonderful pattern of true living will be the 26 foot wide country kitchen. The spacious, L-shaped kitchen has its efficiency enhanced by the island counter work surface. Beamed ceilings, fireplace and sliding glass doors add to the cozy atmosphere of this area. The laundry, dining room and entry hall are but a step or two away. The big keeping room also has a fireplace and can function with the terrace. Observe the 2½ baths.

Design T172957

2,557 Sq. Ft. - First Floor
1,939 Sq. Ft. - Second Floor; 80,159 Cu. Ft.

● The decorative half timbers and stone wall-cladding on this manor are stately examples of Tudor architecture. A grand double staircase is the highlight of the elegant, two-story foyer that opens to each of the main living areas. The living and gathering rooms are anchored by impressive central fireplaces. Handy built-ins, including a lazy susan and desk, and an island workstation with sink and cooktop, are convenient amenities in the kitchen. The adjacent breakfast room opens to the terrace for a sunny start to the day. Functioning with both the kitchen and the formal dining room is the butler's pantry. It has an abundance of cabinet and cupboard space and even a sink for a wet bar. Accessible from both the gathering and living rooms is the quiet study. If desired this could become a media center, sewing room or home office. The outstanding master suite features a cozy bedroom fireplace, picturesque whirlpool bath, and a convenient walk-in closet. Three additional second-floor bedrooms include a guest suite with dressing room and walk-in closet. Every part of this house speaks elegance, formality and the time-honored values for which Tudor is renowned.

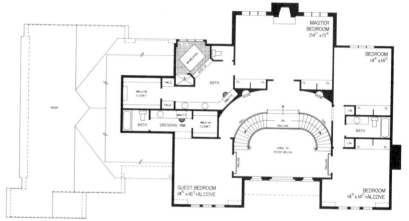

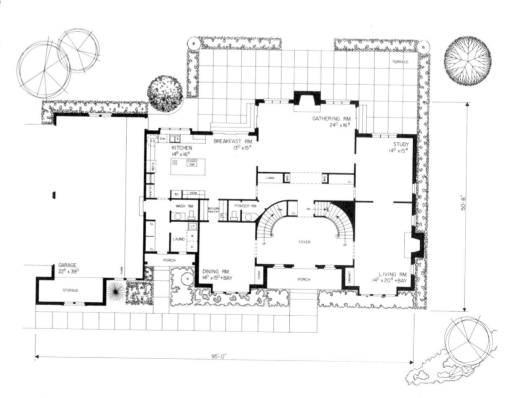

Georgian Houses

As the designs on the following pages depict, Georgian houses took many forms. Georgian characteristics were frequently found on 1½-story as well as two-story houses. New England Georgians were built of wood. Those in the south used brick and even incorporated impressive Greek columns. Federal styling, a later and more sophisticated form of Georgian, is closely related to the Adam style, circa 1780 to 1820.

Design T172132 1,958 Sq. Ft. - First Floor; 1,305 Sq. Ft. - Second Floor 51,428 Cu. Ft.

● This Georgian adaptation gets its appeal from its quietly formal facade. The identifying characteristics of this exterior include the symmetry of the window arrangement, the detailing of the doorway, the massive end chimneys, the tight cornices, the delicate dentils and the raised level of the entrance. The development of the rear yard to include formal gardens is consistent with the atmosphere created by the design of the house itself. Access to the garden area may be gained through the service door, the family room and the garage. This floor plan deserves a full measure of careful study. It will be an enjoyable exercise to visualize how you and your family will live in this home. Each room seems to have its own set of features. The living room, for instance, has as its focal point a corner fireplace and plenty of privacy. An abundance of floor space and two china storage niches are in the dining room. The kitchen area has a beamed ceiling and a big breakfast area. A second fireplace is in the family room. Upstairs, there is a fine master bedroom and two family bedrooms.

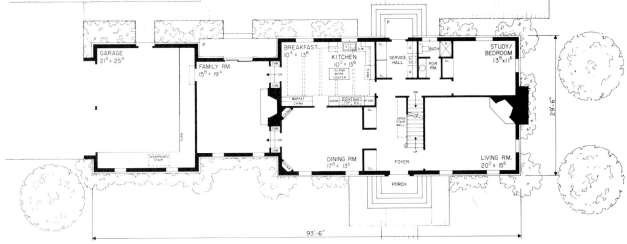

Design T172192 *1,884 Sq. Ft. - First Floor*
1,521 Sq. Ft. - Second Floor; 58,380 Cu. Ft.

● This is surely a fine adaptation from the 18th-Century when formality and elegance were by-words. The authentic detailing of this design centers around the fine proportions, the dentils, the window symmetry, the front door and entranceway, the massive chimneys and the masonry work. The rear elevation retains all the grandeur exemplary of exquisite architecture. The appeal of this outstanding home does not end with its exterior elevations. Consider the formal living room with its corner fireplace. Also, the library with its wall of bookshelves and cabinets. Further, the dining room highlights corner china cabinets. Continue to study this elegant plan.

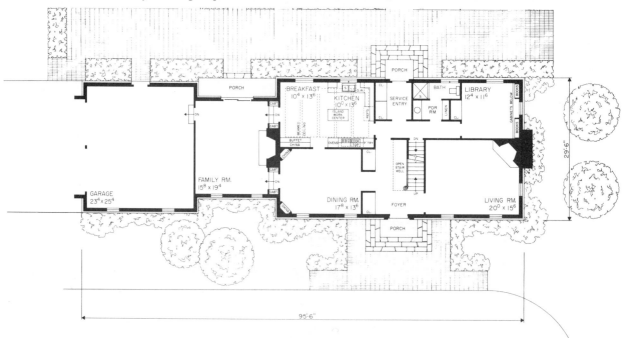

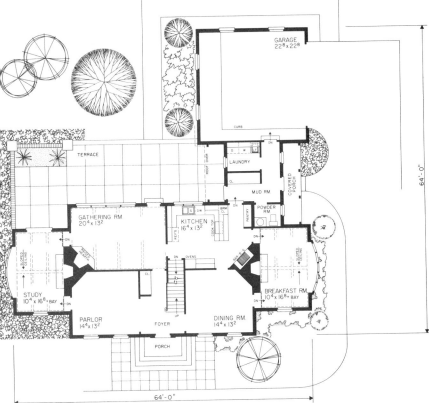

Design T172662

1,735 Sq. Ft. - First Floor; 1,075 Sq. Ft. - Second Floor
746 Sq. Ft. - Third Floor; 49,165 Cu. Ft.

● Influences from both Georgian and Federal architecture are apparent in the design of this home. The exterior is highlighted with multi-paned windows, two classic chimneys and well-proportioned dormers. A curved window is visible in each wing. The interior of this design has been planned just as carefully as the exterior. Study each area carefully and imagine how your family would utilize the space. There is a study, parlor, gathering room, U-shaped kitchen, formal and informal dining rooms plus a powder room and laundry. That is a lot of livability on one floor. Plus - three fireplaces! Three bedrooms and two baths are on the second floor. Two more bedrooms and another bath are on the third floor. A lack of space will never be a problem in this house.

Design T172283

1,559 Sq. Ft. - First Floor
1,404 Sq. Ft. - Second Floor
48,606 Cu. Ft.

● Reminiscent of the stately character of Federal architecture during an earlier period in our history, this two-story is replete with exquisite detailing. The cornice work, the pediment gable, the dentils, the brick quoins at the corners, the beautifully proportioned columns, the front door detailing, the window treatment and massive twin chimneys are among the features which make this design so unique. The formal, center entrance hall controls traffic to all areas. To the left are the formal areas, the living and dining rooms. To the right are the informal family and quiet study rooms. Straight ahead is the kitchen with its informal eating space. Upstairs, there are four bedrooms and two baths with an abundance of storage space. Be sure to notice such other features as the two fireplaces, the mud room, the washroom, the powder room, the beamed ceiling, etc.

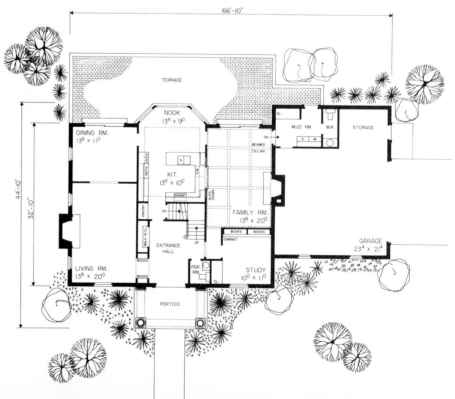

Design T172230 2,288 Sq. Ft. - First Floor

1,863 Sq. Ft. - Second Floor; 79,736 Cu. Ft.

● The gracefulness and appeal of this southern adaptation will be everlasting. The imposing, two-story portico is truly dramatic. Notice the authentic detailing of the tapered Doric columns, balustraded roof deck, denticulated cornice, front entrance and shuttered windows. The architecture of the rear is no less appealing with its formal symmetry and smaller Doric portico. The spacious, formal entrance hall provides a fitting introduction to the scale and elegance of the interior. Observe the openness of the stairwell which provides a view of the curving balusters above. The large living room with its colonial fireplace enjoys a full measure of privacy. Across the hall is the formal dining room with built-in china cabinets. Beamed ceilings and plenty of space produce a country style kitchen. The island work center will be just one of your favorite convenience features. A compartmented full bath is handy to the service entrance and the isolated library, which may double as a guest room when the occasion demands. Functioning between the house and the garage is the sunken family room. It stretches the full width of the house. Two family bedrooms are on the second floor with the master bedroom suite. Imagine yourself occupying this outstanding area. "His" and "her" baths, lounge/dressing room and an abundance of closet space highlight this area.

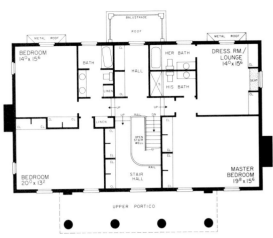

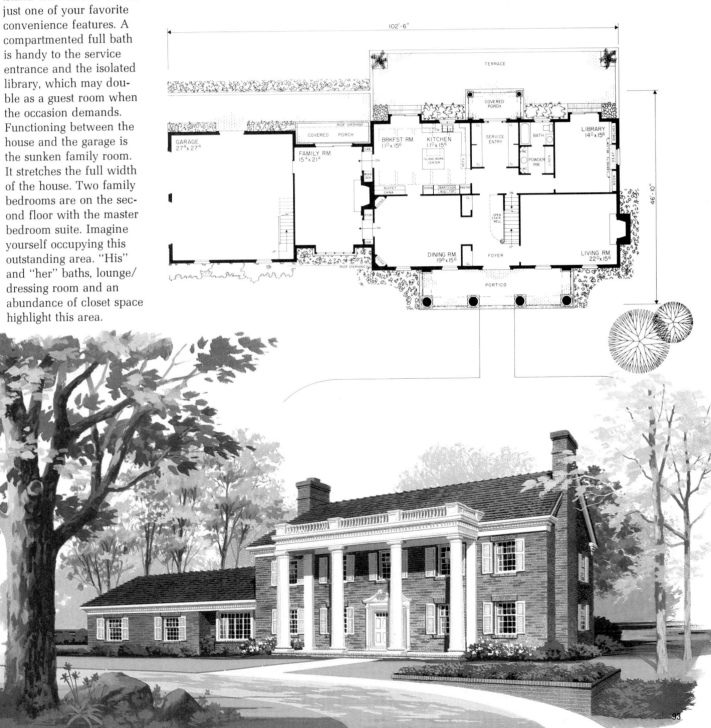

Design T172683 2,126 Sq. Ft. - First Floor; 1,882 Sq. Ft. - Second Floor; 78,828 Cu.Ft.

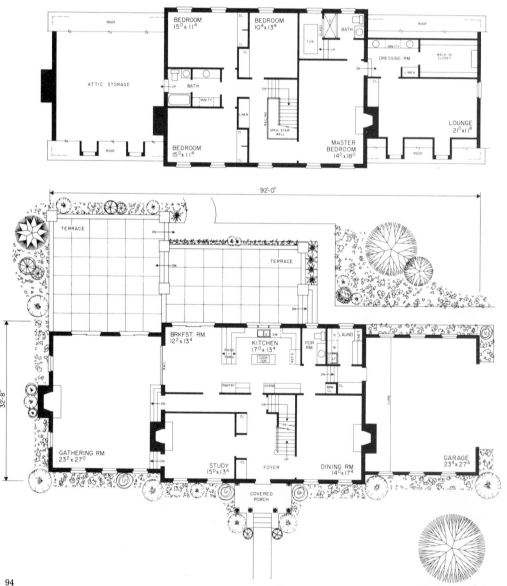

● This historical Georgian home has its roots in the 18th-Century. Dignified symmetry is a hallmark of both front and rear elevations. The full two-story center section is delightfully complimented by the 1½-story wings. Interior livability has been planned to serve today's active family. The elegant gathering room, three steps down from the rest of the house, has ample space for entertaining on a grand scale. It fills an entire wing and is dead-ended so that traffic does not pass through it. Guests and family alike will enjoy the two rooms flanking the foyer, the study and formal dining room. Each of these rooms will have a fireplace as its highlight. The breakfast room, kitchen, powder room and laundry are arranged for maximum efficiency. This area will always have that desired light and airy atmosphere with the sliding glass door and the triple window over the kitchen sink. The second floor houses the family bedrooms. Take special note of the spacious master bedroom suite. It has a deluxe bath, fireplace and sunken lounge with dressing room and walk-in closet. Surely an area to be appreciated.

Design T172984 *3,116 Sq. Ft. - First Floor; 1,997 Sq. Ft. - Second Floor; 95,716 Cu. Ft.*

● Stately Corinthian columns support the impressive pediment gable and help create the inviting portico of this 18th century Georgian manor. Effective window and cornice treatment along with the hip-roof and the massive chimney also help set the delightful character of this two-story home. The projecting end-gathering room and the four-car garage complete the appealing symmetry of the exterior. The spacious central foyer is highlighted by the dramatic open staircase to the second floor. A powder room and walk-in closet are strategically located handy to the front door. Traffic flows efficiently to the formal and informal living areas. A gallery provides the passageway to the immense, sunken 36-foot gathering room and the large study. Each of these rooms has a fireplace. To the rear of the house is the informal living zone. The well-planned kitchen functions with both the family and breakfast rooms. Like the gathering room, each enjoys its direct access through sliding glass doors to the rear terraces. The formal dining room is of nice size and looks out upon the front yard. A first floor laundry has bonus cabinet and counter space. Upstairs, each of the four big bedrooms has its own private bath. Don't miss the sloping ceiling and fireplace of the master bedroom. Note the whirlpool, vanity and twin walk-in closets of the master bath.

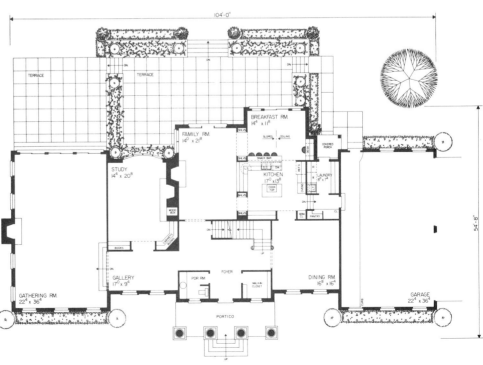

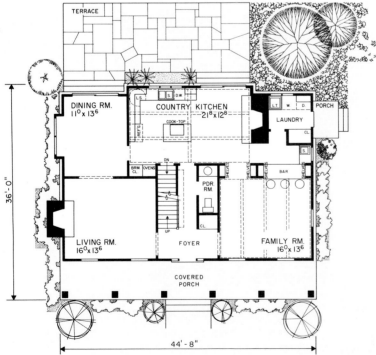

BEDROOM
11⁰ x 12⁴

BEDROOM
12⁰ x 10⁰

WALK-IN CLOSET

BATH

CL.

CL.

DRESSING RM.

LINEN

SEAT

DN

CL.

LIN.

CL.

CL.

LIN.

BEDROOM
16⁰ x 12⁴

BATH

MASTER BEDROOM
16⁰ x 13⁶

COVERED BALCONY

TERRACE

DINING RM.
11⁰ x 13⁶

COUNTRY KITCHEN
21⁸ x 12⁸

COOK-TOP

LAUNDRY

PORCH

W D

CL.

REF'G.

BRM CL.

OVENS

DN

PDR. RM.

SHELVES

BAR

SHELVES

LIVING RM.
16⁰ x 13⁶

FOYER

UP

CL.

FAMILY RM.
16⁰ x 13⁶

COVERED PORCH

36' - 0"

44' - 8"

Design T172664

1,308 Sq. Ft. - First Floor
1,262 Sq. Ft. - Second Floor
49,215 Cu. Ft.

● The exterior of this full two-story is highlighted by the covered, front porch and the covered, second floor balcony. Many enjoyable hours will be spent at these outdoor areas. There is also a rear terrace. It is accessible by way of the two dining areas. The interior is highlighted by a spacious country kitchen. Be sure to notice its island cook-top, fireplace and the beamed ceiling. It is also conveniently located. The laundry, rear terrace, basement stairs and dining room are only steps away. The front of this plan is devoted to the two living areas. To the left of the foyer is the formal living room, to the right, the family room. A built-in bar is in the family room. Sleeping facilities are on the second floor. All four bedrooms are a good size. The spacious master bath is outstanding. Study the many other fine details of this home.

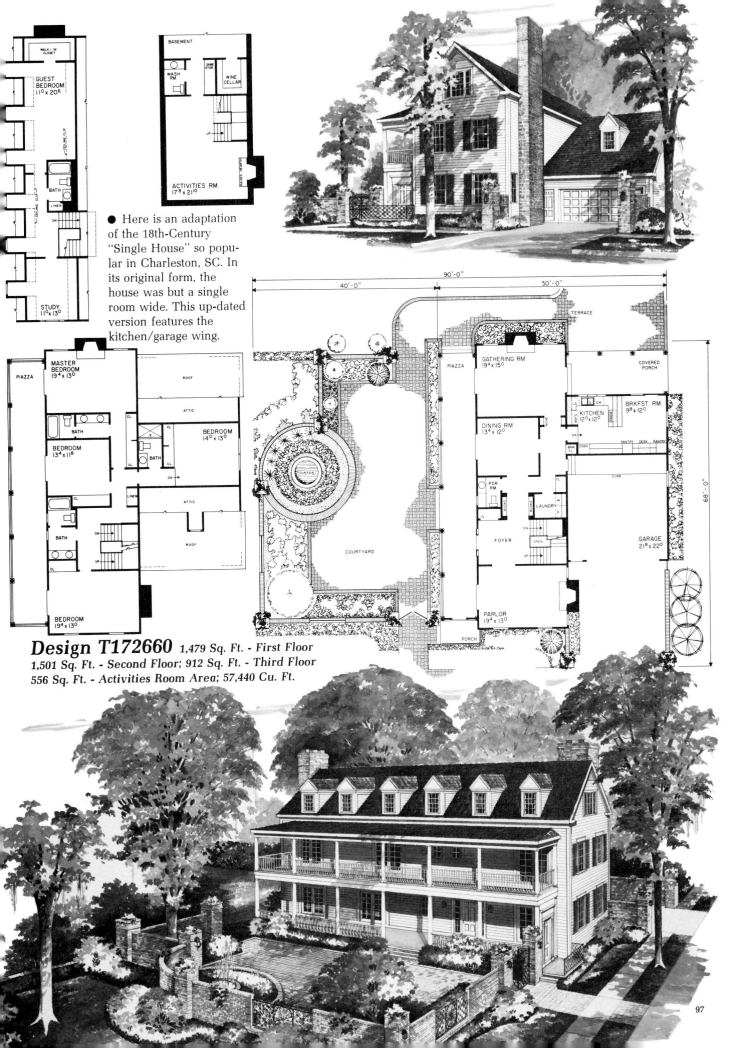

WALK-IN CLOSET

GUEST BEDROOM 11⁰ x 20⁶

BATH

LINEN

DN

STUDY 11⁰ x 13⁰

BASEMENT

WASH RM.

GAME STOR.

WINE CELLAR

UP

ACTIVITIES RM. 17⁸ x 21¹⁰

● Here is an adaptation of the 18th-Century "Single House" so popular in Charleston, SC. In its original form, the house was but a single room wide. This up-dated version features the kitchen/garage wing.

PIAZZA

MASTER BEDROOM 19⁴ x 13⁰

BATH

BEDROOM 13⁴ x 11⁸

BATH

LINEN

DN

UP

BEDROOM 19⁴ x 13⁰

ROOF

ATTIC

BEDROOM 14⁰ x 13⁰

DN

ATTIC

ROOF

90'-0"

40'-0"

50'-0"

68'-0"

TERRACE

PIAZZA

GATHERING RM. 19⁴ x 15⁰

COVERED PORCH

DINING RM. 13⁴ x 12⁰

KITCHEN 12⁰ x 12⁰

BRKFST. RM. 9⁸ x 12⁰

PANTRY DESK PANTRY

OVEN

PDR. RM.

CURB

LAUNDRY

FOYER

OPEN

UP

GARAGE 21⁸ x 22⁰

COURTYARD

FOUNTAIN

PARLOR 19⁴ x 13⁰

PORCH

Design T172660 1,479 Sq. Ft. - First Floor
1,501 Sq. Ft. - Second Floor; 912 Sq. Ft. - Third Floor
556 Sq. Ft. - Activities Room Area; 57,440 Cu. Ft.

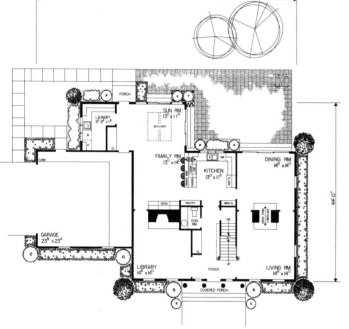

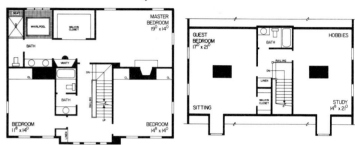

Design T172980 1,648 Sq. Ft. - First Floor
1,368 Sq. Ft. - Second Floor; 567 Sq. Ft. - Third Floor
52,509 Cu. Ft.

● This late Georgian adaptation is reminiscent of the Cowles house built in Farmington, Conn. around 1786. The formal symmetry and rich ornamentation were typical of houses of this period. Ionic columns, a Palladian window, and a pedimented gable are among the details that set the character of this historic house. Inside there are three floors of livability. And, of course, there is no hint of antiquity here. The centered foyer is flanked by wonderfully spacious living areas which flow around the fireplaces. Note the sun room, laundry, and bonus space of the third floor where there is all kinds of livability.

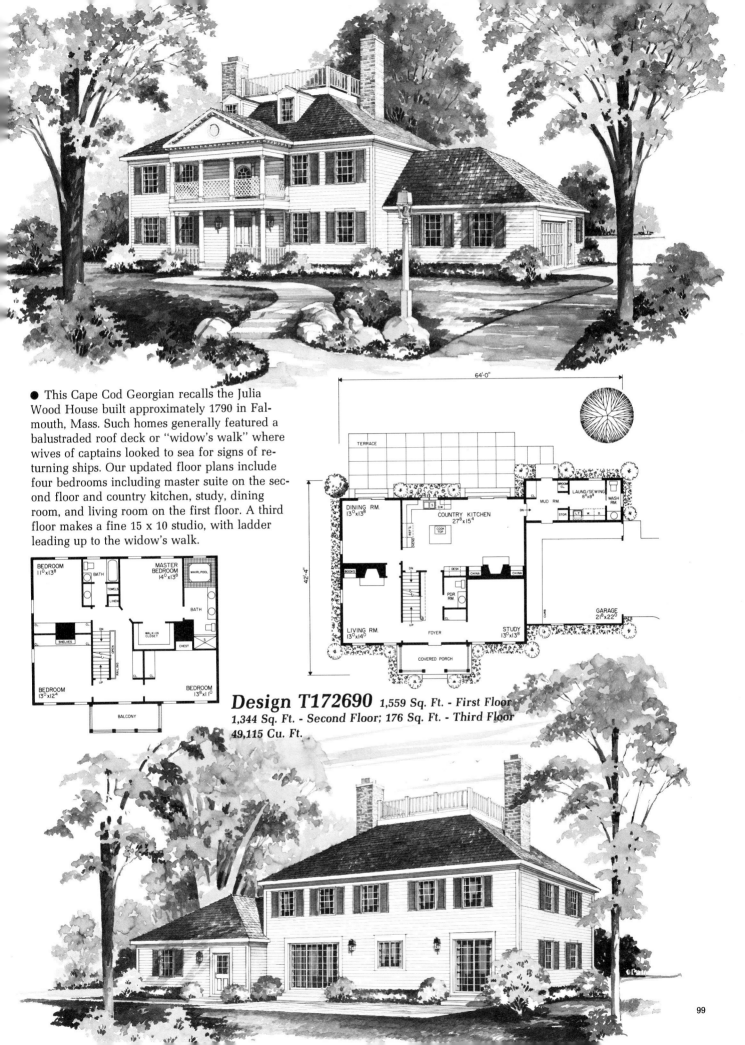

● This Cape Cod Georgian recalls the Julia Wood House built approximately 1790 in Falmouth, Mass. Such homes generally featured a balustraded roof deck or "widow's walk" where wives of captains looked to sea for signs of returning ships. Our updated floor plans include four bedrooms including master suite on the second floor and country kitchen, study, dining room, and living room on the first floor. A third floor makes a fine 15 x 10 studio, with ladder leading up to the widow's walk.

Design T172690 1,559 Sq. Ft. - First Floor
1,344 Sq. Ft. - Second Floor; 176 Sq. Ft. - Third Floor
49,115 Cu. Ft.

A Mount Vernon Reminiscence

● This magnificent manor's streetview illustrates a centralized mansion connected by curving galleries to matching wings. What a grand presentation this home will make! The origin of this house dates back to 1787 and George Washington's stately Mount Vernon. The underlying aesthetics for this design come from the rational balancing of porticoes, fenestration and chimneys. The rear elevation of this home also deserves mention. Six two-story columns, along with four sets of French doors, highlight this view. Study all of the intricate detailing that is featured all around these exteriors.

The flanking wings create a large formal courtyard where guests of today can park their cars. This home, designed from architecture of the past, is efficient and compact enough to fit many suburban lots. Its interior has been well planned and is ready to serve a family of any size.

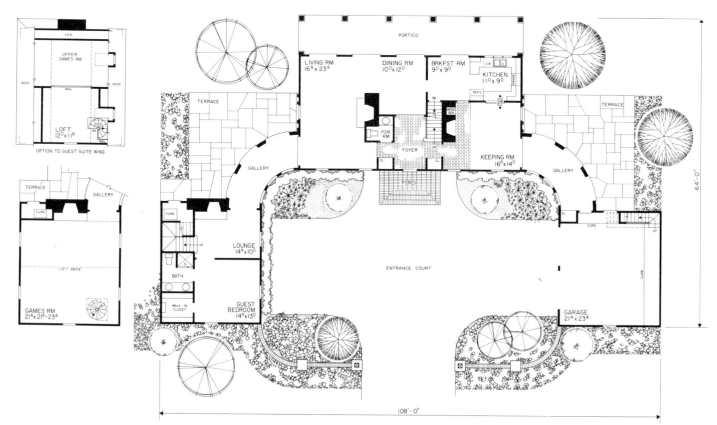

Design T172665 1,152 Sq. Ft. - First Floor
1,152 Sq. Ft. - Second Floor; 38,754 Cu. Ft. (Excludes Guest Suite and Galleries)

● The main, two-story section of this home houses the living areas. First - there is the large, tiled foyer with two closets and powder room. Then there is the living room which is the entire width of the house. This room has a fireplace and leads into the formal dining room. Three sets of double French doors lead to the rear portico from this formal area. The kitchen and breakfast room will function together. There is a pass-thru from the kitchen to the keeping room. All of the sleeping facilities, four bedrooms, are on the second floor. The gallery on the right leads to the garage; the one on the left, to a lounge and guest suite with studio above. The square and cubic footages quoted above do not include the guest suite or gallery areas. The first floor of the guest suite contains 688 sq. ft.; the second floor studio, 306 sq. ft. The optional plan shows a game room with a loft above having 162 sq. ft.

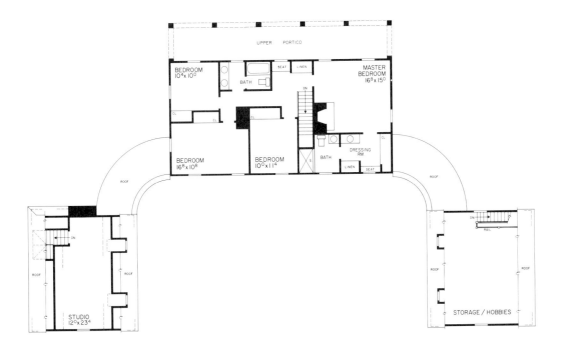

Design T172668 1,206 Sq. Ft. - First Floor
1,254 Sq. Ft. - Second Floor; 47,915 Cu. Ft.

● This elegant exterior houses a very livable plan. Every bit of space has been put to good use. The front country kitchen is a good place to begin. It is efficiently planned with its island cook top, built-ins and pass-thru to the dining room. The large great room will be the center of all family activities. Quiet times can be enjoyed in the front library. Study the second floor sleeping areas.

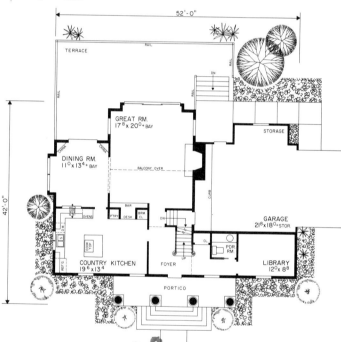

Design T172889

2,529 Sq. Ft. - First Floor
1,872 Sq. Ft. - Second Floor
80,670 Cu. Ft.

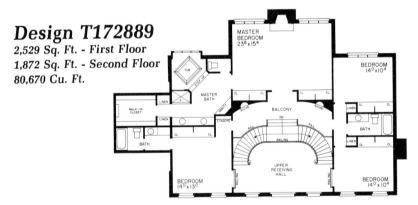

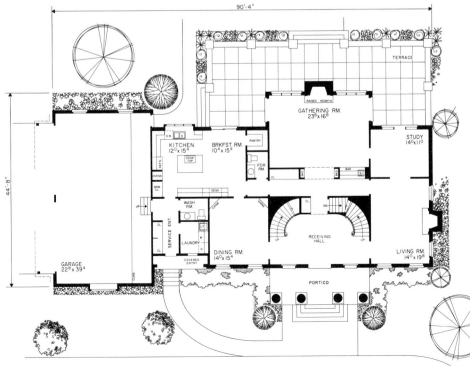

● This is truly classical, Georgian design at its best. Some of the exterior highlights of this two-story include the pediment gable with cornice work and dentils, the beautifully proportioned columns, the front door detailing and the window treatment. These are just some of the features which make this design so unique and appealing. Behind the facade of this design is an equally elegant interior. Imagine greeting your guests in the large receiving hall. It is graced by two curving staircases and opens to the formal living and dining rooms. Beyond the living room is the study. It has access to the rear terrace. Those large, informal occasions for family get-togethers or entertaining will be enjoyed in the spacious gathering room. It has a centered fireplace flanked by windows on each side, access to the terrace and a wet bar. Your appreciation for this room will be never-ending. The work center is efficient: the kitchen with island cook top, breakfast room, washroom, laundry and service entrance. The second floor also is outstanding. Three family bedrooms and two full baths are joined by the feature-filled master bedroom suite. Study this area carefully. If you like this basic floor plan but would prefer a French exterior, see Design T172543 on page 285.

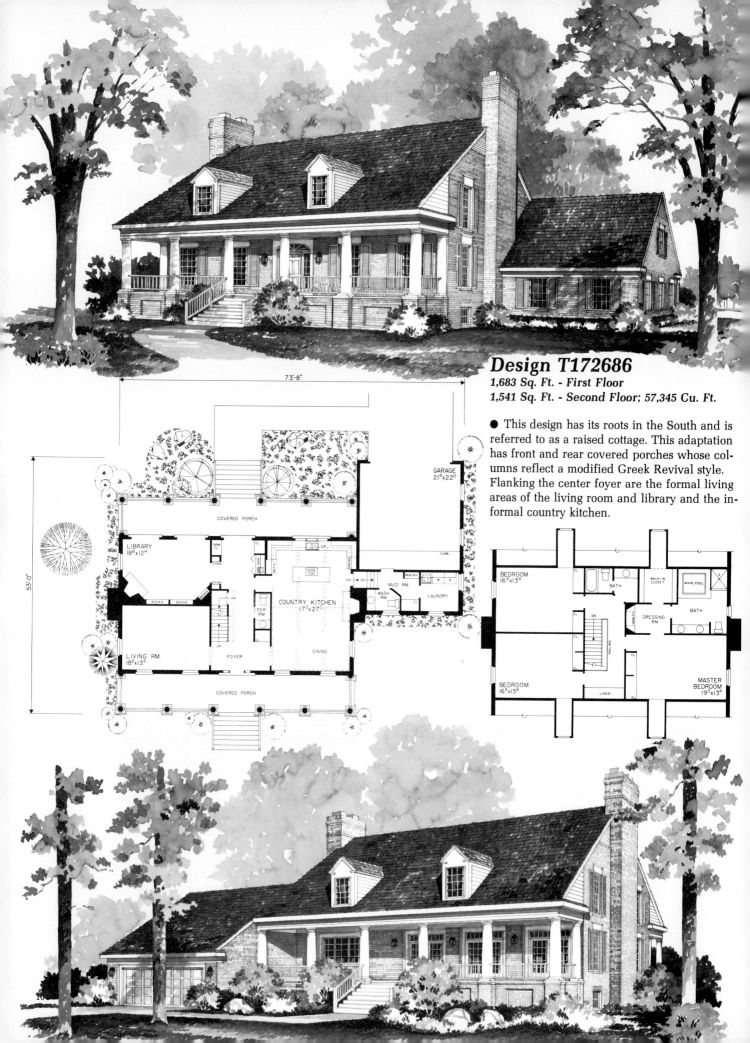

Design T172686

1,683 Sq. Ft. - First Floor
1,541 Sq. Ft. - Second Floor; 57,345 Cu. Ft.

● This design has its roots in the South and is referred to as a raised cottage. This adaptation has front and rear covered porches whose columns reflect a modified Greek Revival style. Flanking the center foyer are the formal living areas of the living room and library and the informal country kitchen.

73'-8"

53'-0"

GARAGE
21⁴x22⁰

COVERED PORCH

LIBRARY
18⁸x12⁴

BRM CL

CHINA

BOOKS   BOOKS

CHINA

LIVING RM.
18⁸x13⁴

FOYER

COOK TOP

CL

DN   DN

PDR RM

UP

DINING

COUNTRY KITCHEN
17⁰x27⁰

MUD RM

WASH RM

CL

PANTRY

T W D

LAUNDRY

CURB

COVERED PORCH

BEDROOM
16⁴x13⁴

CL

BATH

WALK-IN CLOSET

WHIRLPOOL

DRESSING RM

BATH

CL

DN

CL

RAILING

BEDROOM
16⁴x13⁴

LINEN

CL

MASTER BEDROOM
19⁰x13⁴

Design T172684 *1,600 Sq. Ft. - First Floor*
1,498 Sq. Ft. - Second Floor; 47,395 Cu. Ft.

● Highlighting this plan is the spacious, country kitchen. Its features are many, indeed. Also worth a special note is the second floor studio/office. It is accessible by way of a staircase in the back of the plan. Just imagine the many uses for this area. There is a great deal of livability in this plan. Don't miss the three fireplaces or the first floor laundry.

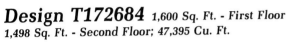

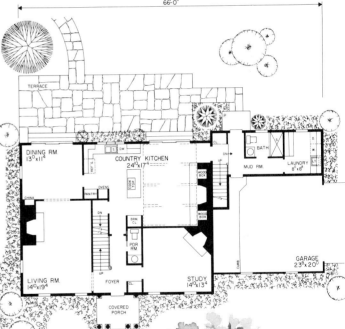

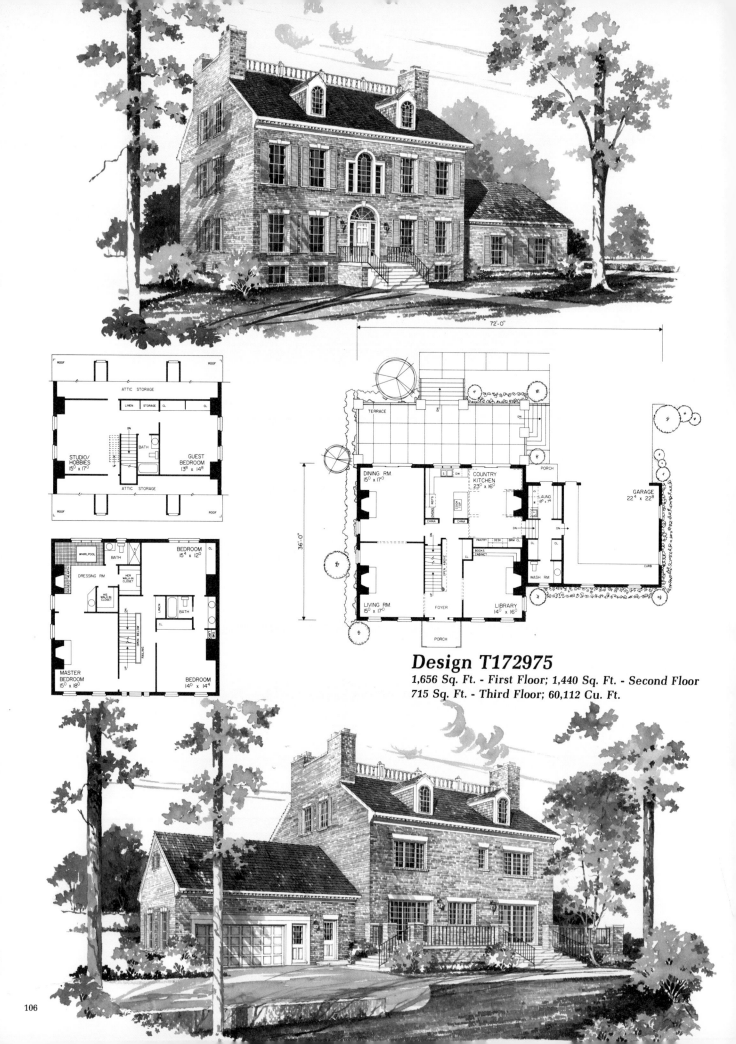

ATTIC STORAGE

LINEN | STORAGE | CL | CL

STUDIO/ HOBBIES 15⁰ x 17⁰

BATH

GUEST BEDROOM 13⁸ x 14⁸

ATTIC STORAGE

WHIRLPOOL | BATH | BEDROOM 15⁴ x 12⁰

DRESSING RM

HER WALK-IN CLOSET

HIS WALK-IN CLOSET | LINEN | BATH

MASTER BEDROOM 15⁰ x 18⁰

BEDROOM 14⁰ x 14⁴

72'-0"

36'-0"

TERRACE

DINING RM 15⁰ x 17⁰

COUNTRY KITCHEN 23⁰ x 16⁰

PORCH

LAUND 8⁰ x 7⁴

GARAGE 22⁴ x 22⁸

CHINA | CHINA

PANTRY | DESK | BRM CL

BOOKS CABINET

WASH RM

CURB

LIVING RM 15⁰ x 17⁰

FOYER

LIBRARY 14⁰ x 16⁰

PORCH

Design T172975
1,656 Sq. Ft. - First Floor; 1,440 Sq. Ft. - Second Floor
715 Sq. Ft. - Third Floor; 60,112 Cu. Ft.

Design T172139
1,581 Sq. Ft. - First Floor
991 Sq. Ft. - Second Floor
36,757 Cu. Ft.

● Four bedrooms and two baths make-up the second floor of this two-story design. The first floor has all of the living areas and work center. Note the convenience of the powder room.

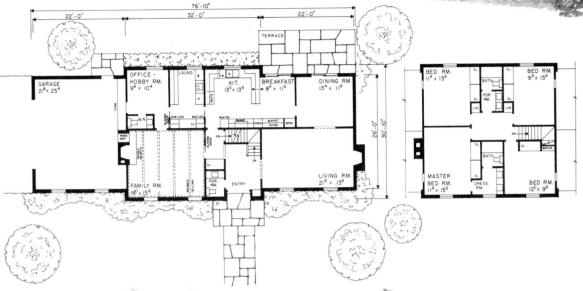

Design T172176
1,485 Sq. Ft. - First Floor
1,175 Sq. Ft. - Second Floor
41,646 Cu. Ft.

● A big, end living room featuring a fireplace and sliding glass doors is the focal point of this Georgian design. Adjacent is the formal dining room strategically located but a couple of steps from the efficient kitchen. Functioning closely with the kitchen is the family room.

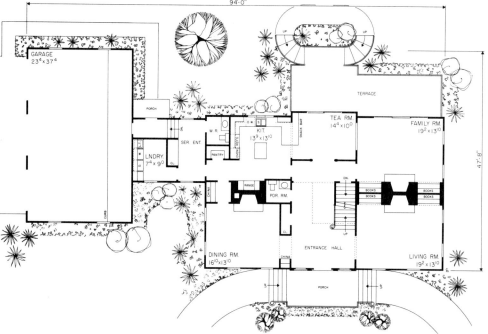

Design T172301

2,044 Sq. Ft. - First Floor
1,815 Sq. Ft. - Second Floor
69,925 Cu. Ft.

● Reminiscent of architecture with roots in the deep South, this finely detailed home is exquisite, indeed. Study the contemporary floor plan and the living patterns it offers.

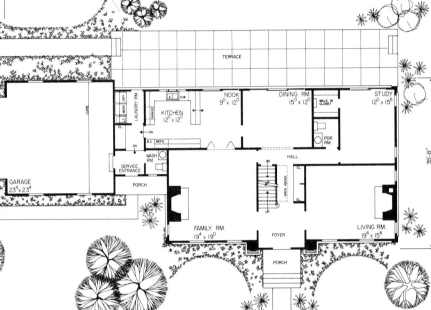

Design T172522

1,835 Sq. Ft. - First Floor
1,625 Sq. Ft. - Second Floor
58,700 Cu. Ft.

● This wood frame Georgian adaptation revives the architecture of an earlier period in New England. Its formal facade houses an abundance of spacious livability.

First Floor

85'-8"

35'-8"

TERRACE

NOOK 9⁰ x 12⁰

DINING RM. 15⁰ x 12⁰

WALK IN CLOSET

STUDY 12⁰ x 15⁶

LAUNDRY RM.

WASH DRY

KITCHEN 12⁰ x 12⁰

RANGE

DW

DN

B.C. REFG.

PDR. RM.

DN

WASH RM.

SERVICE ENTRANCE

HALL

CL

OPEN ABOVE

DN UP

CL

GARAGE 23⁴ x 23⁴

PORCH

FAMILY RM. 19⁴ x 19⁰

FOYER

LIVING RM. 19⁴ x 15⁶

PORCH

Second Floor

BATH

VANITY

BED RM. 13⁴ x 12⁰

WALK-IN CLOSET

SHELVES

BED RM. 11⁴ x 15⁶

BATH

VANITY

CL

DN

DN

RAILING

HALL

LINEN

CL

CL

MASTER BED RM. 19⁴ x 15⁶

SITTING RM. 10⁰ x 9⁴

BED RM. 17⁰ x 15⁶

● A Georgian Colonial adaptation on the grand scale. The authentic front entrance is delightfully detailed. Two massive end chimneys, housing four fireplaces, are in keeping with the architecture of its day.

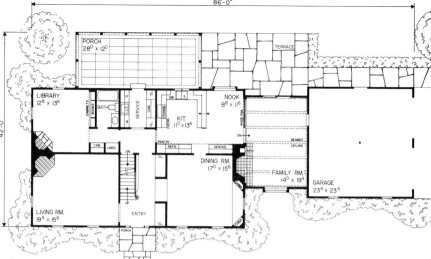

Design T172221 1,726 Sq. Ft. - First Floor
1,440 Sq. Ft. - Second Floor; 50,204 Cu. Ft.

Design T171852 1,802 Sq. Ft. - First Floor
1,603 Sq. Ft. - Second Floor; 51,361 Cu. Ft.

● This is an impressive Georgian adaptation. The front entrance detailing, the window treatment and the masses of brick help put this house in a class of its own.

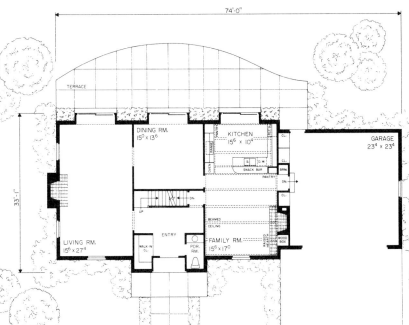

TERRACE

DINING RM.
15⁰ x 13⁶

KITCHEN
15⁶ x 10⁴

SNACK BAR

PANTRY

GARAGE
23⁴ x 23⁴

LIVING RM.
15⁶ x 27⁴

WALK IN CL.

ENTRY

PDR. RM.

FAMILY RM.
15⁶ x 17⁰

BEAMED CEILING

WOOD BOX

UP

DN.

74'-0"

33'-1"

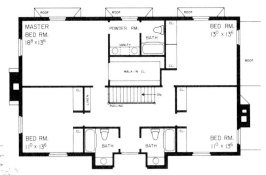

MASTER BED RM.
18⁸ x 13⁶

POWDER RM.

BED RM.
13⁰ x 13⁶

VANITY

BATH

WALK-IN CL.

CL.

LINEN

RAILING

DN.

ROOF

BED RM.
11⁰ x 13⁶

BATH

BATH

BED RM.
11⁰ x 13⁶

● This stately home, whose roots go back to an earlier period in American architecture, will forever retain its aura of distinction. The spacious front entry effectively separates the formal and informal living zones. Four bedrooms on second floor.

Design T172250
1,442 Sq. Ft. - First Floor
1,404 Sq. Ft. - Second Floor; 46,326 Cu. Ft.

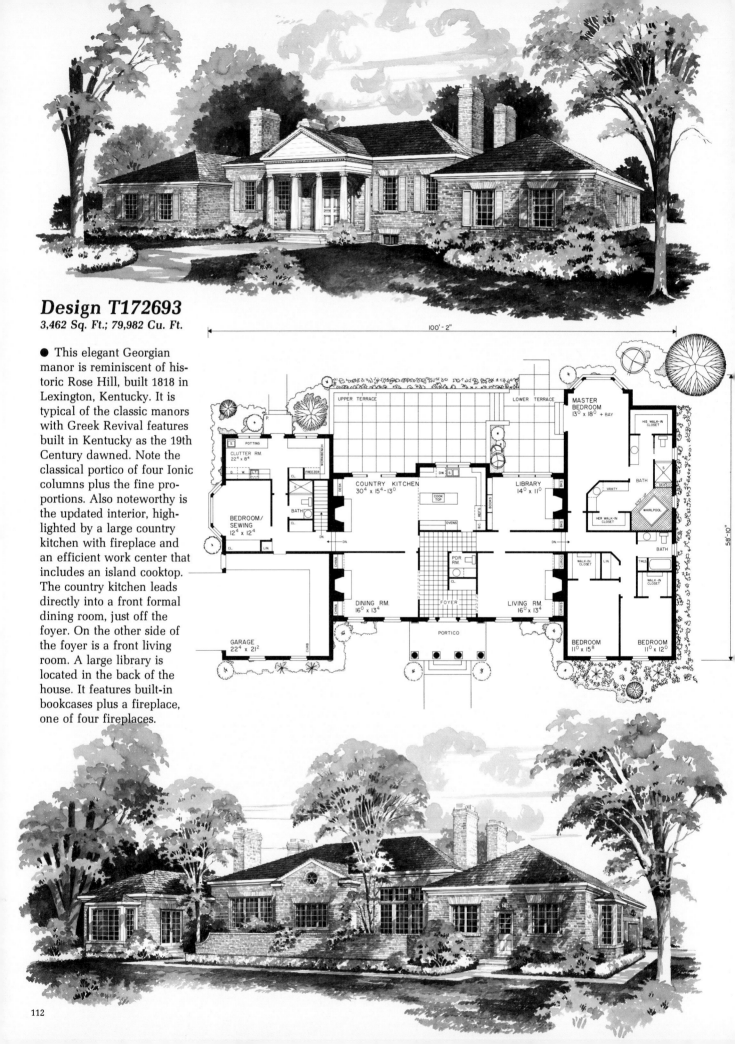

Design T172693
3,462 Sq. Ft.; 79,982 Cu. Ft.

● This elegant Georgian manor is reminiscent of historic Rose Hill, built 1818 in Lexington, Kentucky. It is typical of the classic manors with Greek Revival features built in Kentucky as the 19th Century dawned. Note the classical portico of four Ionic columns plus the fine proportions. Also noteworthy is the updated interior, highlighted by a large country kitchen with fireplace and an efficient work center that includes an island cooktop. The country kitchen leads directly into a front formal dining room, just off the foyer. On the other side of the foyer is a front living room. A large library is located in the back of the house. It features built-in bookcases plus a fireplace, one of four fireplaces.

100' - 2"

58' - 10"

POTTING
CLUTTER RM. 22⁴ x 8⁴
FREEZER
WORKBENCH
BEDROOM/ SEWING 12⁴ x 12⁴
BATH
DESK
COUNTRY KITCHEN 30⁴ x 15⁴ - 13⁰
COOK TOP
OVENS
DW
UPPER TERRACE
LOWER TERRACE
MASTER BEDROOM 13⁰ x 18⁰ + BAY
HIS WALK-IN CLOSET
LIBRARY 14⁰ x 11⁰
BOOKS
BATH
VANITY
WHIRLPOOL
HER WALK-IN CLOSET
BATH
GARAGE 22⁴ x 21²
CHINA
DINING RM. 16⁰ x 13⁴
CHINA
PDR. RM.
FOYER
LIVING RM. 16⁰ x 13⁴
WALK-IN CLOSET
LIN
WALK-IN CLOSET
PORTICO
BEDROOM 11⁰ x 15⁸
BEDROOM 11⁰ x 12⁰

Design T172977 4,104 Sq. Ft. - First Floor; 979 Sq. Ft. - Second Floor; 104,801 Cu. Ft.

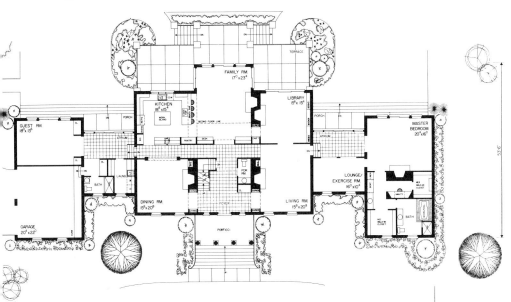

● Both front and rear facades of this elegant brick manor depict classic Georgian symmetry. A columned, Greek entry opens to an impressive two-story foyer. Fireplaces, built-in shelves, and cabinets highlight each of the four main gathering areas: living room, dining room, family room, and library.

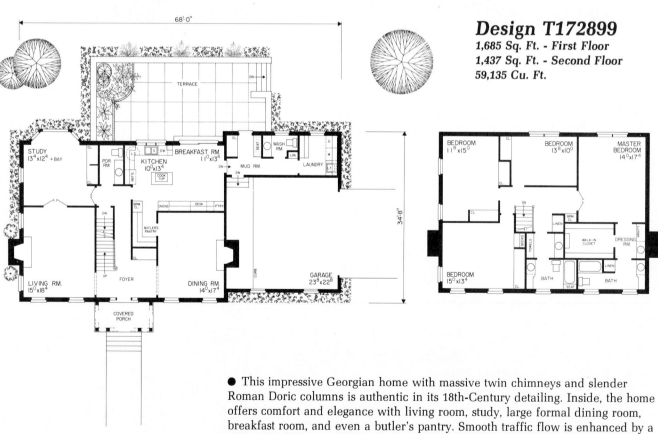

Design T172899
1,685 Sq. Ft. - First Floor
1,437 Sq. Ft. - Second Floor
59,135 Cu. Ft.

● This impressive Georgian home with massive twin chimneys and slender Roman Doric columns is authentic in its 18th-Century detailing. Inside, the home offers comfort and elegance with living room, study, large formal dining room, breakfast room, and even a butler's pantry. Smooth traffic flow is enhanced by a central foyer that opens to stairs leading to the second story. Downstairs there's also a mud room adjacent to the laundry. Upstairs is thoughtfully zoned, too, with a central bath to accommodate a master bedroom and three other bedrooms there.

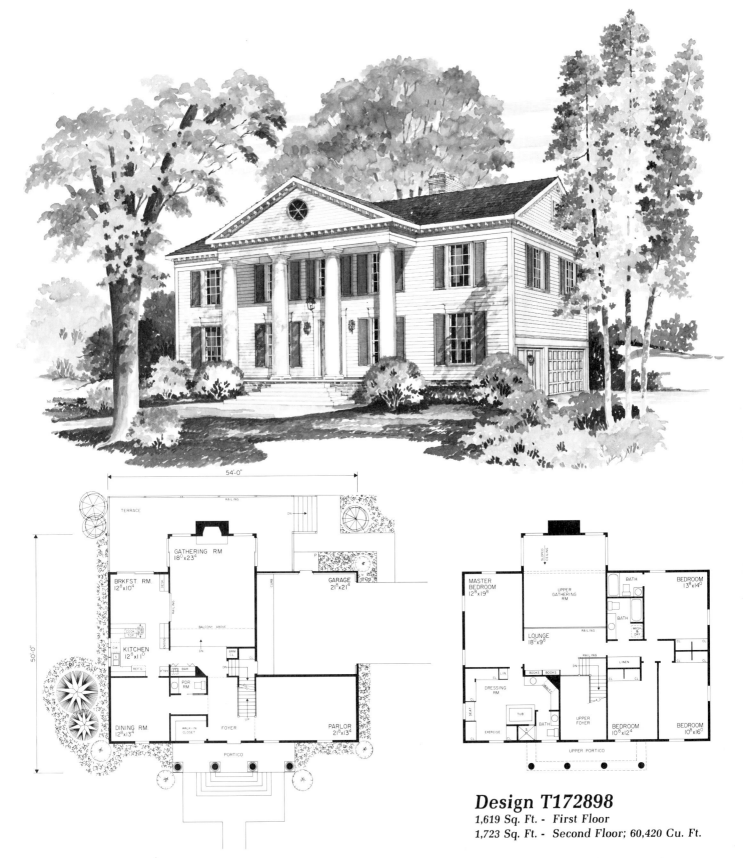

Design T172898
1,619 Sq. Ft. - *First Floor*
1,723 Sq. Ft. - *Second Floor; 60,420 Cu. Ft.*

● Four soaring Doric columns highlight the exterior of this Greek Revival dwelling. The elevation reflects a balanced design that incorporates four bedrooms and a two-car garage in one central unit. The stylish heart of this dwelling is a two-story gathering room. A balcony lounge on the second floor offers a quiet aerie overlooking this living area. Both of these areas will have sunlight streaming through the high windows. A second living area is the parlor. It could serve as the formal area whereas the gathering room could be considered informal. Entrance to all of these areas will be through the foyer. It has an adjacent powder room and spacious walk-in closet. The U-shaped kitchen will conveniently serve the breakfast and dining rooms. Second floor livability is outstanding. Study all of the features in the master bedroom: dressing room, tub and shower, large vanity and exercise area. Three more bedrooms, another has a private bath which would make it an ideal guest room.

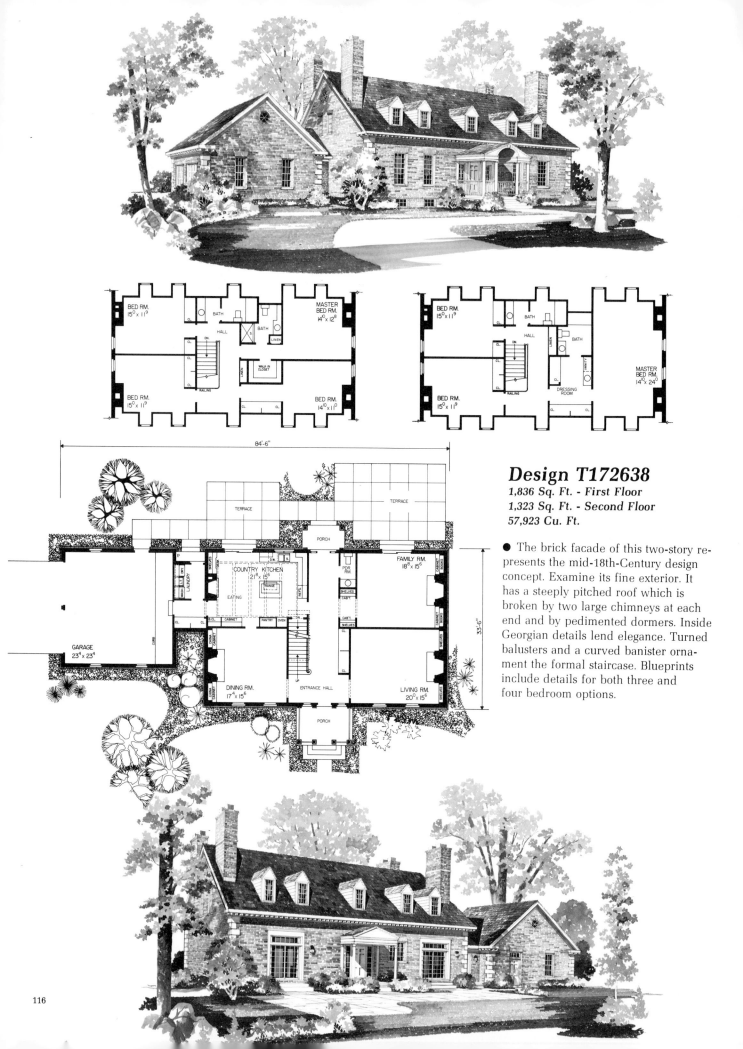

BED RM. 15⁰ x 11⁹

BED RM. 15⁰ x 11⁹

BATH

HALL

BATH

MASTER BED RM. 14⁰ x 12⁸

LINEN

WALK IN CLOSET

BED RM. 14¹⁰ x 11⁰

BED RM. 15⁰ x 11⁹

BED RM. 15⁰ x 11⁹

BATH

HALL

LINEN

BATH

VANITY

DRESSING ROOM

MASTER BED RM. 14¹⁰ x 24⁰

84'-6"

TERRACE

TERRACE

PORCH

COUNTRY KITCHEN 21⁸ x 15⁶

LAUNDRY

EATING

RANGE

PANTRY

OVEN

PDR. RM.

FAMILY RM. 18⁸ x 15⁶

GARAGE 23⁴ x 23⁴

33'-6"

DINING RM. 17⁴ x 15⁶

ENTRANCE HALL

UP

LIVING RM. 20⁰ x 15⁶

PORCH

Design T172638

1,836 Sq. Ft. - First Floor
1,323 Sq. Ft. - Second Floor
57,923 Cu. Ft.

● The brick facade of this two-story re-presents the mid-18th-Century design concept. Examine its fine exterior. It has a steeply pitched roof which is broken by two large chimneys at each end and by pedimented dormers. Inside Georgian details lend elegance. Turned balusters and a curved banister orna-ment the formal staircase. Blueprints include details for both three and four bedroom options.

Design T172688 1,588 Sq. Ft. - First Floor
1,101 Sq. Ft. - Second Floor; 44,021 Cu. Ft.

● Here are two floors of excellent livability. Start at the country kitchen. It will be the center for family activities. It has an island, desk, raised hearth fireplace, conversation area and sliding glass doors to the terrace. Adjacent to this area is the washroom and laundry. Quieter areas are available in the living room and library. Three bedrooms are housed on the second floor.

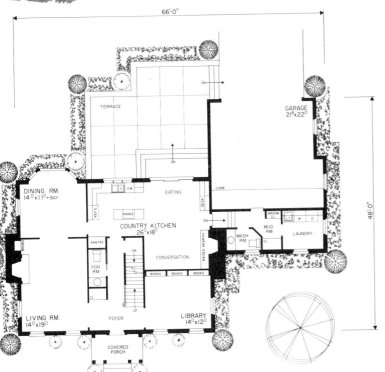

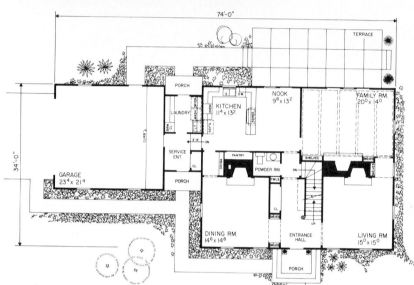

● Here is a New England Georgian adaptation with an elevated doorway highlighted by pilasters and a pediment. It gives way to a second-story Palladian window, capped in turn by a pediment projecting from the hipped roof. The interior is decidely up-to-date with even an upstairs lounge.

Design T172639 1,556 Sq. Ft. - First Floor; 1,428 Sq. Ft. - Second Floor; 46,115 Cu. Ft.

Design T172667 1,827 Sq. Ft. - First Floor
697 Sq. Ft. - Second Floor; 46,290 Cu. Ft.

● Two one-story wings flank the two-story center section of this design which echoes the architectural forms of 18th-Century Tidewater Virginia. The left wing is a huge living room; the right, the master bedroom suite, service area and garage. Kitchen, dining room and family room are centrally located with the three bedrooms above. Study both plans and envision your family occupying them.

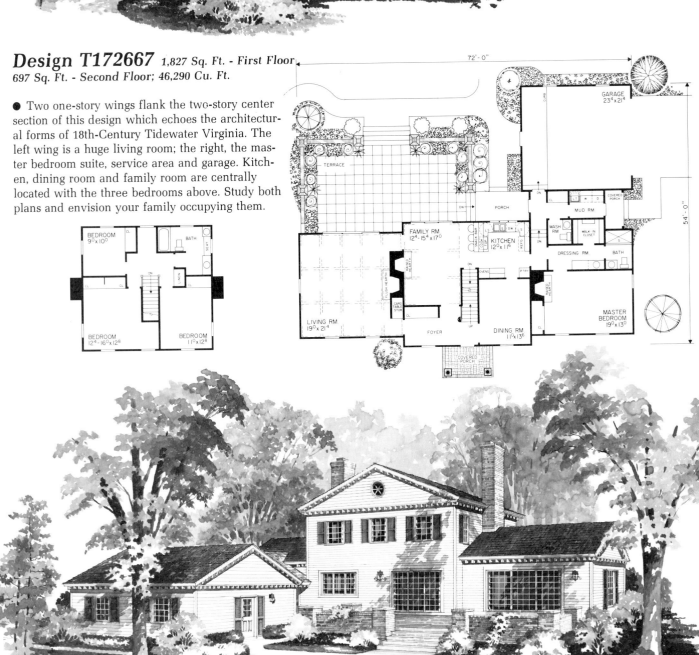

Design T171858

1,794 Sq. Ft. - First Floor
1,474 Sq. Ft. - Second Floor
424 Sq. Ft. - Studio
54,878 Cu. Ft.

● You'll never regret your choice of this Georgian design. Its stately facade seems to foretell all of the exceptional features to be found inside. From the delightful spacious front entry hall, to the studio or maid's room over the garage, this home is unique all along the way. Imagine four fireplaces, three full baths, two extra washrooms, a family room, plus a quiet library. Don't miss the first floor laundry. Note the separate set of stairs to the studio, or maid's room. The center entrance leads to the vestibule and the wonderfully spacious entry hall. All the major areas are but a step or two from this formal hall. The kitchen is well-planned and strategically located between the separate dining room and the breakfast room. Sliding glass doors permit easy access to the functional rear terraces.

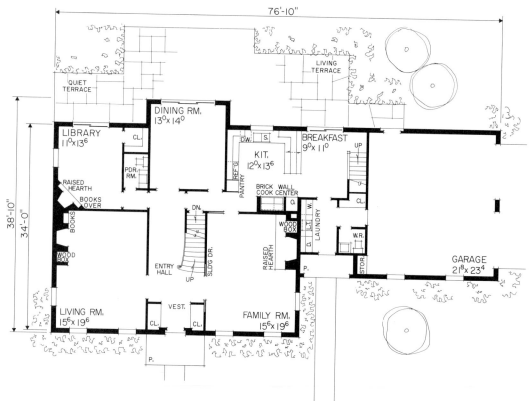

Spanish Houses

Here is a selection of designs that capture the feeling of the southwest. To one degree or another, most of these designs feature a variety of Spanish architectural features. Others, however, reflect an ambience of the western ranch. Nevertheless, all designs are fine examples of what good indoor/outdoor living relationships should be. Notice the visor-like wide overhanging roofs.

Design T172820 2,261 Sq. Ft.; 46,830 Cu. Ft.

● A privacy wall around the courtyard with pool and trellised planter area is a gracious area by which to enter this one-story design. The Spanish flavor is accented by the grillework and the tiled roof. Interior livability has a great deal to offer. The front living room has sliding glass doors which open to the entrance court; the adjacent dining room features a bay window. Informal activities will be enjoyed in the rear family room. Its many features include a sloped, beamed ceiling, raised hearth fireplace, sliding glass doors to the terrace and a snack bar for those very informal meals. A laundry and powder room are adjacent to the U-shaped kitchen. The sleeping wing can remain quiet away from the plan's activity centers. Notice the three-car garage with an extra storage area.

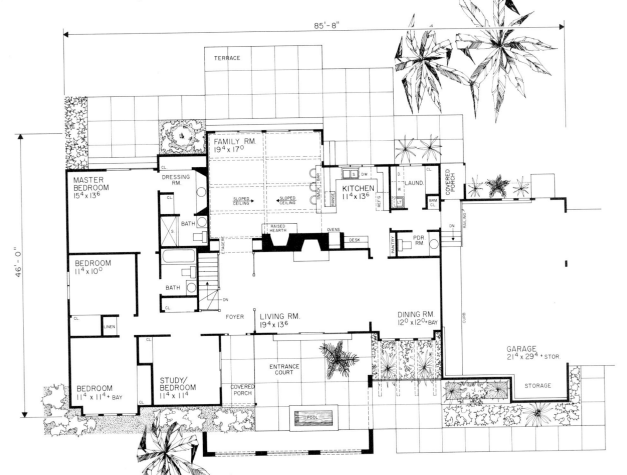

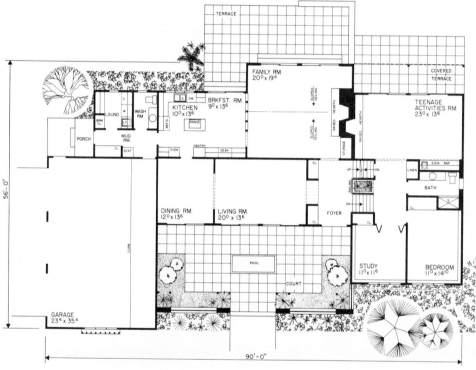

Design T172850

1,530 Sq. Ft. - Main Level; 984 Sq. Ft. - Upper Level; 951 Sq. Ft. - Lower Level; 53,780 Cu. Ft.

● Entering through the entry court of this Spanish design is very impressive. Partially shielded from the street, this court features planting areas and a small pool. Enter into the foyer and this split-level interior will begin to unfold. Down six steps from the foyer is the lower level housing a bedroom and full bath, study and teenage activities room. Adults, along with teenagers, will enjoy the activities room which has a raised hearth fireplace, soda bar and sliding glass doors leading to a covered terrace. Six steps up from the foyer is the upper level bedroom area. The main level has the majority of the living areas. Formal living and dining rooms, informal family room, kitchen with accompanying breakfast room and mud room consisting of laundry and wash room. This home even has a three-car garage. Livability will be achieved with the greatest amount of comfort in this home.

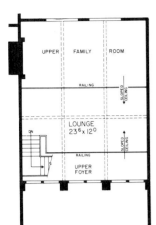

Design T172670
3,058 Sq. Ft.; 44,210 Cu. Ft.

● A centrally located interior atrium is one of the most interesting features of this Spanish design. The atrium has a built-in seat and will bring light to its adjacent rooms, living, dining and breakfast room. Beyond the foyer, sunken one step, is a tiled reception hall that includes a powder room. This area leads to the sleeping wing and up one step to the family room. Overlooking the family room is a railed lounge, 279 square feet, which can be used for various activities. The work center area will be convenient to work in.

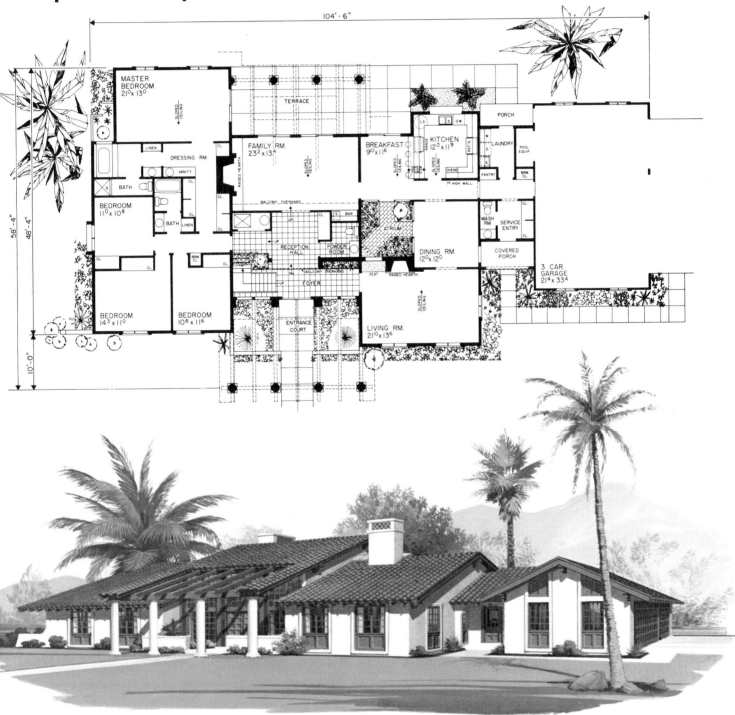

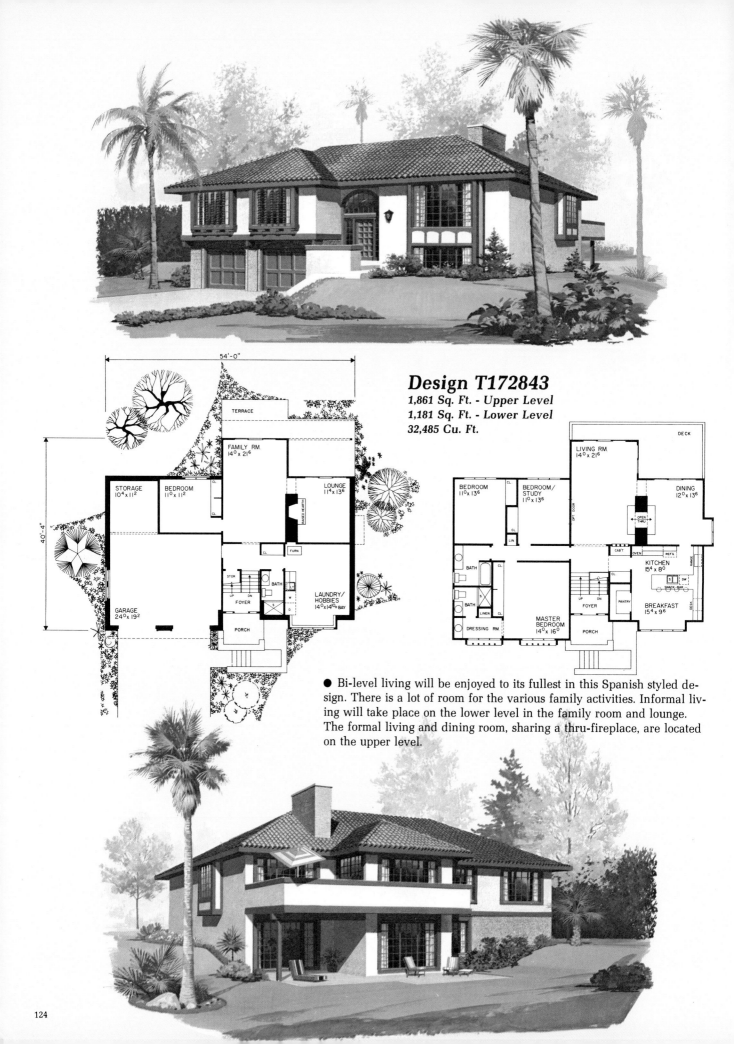

Design T172843

1,861 Sq. Ft. - Upper Level
1,181 Sq. Ft. - Lower Level
32,485 Cu. Ft.

54'-0"

40'-4"

TERRACE

FAMILY RM.
14⁰ x 21⁶

LOUNGE
11⁴ x 13⁶

STORAGE
10⁴ x 11²

BEDROOM
11⁰ x 11²

RAISED HEARTH

GARAGE
24⁰ x 19²

STOR

CL   FURN

UP   DN
FOYER

BATH

LAUNDRY/
HOBBIES
14⁰ x 14¹⁰ BAY

PORCH

DECK

LIVING RM.
14⁰ x 21⁶

BEDROOM
11⁰ x 13⁶

BEDROOM/
STUDY
11⁰ x 13⁶

DINING
12⁰ x 13⁶

OPEN
THRU

BATH

CAB'T   OVEN   REF'G.

KITCHEN
15⁴ x 8⁰

RANGE

BATH

LINEN

UP   DN
FOYER

CL

PANTRY

SNACK BAR   DW

BREAKFAST
15⁴ x 9⁶

DRESSING RM.

MASTER
BEDROOM
14⁰ x 16⁰

PORCH

● Bi-level living will be enjoyed to its fullest in this Spanish styled design. There is a lot of room for the various family activities. Informal living will take place on the lower level in the family room and lounge. The formal living and dining room, sharing a thru-fireplace, are located on the upper level.

DECK

FAMILY RM. 12⁰ x 17⁶	KITCHEN 11⁰ x 16⁰

66'-0"

FAMILY RM. 12⁰ x 17⁶

KITCHEN 11⁰ x 16⁰

DINING RM. 11⁴ x 14⁰

LIVING RM. 16⁰ x 17⁶

COVERED PORCH

MASTER BEDROOM 13⁸ x 15⁰

BEDROOM 12⁰ x 11²

PANTRY

OPEN OVER PLANTER

FOYER

PDR RM.

LINEN

WALK-IN CLOSET

LINEN TUB

BATH

COVERED PORCH

STUDY 12⁰ x 12⁰

BATH

BEDROOM 12⁰ x 11⁴

LAUNDRY

OPEN ABOVE

OPEN ABOVE

OPEN ABOVE

COURT

CURB

GARAGE 23⁴ x 22⁰

COVERED TERRACE

LOUNGE 22⁶ x 17⁶

GUEST BEDROOM 11⁶ x 14⁰

BASEMENT

UNEXCAVATED

AIR COND

SNACK BAR

SUMMER KITCHEN 14⁸ x 9⁸

UP

LINEN

BATH

STORAGE

UNEXCAVATED

HOBBIES / SHOP

GAMES RM. 21⁸ x 15⁰

Design T172846
2,341 Sq. Ft. - Main Level; 1,380 Sq. Ft. - Lower Level; 51,290 Cu. Ft.

● The street view of this Spanish design shows a beautifully designed one-story home, but now take a look at the rear elevation. This home has been designed to be built into a hill so the lower level can be opened to the sun. By so doing, the total livability is almost doubled.

Design T172294 *3,056 Sq. Ft.; 34,533 Cu. Ft.*

● Here is a Western ranch with an authentic Spanish flavor. Striking a note of distinction, the arched privacy walls provide a fine backdrop for the long, raised planter. Behind the open arches with their patterned grille-work are two spacious outdoor living areas. The central, open courtyard will be a delightful challenge to your gardening instincts. The wide, covered loggia, in addition to providing a covered walkway to the double front doors, functions as a sheltered outdoor sitting area. The quiet terrace is a marvelous outdoor extension to the bedroom area. The low-pitched roof features tile and has a wide overhang with exposed rafter tails. The interior is wonderfully zoned. The all-purpose family rooom is flanked by the sleeping wing and the living wing. Study each area carefully. The planning is excellent and the features are many. Imagine, a 24 foot master bedroom with sloping ceiling!

Design T172236 2,307 Sq. Ft.; 28,800 Cu. Ft.

● Living in this Spanish adaptation truly will be fun for the whole family. It will matter very little whether the backdrop matches the mountains as shown or becomes the endless prairie, turns out to be the rolling farmland, or is the backdrop of suburbia, U.S.A.

A family's flair for distinction will be satisfied by this picturesque exterior, while its requirements for everyday living will be gloriously catered to by its floor plan. The hub of the plan will be the kitchen-family room area. The beamed ceiling and raised hearth fire-

place will contribute to the cozy, informal atmosphere. The separate dining room and the sunken living room function together formally. The master bedroom will enjoy its privacy from the three children's rooms located at the opposite end of the plan.

Design T172741 1,842 Sq. Ft.; 37,045 Cu. Ft.

● Here is an example of what 1,800 square feet can deliver in comfort and convenience. The setting reminds one of the sun country of Arizona. However, this design would surely be an attractive and refreshing addition to any region. The covered front porch with its adjacent open trellis area shelters the center entry. From here traffic flows efficiently to the sleeping, living and kitchen zones. There is much to recommend each area. The sleeping with its fine bath and closet facilities; the living with its spaciousness, fireplace and adjacent dining room; the kitchen with its handy nook, excellent storage, nearby laundry and extra wash room. Be sure to notice that each of the rear rooms have sliding glass doors opening onto the terraces. Note the privacy wall.

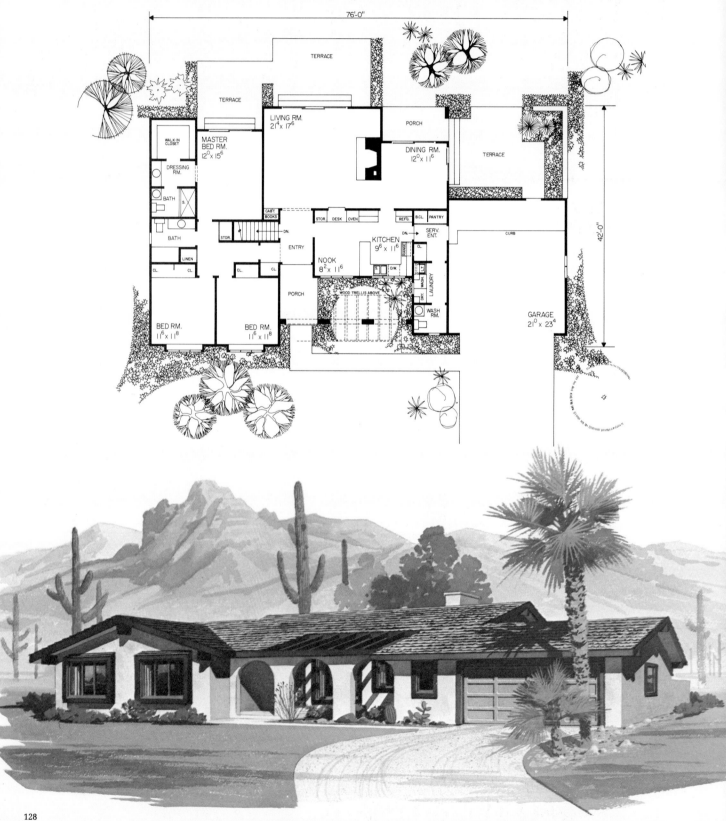

Design T172200
1,695 Sq. Ft.; 18,916 Cu. Ft.

● The two plans featured here are both housed in this L-shaped ranch home. Its exterior shows a Spanish influence by utilizing a stucco exterior finish, grilled windows and an arched entryway. Beyond the arched entryway is the private front court which leads to the tiled foyer. Interior livability has been well planned in both designs.

BED RM. | LIVING RM.

FOYER

OPTIONAL BASEMENT PLAN

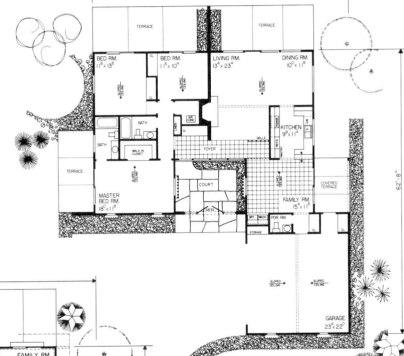

58'-8"

TERRACE | TERRACE

BED RM. 11⁸x13⁸ | BED RM. 11⁶x10⁴ | LIVING RM. 13⁴x23⁴ | DINING RM. 10⁰x11⁸

SLOPED CEILING | SLOPED CEILING | SLOPED CEILING

BATH | KITCHEN 9⁸x11⁴

BATH | WALK IN CLOSET | FOYER | REF'G. | RANGE

TERRACE | GRILLE

MASTER BED RM. 18⁴x11⁸ | COURT | SLOPED CEILING | COVERED TERRACE

GATES | FAMILY RM. 15⁴x11⁸

DRY. WASH. | PDR. RM.

STORAGE

SLOPED CEILING | SLOPED CEILING

GARAGE 23⁴x22

62'-8"

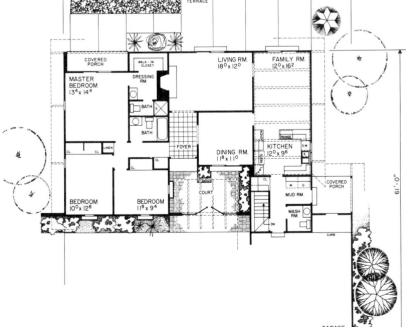

62'-0"

TERRACE

COVERED PORCH | WALK-IN CLOSET | LIVING RM. 18⁰x12⁰ | FAMILY RM. 12⁰x16²

MASTER BEDROOM 13⁴x14⁴ | DRESSING RM.

BATH

BATH

LINEN | FOYER | DINING RM. 11⁸x11⁰ | KITCHEN 12⁰x9⁶ | RANGE | D.W.

CL. | CL.

BEDROOM 10⁰x12⁸ | BEDROOM 11⁸x9⁴ | COURT | MUD RM. | COVERED PORCH

W. | D.

WASH. RM. | DN.

CURB

61'-0"

GARAGE 21⁴x22⁸

Design T172677
1,634 Sq. Ft.; 26,770 Cu. Ft.

● Notice the difference in these plan's livability. Design T172200 has a shared living dining room overlooking the backyard and a front master bedroom with a side terrace where Design T172677 has a separate front dining room, family room with access to the rear terrace and a rear master bedroom with an adjacent covered porch. Both designs have two additional bedrooms besides the master bedroom. Access to the basement varies in each plan.

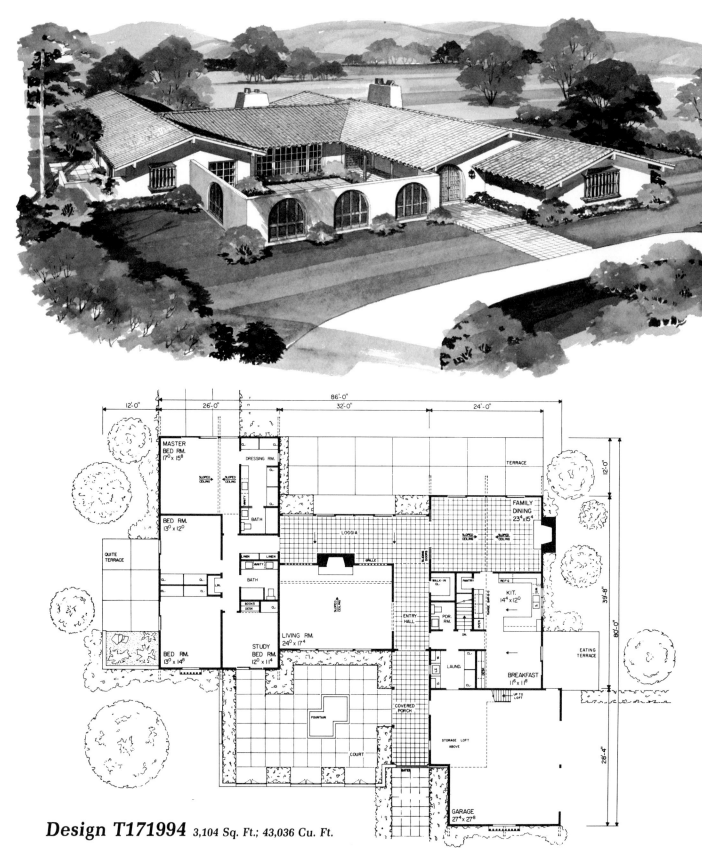

Design T171994 3,104 Sq. Ft.; 43,036 Cu. Ft.

● The Spanish flavor of the old Southwest is delightfully captured by this sprawling ranch house. Its L-shape and high privacy wall go together to form a wide open interior court. This will be a great place to hold those formal and/or informal garden parties. The plan itself is wonderfully zoned. The center portion of the house is comprised of the big, private living room with sloped ceiling. Traffic patterns will noiselessly skirt this formal area. The two wings—the sleeping and informal living—are connected by the well-lighted and spacious loggia. In the sleeping wing, observe the size of the various rooms and the fine storage. In the informal living wing, note the big family room and breakfast room that family members will enjoy.

Design T172335 2,674 Sq. Ft.; 41,957 Cu. Ft.

● Surely a winner for those who have a liking for the architecture of the Far West. With or without the enclosure of the front court, this home with its stucco exterior, brightly colored roof tiles, and exposed rafter tails will be impressive, indeed. The floor plan reflects a wonderfully zoned interior. This results in a fine separation of functions which helps assure convenient living. The traffic patterns which flow from the spacious foyer are most efficient. Study them. While the sleeping wing is angled to the front line of the house, the sunken living room projects, at an angle, from the rear. Worthy of particular notice are such highlights as the two covered porches, the raised hearth fireplaces, the first floor laundry, the partial basement and the oversized garage with storage space.

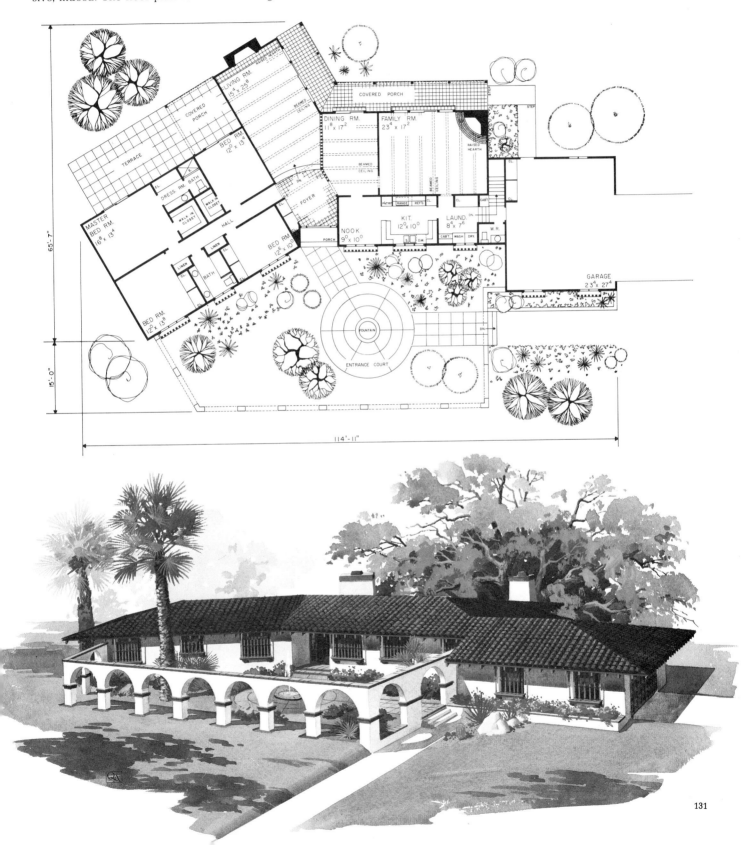

● Westward Ho! Here's a plan that will stir your imagination. If you desire to provide your family with living patterns that will be a refreshing break with convention.

Design T172266
2,668 Sq. Ft.; 38,926 Cu. Ft.

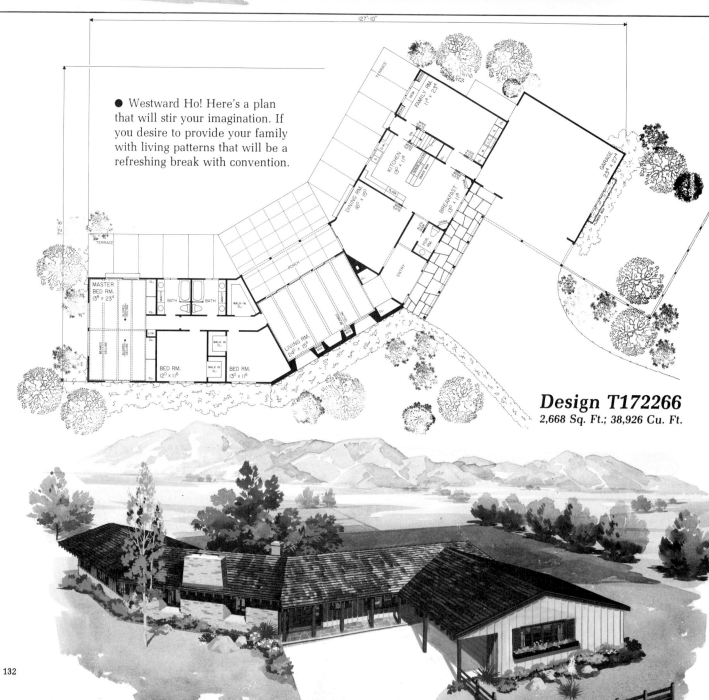

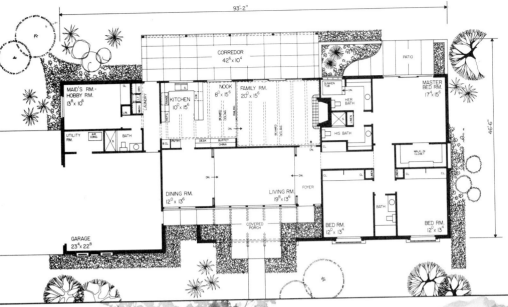

Design T172231
2,740 Sq. Ft.; 31,670 Cu. Ft.

● The features that will appeal to you about this flat-roofed Spanish hacienda are almost endless. Of course, the captivating qualities of the exterior speak for themselves. The extension of the front bedroom wall to form the inviting arch is distinctive. Once inside, any list of features will continue to grow rapidly. Both the family and living rooms are sunken. Private patio adjacent to the master suite.

Design T172258 2,504 Sq. Ft.; 26,292 Cu. Ft.

● Here's a real Western Ranch House with all the appeal of its forebears. As for the livability offered by this angular design, the old days of the rugged west never had anything like this.

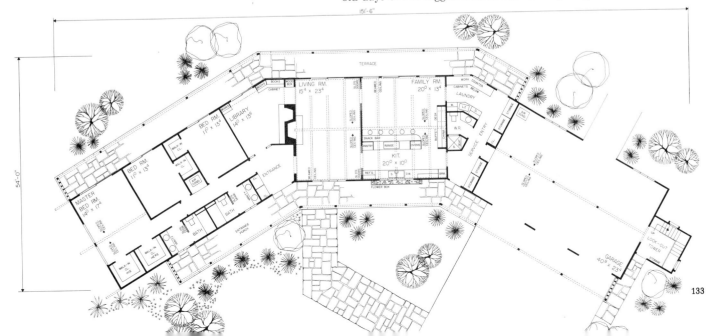

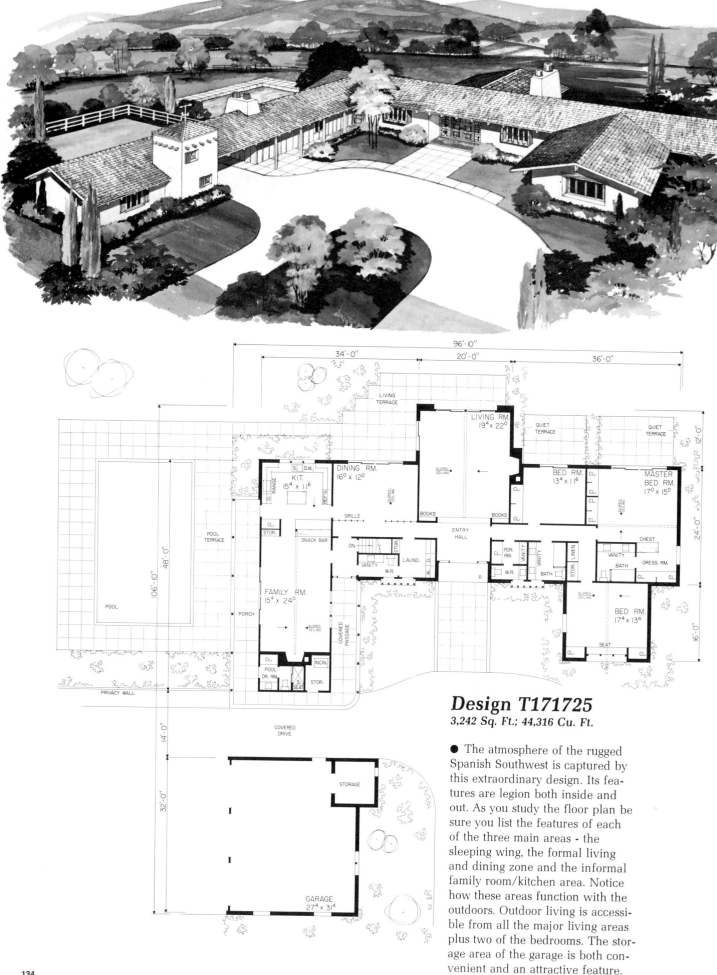

Design T171725
3,242 Sq. Ft.; 44,316 Cu. Ft.

● The atmosphere of the rugged Spanish Southwest is captured by this extraordinary design. Its features are legion both inside and out. As you study the floor plan be sure you list the features of each of the three main areas - the sleeping wing, the formal living and dining zone and the informal family room/kitchen area. Notice how these areas function with the outdoors. Outdoor living is accessible from all the major living areas plus two of the bedrooms. The storage area of the garage is both convenient and an attractive feature.

● Echoing design themes of old Spain, this history house distills the essence of country houses built by rancheros in Early California. Yet its floor plan provides all the comfort and convenience essential to our contemporary living.

Among its charming features is a secluded court, or patio; a greenhouse tucked in behind the garage; a covered rear porch; a low-pitched wide overhanging roof with exposed rafter tails; sloping beamed ceilings. Contri-

buting to the authenticity of the design are the two sets of panelled doors. The covered walk to the front doors provides a sheltered area adjacent to the court. Once inside, the feeling of space continues to impress.

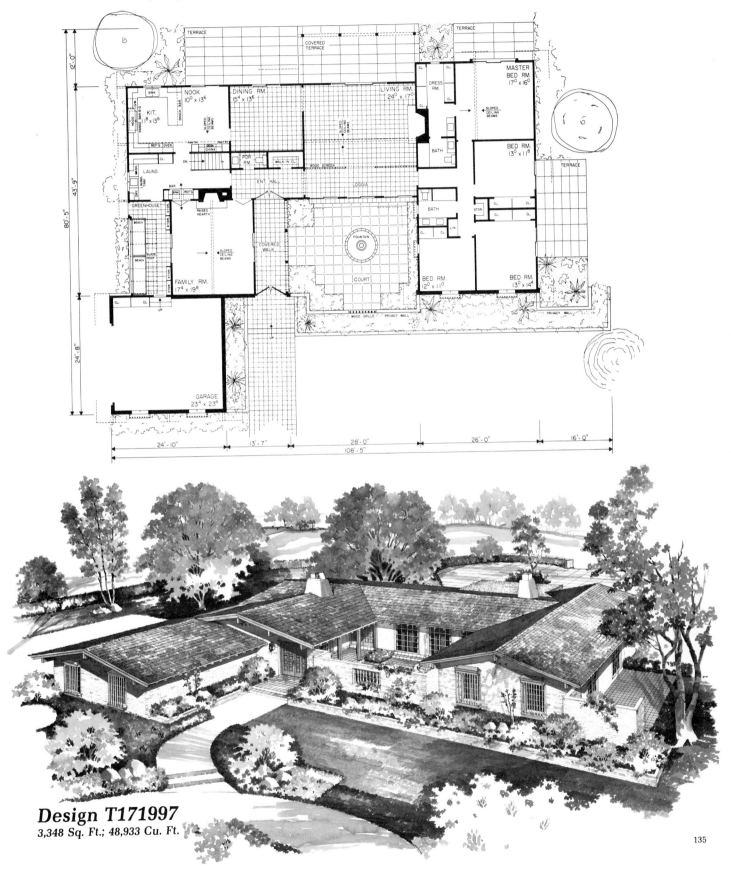

Design T171997
3,348 Sq. Ft.; 48,933 Cu. Ft.

Design T172518

1,630 Sq. Ft. - First Floor
1,260 Sq. Ft. - Second Floor
43,968 Cu. Ft.

● For those who have a predilection for the Spanish influence in their architecture. Outdoor oriented, each of the major living areas on the first floor have direct access to the terraces. Traffic patterns are excellent.

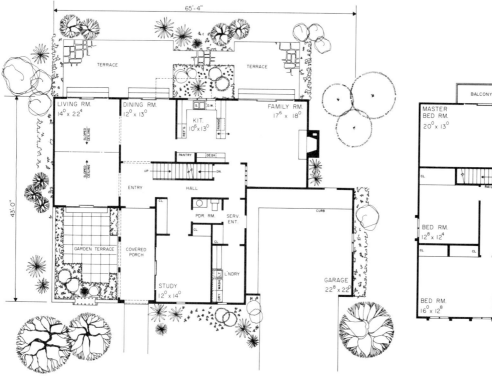

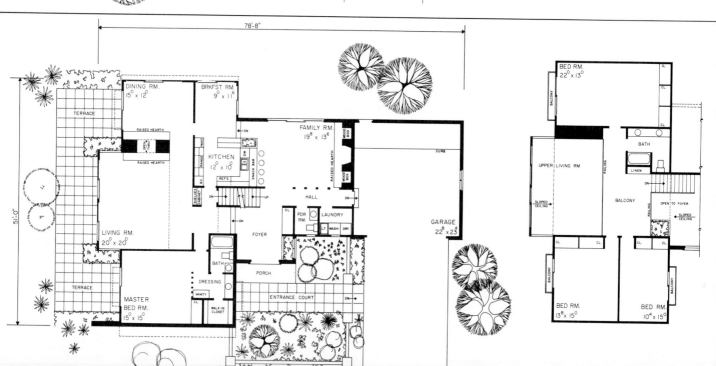

Design T172517

1,767 Sq. Ft. - First Floor
1,094 Sq. Ft. - Second Floor
50,256 Cu. Ft.

● Wherever built - north, east,
south, or west - this home will surely command all the attention it
deserves. And little wonder with
such a well-designed exterior and
such an outstanding interior. List
your favorite features.

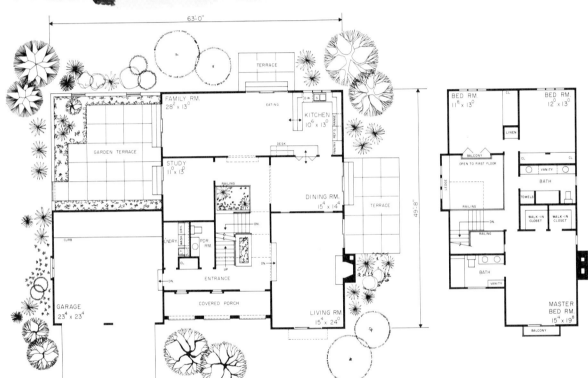

Design T172512

2,074 Sq. Ft. - First Floor
1,116 Sq. Ft. - Second Floor
41,500 Cu. Ft.

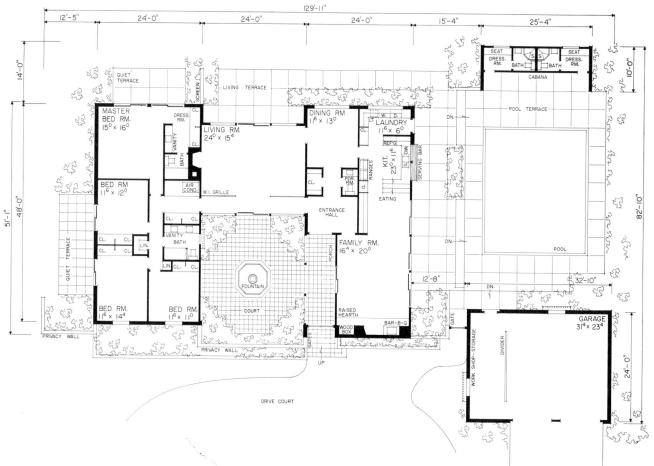

Design T171756 *2,736 Sq. Ft.; 29,139 Cu. Ft.*

● Reminiscent of the West and impressive, indeed. If you are after something that is luxurious in both its appearance and its livability this design should receive your consideration. This rambling ranch house, which encloses a spacious and dramatic flower court, is designed for comfort and privacy indoors and out. Study the outdoor areas. Notice the seclusion each of them provides. Three bedrooms, plus a master suite with dressing room and bath form a private bedroom wing. Formal and informal living areas serve ideally for various types of entertaining. There is excellent circulation of traffic throughout the house. The kitchen is handy to the formal dining room and the informal family room. Don't miss raised hearth fireplace.

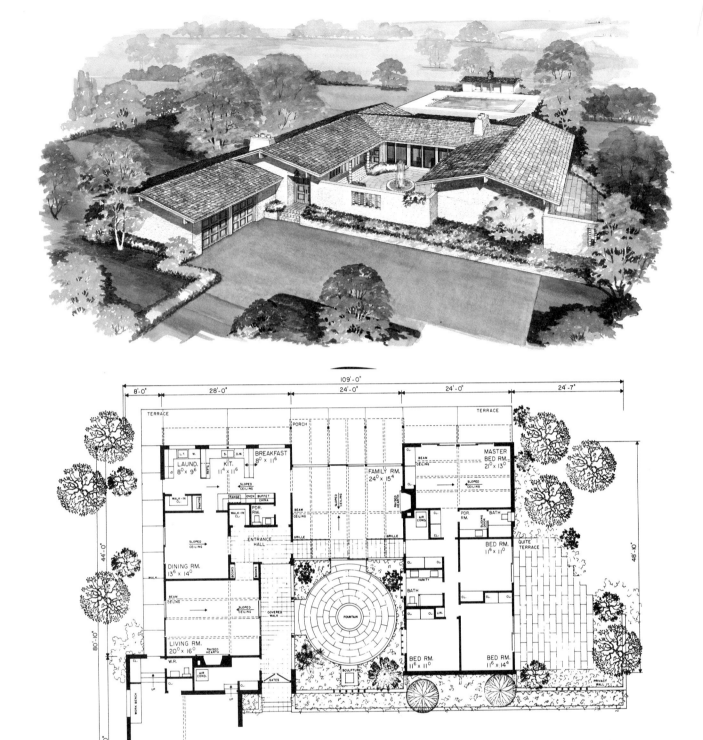

Design T171264
3,108 Sq. Ft.; 31,857 Cu. Ft.

● A romantic adaptation from the Spanish Southwest. This design is truly distinctive, both in its exterior styling and in its gracious floor plan. Its exterior beauty is characterized by the series of low-pitched, overhanging roofs, the extended rafter ends, the blank masonry wall masses and the paneled double front gates. Behind the front privacy wall is the unique, enclosed court. The stroll up the covered walk to the entrance hall will be a delightful experience, indeed. The entrance hall routes traffic to the formal dining and living rooms, the efficient work center and to the passageway between the family room and court to the four bedroom sleeping wing. Study the many other features. You will be able to make a long list.

Design T172594
2,294 Sq. Ft.; 42,120 Cu. Ft.

● A spectacular foyer! It is fully 21' long and offers double entry to the heart of this home. Other highlights include a 21' by 21' gathering room complete with sloped ceiling, raised hearth fireplace and sliding glass doors. There's a formal dining room, too. Plus a well-located study which insures space for solitude or undisturbed work. The kitchen features a snack bar and a breakfast nook with another set of sliding doors. For more convenience, a pantry and first-floor laundry. In the master suite, a dressing room with entry to the bath, four closets and sliding doors onto the terrace! Two more bedrooms if you wish to convert the study or one easily large enough for two children with a dressing area and private entry to the second bath.

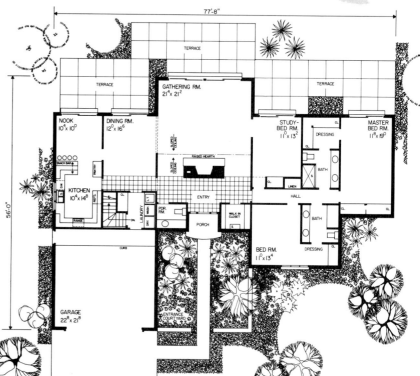

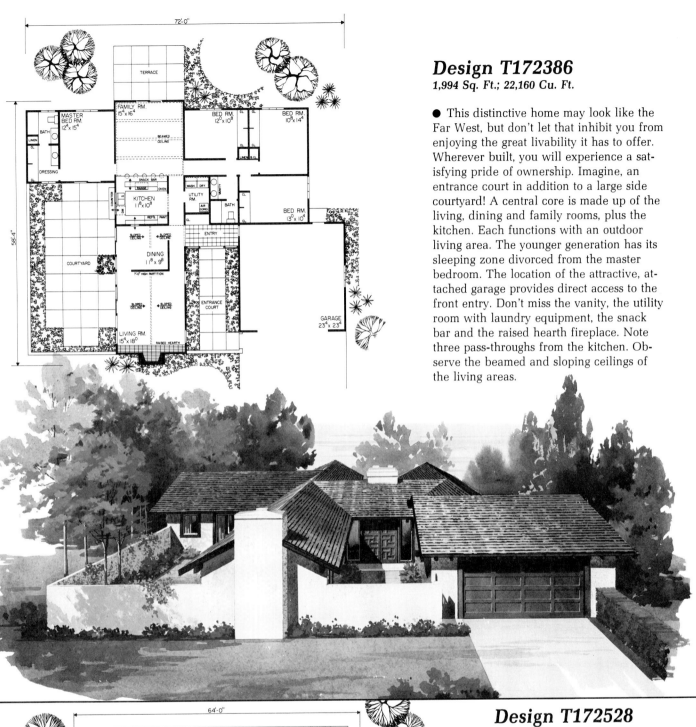

Design T172386
1,994 Sq. Ft.; 22,160 Cu. Ft.

● This distinctive home may look like the Far West, but don't let that inhibit you from enjoying the great livability it has to offer. Wherever built, you will experience a satisfying pride of ownership. Imagine, an entrance court in addition to a large side courtyard! A central core is made up of the living, dining and family rooms, plus the kitchen. Each functions with an outdoor living area. The younger generation has its sleeping zone divorced from the master bedroom. The location of the attractive, attached garage provides direct access to the front entry. Don't miss the vanity, the utility room with laundry equipment, the snack bar and the raised hearth fireplace. Note three pass-throughs from the kitchen. Observe the beamed and sloping ceilings of the living areas.

Design T172528
1,754 Sq. Ft.; 37,832 Cu. Ft.

● This inviting, U-shaped western ranch adaptation offers outstanding living potential behind its double, front doors and flanking glass panels. In but 1,754 square feet there are three bedrooms, 2½ baths, a formal living room and an informal family room, an excellently functioning interior kitchen, an adjacent breakfast nook and good storage facilities. The open stairwell to the lower level basement can be an interesting, interior feature. Note raised hearth fireplace and sloped ceiling.

Design T172143 832 Sq. Ft. - Main Level; 864 Sq. Ft. - Upper Level; 864 Sq. Ft. - Lower Level; 27,473 Cu. Ft.

● Here the Spanish Southwest comes to life in the form of an enchanting multi-level home. There is much to rave about. The architectural detailing is delightful, indeed. The entrance courtyard, the twin balconies and the roof treatment are particularly noteworthy. Functioning at the rear of the house are the covered patio and the balcony with its lower patio. Well zoned, the upper level has three bedrooms and two baths; the main level has its formal living and dining rooms to the rear and kitchen area looking onto the courtyard; the lower level features the family room, study and laundry. Be sure to notice the extra wash room and the third full bath. There are two fireplaces each with a raised hearth. A dramatic house wherever built!

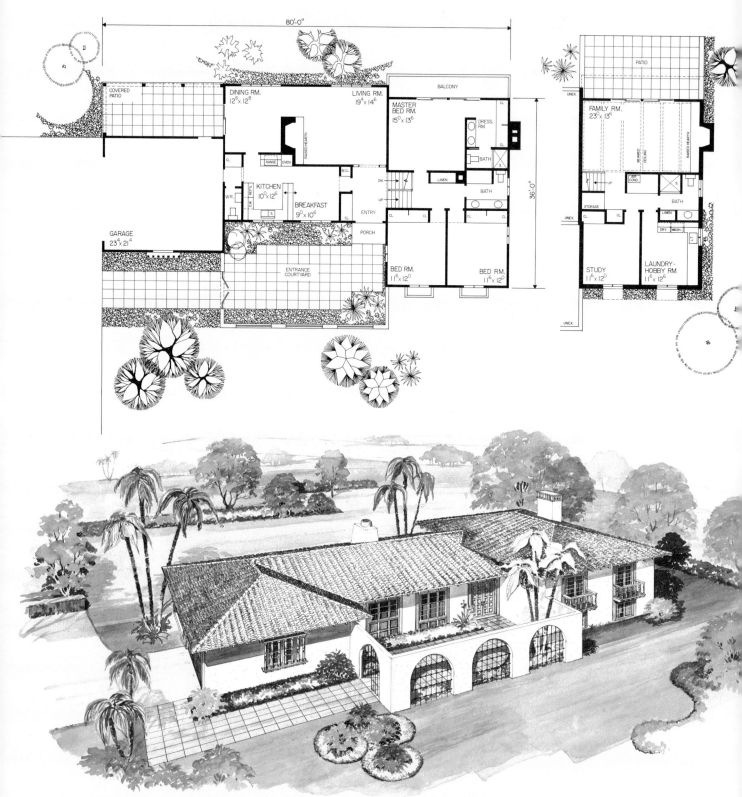

Design T171754 2,080 Sq. Ft.; 21,426 Cu. Ft.

● Boasting a traditional Western flavor, this rugged U-shaped ranch home has the features to assure grand living. The front flower court, inside the high brick wall, creates a delightfully dramatic atmosphere which carries inside. The floor plan is positively unique and exceptionally livable. Wonderfully zoned, the three bedrooms enjoy their full measure of privacy. The formal living and dining rooms function together in a most pleasing fashion. The laundry, kitchen, informal eating and family room fit together to guarantee efficient living patterns.

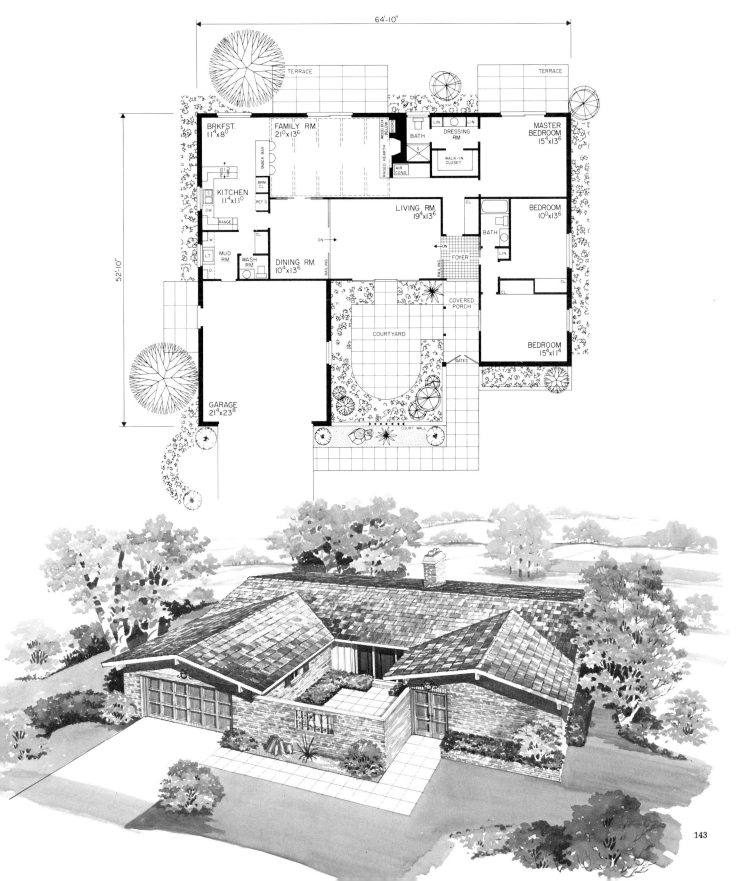

Design T172214

3,011 Sq. Ft. - First Floor
2,297 Sq. Ft. - Second Floor; 78,585 Cu. Ft.

● A Spanish hacienda with all the appeal and all the comforts one would want in a new home. This is a house that looks big and really is big. Measuring 100 feet across the front with various appendages and roof planes.

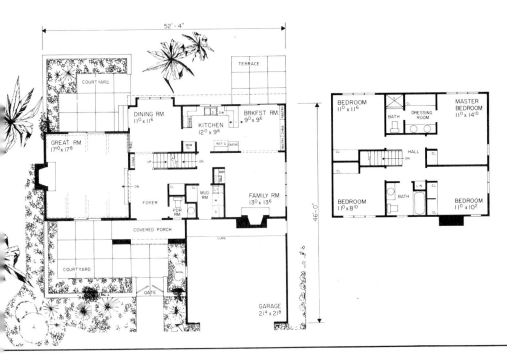

Design T172801

1,172 Sq. Ft. - First Floor
884 Sq. Ft. - Second Floor
32,510 Cu. Ft.

● The great room in this design will be just that. It is sunken two steps, has a beamed ceiling, the beauty of a fireplace and two sets of sliding glass doors to a front and rear courtyard. A built-in wet bar and fireplace are the features of the family room. The foyer of this Spanish design is very spacious and houses a powder room. Four bedrooms and two baths are on the second floor. Don't miss the two enclosed courtyards.

Design T172136

1,688 Sq. Ft. - First Floor
1,688 Sq. Ft. - Second Floor; 50,353 Cu. Ft.

● This authentic, Spanish Colonial adaptation has its roots in the past. Here is a design whose exterior captures the romance of a bygone era, while its floor plan offers all of the up-to-date conveniences of today's living.

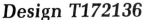

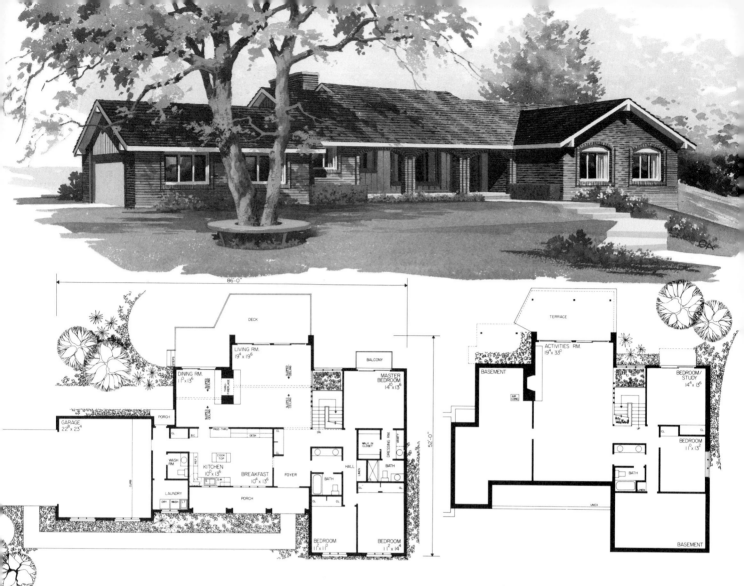

● This hillside home gives all the appearances of being a one-story ranch home; and what a delightful one at that! Should the contours of your property slope to the rear, this plan permits the exposing of the lower level. This results in the activities room and bedroom/study gaining direct access to outdoor living. Certainly a most desirable aspect for active, outdoor family living. The large and growing family will be admirably served with five bedrooms and three baths. An extra washroom and separate laundry add to the convenient living potential.

Design T172549
2,260 Sq. Ft. - Main Level
1,406 Sq. Ft. - Lower Level; 51,857 Cu. Ft.

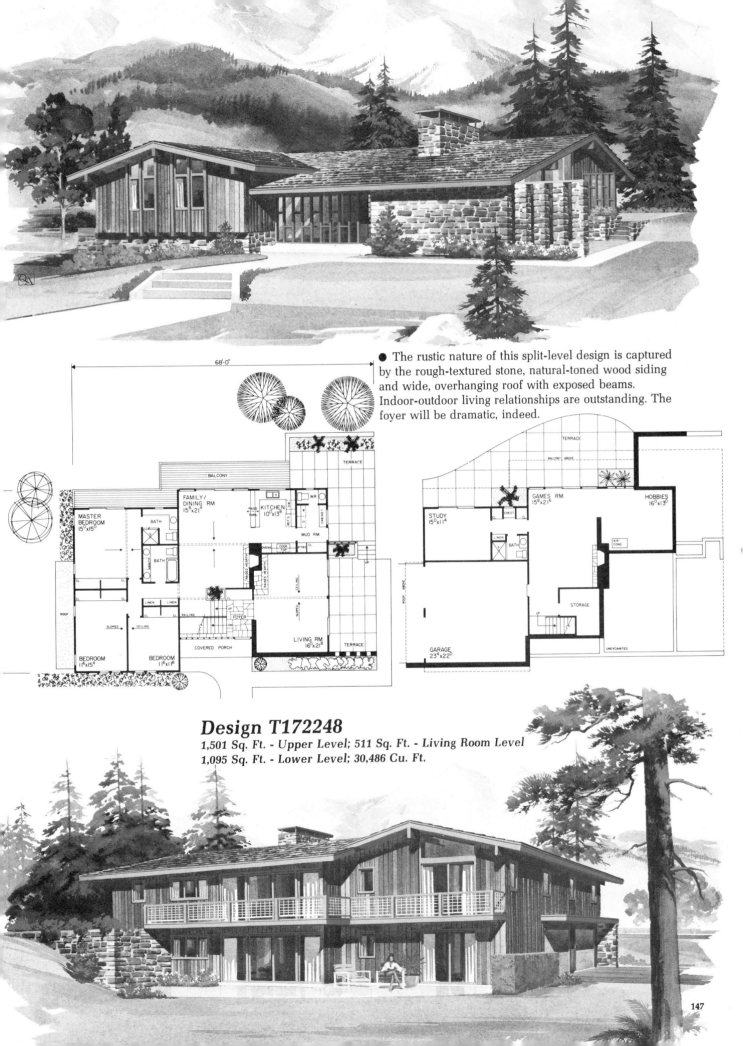

● The rustic nature of this split-level design is captured by the rough-textured stone, natural-toned wood siding and wide, overhanging roof with exposed beams. Indoor-outdoor living relationships are outstanding. The foyer will be dramatic, indeed.

Design T172248
1,501 Sq. Ft. - Upper Level; 511 Sq. Ft. - Living Room Level
1,095 Sq. Ft. - Lower Level; 30,486 Cu. Ft.

Design T172232
1,776 Sq. Ft.; 17,966 Cu. Ft.

● This appealing, flat roof design has its roots in the Spanish Southwest. The arched, covered porch with its heavy beamed ceiling sets the note of distinction. The center foyer routes traffic effectively to the main zones of the house. Down a step is the sunken living room. Privacy will be the byword here. The cluster of three bedrooms features two full baths and good storage facilities.

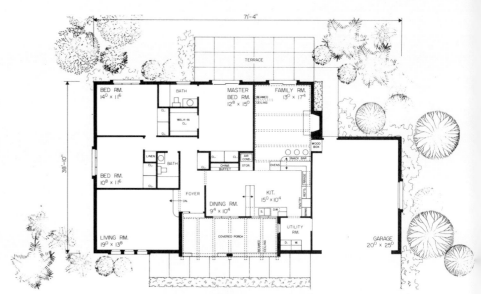

Design T172557
1,955 Sq. Ft.; 43,509 Cu. Ft.

● This eye-catching design has a flavor of the Spanish Southwest. The character of the exterior is set by the wide, overhanging roof with its exposed beams; the massive, arched pillars; the arching of the brick over the windows; the panelled door and the horizontal siding that contrasts with the brick. The master bedroom/study suite is a focal point of the interior. However, if necessary, the study could become the fourth bedroom. The living and dining rooms are large and separated by a massive raised hearth fireplace.

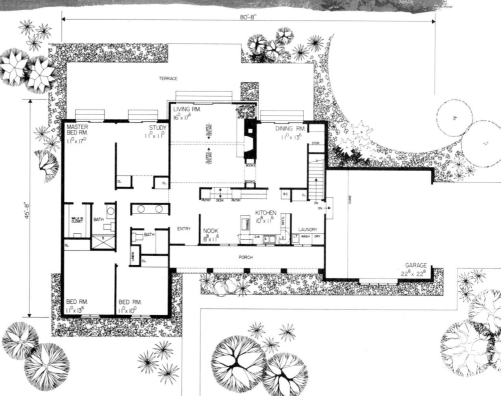

Design T171726
1,910 Sq. Ft.; 19,264 Cu. Ft.

● The U-shaped plan has long been honored for its excellent zoning. As the floor plan for this fine Spanish adaptation illustrates, it not only provides separation between parents' area and children's wing, but also it places a buffer area in the center. This makes the kitchen the "control center" for the home - handy to the family room, living room and the dining alcove.

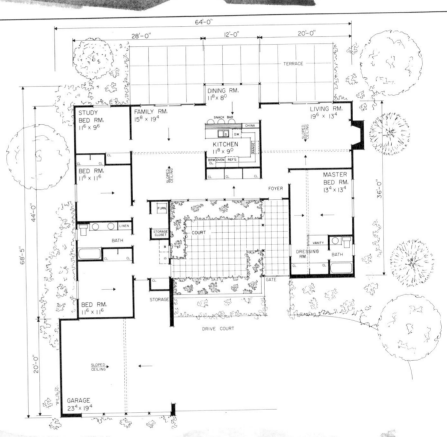

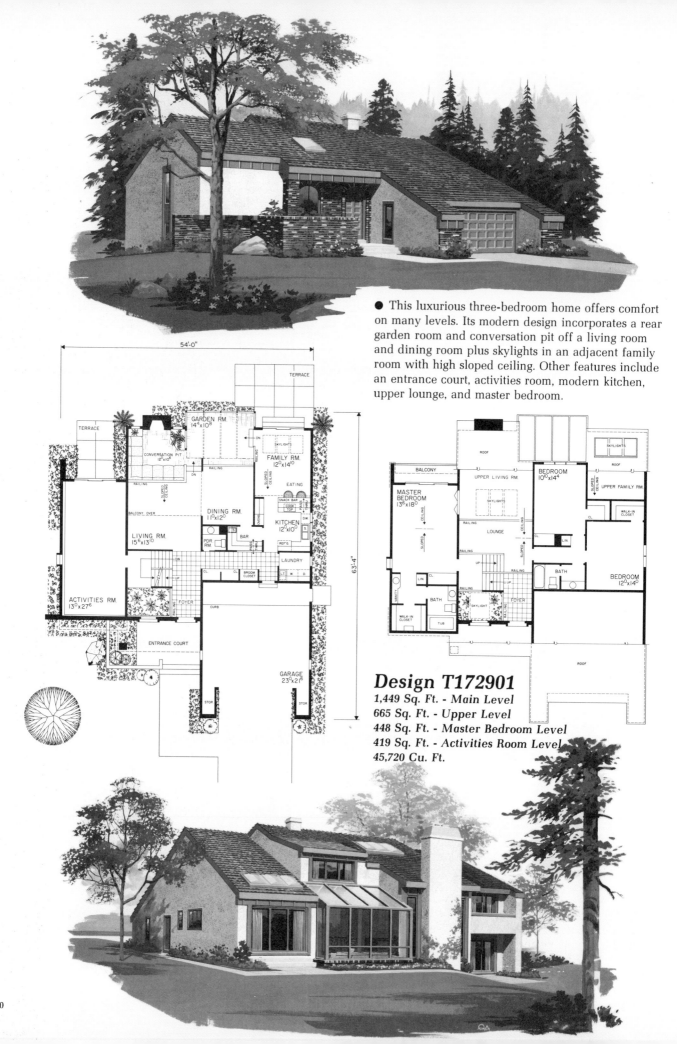

● This luxurious three-bedroom home offers comfort on many levels. Its modern design incorporates a rear garden room and conversation pit off a living room and dining room plus skylights in an adjacent family room with high sloped ceiling. Other features include an entrance court, activities room, modern kitchen, upper lounge, and master bedroom.

Design T172901
1,449 Sq. Ft. - Main Level
665 Sq. Ft. - Upper Level
448 Sq. Ft. - Master Bedroom Level
419 Sq. Ft. - Activities Room Level
45,720 Cu. Ft.

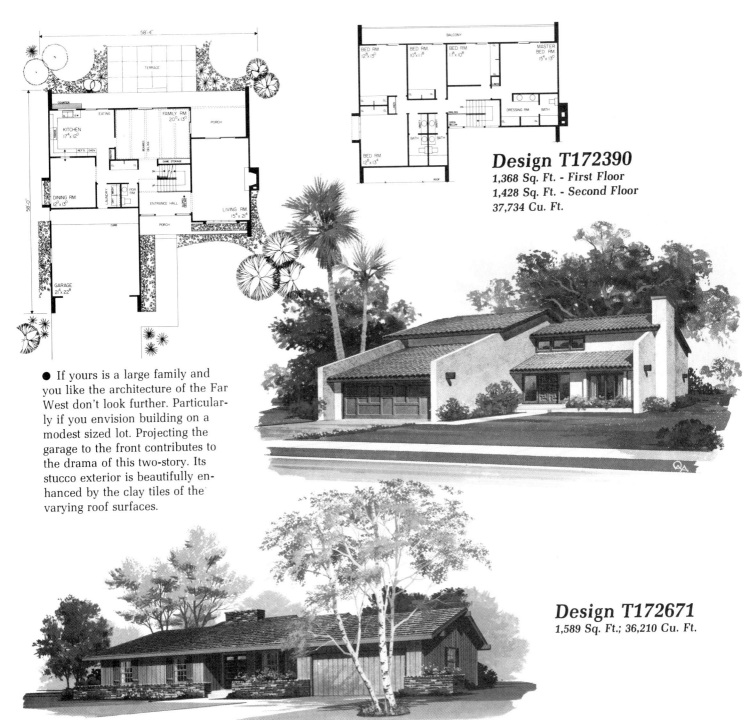

Design T172390

1,368 Sq. Ft. - First Floor
1,428 Sq. Ft. - Second Floor
37,734 Cu. Ft.

● If yours is a large family and you like the architecture of the Far West don't look further. Particularly if you envision building on a modest sized lot. Projecting the garage to the front contributes to the drama of this two-story. Its stucco exterior is beautifully enhanced by the clay tiles of the varying roof surfaces.

Design T172671

1,589 Sq. Ft.; 36,210 Cu. Ft.

● The rustic exterior of this one-story home features vertical wood siding. The entry foyer is floored with flagstone and leads to the three areas of the plan: sleeping, living and work center. The sleeping area has three bedrooms. The master bedroom has sliding glass doors to the rear terrace. The living area, consisting of gathering and dining rooms, also has access to the terrace. The work center is efficiently planned. It houses the kitchen with snack bar, breakfast room with built-in china cabinet and stairs to the basement. This is a very livable plan.

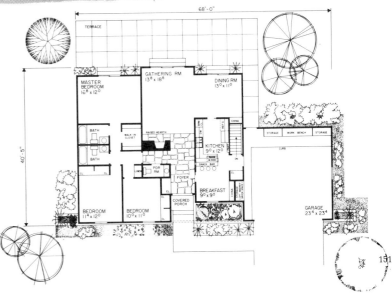

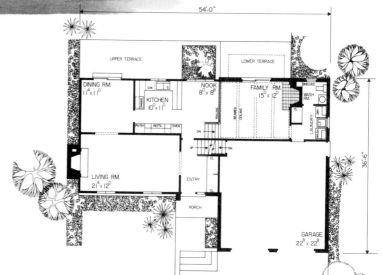

Design T172608

728 Sq. Ft. - Main Level; 874 Sq. Ft. - Upper Level
310 Sq. Ft. - Lower Level; 27,705 Cu. Ft.

● Here is tri-level livability with a fourth basement level for bulk storage and, perhaps, a shop area. There are four bedrooms, a handy laundry, two eating areas, formal and informal living areas and two fireplaces. Sliding glass doors in the formal dining room and the family room open to a terrace. The U-shaped kitchen has a built-in range/oven and storage pantry. The breakfast nook overlooks the family room.

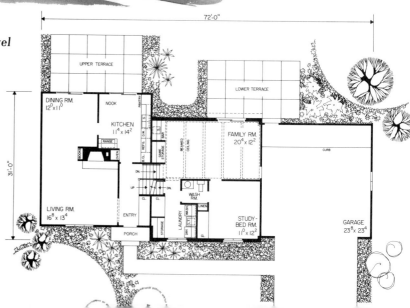

Design T172628

649 Sq. Ft. - Main Level; 672 Sq. Ft. - Upper Level
624 Sq. Ft. - Lower Level; 25,650 Cu. Ft.

● Traditional, yet contemporary! With lots of extras, too. Like a wet bar and game storage in the family room. A beamed ceiling, too, and a sliding glass door onto the terrace. In short, a family room designed to make your life easy and enjoyable. There's more. A living room with a traditionally styled fireplace and built-in bookshelves. And a dining room with a sliding glass door that opens to a second terrace. Here's the appropriate setting for those times when you want a touch of elegance.

Early Colonial Houses

Saltboxes, gambrel-roofed and gable-roofed designs, early stone and front-porch farmhouses comprise this selection of houses. For purposes of categorization, these designs cover a wide period — from medieval styles of the 17th century to the 18th century with its early Georgian and farmhouse adaptations. As delightfully dated as these exterior styles may be, their interior plans are exemplary of today's living patterns.

Design T172211
1,214 Sq. Ft. - First Floor
1,146 Sq. Ft. - Second Floor
32,752 Cu. Ft.

● The appeal of this Colonial home will be virtually everlasting. It will improve with age and service the growing family well. Imagine your family living here. There are four bedrooms, 2½ baths, plus plenty of first floor living space. Formal and informal activities will have their place. Entertaining can be done in the front living room. It is spacious and has an end fireplace. When dinner is ready, your guests can flow to the adjacent dining room. Maybe an after dinner drink could be served on the terrace. There are sliding glass doors in the dining room which lead to this outdoor area. There is a second set of doors to the terrace in the family room. This will be a warm and comfortable area for family and friends alike. The adjacent work center is efficient. Note the powder room which is convenient to all of the first floor areas.

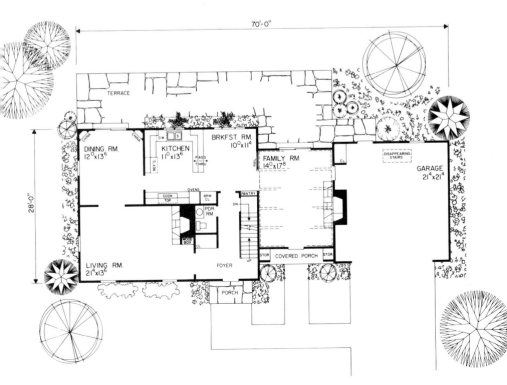

Design T172320 *1,856 Sq. Ft. - First Floor; 1,171 Sq. Ft. - Second Floor; 46,699 Cu. Ft.*

● A charming Colonial adaptation with a Gambrel roof front exterior and a Salt Box rear. The focal point of family activities will be the spacious family kitchen with its beamed ceiling and fireplace. Blueprints include details for both three and four bedroom options. In addition to the family kitchen, note the family room with beamed ceiling and fireplace. Don't miss the study with built-in book shelves and cabinets. Gracious living will be enjoyed throughout this design.

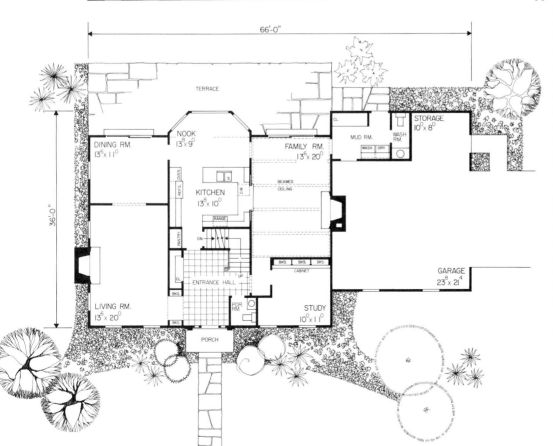

Design T172610

1,505 Sq. Ft. - First Floor
1,344 Sq. Ft. - Second Floor
45,028 Cu. Ft.

● This full two-story traditional will be worthy of note wherever built. It strongly recalls images of New England from yesteryear. And well it might; for the window treatment is delightful. The front entrance detail is inviting. The narrow horizontal siding and the corner boards are appealing as are the two massive chimneys. The center entrance hall is large with a handy powder room nearby. The study has built-in bookshelves and offers a full measure of privacy. The interior kitchen has a pass-thru to the family room and enjoys all that natural light from the bay window of the nook. A beamed ceiling, fireplace and sliding glass doors are features of the family room. The mud room highlights a closet, laundry equipment and an extra wash room. Study the upstairs with those four bedrooms, two baths and plenty of closets.

Design T172865

1,703 Sq. Ft. - First Floor
1,044 Sq. Ft. - Second Floor
47,179 Cu. Ft.

● This comfortable farmhouse with post-rail, covered wrap-around porch is charming, indeed! Fine proportioning and zoning is evident on both floors. Three bedrooms are isolated upstairs to allow privacy and quiet. Two bedrooms enjoy their own window seats, as traditional dormers pierce the roof line. A study downstairs could double as a fourth bedroom. Downstairs one also finds a front living room with its own fireplace and a large back family room with it own fireplace. A formal dining room is positioned in front just off the foyer. A modern kitchen features pass-thru to a breakfast room. A mud room is positioned just off the double garage and adjacent to the kitchen. This traditional design offers plenty of modern comfort for contemporary families.

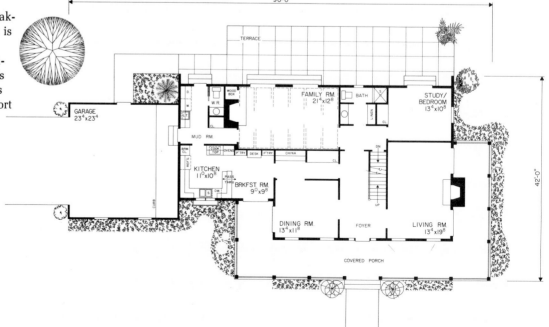

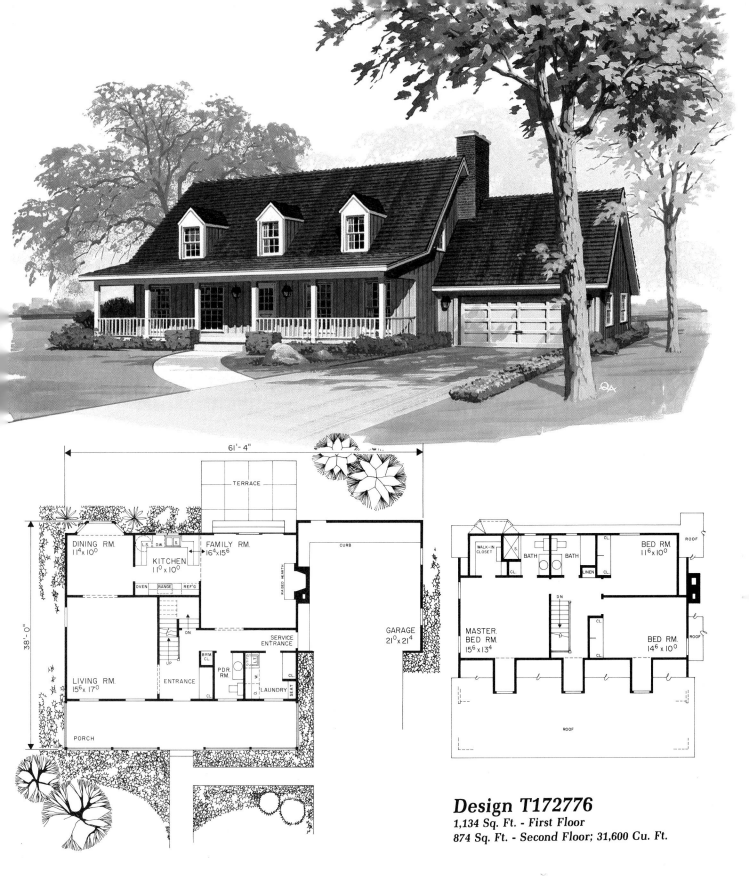

Design T172776

1,134 Sq. Ft. - First Floor
874 Sq. Ft. - Second Floor; 31,600 Cu. Ft.

● This board-and-batten farmhouse design has all of the country charm of New England. The large front covered porch surely will be appreciated during the beautiful warm weather months. Immediately off the front entrance is the delightful corner living room. The dining room with bay window will be easily served by the U-shaped kitchen. Informal family living enjoyment will be obtained in the family room which features a raised hearth fireplace, sliding glass doors to the rear terrace and easy access to the work center of powder room, laundry and service entrance. The second floor houses all of the sleeping facilities. There is a master bedroom with a private bath and walk-in closet. Two other bedrooms share a bath. This is an excellent one-and-a-half story design.

Design T172623

1,368 Sq. Ft. - First Floor
1,046 Sq. Ft. - Second Floor; 35,130 Cu. Ft.

● Take note of this four bedroom Salt Box design. Enter through the large entrance hall to enjoy this home. Imagine a living room 13 x 27 feet. Plus a family room. Both having a fireplace. Also, sliding glass doors in both the family room and nook leading to the rear terrace. U-shaped kitchen is efficient.

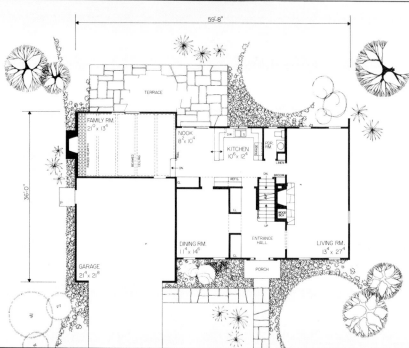

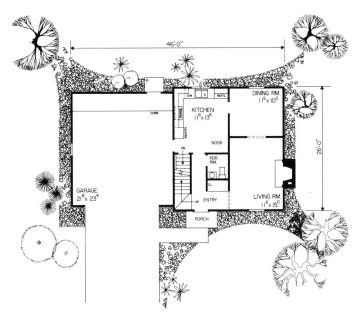

Design T172622

624 Sq. Ft. - First Floor
624 Sq. Ft. - Second Floor; 19,864 Cu. Ft.

● Appealing design can envelope little packages, too. Here is a charming, Early Colonial adaptation with an attached two-car garage to serve the young family with a modest building budget.

Design T172751 *1,202 Sq. Ft. - First Floor*
964 Sq. Ft. - Second Floor; 33,830 Cu. Ft.

● This Gambrel roof version of a Colonial is sure to serve your family efficiently. The U-shaped kitchen with pass-thru to breakfast nook will be convenient to the busy homemaker. The terrace is accessible by way of sliding glass doors in the nook and family room.

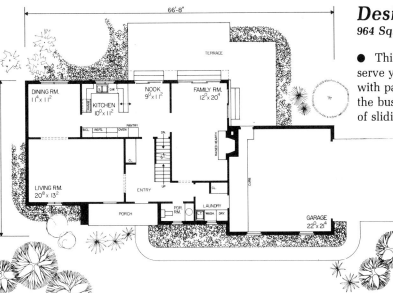

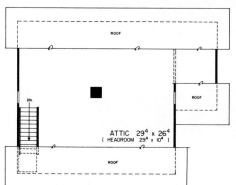

ROOF

DN.

ATTIC 29⁴ x 26⁴
(HEADROOM 29⁴ x 10⁴)

ROOF

ROOF

BEDROOM / STUDY 11⁰ x 13²

BATH DRESS. RM. VANITY

MASTER BEDROOM 13⁰ x 13²

CL.

BATH

CL.

LIN

DN.

CL.

UP TO ATTIC

BEDROOM 10⁰ x 10⁶

CL.

BEDROOM 13⁰ x 10⁶

Design T172774

1,370 Sq. Ft. - First Floor
969 Sq. Ft. - Second Floor
38,305 Cu. Ft.

● A Farmhouse adaptation with all of the most up-to-date features expected in a new home. Beginning with the formal areas, this design offers pleasures for the entire family. There is the quiet, corner living room which has an opening to the sizable dining room. This room will have plenty of natural light from the delightful bay window which overlooks the rear yard. It is also conveniently located with the efficient, U-shaped kitchen just a step away. The kitchen features many built-ins with a pass-thru to the beamed ceiling breakfast room. Sliding glass doors to the terrace are fine attractions in both the sunken family room and breakfast room. The service entrance to the garage has a storage closet on each side, plus there is a secondary entrance through the laundry area. Recreational activities and hobbies can be pursued in the basement area. Four bedrooms and two baths are on the second floor.

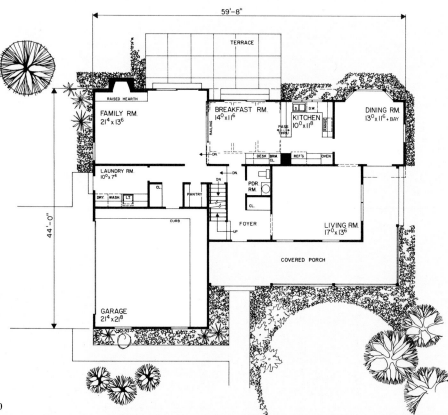

59'-8"

TERRACE

RAISED HEARTH

FAMILY RM. 21⁴ x 13⁶

BREAKFAST RM. 14⁰ x 11⁶

KITCHEN 10⁰ x 11⁸

DINING RM. 13⁰ x 11⁶ + BAY

RAILING

DESK BRM. REF'G OVEN

LAUNDRY RM. 10⁰ x 7⁶

DN.

DN.

PDR. RM.

DRY. WASH.

PANTRY

CURB

FOYER

UP

LIVING RM. 17⁰ x 13⁶

44'-0"

GARAGE 21⁴ x 21⁸

COVERED PORCH

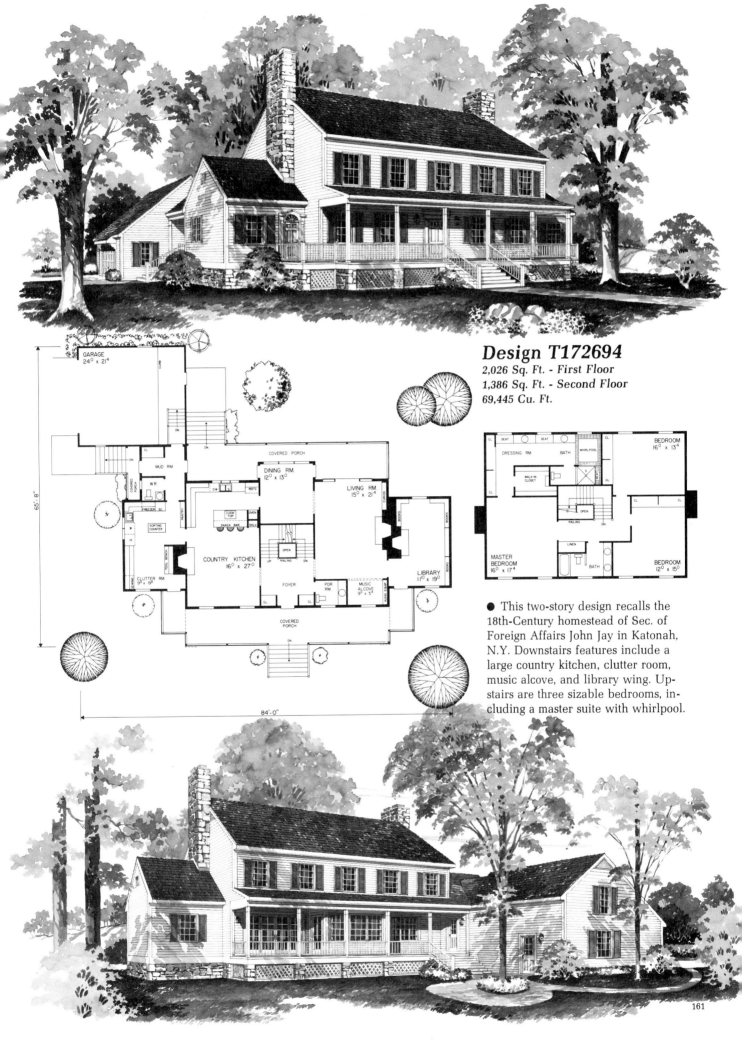

Design T172694

2,026 Sq. Ft. - First Floor
1,386 Sq. Ft. - Second Floor
69,445 Cu. Ft.

First Floor Plan

- GARAGE 24⁰ x 21⁴
- MUD RM
- W R
- FREEZER
- SORTING COUNTER
- PANTRY
- CLUTTER RM 9⁰ x 19⁰
- TOOL BENCH
- COOK TOP
- OVEN
- SNACK BAR
- SHLV
- COUNTRY KITCHEN 16⁰ x 27⁰
- DW
- REFS
- COVERED PORCH
- DINING RM. 12⁰ x 13⁰
- LIVING RM. 15⁰ x 21⁴
- BOOKS
- OPEN RAILING
- UP
- DN
- FOYER
- POR RM
- MUSIC ALCOVE 9⁰ x 5⁴
- LIBRARY 11⁰ x 19⁰
- CL
- COVERED PORCH
- DN

65'- 8"

84'- 0"

Second Floor Plan

- SEAT
- SEAT
- CL
- BEDROOM 16⁰ x 13⁴
- DRESSING RM
- BATH
- WHIRLPOOL
- WALK-IN CLOSET
- S
- OPEN RAILING
- DN
- LINEN
- BATH
- MASTER BEDROOM 16⁰ x 17⁴
- BEDROOM 12⁰ x 15⁰

● This two-story design recalls the 18th-Century homestead of Sec. of Foreign Affairs John Jay in Katonah, N.Y. Downstairs features include a large country kitchen, clutter room, music alcove, and library wing. Upstairs are three sizable bedrooms, including a master suite with whirlpool.

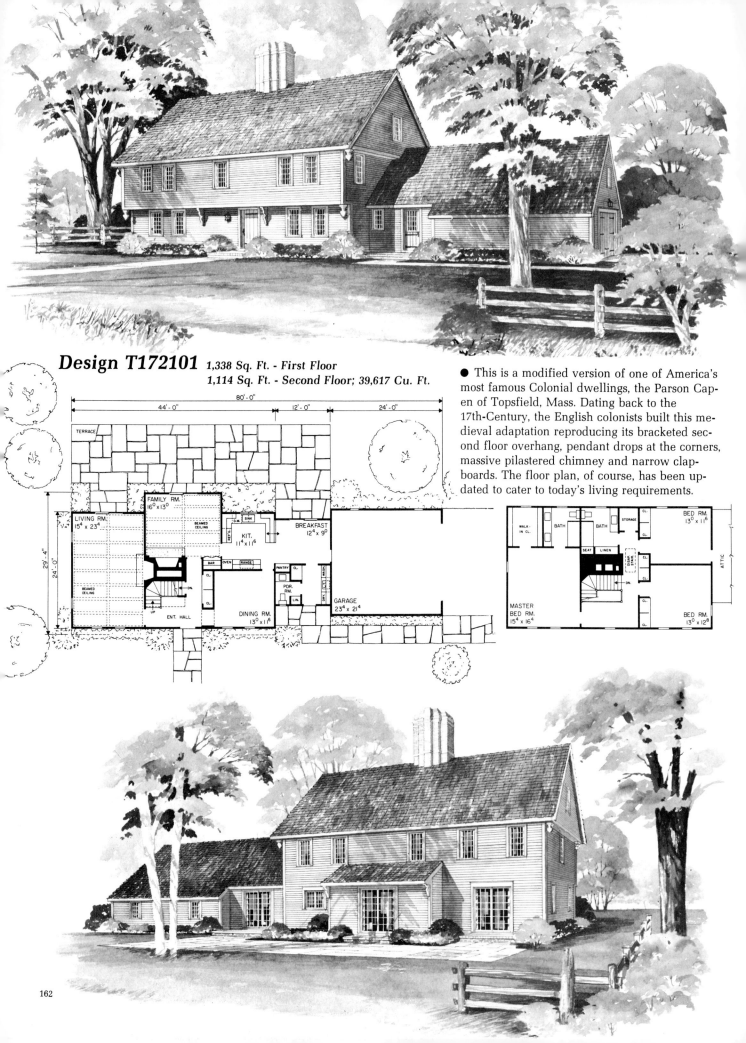

Design T172101
1,338 Sq. Ft. - First Floor
1,114 Sq. Ft. - Second Floor; 39,617 Cu. Ft.

● This is a modified version of one of America's most famous Colonial dwellings, the Parson Capen of Topsfield, Mass. Dating back to the 17th-Century, the English colonists built this medieval adaptation reproducing its bracketed second floor overhang, pendant drops at the corners, massive pilastered chimney and narrow clapboards. The floor plan, of course, has been updated to cater to today's living requirements.

Floor plan labels (first floor):

- 80'-0"
- 38'-0"
- PORCH
- FAMILY RM. 16⁰ x 17⁰
- BEAMED CEILING
- KITCHEN 11⁴ x 15⁶
- NOOK 12⁰ x 9⁸
- CEIL'G CLIP
- CEIL'G CLIP
- BEAMED CEILING
- BAR
- OVEN
- RANGE
- PANTRY
- PDR. RM.
- LAUNDRY
- DINING 15⁴ x 11⁶
- GARAGE 23⁴ x 23⁴
- CEIL'G CLIP
- LIVING RM. 15⁴ x 23⁴
- ENTRANCE HALL
- UP
- DN.
- FOYER
- SEAT
- CL.

Floor plan labels (second floor):

- WALK-IN CL.
- BATH
- VANITY
- BATH
- STOR.
- BED RM. 13⁰ x 11⁶
- SEAT
- LINEN
- OPEN STAIRWELL
- DN.
- MASTER BED RM. 15⁴ x 16⁴
- BED RM. 13⁰ x 13⁰
- LOUNGE
- SEAT
- CL.

Design T172191

1,553 Sq. Ft. - *First Floor*
1,197 Sq. Ft. - *Second Floor*
47,906 Cu. Ft.

● This exquisite house reproduces the architectural details from the 17th-Century. Medieval and Tudor influences, brought to the New World by the first English colonists, distinguish this adaptation. The interior has been designed to serve today's active family.

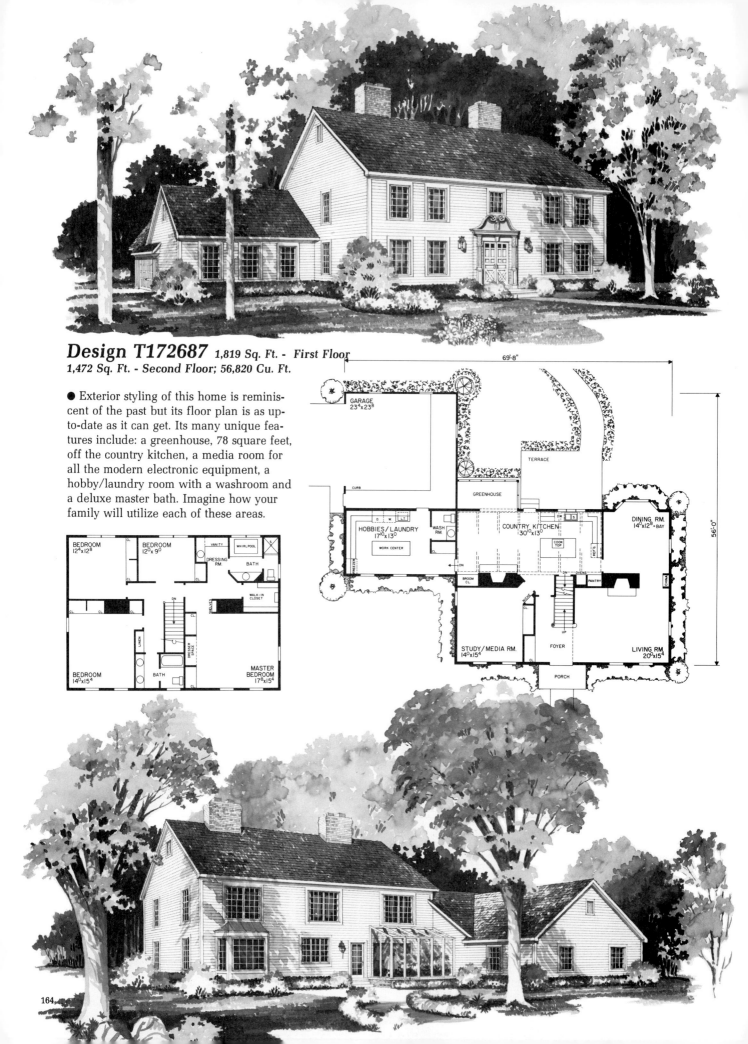

Design T172687
1,819 Sq. Ft. - First Floor
1,472 Sq. Ft. - Second Floor; 56,820 Cu. Ft.

● Exterior styling of this home is reminiscent of the past but its floor plan is as up-to-date as it can get. Its many unique features include: a greenhouse, 78 square feet, off the country kitchen, a media room for all the modern electronic equipment, a hobby/laundry room with a washroom and a deluxe master bath. Imagine how your family will utilize each of these areas.

Design T172659

1,023 Sq. Ft. - First Floor; 1,008 Sq. Ft. - Second Floor
476 Sq. Ft. - Third Floor; 31,510 Cu. Ft.

● The facade of this three-storied, pitch-roofed house has a symmetrical placement of windows and a restrained but elegant central entrance. The central hall, or foyer, expands midway through the house to a family kitchen. Off the foyer are two rooms, a living room with fireplace and a study. The windowed third floor attic can be used as a study and studio. Three bedrooms are housed on the second floor.

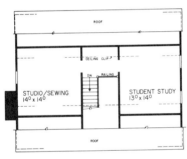

Design T172539

1,450 Sq. Ft. - First Floor
1,167 Sq. Ft. - Second Floor; 46,738 Cu. Ft.

● This appealingly proportioned Gambrel exudes an aura of coziness. The beauty of the main part of the house is delightfully symmetrical and is enhanced by the attached garage and laundry room. The center entrance routes traffic directly to all major zones of the house.

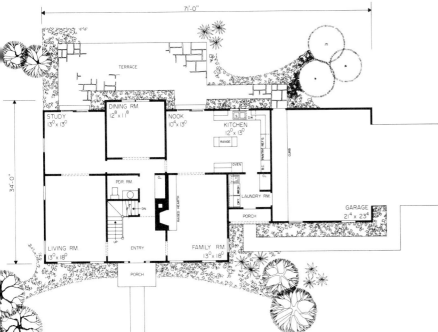

Design T172538

1,503 Sq. Ft. - First Floor
1,095 Sq. Ft. - Second Floor; 44,321 Cu. Ft.

● This Salt Box is charming, indeed. The livability it has to offer to the large and growing family is great. The entry is spacious and is open to the second floor balcony. For living areas, there is the study in addition to the living and family rooms.

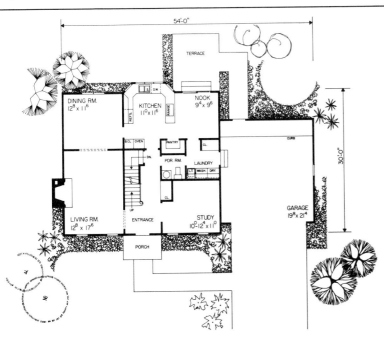

Design T172731

1,039 Sq. Ft. - First Floor
973 Sq. Ft. - Second Floor; 29,740 Cu. Ft.

● The multi-paned windows with shutters of this two-story highlight the exterior delightfully. Inside the livability is ideal. Formal and informal areas are sure to serve your family with ease. Note efficient U-shaped kitchen with handy first-floor laundry. Sleeping facilities on second floor.

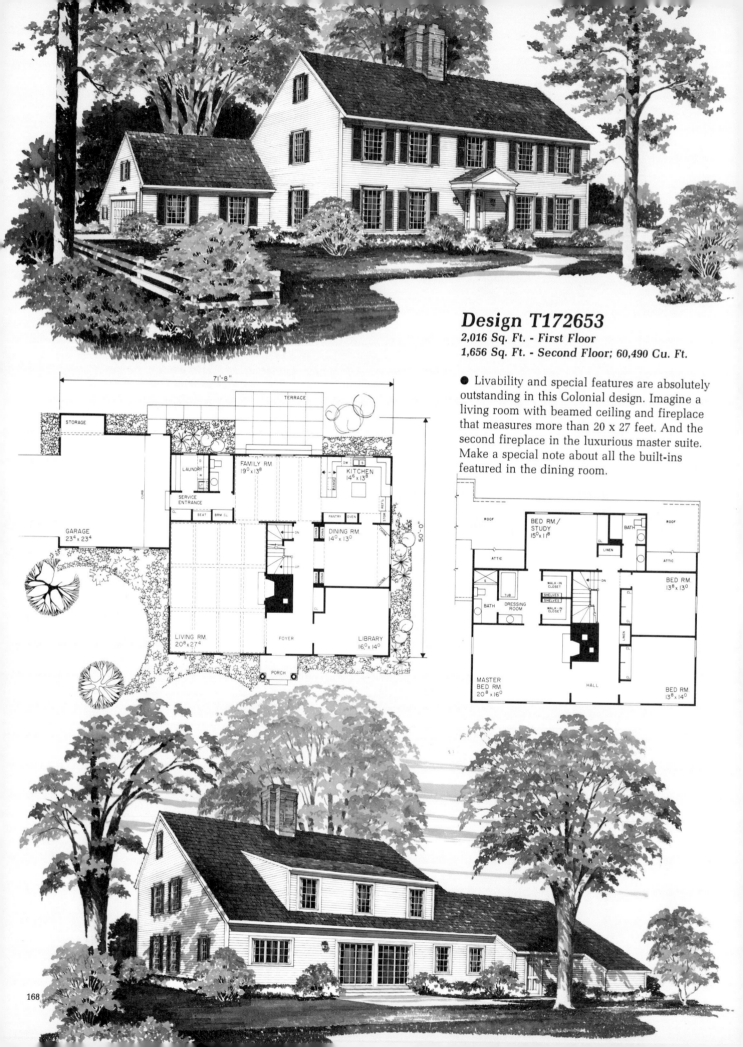

Design T172653

2,016 Sq. Ft. - First Floor
1,656 Sq. Ft. - Second Floor; 60,490 Cu. Ft.

● Livability and special features are absolutely outstanding in this Colonial design. Imagine a living room with beamed ceiling and fireplace that measures more than 20 x 27 feet. And the second fireplace in the luxurious master suite. Make a special note about all the built-ins featured in the dining room.

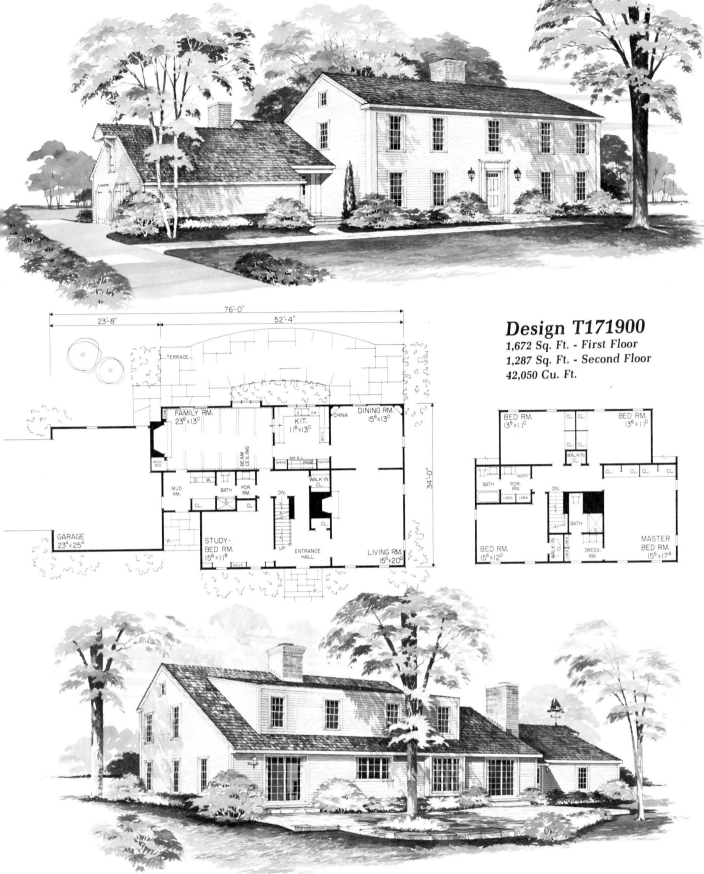

Design T171900

1,672 Sq. Ft. - First Floor
1,287 Sq. Ft. - Second Floor
42,050 Cu. Ft.

Floor plan labels (first floor): TERRACE, FAMILY RM. 23⁶x13⁰, KIT. 11⁸x13⁰, CHINA, DINING RM. 15⁶x13⁰, BEAM CEILING, OVENS, RANGE, PANTRY, WALK-IN CL., MUD RM., BATH, PDR. RM., WOOD BOX, STUDY-BED RM. 15⁶x11⁸, UP, DN., ENTRANCE HALL, LIVING RM. 15⁶x20⁰, GARAGE 23⁴x25⁴. Dimensions: 76'-0", 23'-8", 52'-4", 34'-0"

Floor plan labels (second floor): BED RM. 13⁸x11⁰, CL., WALK-IN CL., BED RM. 13⁸x11⁰, BATH, PDR. RM., VANITY, LINEN, DN., BED RM. 15⁶x12⁰, WALK-IN CL., BATH, DRESS. RM., MASTER BED RM. 15⁶x17⁸

● The history of the Colonial Salt Box goes back some 200 years. This unusually authentic adaptation captures all the warmth and charm of the early days both inside as well as outside. To reflect today's living patterns, an up-dating of the floor plan was inevitable. The result is a room arrangement which will serve the active family wonderfully. Formal living and dining take place at one end of the house which is free of cross-room traffic. Informal living activities will center around the family room and expand through sliding glass doors to the terrace. The mud room area is strategically located and includes the laundry and a full bath. An extra study/bedroom supplements four bedrooms upstairs. Count the closets and the other storage areas.

Design T171986 896 Sq. Ft. - First Floor
1,148 Sq. Ft. - Second Floor; 28,840 Cu. Ft.

● This design with its distinctive Gambrel roof will spell charm wherever it may be situated - far out in the country, or on a busy thoroughfare. Compact and economical to build, it will be easy on the budget. Note the location of the family room. It is over the garage on the second floor.

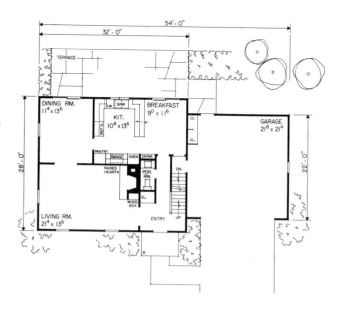

Design T171777 1,142 Sq. Ft. - First Floor
1,010 Sq. Ft. - Second Floor; 28,095 Cu. Ft.

● If it's charm you are after, you'll find this design with a Gambrel roof difficult to top. Its distinctive air is enhanced by the attached family room unit and the two-car garage. The wide vertical siding delightfully contrasts with the narrow horizontal siding.

Design T172531 1,353 Sq. Ft. - First Floor
1,208 Sq. Ft. - Second Floor; 33,225 Cu. Ft.

● This design has its roots in the early history of New England. While its exterior is decidedly and purposely dated, the interior reflects an impressive 20th-Century floor plan. All of the elements are present to guarantee outstanding living patterns for today's large, active family.

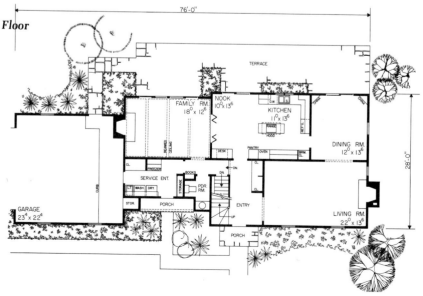

171

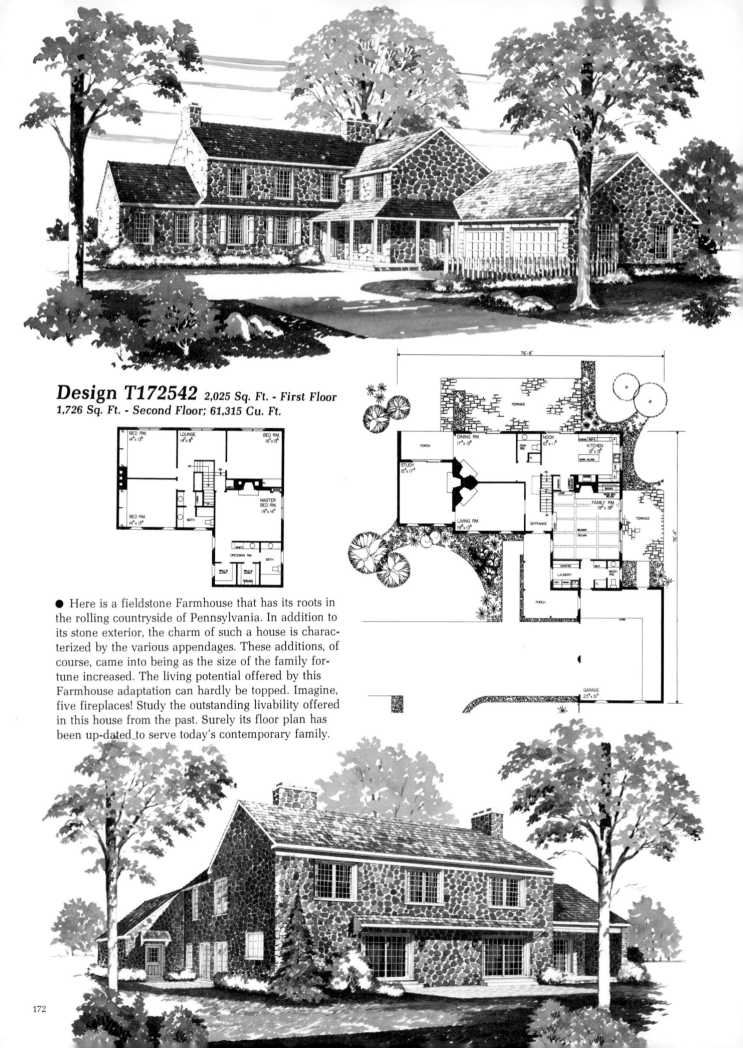

Design T172542
2,025 Sq. Ft. - First Floor
1,726 Sq. Ft. - Second Floor; 61,315 Cu. Ft.

● Here is a fieldstone Farmhouse that has its roots in the rolling countryside of Pennsylvania. In addition to its stone exterior, the charm of such a house is characterized by the various appendages. These additions, of course, came into being as the size of the family fortune increased. The living potential offered by this Farmhouse adaptation can hardly be topped. Imagine, five fireplaces! Study the outstanding livability offered in this house from the past. Surely its floor plan has been up-dated to serve today's contemporary family.

Design T172633

1,338 Sq. Ft. - First Floor
1,200 Sq. Ft. - Second Floor
506 Sq. Ft. - Third Floor
44,525 Cu. Ft.

● This is certainly a pleasing Georgian. Its facade features a front porch with a roof supported by 12" diameter wooden columns. The garage wing has a sheltered service entry and brick facing which complements the design. Sliding glass doors link the terrace and family room, providing an indoor/outdoor area for entertaining as pictured in the rear elevation. The floor plan has been designed to serve the family efficiently. The stairway in the foyer leads to four second-floor bedrooms. The third floor is windowed and can be used as a studio and study.

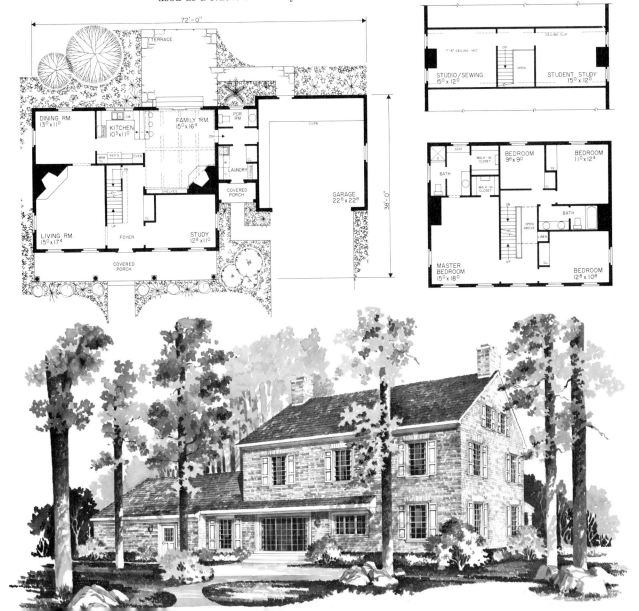

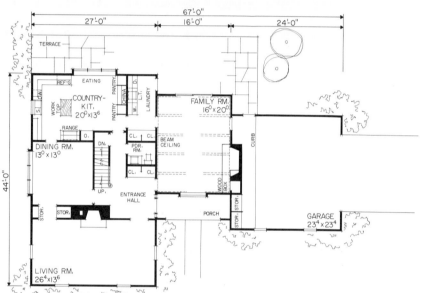

Design T171887

1,518 Sq. Ft. - First Floor
1,144 Sq. Ft. - Second Floor
40,108 Cu. Ft.

● This Gambrel roof Colonial is steeped in history. And well it should be, for its pleasing proportions are a delight to the eye. The various roof planes, the window treatment, and the rambling nature of the entire house revive a picture of rural New England. The covered porch protects the front door which opens into a spacious entrance hall. Traffic then flows in an orderly fashion to the end living room, the separate dining room, the cozy family room, and to the spacious country-kitchen. There is a first floor laundry, plenty of coat closets, and a handy powder room. Two fireplaces enliven the decor of the living areas. Upstairs there is an exceptional master bedroom layout, and abundant storage. Note the walk-in closets.

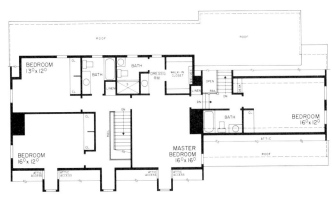

Design T172680
1,707 Sq. Ft. - First Floor
1,439 Sq. Ft. - Second Floor; 53,865 Cu. Ft.

● This Early American, Dutch Colonial not only has charm, but offers many fine features. The foyer allows easy access to all rooms on the first floor - excellent livability. Note the large country kitchen with beamed ceiling, fireplace and island cook top. A large, formal dining room and powder room are only a few steps away. A fireplace also will be found in the study and living room. The service area, mud room, wash room and laundry are tucked near the garage. Two bedrooms, full bath and master bedroom suite will be found on the second floor. A fourth bedroom and bath are accessible through the master bedroom or stairs in the service entrance.

Design T172650

1,451 Sq. Ft. - First Floor
1,091 Sq. Ft. - Second Floor; 43,555 Cu. Ft.

● The rear view of this design is just as appealing as the front. The dormers and the covered porch with pillars is a charming way to introduce this house to the on-lookers. Inside, the appeal is also outstanding. Note the size (18 x 25) of the gathering room which is open to the dining room. Kitchen-nook area is very spacious and features an island range, built-in desk and more. It is a great convenience having the laundry in the service area which is close to the kitchen. Imagine, a fireplace in both the gathering room and the master bedroom! Make special note of the front and rear service entrances.

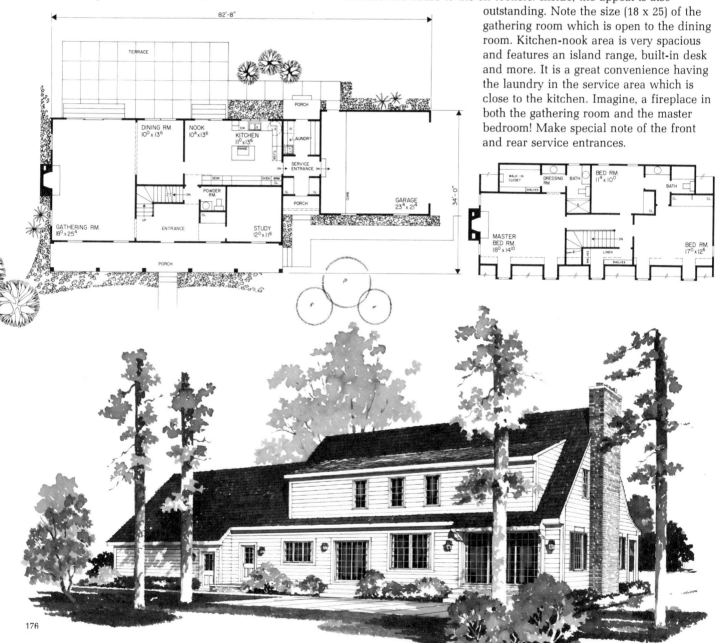

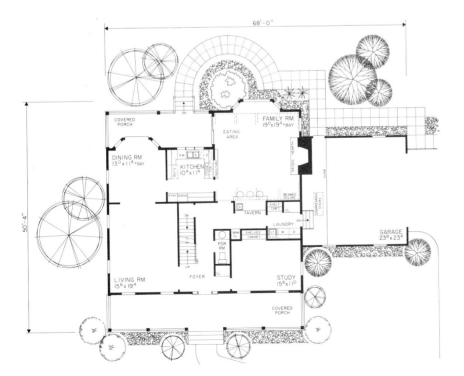

Design T172890

1,612 Sq. Ft. - First Floor
1,356 Sq. Ft. - Second Floor
47,010 Cu. Ft.

● An appealing Farm-house that is complimented by an inviting front porch. Many memorable summer evenings will be spent here. Entering this house, you will notice a nice-sized study to your right and spacious living room to the left. The adjacent dining room is enriched by an attractive bay window. Just a step away, an efficient kitchen will be found. Many family activities will be enjoyed in the large family room. The tavern/snack bar will make entertaining guests a joy. A powder room and laundry are also on the first floor. Upstairs you'll find a master bedroom suite featuring a bath with an oversized tub and shower and a dressing room. Also on this floor; two bedrooms, full bath and a large attic.

Design T172641

1,672 Sq. Ft. - First Floor
1,248 Sq. Ft. - Second Floor; 45,306 Cu. Ft.

● This Georgian adaptation is from the early 18th Century and has plenty of historical background. The classical details are sedately stated. The plan promises up-to-date livability. The size of your site need not be large, either.

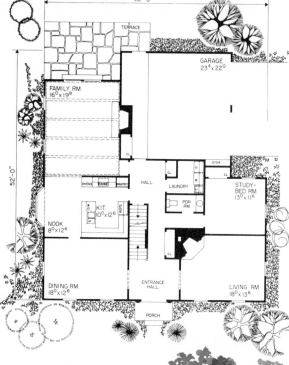

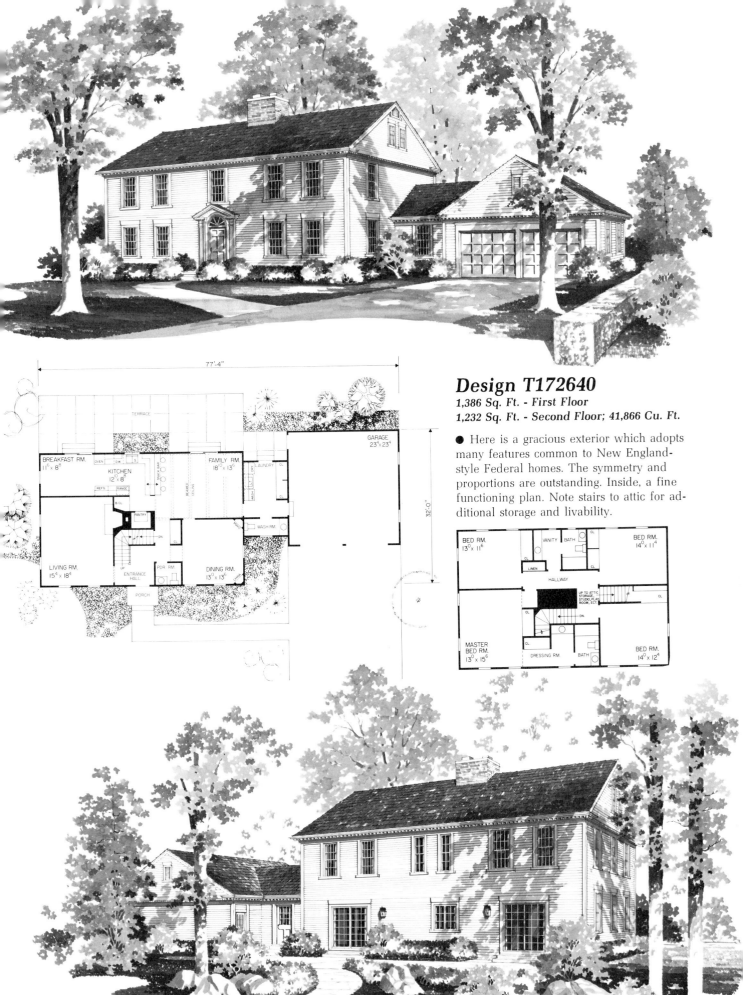

Design T172640

1,386 Sq. Ft. - First Floor
1,232 Sq. Ft. - Second Floor; 41,866 Cu. Ft.

● Here is a gracious exterior which adopts many features common to New England-style Federal homes. The symmetry and proportions are outstanding. Inside, a fine functioning plan. Note stairs to attic for additional storage and livability.

Design T172654

1,152 Sq. Ft. - First Floor
844 Sq. Ft. - Second Floor; 31,845 Cu. Ft.

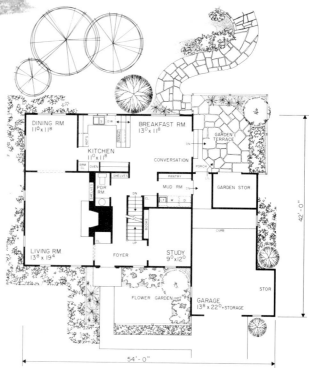

● This is certainly an authentic traditional salt-box. It features a symmetrical design with a center fireplace, a wide, paneled doorway and multi-paned, double-hung windows. Tucked behind the one-car garage is a garden shed which provides work and storage space. The breakfast room features French doors which open onto a flagstone terrace. The U-shaped kitchen has built-in counters which make efficient use of space. The upstairs plan houses three bedrooms.

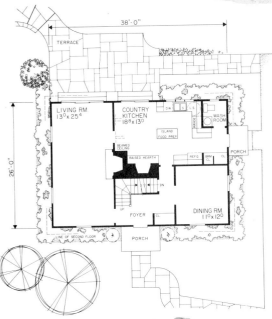

Design T172666 988 Sq. Ft. - First Floor
1,147 Sq. Ft. - Second Floor; 35,490 Cu. Ft.

● A spacious country-kitchen highlights the interior of this two-story. Its features include an island work center, fireplace, beamed ceiling and sliding glass doors leading to the rear terrace. A wash room and a side door are only steps away. A second fireplace is in the large living room. It, too, has sliding glass doors in the rear.

Design T172713

1,830 Sq. Ft. - First Floor
1,056 Sq. Ft. - Second Floor; 41,370 Cu. Ft.

● This home with its Gambrel roof and paned windows is sure to be a pleasure for the entire family. Along with the outside, the inside is a delight. The spacious family room creates an inviting atmosphere with sliding glass doors to the terrace, beamed ceiling and a raised hearth fireplace that includes a built-in wood box. A spectacular kitchen, too. Presenting a cooking island as well as a built-in oven, desk and storage pantry. A sunny breakfast nook, too, also with sliding glass doors leading to the terrace. A service entrance and laundry are adjacent. Note the size of the formal dining room and the fireplace in the living room. A first floor study/bedroom has a private terrace. Upstairs, there is the master suite and two more bedrooms and a bath.

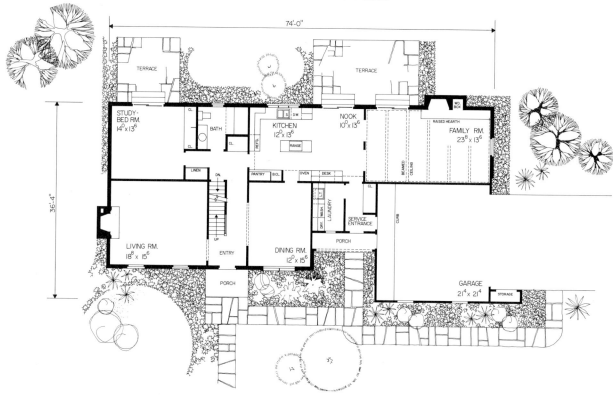

STORAGE
18⁴ X 18⁸

POTENTIAL PLAYROOM, STUDIO, GUEST ROOM
22⁸ X 18⁸

ROOF

ROOF

BED RM - SITTING RM.
15⁴ x 10²

BED RM.
16⁰ x 10²

BATH

DRESSING RM.

LIN.

LIN.

VANITY

BATH

MASTER BED RM.
18⁴ x 12¹⁰

HALL

BED RM.
16⁰ x 12¹⁰

78'-4"

44'-4"

TERRACE

PORCH

FAMILY RM.
18⁴ x 15⁶

NOOK
12² x 13²

BEAMED CEILING

KITCHEN
14⁶ x 13²

RANGE

LAUNDRY

COUNTER

DISAPPEARING STAIR

CABINET

BOOKS

BOOKS

CABINET

RAISED HEARTH

PDR. RM.

PANTRY

CHINA CABINET

SERV. ENT.

GARAGE
23⁴ x 21⁴

LIVING RM.
18⁴ x 12¹⁰

ENTRY

DINING RM.
16⁰ x 12¹⁰

CHINA

CHINA

PORCH

PORCH

Design T172556

1,675 Sq. Ft. - First Floor

1,472 Sq. Ft. - Second Floor

59,260 Cu. Ft.

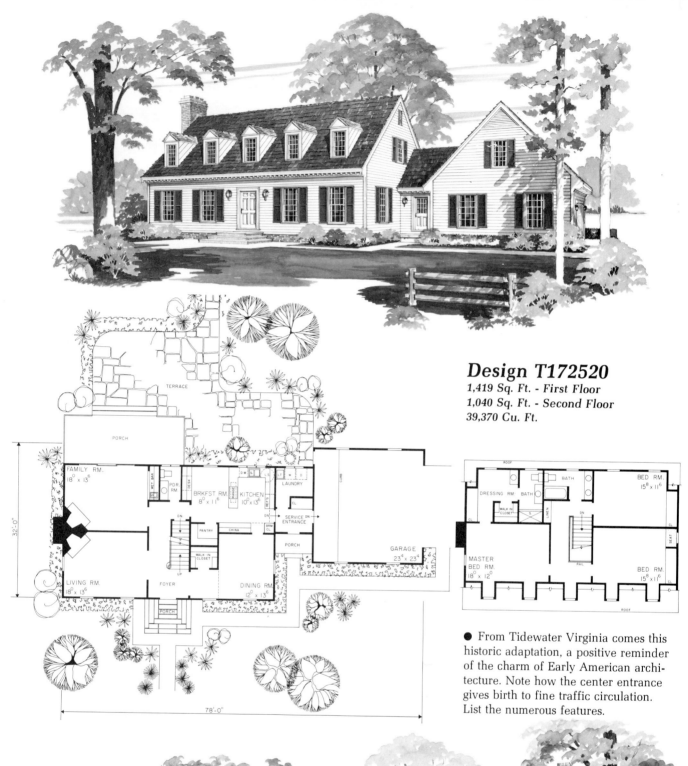

Design T172520

1,419 Sq. Ft. - First Floor
1,040 Sq. Ft. - Second Floor
39,370 Cu. Ft.

● From Tidewater Virginia comes this historic adaptation, a positive reminder of the charm of Early American architecture. Note how the center entrance gives birth to fine traffic circulation. List the numerous features.

Traditional Adaptations

Many of today's most charming houses are those whose pleasing proportions have retained the architectural detailing of earlier period houses. These traditional adaptations typically feature double-hung and muntined windows, panelled doors with and without sidelights, shutters, wood siding with corner boards, cupolas, dovecotes, etc. This group of one-story, two-story and split-level designs show how houses of varying sizes and shapes can capture all the warmth and charm of an earlier period.

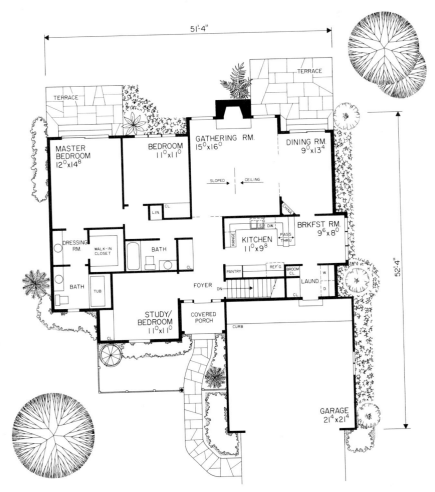

Design T172878
1,521 Sq. Ft.; 34,760 Cu. Ft.

● There is a great deal of livability in this one-story design. The efficient floor plan makes optimum use of limited floor space. Ideally located, the gathering room is warmed by a fireplace. Its sloped-ceiling gives it a spacious appeal. Adjacent is the dining room which opens up to the rear terrace via sliding glass doors for dining alfresco. Ready to serve the breakfast room and dining room, there is the interior kitchen. The laundry, basement stairs and garage door are nearby. Two with an optional third bedroom are tucked away from the more active areas of the house. The master bedroom has sliding glass doors to the terrace for outdoor enjoyment. Study this cozy, clapboard cottage and imagine it as your next home.

Design T172558

1,030 Sq. Ft. - First Floor
840 Sq. Ft. - Second Floor
27,120 Cu. Ft.

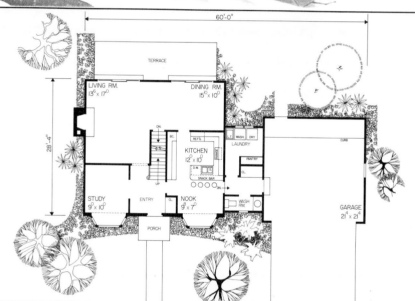

● This relatively low-budget house is long on exterior appeal and interior livability. It has all the features to assure years of Convenient Living. List them. Which are your favorites?

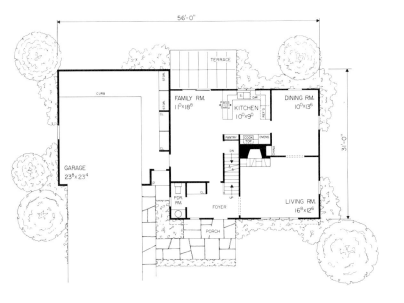

Design T171719
864 Sq. Ft. - First Floor
896 Sq. Ft. - Second Floor
26,024 Cu. Ft.

● Truly a picture house. This attractive home with it authentic detailing illustrates how good, good floor planning really can be. All the elements are present for efficient and comfortable living.

Design T172609
1,534 Sq. Ft. - First Floor
1,005 Sq. Ft. - Second Floor
36,800 Cu. Ft.

● This two-story, L-shaped Colonial home features massive twin chimneys, contrasting exterior materials, and comfortable interior highlighted by four bedrooms.

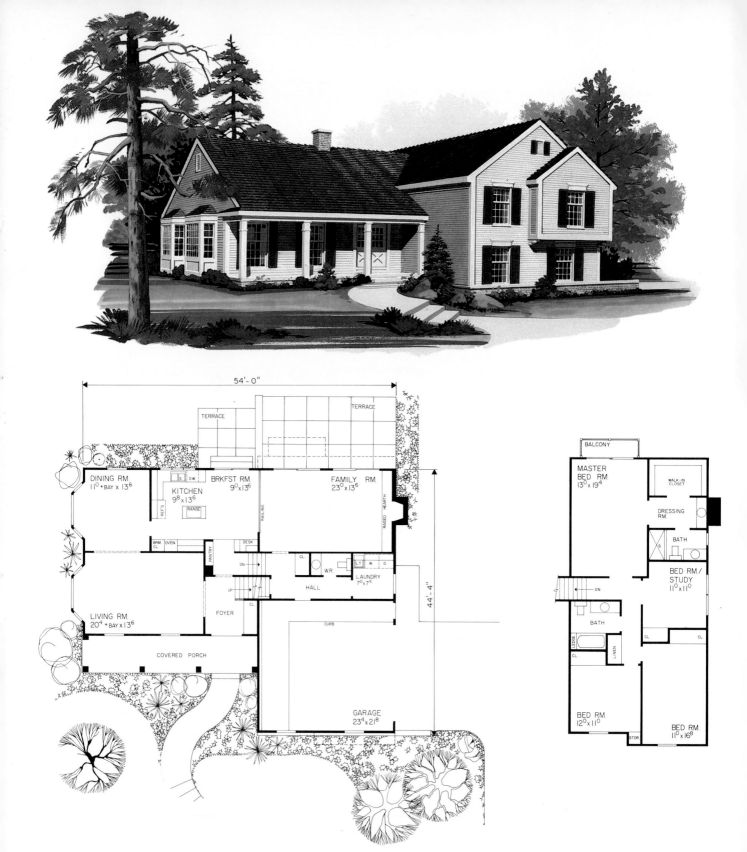

Image labels (floor plans):

Main Level:
- 54'-0"
- TERRACE
- TERRACE
- DINING RM. 11⁰ + BAY x 13⁶
- KITCHEN 9⁸ x 13⁶
- BRKFST RM. 9⁰ x 13⁶
- FAMILY RM. 23⁰ x 13⁶
- RAISED HEARTH
- REF'G
- RANGE
- BRM. CL.
- OVEN
- PANTRY
- DESK
- RAILING
- DN
- CL.
- W.R.
- LT W D
- LAUNDRY 7⁰ x 7⁶
- UP
- CL.
- HALL
- FOYER
- LIVING RM. 20⁴ + BAY x 13⁶
- COVERED PORCH
- CURB
- GARAGE 23⁴ x 21⁸
- 44'-4"

Upper Level:
- BALCONY
- MASTER BED RM. 13⁰ x 19⁴
- WALK-IN CLOSET
- DRESSING RM.
- BATH
- BED RM./STUDY 11⁰ x 11⁰
- DN
- BATH
- LEDGE
- CL.
- LINEN
- CL.
- CL.
- BED RM. 12⁰ x 11⁰
- BED RM. 11⁰ x 16⁸
- STOR

Design T172786 *871 Sq. Ft. - Main Level; 1,132 Sq. Ft. - Upper Level; 528 Sq. Ft. - Lower Level; 44,000 Cu. Ft.*

● A bay window in each of the formal living room and dining room. A great interior and exterior design feature to attract attention to this tri-level home. The exterior also is enhanced by a covered front porch to further the Co-lonial charm. The interior livability is outstanding, too. An abundance of built-ins in the kitchen create an efficient work center. Features include an island range, pantry, broom closet, desk and breakfast room with sliding glass doors to the rear terrace. The lower level houses the informal family room, washroom and laundry. Further access is available to the outdoors by the family room to the terrace and laundry room to the side yard.

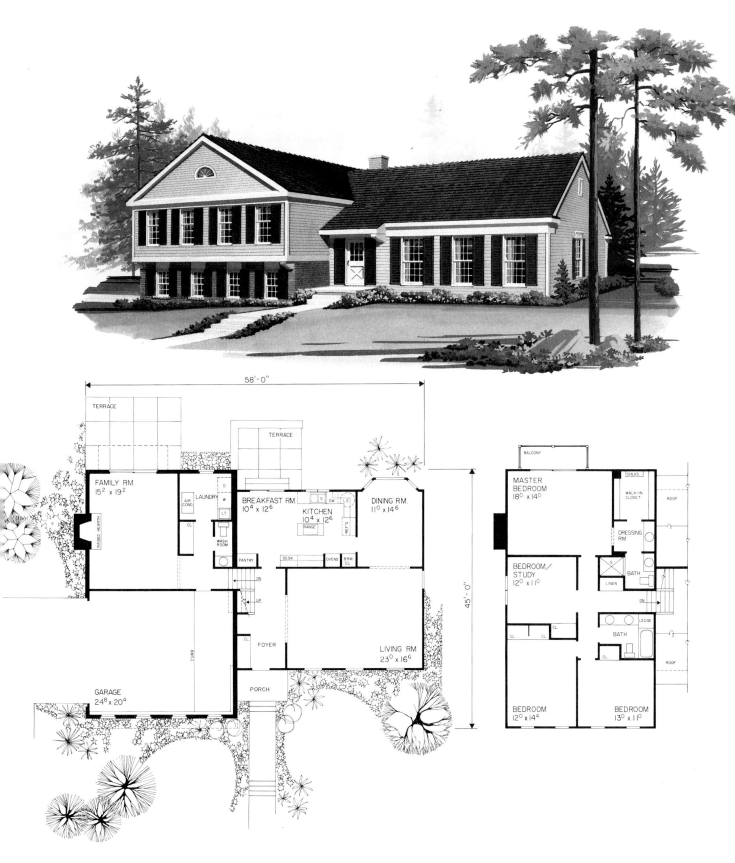

Design T172787 976 Sq. Ft. - Main Level; 1,118 Sq. Ft. - Upper Level; 524 Sq. Ft. - Lower Level; 36,110 Cu. Ft.

189

Design T172550
1,892 Sq. Ft.; 39,590 Cu. Ft.

● An enchanting low-slung traditional ranch with exceptional appeal. Inside, there are four bedrooms and two full baths in the sleeping wing. The L-shaped living area is spacious and features a sloping ceiling for the gathering and dining rooms. The open stairwell to the basement recreation area is attractive. The pleasant kitchen is flanked by nook and laundry.

Design T172181
2,612 Sq. Ft.; 42,230 Cu. Ft.

● It is hard to imagine a home with any more eye-appeal than this one. It is the complete picture of charm. The interior is no less outstanding. Sliding glass doors permit the large master bedroom, the quiet living room, and the all-purpose family room to function directly with the outdoors. The two fireplaces, the built-in china cabinets, the bookshelves, are extra features.

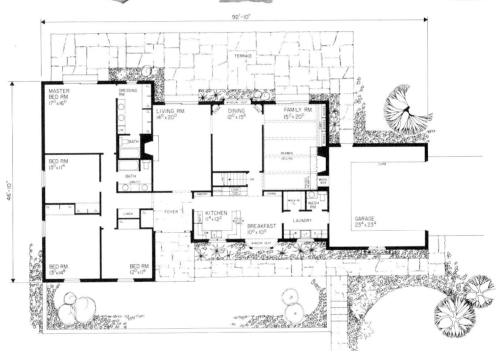

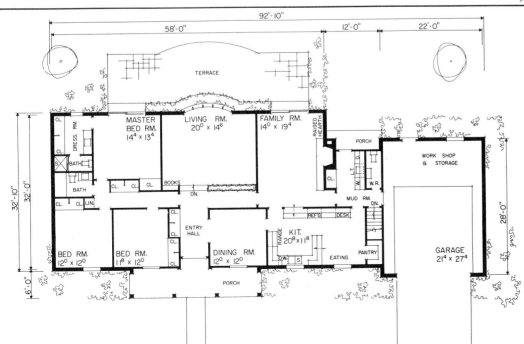

Design T171788
2,218 Sq. Ft.; 36,002 Cu. Ft.

● Charm is but one of many words which may be used to correctly describe this fine design. In addition to its attractive facade, it has a practical and smoothly functioning floor plan. The detail of the front entrance, highlighted by columns, supporting the projecting pediment gable, is outstanding. Observe the window treatment and the double front doors. Also the sunken living room.

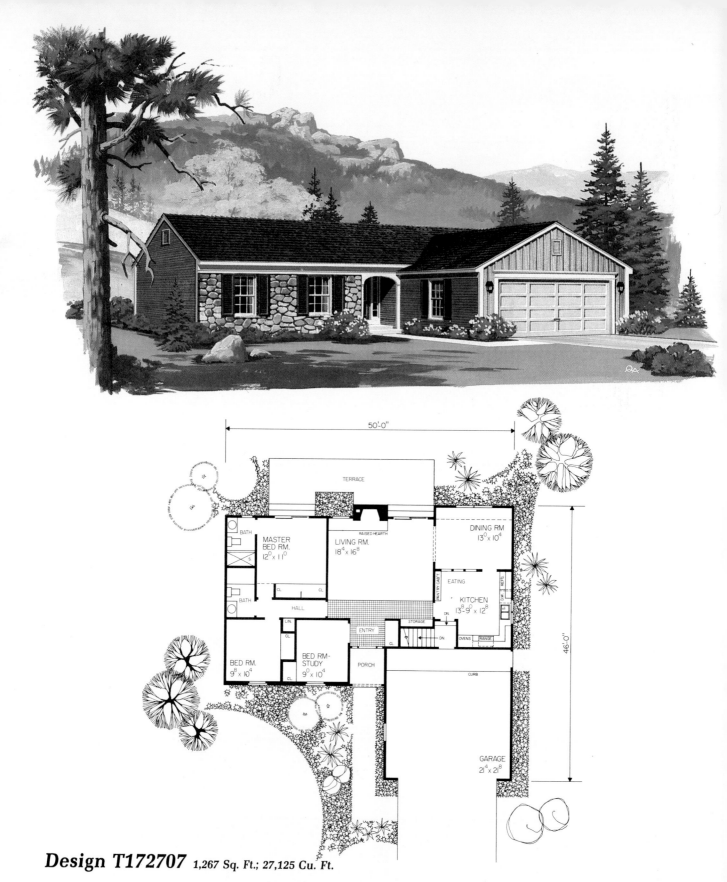

Design T172707 1,267 Sq. Ft.; 27,125 Cu. Ft.

● Here is a charming Early American adaptation that will serve as a picturesque and practical retirement home. This plan is also perfect for those with a small family in search of an efficient, economically built home. The centrally located living area, highlighted by the raised hearth fireplace, is spacious. The kitchen features eating space and easy access to the garage and basement. Adjacent to the kitchen, the dining room has an excellent view of the rear yard. The bedroom wing offers three bedrooms and two full baths.

Don't miss the sliding glass doors to the terrace from the living room and the master bedroom. Storage units are plentiful including a pantry cabinet in the eating area of the kitchen. There is a good-sized basement for recreation and hobby pursuits.

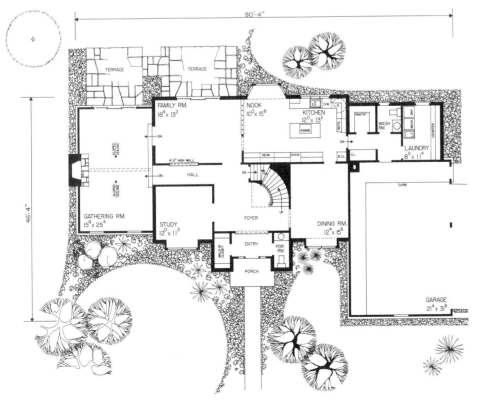

Design T172599
2,075 Sq. Ft. - First Floor
1,398 Sq. Ft. - Second Floor
55,000 Cu. Ft.

● This traditional two-story with its projecting one-story wings is delightfully proportioned. The symmetrical window treatment is most appealing. The massive field-stone arch projects from the front line of the house providing a sheltered front entrance. Inside, there is the large foyer with the curving, open staircase to the second floor. Flexibility will be the byword to describe the living patterns. Not only are there the formal living and informal family rooms, but there is the quiet study and the upstairs sitting room. As for eating, there is a sizeable breakfast nook and a separate dining room. The second floor offers the option to function as either a three, or four, bedroom sleeping zone. That's a fine master bedroom suite when the sitting room is included.

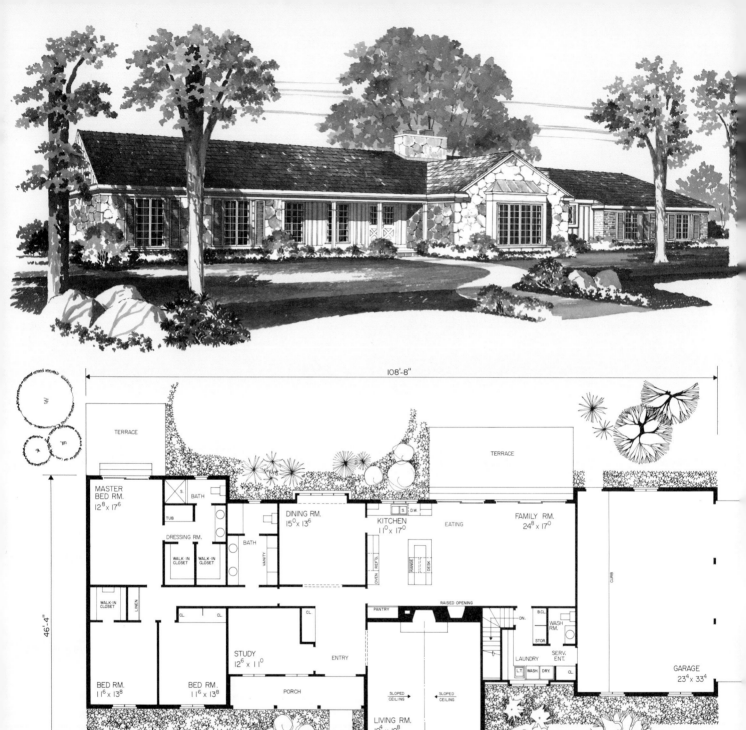

Design T172767 *3,000 Sq. Ft.; 58,460 Cu. Ft.*

● What a sound investment this impressive home will be. And while its value withstands the inflationary pressures of ensuing years, it will serve your family well. It has all the amenities to assure truly pleasurable living. The charming exterior will lend itself

to treatment other than the appealing fieldstone, brick and frame shown. Inside, the plan will impress you with large, spacious living areas, formal and informal dining areas, three large bedrooms, two full baths with twin lavatories, walk-in closets and a fine study.

The kitchen features an island work center with range and desk. The two fireplaces will warm their surroundings in both areas. Two separate terraces for a variety of uses. Note laundry, wash room and three-car garage with extra curb area.

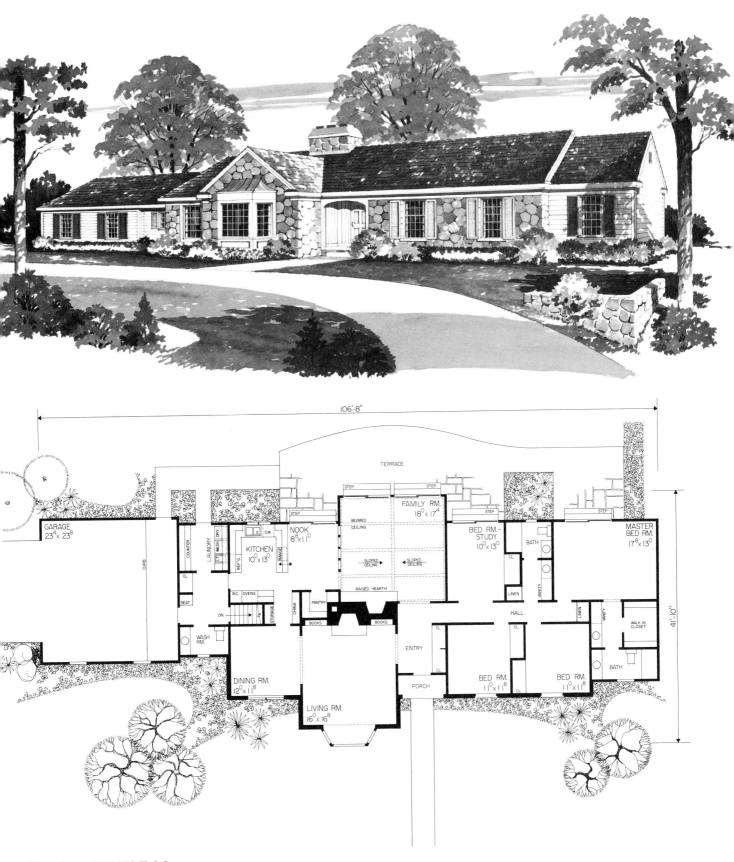

Design T172544 *2,527 Sq. Ft.; 61,943 Cu. Ft.*

● A blend of exterior materials enhance the beauty of this fine home. Here, the masonry material used is fieldstone to contrast effectively with the horizontal siding. You may substitute brick or quarried stone if you wish. Adding to the appeal are the various projections and their roof planes, the window treatment and the recessed front entrance. Two large living areas highlight the interior. Each has a fireplace. The homemaking effort will be easily and enjoyably dispatched with such features as the efficient kitchen, the walk-in pantry, the handy storage areas, the first floor laundry and extra washroom. The sleeping zone has four bedrooms, two baths with vanities and good closet accommodations. There's a basement for additional storage and recreation activities.

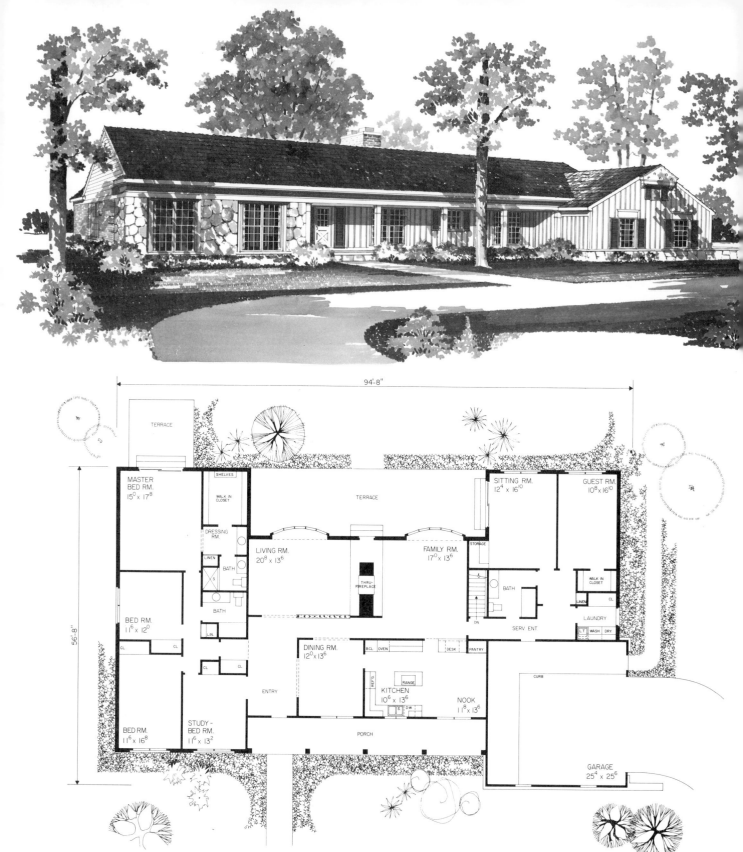

Design T172768 3,436 Sq. Ft.; 65,450 Cu. Ft.

● Besides its elegant traditionally styled exterior with its delightfully long covered front porch, this home has an exceptionally livable interior. There is the outstanding four bedroom and two-bath sleeping wing. Then, the efficient front kitchen with island range flanked by the formal dining room and the informal breakfast nook. Separated by the two-way, thru fireplace are the living and family rooms which look out on the rear yard. Worthy of particular note is the development of a potential live-in relative facility. These two rooms would also serve the large family well as a hobby room and library or additional bedrooms. A full bath is adjacent as well as the laundry. Note curb area in the garage for the storage of outdoor equipment.

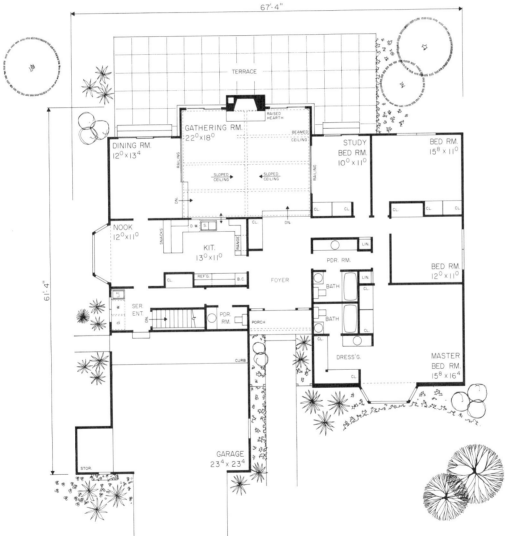

Design T172527 *2,392 Sq. Ft.; 42,579 Cu. Ft.*

● Vertical boards and battens, field-stone, bay window, a dovecote, a gas lamp and a recessed front entrance are among the appealing exterior features of this U-shaped design. Through the double front doors, flanked by

glass side lites, one enters the spacious foyer. Straight ahead is the cozy sunken gathering room with its sloping, beamed ceiling, raised hearth fireplace and two sets of sliding glass doors to the rear terrace. To the right of

the foyer is the sleeping wing with its three bedrooms, study (make it the fourth bedroom if you wish) and two baths. To the left is the strategically located powder room and large kitchen with its delightful nook and bay window.

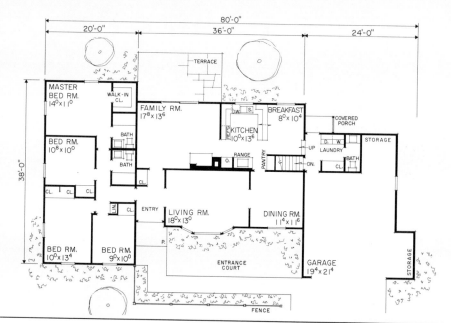

Design T171829
1,800 Sq. Ft.; 32,236 Cu. Ft.

● All the charm of a traditional heritage is wrapped up in this U-shaped home with its narrow, horizontal siding, delightful window treatment and high-pitched roof. The massive center chimney, the bay window and the double front doors are plus features. Inside, the living potential is outstanding. The sleeping wing is self-contained and has four bedrooms and two baths. The large family and living rooms cater to the divergent age groups.

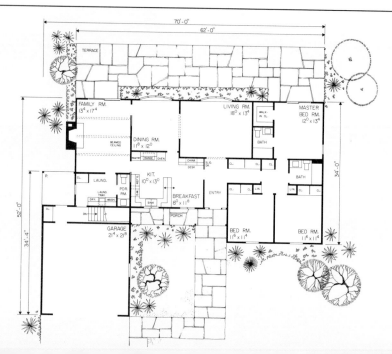

Design T171980
1,901 Sq. Ft.; 36,240 Cu. Ft.

● Planned for easy living, the daily living patterns of the active family will be pleasant ones, indeed. All the elements are present to assure a wonderful family life. The impressive exterior is enhanced by the recessed front entrance area with its covered porch. The center entry results in a convenient and efficient flow of traffic. A secondary entrance leads from the covered side porch, or the garage, into the first floor laundry. Note the powder room nearby.

Design T172360
1,936 Sq. Ft.; 37,026 Cu. Ft.

● There is no such thing as taking a fleeting glance at this charming home. Fine proportion and pleasing lines assure a long and rewarding study. Inside, the family's everyday routine will enjoy all the facilities which will surely guarantee pleasurable living. Note the sunken living room with its fireplace flanked by storage cabinets and book shelves. Observe the excellent kitchen just a step from the dining room and the nook.

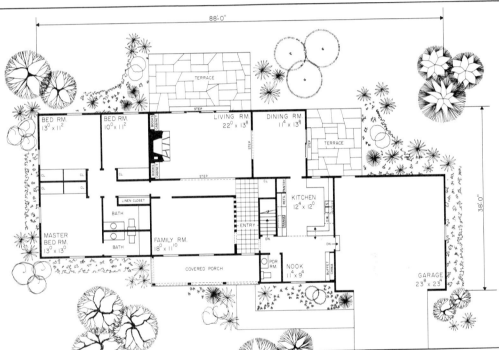

Design T172739 *3,313 Sq. Ft.; 65,230 Cu. Ft.*

● If you and your family are looking for new living patterns, try to envision your days spent in this traditionally styled home. Its Early American flavor is captured by effective window and door treatment, cornice work and porch pillars. Its zoning is interesting.

The spacious interior leaves nothing to be desired. There are three bedrooms and two full baths in the sleeping area. A quiet, formal living room is separated from the other living areas. The gathering and dining rooms are adjacent to each other and function with

the excellent kitchen and its breakfast eating area. Note work island, pantry and pass-thru. Then, there is an extra guest room sunken one step. A live-in relative would enjoy the privacy of this room. Full bath is nearby. This is definitely a home for all to enjoy.

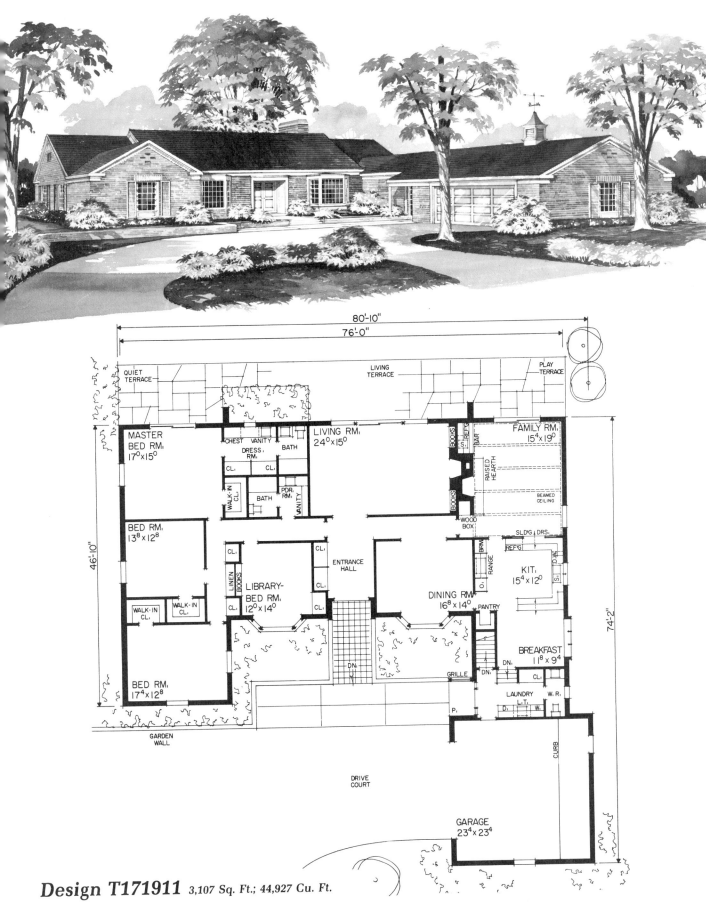

Design T171911 3,107 Sq. Ft.; 44,927 Cu. Ft.

● For luxurious, country-estate living it would be difficult to beat the livability offered by these two impressive traditional designs. To begin with, their exterior appeal is, indeed, gracious. Their floor plans highlight plenty of space, excellent room arrangements, fine traffic circulation, and an abundance of convenient living features. It is interesting to note that each design features similar livability facilities. Both may function as four bedroom homes . . .

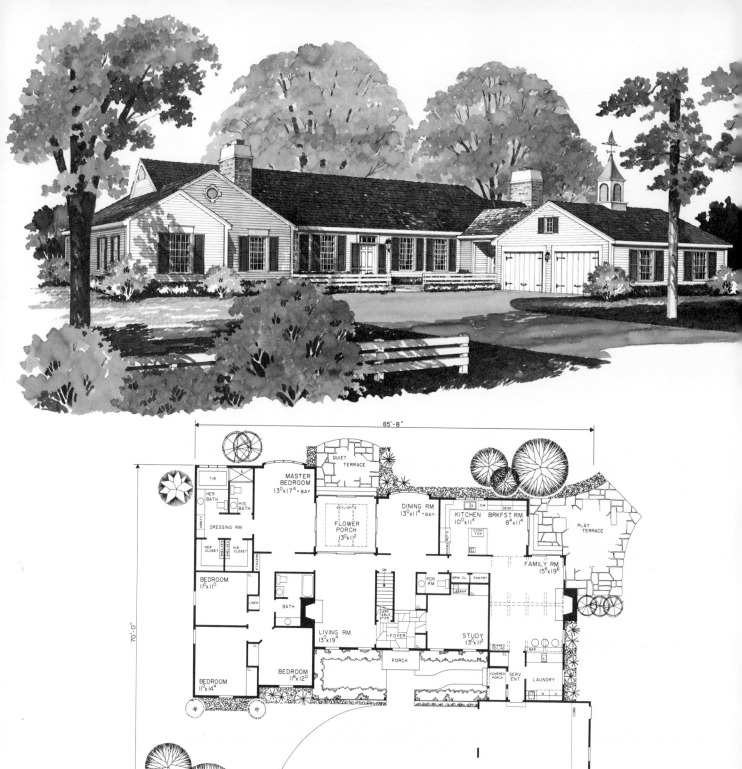

Design T172888
3,018 Sq. Ft.; 59,769 Cu. Ft.

● This is an outstanding Early American design for the 20th-Century. The exterior detailing with narrow clapboards, multi-paned windows and cupola are the features of yesteryear. Interior planning, though, is for today's active family. Formal living room, in-

formal family room plus a study are present. Every activity will have its place in this home. Picture yourself working in the kitchen. There's enough counter space for two or three helpers. Four bedrooms are in the private area. Stop and imagine your daily routine if

you occupied the master bedroom. Both you and your spouse would have plenty of space and privacy. The flower porch, accessible from the master bedroom, living and dining rooms, is a very delightful "plus" feature. Study this design's every detail.

Design T172778 2,761 Sq. Ft.; 41,145 Cu. Ft.

● No matter what the occasion, family and friends alike will enjoy the sizable gathering room which is featured in this plan. A spacious 20' x 23', this room has a thru-fireplace to the study and two sets of sliding glass doors to the large rear terrace. Indoor-outdoor living can also be enjoyed from the dining room, study and master bedroom; all located to face the rear yard. There is a covered dining porch, too, accessible through sliding glass doors in the dining and breakfast rooms. A total of three bedrooms are planned for this design. Each has plenty of closet space. Notice the hightlights of the master suite: large walk-in closet, tub plus stall shower and exercise area.

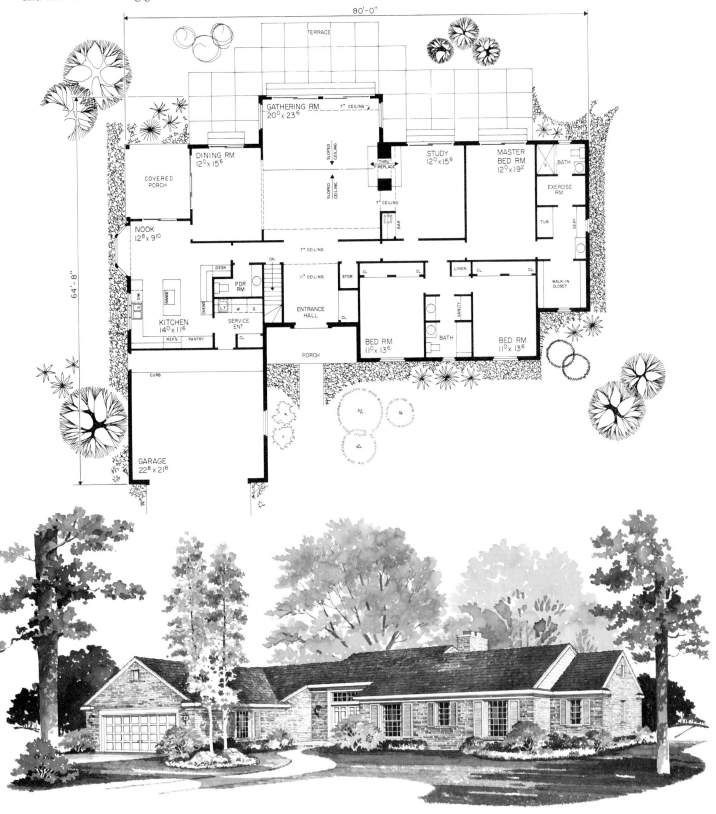

Design T172883 *1,919 Sq. Ft. - First Floor*
895 Sq. Ft. - Second Floor; 46,489 Cu. Ft.

● A country-style home is part of America's fascination with the rural past. This home's emphasis of the traditional home is in its gambrel roof, dormers and fanlight windows. Having a traditional exterior from the street view, this home has window

walls and a greenhouse, which opens the house to the outdoors in a thoroughly contemporary manner. The interior meets the requirements of today's active family. Like the country houses of the past, it has a gathering room for family get-togethers or entertaining. The adjacent two-story greenhouse doubles as the dining room. There is a pass-thru snack bar to the country kitchen here. This country kitchen just might be the heart of the house with its two areas - work zone and sitting room. There are four bedrooms on the two floors - the master bedroom suite on the first floor; three more on the second floor. A lounge, overlooking the gathering room and front foyer, is also on the second floor.

Design T172826
1,112 Sq. Ft. - First Floor
881 Sq. Ft. - Second Floor; 32,770 Cu. Ft.

ALTERNATE KITCHEN / DINING RM / BREAKFAST RM. FLOOR PLAN

● This is an outstanding example of the type of informal, traditional-style architecture that has captured the modern imagination. The interior plan houses all the features that people want most - a spacious gathering room, formal and informal dining areas, efficient, U-shaped kitchen, master bedroom, two children's bedrooms, second-floor lounge, entrance court and rear terrace and deck. Study all areas of this plan carefully.

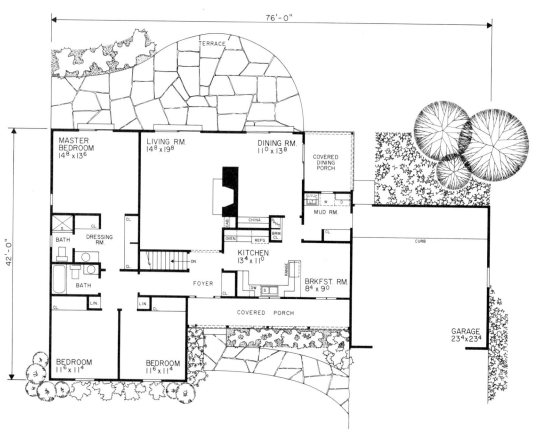

Design T172672 *1,717 Sq. Ft.; 37,167 Cu. Ft.*

● The traditional appearance of this one-story is emphasized by its covered porch, multi-paned windows, narrow clapboard and vertical wood siding. Not only is the exterior eye-appealing but the interior has an efficient plan and is very livable. The front U-shaped kitchen will work with the breakfast room and mud room, which houses the laundry facilities. An access to the garage is here. Outdoor dining can be enjoyed on the covered porch adjacent to the dining room. Both of these areas, the porch and dining room, are convenient to the kitchen. Sleeping facilities consist of three bedrooms and two full baths. Note the three sets of sliding glass doors leading to the terrace.

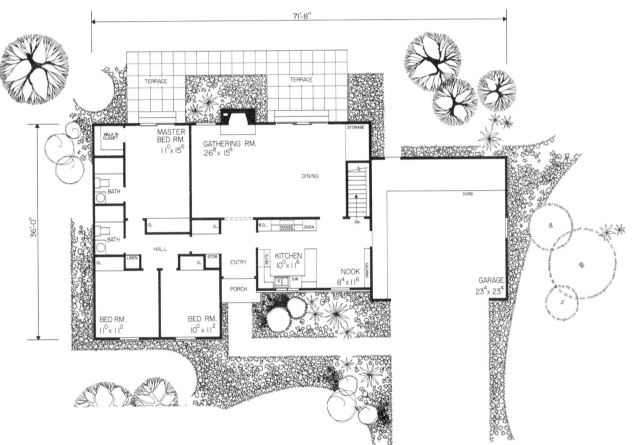

Design T172597 1,515 Sq. Ft.; 32,000 Cu. Ft.

● Whether it be a starter house you are after, or one in which to spend your retirement years, this pleasing frame home will provide a full measure of pride in ownership. The contrast of vertical and horizontal lines, the double front doors and the coach lamp post at the garage create an inviting exterior. The floor plan functions in an orderly and efficient manner. The 26 foot gathering room has a delightful view of the rear yard and will take care of those formal dining occasions. There are two full baths serving the three bedrooms. There are plenty of storage facilities, two sets of glass doors to the terraces, a fireplace in the gathering room, a basement and an attached two-car garage to act as a buffer against the wind. A delightful home, indeed.

Design T172777
2,006 Sq. Ft.; 44,580 Cu. Ft.

● Many years of delightful living will be enjoyed in this one-story traditional home. The covered, front porch adds a charm to the exterior as do the paned windows and winding drive. Inside, there is livability galore. An efficient kitchen with island range and adjacent laundry make this work area very pleasing. A breakfast nook with bay window and built--in desk will serve the family when informal dining is called upon. A formal dining room with sliding glass doors leads to the rear terrace. The large gathering room with raised hearth fireplace can serve the family on any occasion gracefully. The sleeping wing consists of two bedrooms and a study (or make it three bedrooms). The master bedroom in-cludes all of the fine fea-tures one would expect: a huge walk-in closet, a vanity, a bath and sliding glass doors to a private terrace.

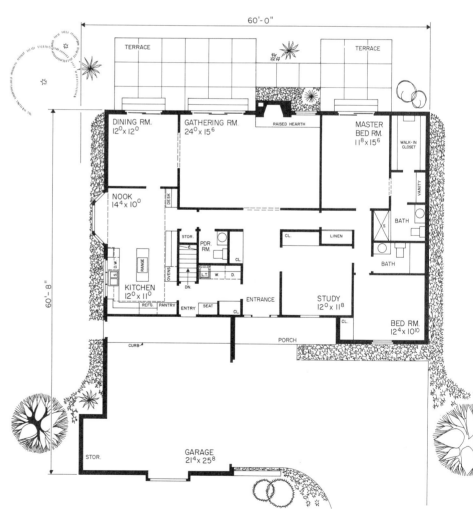

Design T172867 *2,388 Sq. Ft.; 49,535 Cu. Ft.*

● A live-in relative would be very comfortable in this home. This design features a self-contained suite (473 sq. ft.) consisting of a bedroom, bath, living room and kitchenette with dining area. This suite is nestled behind the garage away from the main areas of the house. The rest of this traditional, one-story house, faced with fieldstone and vertical wood siding, is also very livable. One whole wing houses the four family bedrooms and bath facilities. The center of the plan has a front, U-shaped kitchen and breakfast room. The formal dining room and large gathering room will enjoy the view, and access to, the backyard. The large, covered porch will receive much use.

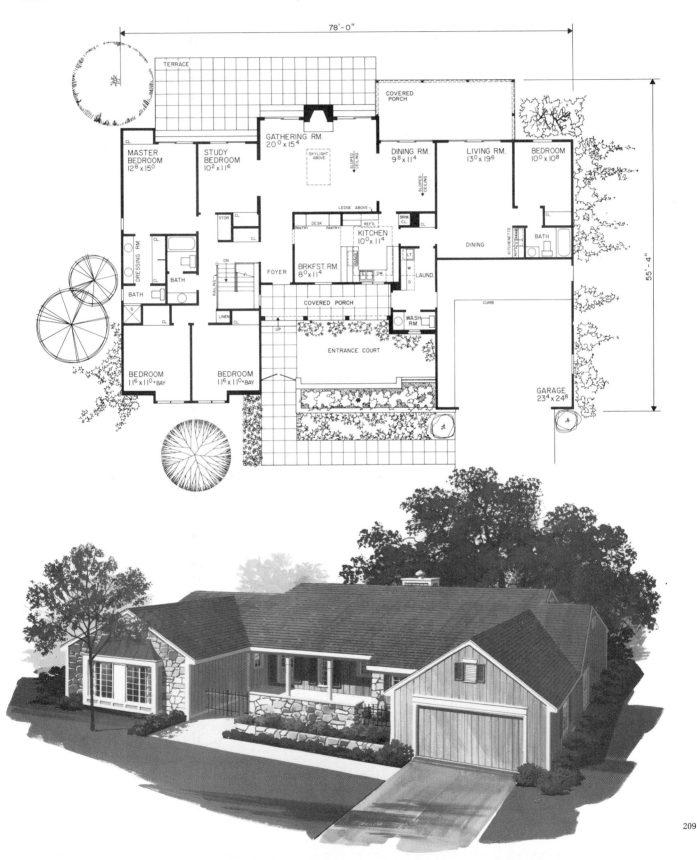

Design T172802
1,729 Sq. Ft.; 42,640 Cu. Ft.

● The three exteriors shown at the left house the same, efficiently planned one-story floor plan shown below. Be sure to notice the design variations in the window placement and roof pitch. The Tudor design to the left is delightful. Half-timbered stucco and brick comprise the facade of this English Tudor variation of the plan. Note authentic bay window in the front bedroom.

Design T172803
1,679 Sq. Ft.; 36,755 Cu. Ft.

● Housed in varying facades, this floor plan is very efficient. The front foyer leads to each of the living areas. The sleeping area of two, or optional three, bedrooms is ready to serve the family. Then there is the gathering room. This room is highlighted by its size, 16 x 20 feet. A contemporary mix of fieldstone and vertical wood siding characterizes this exterior. The absence of columns or posts gives a modern look to the covered porch.

Design T172804
1,674 Sq. Ft.; 35,465 Cu. Ft.

● Stuccoed arches, multi-paned windows and a gracefully sloped roof accent the exterior of this Spanish-inspired design. Like the other two designs, the interior kitchen will efficiently serve the dining room, covered dining porch and breakfast room with great ease. Blueprints for all three designs include details for an optional non-basement plan.

OPTIONAL NON - BASEMENT

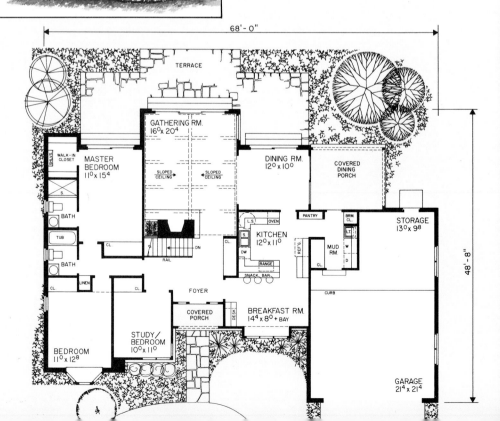

Design T172805
1,547 Sq. Ft.; 40,880 Cu. Ft.

● Three completely different exterior facades share one compact, practical and economical floor plan. The major design variations are roof pitch, window placement and garage openings. Each design will hold its own when comparing the three exteriors. The design to the right is a romantic stone-and-shingle cottage design. This design, along with the other two designs presented here, is outstanding.

Design T172806
1,584 Sq. Ft.; 41,880 Cu. Ft.

● Even though these exteriors are extremely different in their styling and also have a few design variations, their floor plans are identical. Each will provide the family with a livable plan. In this brick and half-timbered stucco Tudor version, like the other two, the living-dining room expands across the rear of the plan and has direct access to the covered porch. Notice the built-in planter adjacent to the open staircase leading to the basement.

Design T172807
1,576 Sq. Ft.; 35,355 Cu. Ft.

● Along with the living-dining areas of the other two plans, this sleek contemporary styled home's breakfast room also will have a view of the covered porch. A desk, snack bar and mud room housing the laundry facilities are near the U-shaped kitchen. Clustering these work areas together is very convenient. The master bedroom has a private bath.

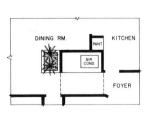

OPTIONAL NON-BASEMENT

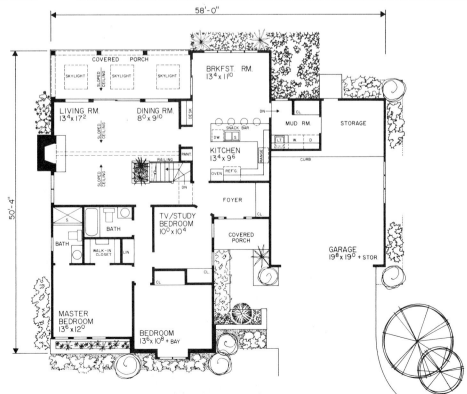

Design T171715   1,276 Sq. Ft. - First Floor; 1,064 Sq. Ft. - Second Floor; 31,295 Cu. Ft.

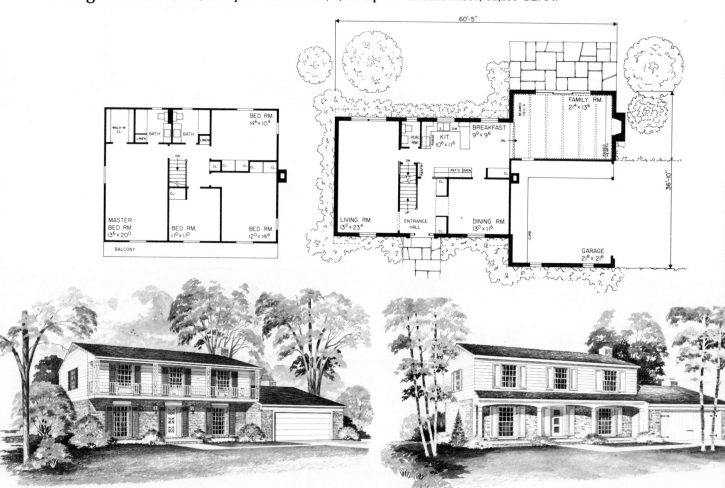

● The blueprints you order for this design show details for building each of these three appealing exteriors. Which do you like best? Whatever your choice, the interior will provide the growing family with all the facilities for fine living.

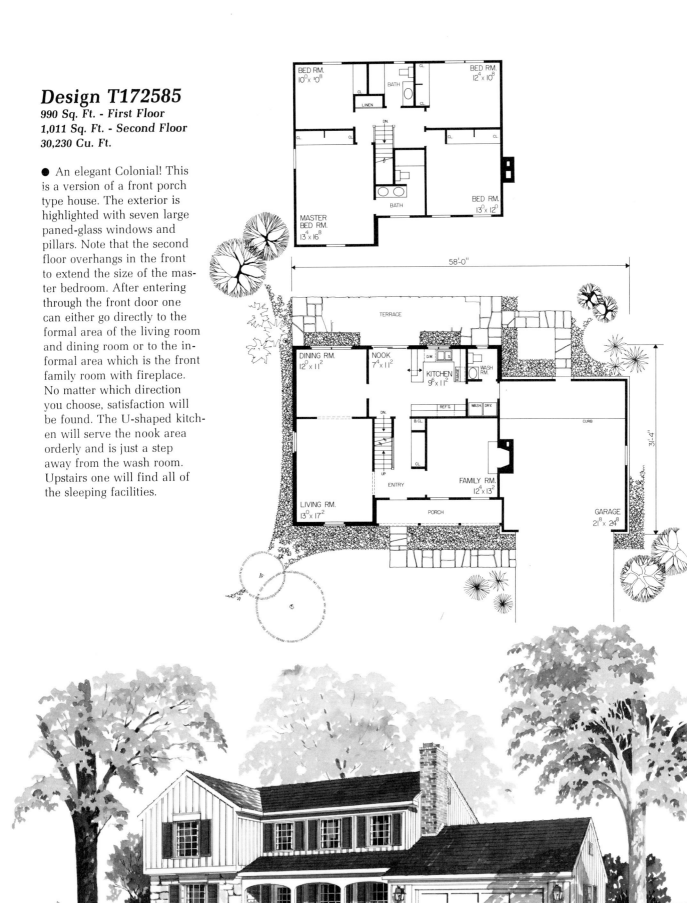

Design T172585

990 Sq. Ft. - First Floor
1,011 Sq. Ft. - Second Floor
30,230 Cu. Ft.

● An elegant Colonial! This is a version of a front porch type house. The exterior is highlighted with seven large paned-glass windows and pillars. Note that the second floor overhangs in the front to extend the size of the master bedroom. After entering through the front door one can either go directly to the formal area of the living room and dining room or to the informal area which is the front family room with fireplace. No matter which direction you choose, satisfaction will be found. The U-shaped kitchen will serve the nook area orderly and is just a step away from the wash room. Upstairs one will find all of the sleeping facilities.

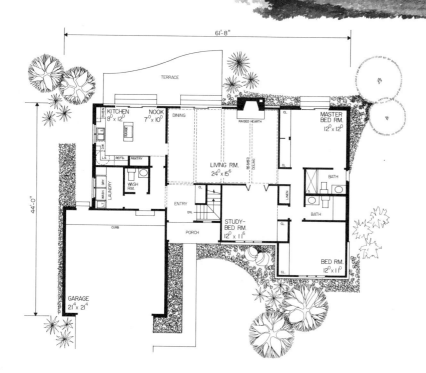

Design T172565
1,540 Sq. Ft.; 33,300 Cu. Ft.

● This modest sized floor plan has much to offer in the way of livability. It may function as either a two or three bedroom home. The living room is huge and features a fine, raised hearth fireplace. The open stairway to the basement is handy and will lead to what may be developed as the recreation area. In addition to the two full baths, there is an extra wash room. Adjacent is the laundry room and the service entrance from the garage. The blueprints you order for this design will show details for each of the three delightful elevations above. Which is your favorite? The Tudor, the Colonial or the Contemporary?

Design T172505

1,366 Sq. Ft.; 29,329 Cu. Ft.

● This design offers you a choice of
three distinctively different exteriors.
Which is your favorite? Blueprints
show details for all three optional
elevations. A study of the floor plan
reveals a fine measure of livability.
In less than 1,400 square feet there
are features galore. An excellent return on your construction dollar. In
addition to the two eating areas and
the open planning of the gathering
room, the indoor-outdoor relationships are of great interest. The basement may be developed for recreational activities. Be sure to note the
storage potential, particularly the lin-
en closet, the pantry, the china cabinet and the broom closet.

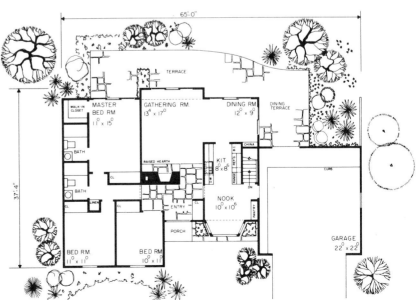

Design T171920
1,600 Sq. Ft.; 18,966 Cu. Ft.

● A charming exterior with a truly great floor plan. The front entrance with its covered porch seems to herald all the outstanding features to be found inside. Study the sleeping zone with its three bedrooms and two full baths. Each of the bedrooms has its own walk-in closet. Note the efficient U-shaped kitchen with the family and dining rooms to each side. Observe the laundry and the extra wash room. Blueprints for this design include details for both basement and non-basement construction.

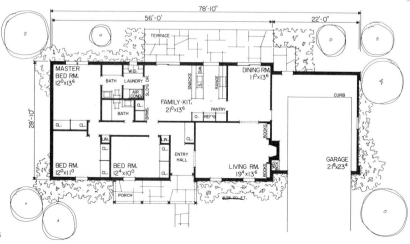

Design T171890
1,628 Sq. Ft.; 20,350 Cu. Ft.

● The pediment gable and columns help set the charm of this modestly sized home. Here is graciousness normally associated with homes twice its size. The pleasant symmetry of the windows and the double front doors complete the picture. Inside, each square foot is wisely planned to assure years of convenient living. There are three bedrooms, each with twin wardrobe closets. There are two full baths economically grouped with the laundry and heating equipment. A fine feature.

Contemporary One-Story Houses

Contemporary planning and styling can be both practical and dramatic. Here is an exciting group of designs whose configurations have resulted in eye-catching exteriors and interesting, efficient living patterns. Notice how the unusual shapes of these designs have led to refreshing roof lines, appealing glass areas, effective uses of exterior materials, and outstanding indoor-outdoor living relationships. Note, also, the unique zoning of many of the plans.

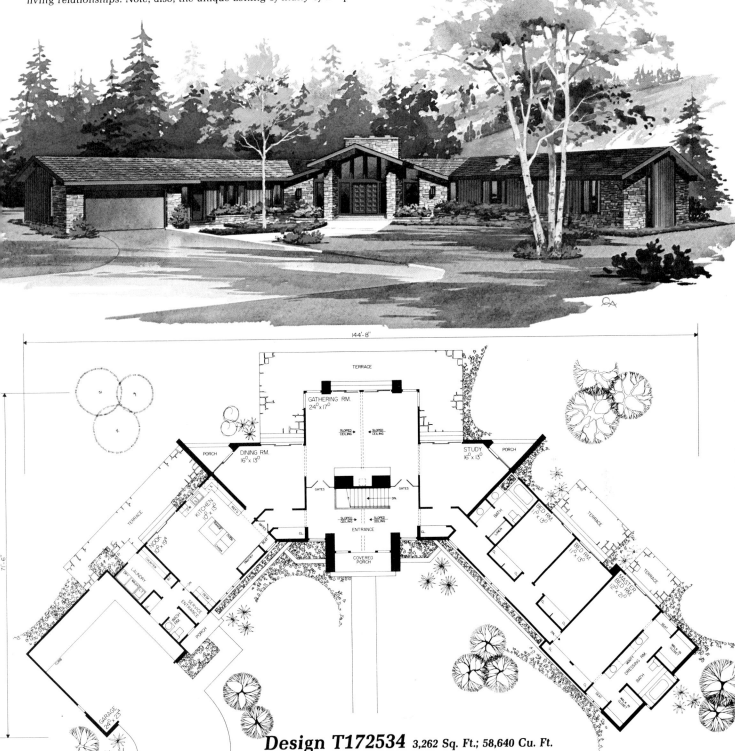

Design T172534 3,262 Sq. Ft.; 58,640 Cu. Ft.

● The angular wings of this ranch home surely contribute to the unique character of the exterior. These wings effectively balance what is truly a dramatic and inviting front entrance. Massive masonry walls support the wide overhanging roof with its exposed wood beams. The patterned double front doors are surrounded by delightful expanses of glass. The raised planters and the masses of quarried stone (make it brick if you prefer) enhance the exterior appeal. Inside, a distinctive and practical floor plan stands ready to shape and serve the living patterns of the active family. The spacious entrance hall highlights sloped ceiling and an attractive open stairway to the lower level recreation area. An impressive fireplace and an abundance of glass are features of the big gathering room.

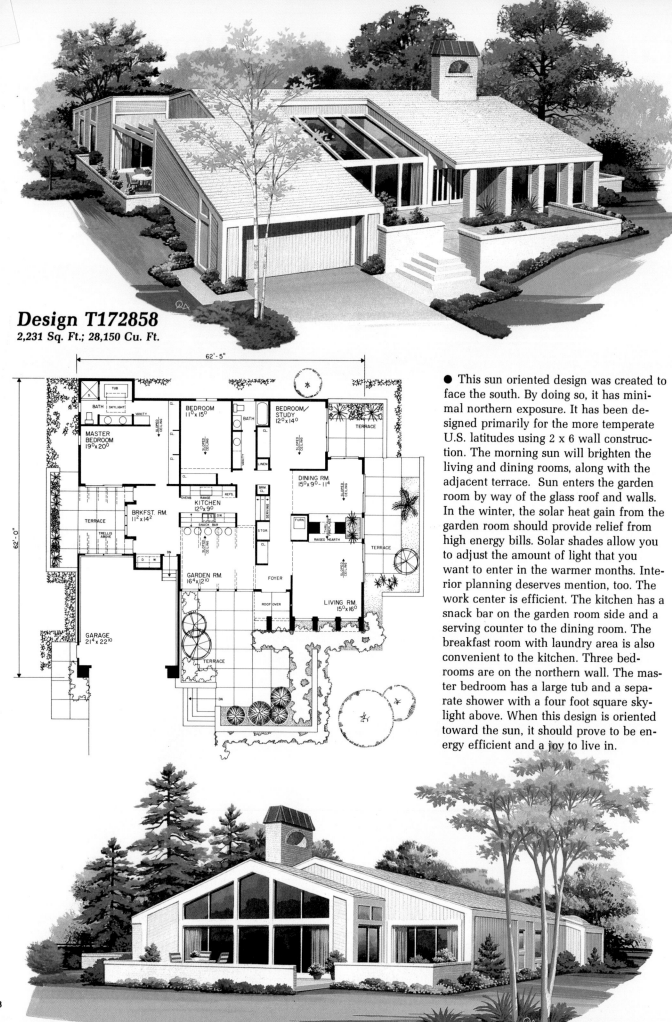

Design T172858

2,231 Sq. Ft.; 28,150 Cu. Ft.

● This sun oriented design was created to face the south. By doing so, it has minimal northern exposure. It has been designed primarily for the more temperate U.S. latitudes using 2 x 6 wall construction. The morning sun will brighten the living and dining rooms, along with the adjacent terrace. Sun enters the garden room by way of the glass roof and walls. In the winter, the solar heat gain from the garden room should provide relief from high energy bills. Solar shades allow you to adjust the amount of light that you want to enter in the warmer months. Interior planning deserves mention, too. The work center is efficient. The kitchen has a snack bar on the garden room side and a serving counter to the dining room. The breakfast room with laundry area is also convenient to the kitchen. Three bedrooms are on the northern wall. The master bedroom has a large tub and a separate shower with a four foot square skylight above. When this design is oriented toward the sun, it should prove to be energy efficient and a joy to live in.

Design T172857
2,982 Sq. Ft.; 60,930 Cu. Ft.

● Imagine yourself occupying this home! Study the outstanding master bedroom. You will be forever pleased by its many features. It has "his" and "her" baths each with a large walk-in closet, sliding glass doors to a private, side terrace (a great place to enjoy a morning cup of coffee) and an adjacent study. Notice that the two family bedrooms are separated from the master bedroom. This allows for total privacy both for the parents and the children. Continue to observe this plan. You will have no problem at all entertaining in the gathering room. Your party can flow to the adjacent balcony on a warm summer evening. The work center has been designed in an orderly fashion. The U-shaped kitchen utilizes the triangular work pattern, said to be the most efficient. Only a few steps away, you will be in the breakfast room, formal dining room, laundry or wash room. Take your time and study every last detail in this home plan.

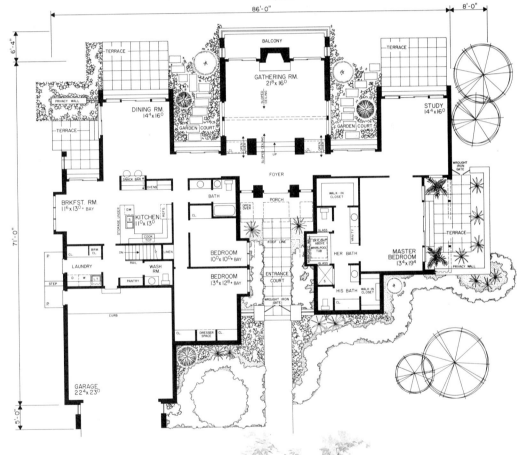

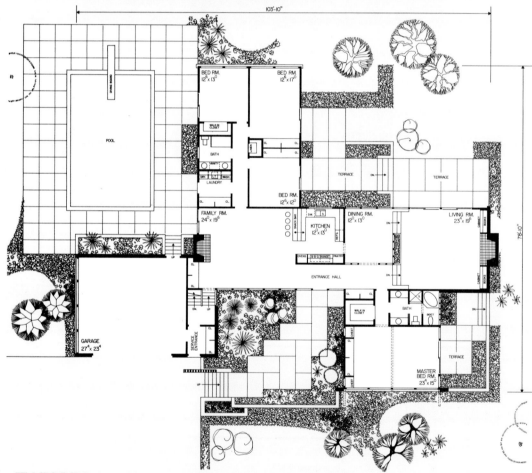

Design T172251 3,112 Sq. Ft.; 36,453 Cu. Ft.

● It will not matter at all where this distinctive ranch home is built. Whether located in the south, east, north or west, the exterior design appeal will be breathtakingly distinctive and the interior livability will be delightfully different. The irregular shape is enhanced by the low-pitched, wide overhanging roof. From the main living area of the house two wings project to help form an appealing entrance court. Variations in grade result in the garage being on a lower level. The plan reflects an interesting study in zoning and a fine indoor-outdoor relationship of the various areas. Notice the bedroom wing and the family room and how these young people's areas function with the pool development. Observe the isolation of the master bedroom with its bath.

Design T172343 3,110 Sq. Ft.; 51,758 Cu. Ft.

● If yours is a growing active family the chances are good that they will want their new home to relate to the outdoors. This distinctive design puts a premium on private outdoor living. And you don't have to install a swimming pool to get the most enjoyment from this home. Developing this area as a garden court will provide the indoor living areas with a breathtaking awareness of nature's beauty. Notice the fine zoning of the plan and how each area has its sliding glass doors to provide an unrestricted view. Three bedrooms plus study are serviced by three baths. The family and gathering rooms provide two great living areas. The kitchen is most efficient.

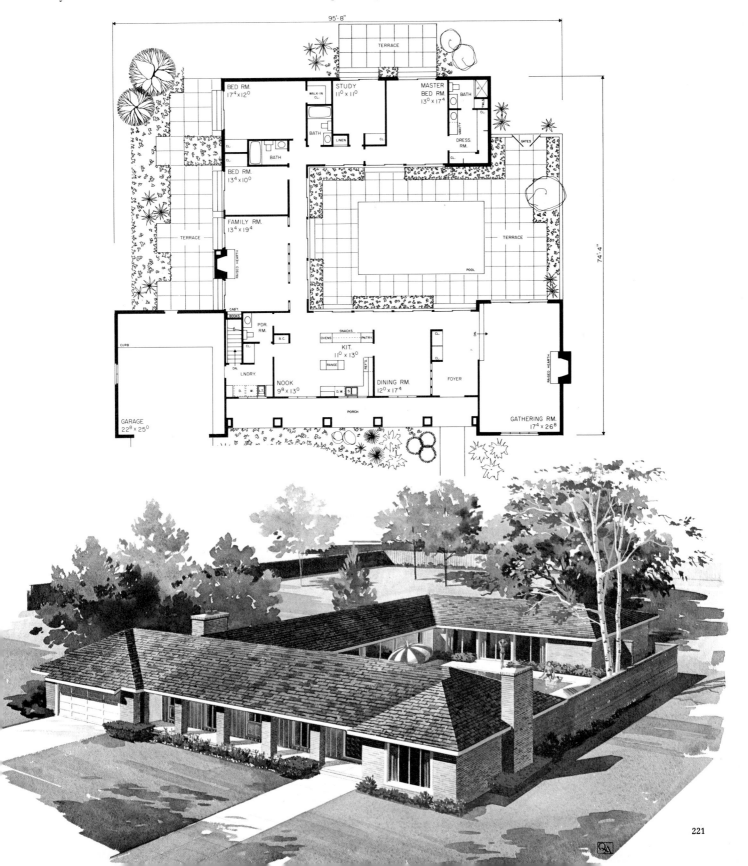

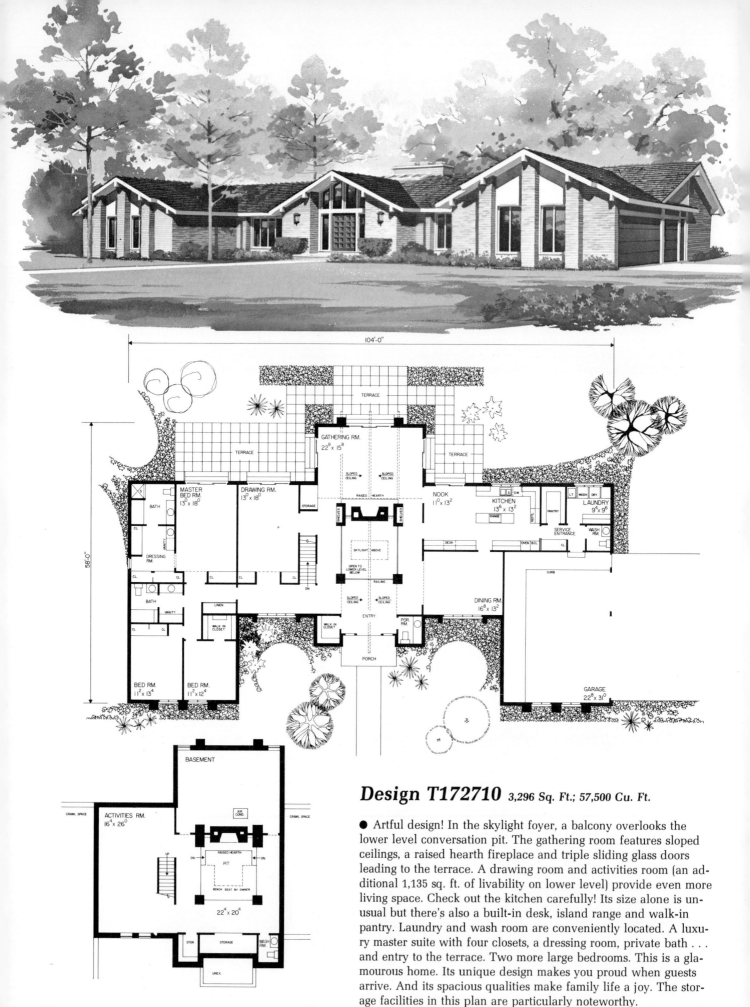

Design T172710 3,296 Sq. Ft.; 57,500 Cu. Ft.

● Artful design! In the skylight foyer, a balcony overlooks the lower level conversation pit. The gathering room features sloped ceilings, a raised hearth fireplace and triple sliding glass doors leading to the terrace. A drawing room and activities room (an additional 1,135 sq. ft. of livability on lower level) provide even more living space. Check out the kitchen carefully! Its size alone is unusual but there's also a built-in desk, island range and walk-in pantry. Laundry and wash room are conveniently located. A luxury master suite with four closets, a dressing room, private bath . . . and entry to the terrace. Two more large bedrooms. This is a glamourous home. Its unique design makes you proud when guests arrive. And its spacious qualities make family life a joy. The storage facilities in this plan are particularly noteworthy.

Design T172791 3,809 Sq. Ft.; 64,565 Cu. Ft.

● The use of vertical paned windows and the hipped roof highlight the exterior of this unique design. Upon entrance one will view a charming sunken atrium with skylight above plus a skylight in the dining room and one in the lounge. Formal living will be graciously accommodated in the living room. It features a raised hearth fireplace, two sets of sliding glass doors to the rear terrace plus two more sliding doors, one to an outdoor dining terrace and the other to an outdoor lounge. Informal living will be enjoyed in the family room with snack bar and in the large library. All will praise the fine planning of the master suite. It features a bay window, "his" and "her" dressing room with private baths and an abundance of closet space.

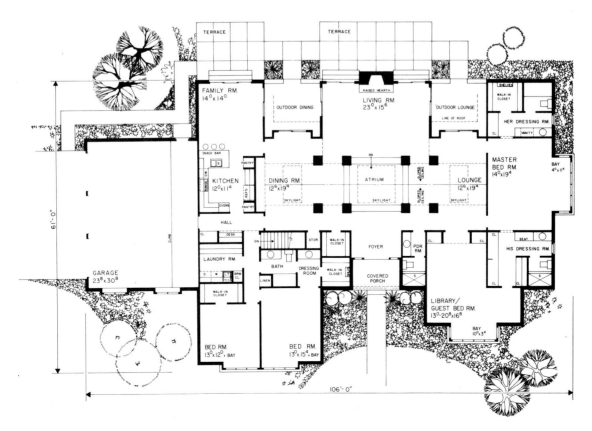

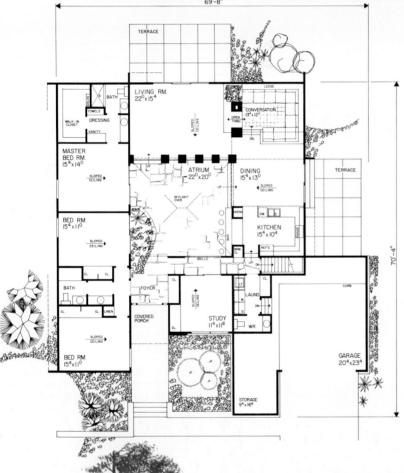

Design T172832
2,805 Sq. Ft. - Excluding Atrium; 52,235 Cu. Ft.

● The advantage of passive solar heating is a significant highlight of this contemporary design. The huge skylight over the atrium provides shelter during inclement weather, while permitting the enjoyment of plenty of natural light to the atrium below and surrounding areas. Whether open to the sky, or sheltered by a glass or translucent covering, the atrium becomes a cheerful spot and provides an abundance of natural light to its adjacent rooms. The stone floor will absorb an abundance of heat from the sun during the day and permit circulation of warm air to other areas at night. During the summer, shades afford protection from the sun without sacrificing the abundance of natural light and the feeling of spaciousness. Sloping ceilings highlight each of the major rooms, three bedrooms, formal living and dining and study. The conversation area between the two formal areas will really be something to talk about. The broad expanses of roof can accommodate solar panels should an active system be desired to supplement the passive features of this design.

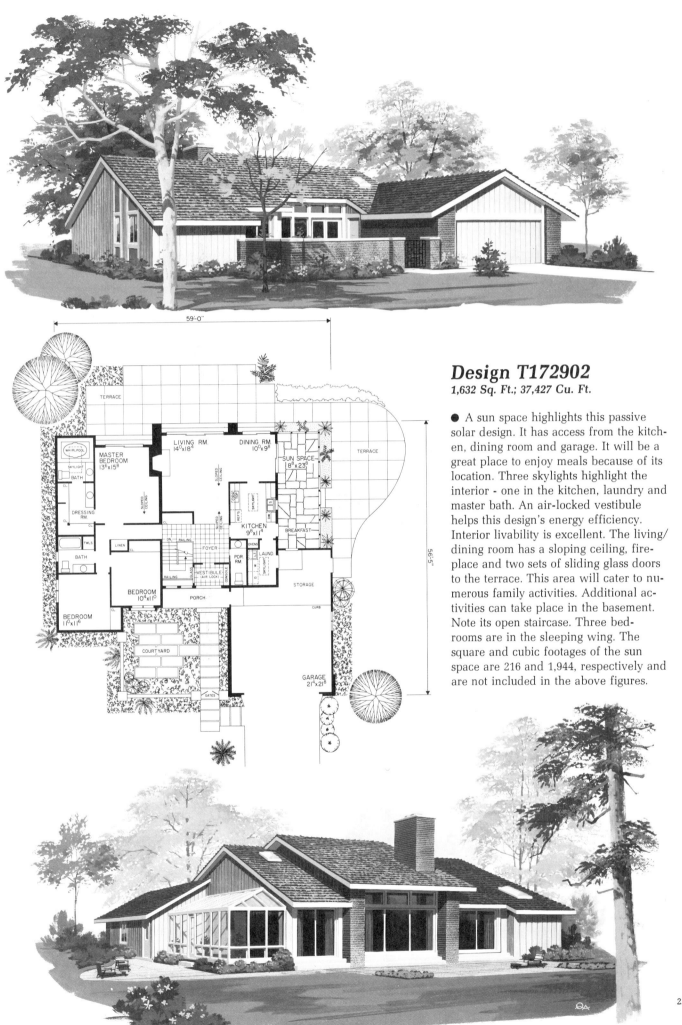

Design T172902
1,632 Sq. Ft.; 37,427 Cu. Ft.

● A sun space highlights this passive solar design. It has access from the kitchen, dining room and garage. It will be a great place to enjoy meals because of its location. Three skylights highlight the interior - one in the kitchen, laundry and master bath. An air-locked vestibule helps this design's energy efficiency. Interior livability is excellent. The living/dining room has a sloping ceiling, fireplace and two sets of sliding glass doors to the terrace. This area will cater to numerous family activities. Additional activities can take place in the basement. Note its open staircase. Three bedrooms are in the sleeping wing. The square and cubic footages of the sun space are 216 and 1,944, respectively and are not included in the above figures.

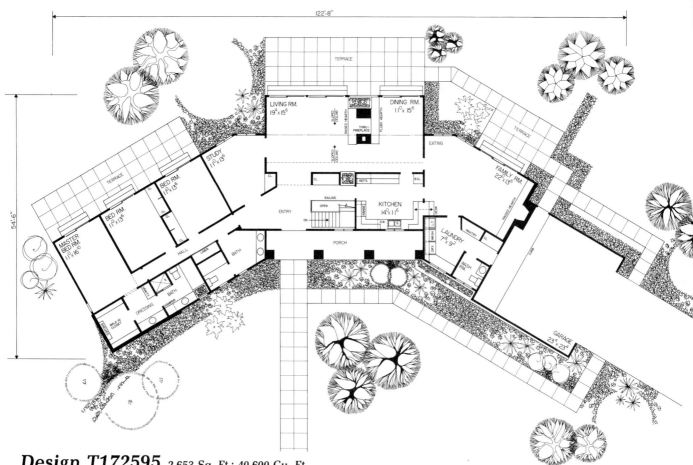

Design T172595 2,653 Sq. Ft.; 40,600 Cu. Ft.

● A winged design puts everything in the right place! At the center, formal living and dining rooms with sloped ceiling share one fireplace for added charm. Sliding glass doors in both rooms open onto the main terrace. In the right wing, there is a spacious family room with another raised hearth fireplace, built-in desk, dining area and adjoining smaller terrace. Also, a first floor laundry with pantry and half bath. A study, the master suite and family bedrooms (all bedrooms having access to a third terrace) plus baths are in the left wing. This home has a floor plan that helps you organize your life. Notice the open staircase leading to the basement.

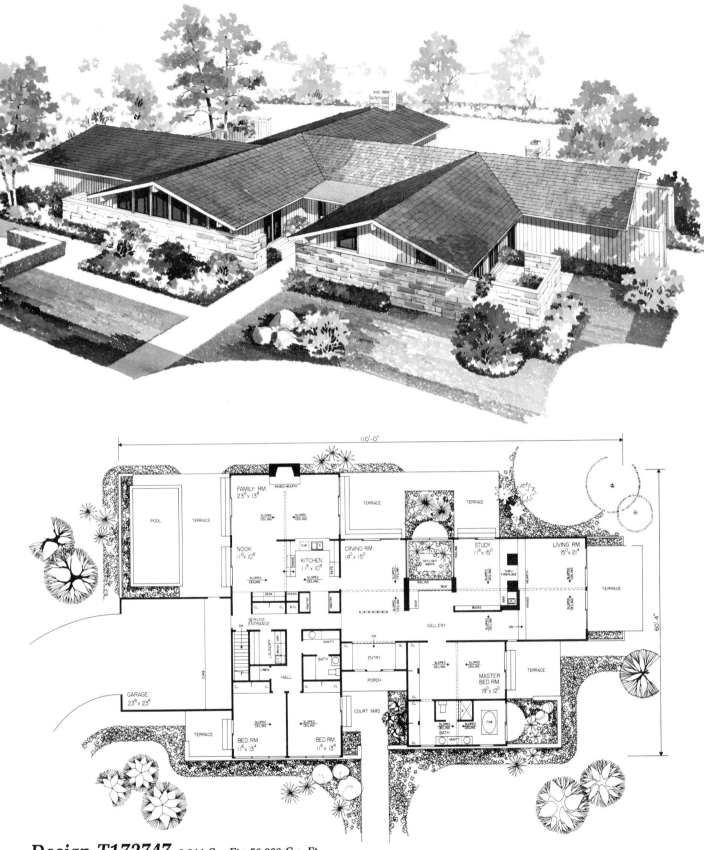

Design T172747 3,211 Sq. Ft.; 50,930 Cu. Ft.

● This home will provide its occupants with a glorious adventure in contemporary living. Its impressive exterior seems to foretell that great things are in store for even the most casual visitor. A study of the plan reveals a careful zoning for both the younger and older family members. The quiet area consists of the exceptional master bedroom suite with private terrace, the study and the isolated living room. For the younger generation, there is a zone with two bedrooms, family room and nearby pool. The kitchen is handy and serves the nook and family rooms with ease. Be sure not to miss the sloping ceilings, the dramatic planter and the functional terrace.

Design T172881 *2,770 Sq. Ft.; 60,315 Cu. Ft.*

● Energy-efficiency will be obtained in this unique, contemporary design. This plan has been designed for a south facing lot in the temperate zones. There is minimal window exposure on the north side of the house so the interior will be protected. The eastern side of the plan, on the other hand, will allow the morning sunlight to enter. As the sun travels from east to west, the various rooms will have light through windows, sliding glass doors or skylights. The garage acts as a buffer against the hot afternoon sun. The living areas are oriented to the front of the plan. They will benefit from the southern exposure during the cooler months. During the summer months, this area will be shielded from the high, hot summer sun by the overhanging roof. If you plan to build in the south, this house would be ideal for a north facing site. This results in a minimum amount of hot sun for the living areas and a maximum amount of protection from the sun on the rear, southern side of the house.

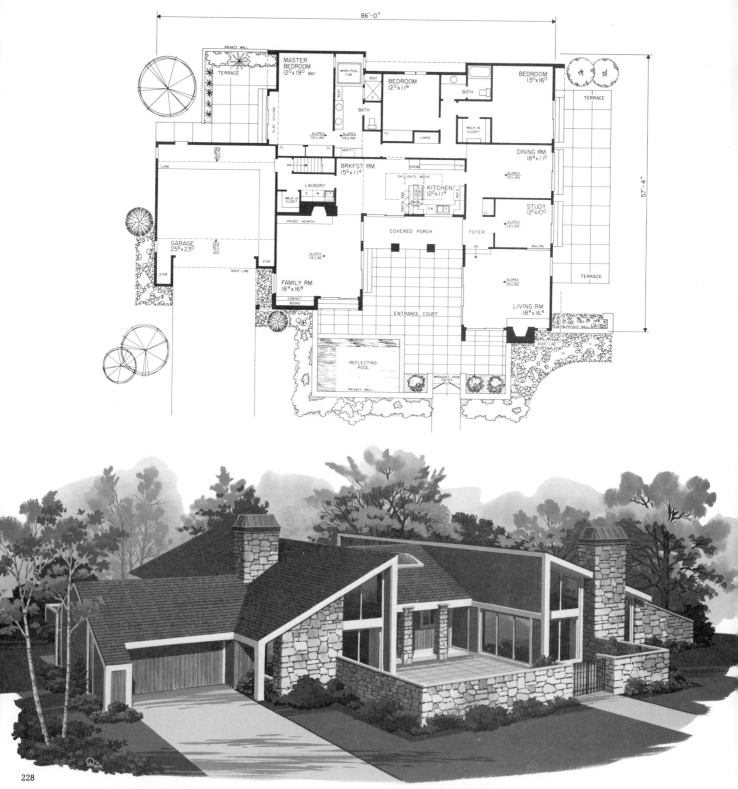

Design T172789 2,732 Sq. Ft.; 54,935 Cu. Ft.

● An attached three car garage! What a fantastic feature of this three bedroom contemporary design. And there's more. As one walks up the steps to the covered porch and through the double front doors the charm of this design will be overwhelming. Inside, a large foyer greets all visitors and leads them to each of the three areas, each down a few steps. The living area has a large gathering room with fireplace and a study adjacent on one side and the for-mal dining room on the other. The work center has an efficient kitchen with island range, breakfast room, laundry and built-in desk and bar. Then there is the sleeping area. Note the raised tub with sloped ceiling.

Design T172793 2,065 Sq. Ft.; 48,850 Cu. Ft.

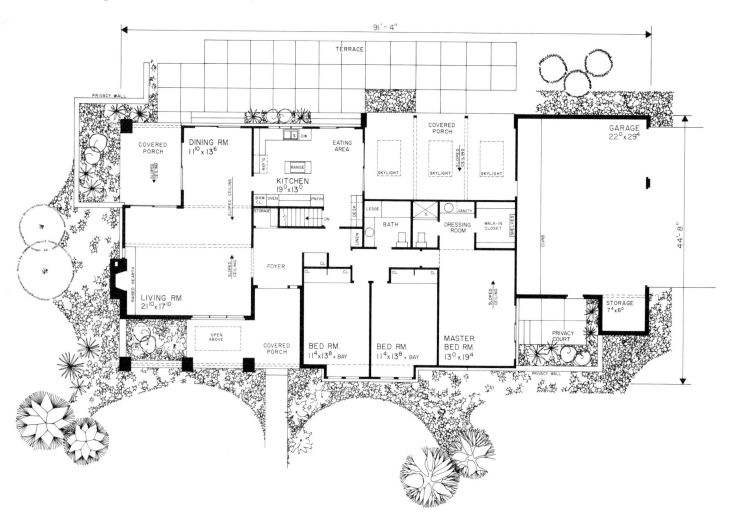

● Privacy will be enjoyed in this home both inside and out. The indoor-outdoor living relationships offered in this plan are outstanding. A covered porch at the entrance. A privacy court off the master bedroom divided from the front yard with a privacy wall. A covered porch serving both the living and dining rooms through sliding glass doors. Also utilizing a privacy wall. Another covered porch off the kitchen eating area. This one is the largest and has skylights above. Also a large rear terrace. The kitchen is efficient with eating space available, an island range and built-in desk. Storage space is abundant. Note storage area in the garage and its overall size. Three front bedrooms. Raised hearth fireplace in the living room.

Design T172765   3,365 Sq. Ft.; 59,820 Cu. Ft.

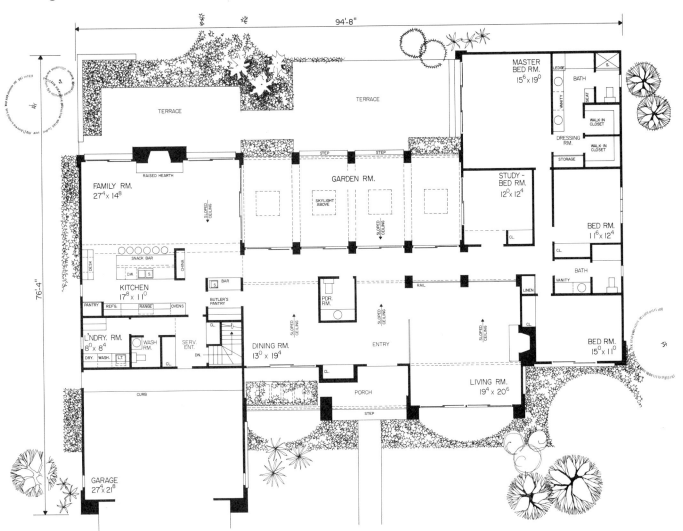

● This three (optional four) bedroom contemporary is a most appealing design. It offers living patterns that will add new dimensions to your everyday routine. The sloped ceilings in the family room, dining room and living room add much spaciousness to this home.

The efficient kitchen has many fine features including the island snack bar and work center, built-in desk, china cabinet and wet bar. Adjacent to the kitchen is a laundry room, washroom and stairs to the basement. Formal and informal living will each have its own

area. A raised hearth fireplace and sliding glass doors to the rear terrace are in the informal family room. Another fireplace is in the front formal living room. You will enjoy all that natural light in the garden room from the skylights in the sloped ceiling.

Clutter Room, Media Room To The Fore

● Something new? Something new, indeed!! Here is the introduction of two rooms which will make a wonderful contribution to family living. The clutter room is strategically placed between the kitchen and garage. It is the nerve center of the work area. It houses the laundry, provides space for sewing, has a large sorting table, and even plenty of space for the family's tool bench. A handy potting area is next to the laundry tray. Adjacent to

the clutter room, and a significant part of the planning of this whole zone, are the pantry and freezer with their nearby counter space. These facilities surely will expedite the unloading of groceries from the car and their convenient storing. Wardrobe and broom closets, plus washroom complete the outstanding utility of this area. The location of the clutter room with all its fine cabinet and counter space means that the often numerous family projects

can be on-going. This room is ideally isolated from the family's daily living patterns. The media room may be thought of as the family's entertainment center. While this is the room for the large or small TV, the home movies, the stereo and VCR equipment, it will serve as the library or study. It would be ideal as the family's home office with its computer equipment. Your family will decide just how it will utilize this outstanding area.

Design T172915 2,758 Sq. Ft.; 60,850 Cu Ft.

● The features of this appealing contemporary design go far beyond the clutter and media rooms. The country kitchen is spacious and caters to the family's informal living and dining activities. While it overlooks the rear yard it is just a step from the delightful greenhouse. Many happy hours will be spent here enjoying to the fullest the outdoors from within. The size of the greenhouse is 8'x18' and contains 149 sq. ft. not included in the square footage quoted above. The formal living and dining areas feature spacious open planning. Sloping ceiling in the living room, plus the sliding glass doors to the outdoor terrace enhance the cheerfulness of this area. The foyer is large and routes traffic efficiently to all areas. Guest coat closets and a powder room are handy. The sleeping zone is well-planned. Two children's bedrooms have fine wall space, good wardrobe facilities and a full bath.

The master bedroom is exceptional. It is large enough to accommodate a sitting area and has access to the terrace. Two walk-in closets, a vanity area with lavatory and a compartmented bath are noteworthy features. Observe the stall shower in addition to the dramatic whirlpool installation. The floor plan below is identical with that on the opposite page and shows one of many possible ways to arrange furniture.

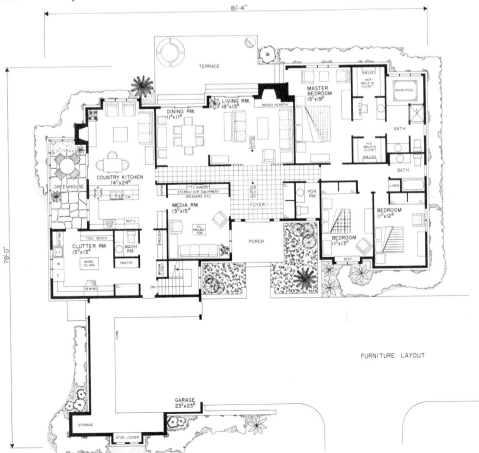

FURNITURE LAYOUT

233

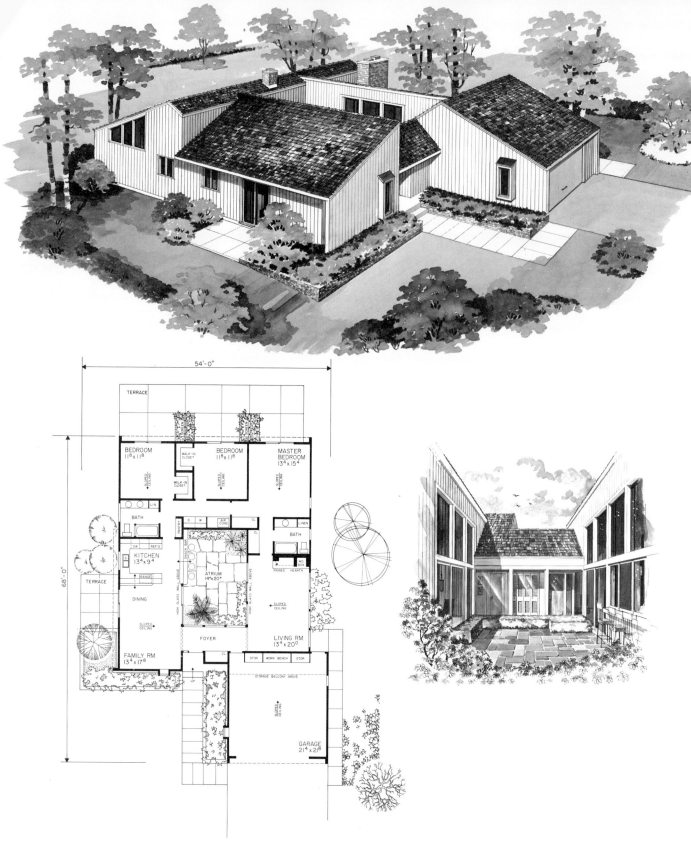

Design T172182 *1,558 Sq. Ft.; 280 Sq. Ft. - Atrium; 18,606 Cu. Ft.*

● What a great new dimension in living is represented by this unique contemporary design! Each of the major zones comprise a separate unit which, along with the garage, clusters around the atrium. High sloped ceilings and plenty of glass areas assure a feeling of spaciousness. The quiet living room will enjoy its privacy, while activities in the informal family room will be great fun functioning with the kitchen. A snack bar opens the kitchen to the atrium. The view, above right, shows portions of snack bar and the front entry looking through the glass wall. There are two full baths strategically located to service all areas conveniently. Storage facilities are excellent, indeed. Don't miss the storage potential found in the garage. There is a work bench and storage balcony above.

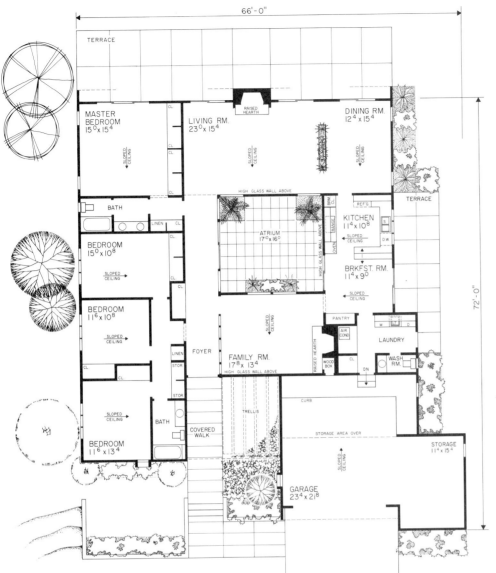

TERRACE

66'-0"

MASTER BEDROOM
15⁰ x 15⁴
SLOPED CEILING

LIVING RM.
23⁰ x 15⁴
SLOPED CEILING

RAISED HEARTH

DINING RM.
12⁴ x 15⁴
SLOPED CEILING

CL

BATH
LINEN CL

BEDROOM
15⁰ x 10⁸
SLOPED CEILING

HIGH GLASS WALL ABOVE

ATRIUM
17¹⁰ x 16⁰

HIGH GLASS WALL ABOVE

KITCHEN
11⁴ x 10⁸
SLOPED CEILING

REF'G.
RANGE
OVEN
DW
BRM CL

TERRACE

BRKFST. RM.
11⁴ x 9⁰

BEDROOM
11⁶ x 10⁸
SLOPED CEILING

SLOPED CEILING

SLOPED CEILING

FOYER
LINEN
STOR
STOR

FAMILY RM.
17⁸ x 13⁴
HIGH GLASS WALL ABOVE

PANTRY
AIR COND
RAISED HEARTH
WOOD BOX
CL

LAUNDRY
W D

WASH RM.
DN

CL

BATH

COVERED WALK

TRELLIS

CURB

STORAGE AREA OVER

SLOPED CEILING

STORAGE
11⁴ x 15⁴

BEDROOM
11⁶ x 13⁴
SLOPED CEILING

GARAGE
23⁴ x 21⁸

72'-0"

BRKFST. RM.

FAM. RM.

PANTRY

W   D

LAUNDRY

WOOD BOX

DN
DN

W R

GARAGE

CURB

OPTIONAL PARTIAL BASEMENT

Design T172135
2,495 Sq. Ft. - Excluding Atrium
28,928 Cu. Ft.

● For those seeking a new experience in home ownership. The proud occupants of the contemporary home will forever be thrilled at their choice of such a distinguished exterior and such a practical and exciting floor plan. The variety of shed roof planes contrast dramatically with the simplicity of the vertical siding. Inside there is a feeling of spaciousness resulting from the sloping ceilings. The uniqueness of this design is further enhanced by the atrium. Open to the sky, this outdoor area, indoors, can be enjoyed from all parts of the house. The sleeping zone has four bedrooms, two baths and plenty of closets. The informal living zone has a fine kitchen and breakfast room. The formal zone consists of a large living-dining area with fireplace.

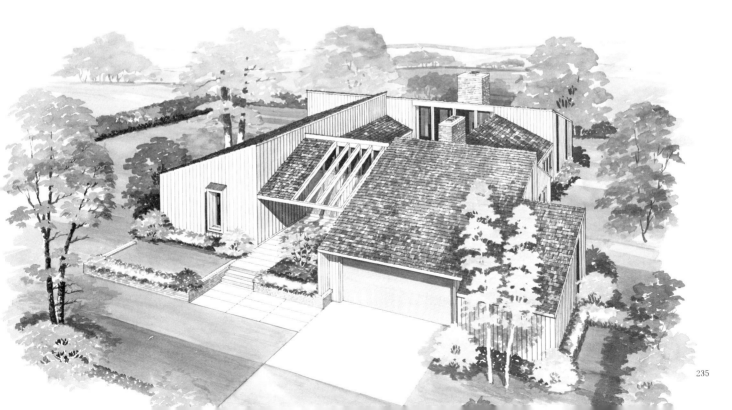

235

Design T172892
1,623 Sq. Ft.; 38,670 Cu. Ft.

● What a striking contemporary! It houses an efficient floor plan with many outstanding features. The foyer has a sloped ceiling and an open staircase to the basement. To the right of the foyer is the work center. Note the snack bar, laundry and covered dining porch, along with the step-saving kitchen. Both the gathering and dining rooms overlook the backyard. Each of the three bedrooms has access to an outdoor area. Now, just think of the potential use of the second floor loft. Its 160 square feet of livability could be used as a den, sewing room, lounge or any of many other activities. It overlooks the gathering room and front foyer and has two large skylights.

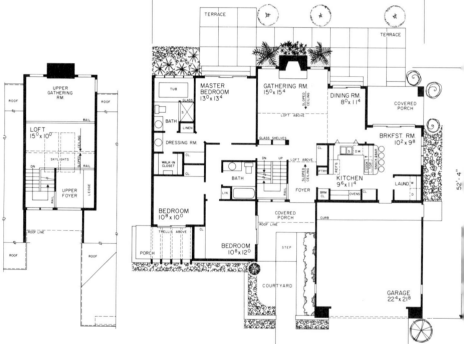

Design T172809
1,551 Sq. Ft.; 42,615 Cu. Ft.

● One-story living can be very rewarding and this contemporary home will be just that. Study the indoor-outdoor living relationships which are offered in the back of the plan. Sliding glass doors are in each of the rear rooms leading to the terrace. The formal dining room has a second set of doors to the porch. Many enjoyable hours will be spent here in the hot tub. A sloped ceiling with skylights is above the hot tub area. Back to the interior, there is a large gathering room. It, too, has a sloped ceiling which will add to its spacious appearance. The interior kitchen is conveniently located between the formal and informal dining areas. Two, or optional three, bedrooms are ready to serve the small family.

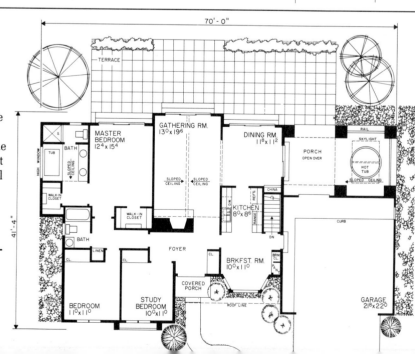

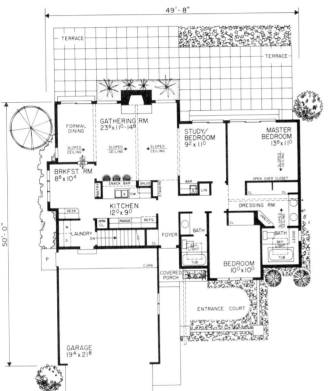

Floor plan labels:
TERRACE
TERRACE
49'-8"
50'-0"
FORMAL DINING
GATHERING RM. 23⁶x11⁰-14⁸
STUDY/ BEDROOM 9²x11⁰
MASTER BEDROOM 13⁸x11⁰
SLOPED CEILING
BRKFST. RM. 8⁸x10⁴
SNACK BAR
SHLVS
BAR
OPEN OVER CLOSET
KITCHEN 12⁰x9⁰
DESK
PANTRY
S
DW
LIN
DRESSING RM.
CL
CL
BRM
RANGE
REF'G
LAUNDRY
W
D
DN
FOYER
CL
BATH
SKY-LIGHT
TUB
VANITY
BATH
SKY-LIGHT
TUB
LEDGE
SLOPED CEILING
P
CURB
COVERED PORCH
BEDROOM 10⁰x10⁰
ENTRANCE COURT
GARAGE 19⁴x21⁸

Design T172864
1,387 Sq. Ft.; 29,160 Cu. Ft.

● Projecting the garage to the front of a house is very economical in two ways. One, it reduces the required lot size for building (in this case the overall width is under 50 feet). And, two, it will protect the interior from street noise and unfavorable winds. Many other characteristics about this design deserve mention, too. The entrance court and covered porch are a delightful way to enter this home. Upon entering, the foyer will take you to the various areas. The interior kitchen has an adjacent breakfast room and a snack bar on the gathering room side. Here, one will enjoy a sloped ceiling and a fireplace. A study with a wet bar is adjacent. If need be, adjust the plan and make the study the third bedroom. Sliding glass doors in the study and master bedroom open to the terrace.

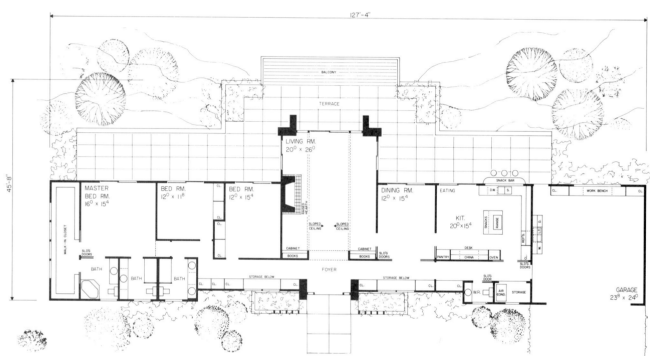

Design T172256 2,632 Sq. Ft.; 35,023 Cu. Ft.

● A dream home for those with young ideas. A refreshing, contemporary exterior with a unique, highly individualized interior. What are your favorite features.

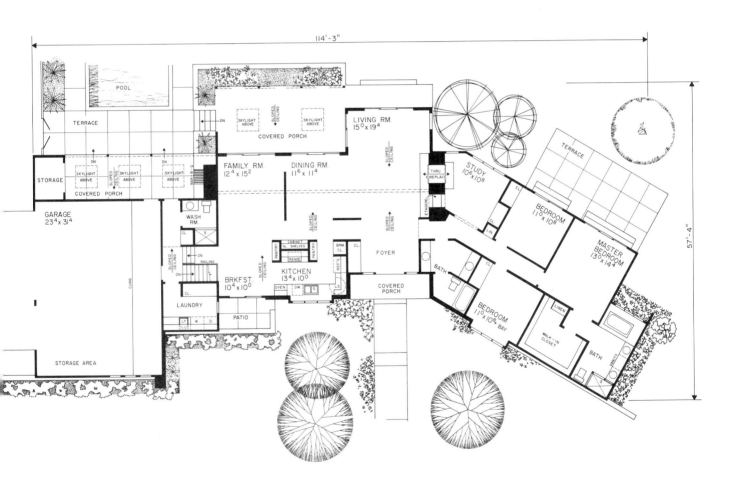

Design T172819 *2,459 Sq. Ft.; 45,380 Cu. Ft.*

● Indoor-outdoor living will be enjoyed to the fullest in this rambling one-story contemporary plan. Each of the rear rooms in this design, excluding the study, has access to a terrace or porch. Even the front breakfast room

has access to a private dining patio. The covered porch off the living areas, family, dining and living rooms, has a sloped ceiling and skylights. A built-in barbecue unit and a storage room will be found on the second covered porch.

Inside, the plan offers exceptional living patterns for various activities. Notice the thru-fireplace that the living room shares with the study. A built-in etagere is nearby. The three-car garage has an extra storage area.

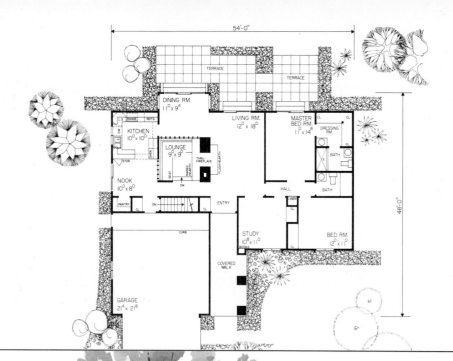

Design T172703
1,445 Sq. Ft.; 30,300 Cu. Ft.

● This modified, hip-roofed contemporary design will be the answer for those who want something both practical, yet different, inside and out. The covered front walk sets the stage for entering a modest sized home with tremendous livability. The focal point will be the pleasant conversation lounge. It is sunken, partically open to the other living areas and shares the enjoyment of the thru-fireplace with the living room. There are two bedrooms, two full baths and a study. The kitchen is outstanding.

Design T172753
1,539 Sq. Ft.; 31,910 Cu. Ft.

● In this day and age of expensive building sites, projecting the attached garage from the front line of the house makes a lot of economic sense. It also lends itself to interesting roof lines and plan configurations. Here, a pleasing covered walkway to the front door results. A privacy wall adds an extra measure of design appeal and provides a sheltered terrace for the study/bedroom. You'll seldom find more livability in 1,539 square feet. Imagine, three bedrooms, two baths, a spacious living/dining area and a family room.

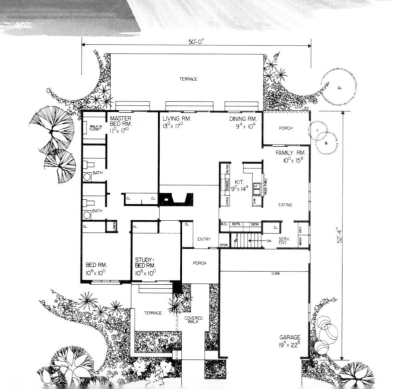

Design T172744
1,381 Sq. Ft.; 17,530 Cu. Ft.

● Here is a practical and an attractive contemporary home for that narrow building site. It is designed for efficiency with the small family or retired couple in mind. Sloping ceilings foster an extra measure of spaciousness. In addition to the master bedroom, there is the study that can also serve as the second bedroom or as an occasional guest room. The single bath is compartmented and its dual access allows it to serve living and sleeping areas more than adequately. Note raised hearth fireplace, snack bar, U-shaped kitchen, laundry, two terraces, etc.

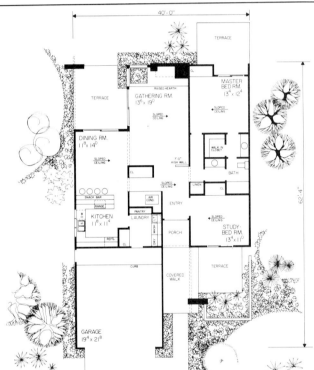

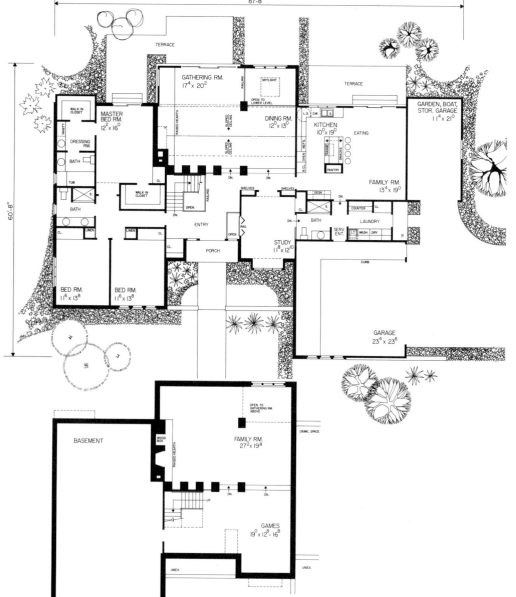

Floor Plan Labels

First Floor:
- TERRACE
- GATHERING RM. 17⁴ x 20²
- SKYLIGHT
- OPEN TO LOWER LEVEL
- RAILING
- SLOPED CEILING
- DINING RM. 12² x 13⁰
- KITCHEN 10⁰ x 19⁰
- EATING
- TERRACE
- GARDEN, BOAT, STOR. GARAGE 11⁴ x 21⁰
- WALK IN CLOSET
- MASTER BED RM. 12² x 16⁰
- DRESSING RM.
- BATH
- VANITY
- TUB
- BATH
- WALK IN CLOSET
- RAISED HEARTH
- PANTRY
- FAMILY RM. 13⁴ x 19⁰
- SHELVES
- DESK
- COUNTER
- BATH
- LAUNDRY
- WASH. DRY.
- SERV. ENT.
- ENTRY
- STUDY 11⁸ x 12¹⁰
- PORCH
- LINEN
- CL.
- BED RM. 11⁶ x 13⁸
- BED RM. 11⁶ x 13⁸
- CURB
- GARAGE 23⁴ x 23⁸

Lower Level:
- BASEMENT
- WOOD BOX
- RAISED HEARTH
- OPEN TO GATHERING RM. ABOVE
- FAMILY RM. 27² x 19⁸
- CRAWL SPACE
- UP
- DN.
- GAMES 19⁰ x 12⁸ - 16⁸
- UNEX.
- UNEX.

Dimensions: 87'-8" (width), 60'-8" (height)

Design T172721
2,667 Sq. Ft.; 53,150 Cu. Ft.

● Visually exciting! A sunken gathering room with a sloped ceiling, raised hearth fireplace, corner balcony and skylight . . . the last two features shared by the formal dining room. There's more. Two family rooms . . . one on the lower level (1,153 sq. ft.) with a raised hearth fireplace, another adjacent to the kitchen with a snack bar! Plus a study and game room. A lavish master suite and two large bedrooms. A first floor laundry and reams of storage space, including a special garage for a boat, sports equipment, garden tools etc. There's plenty of space for family activities in this home. From chic dinner parties for friends to birthday gatherings for kids, there's always the right setting . . . and so much room that adults and children can entertain at the same time.

Design T172730
2,490 Sq. Ft.; 50,340 Cu. Ft.

● Here is a basic one-story home that is really loaded with livability on the first floor and has a bonus of an extra 1,086 sq. ft. of planned livability on a lower level. What makes this so livable is that the first floor adjacent to the stairs leading below is open and forms a balcony looking down into a dramatic planting area. The first floor traffic patterns flow around this impressive and distinctive feature. In addition to the gathering room, study and family room, there is the lounge and activity room. Notice the second balcony open to the activity room below. The master bedroom is outstanding with two baths and two walk-in closets. The attached three-car garage has a bulk storage area and is accessible through the service area.

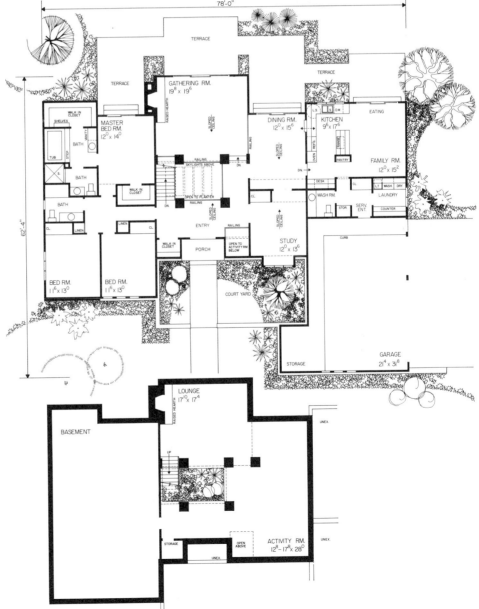

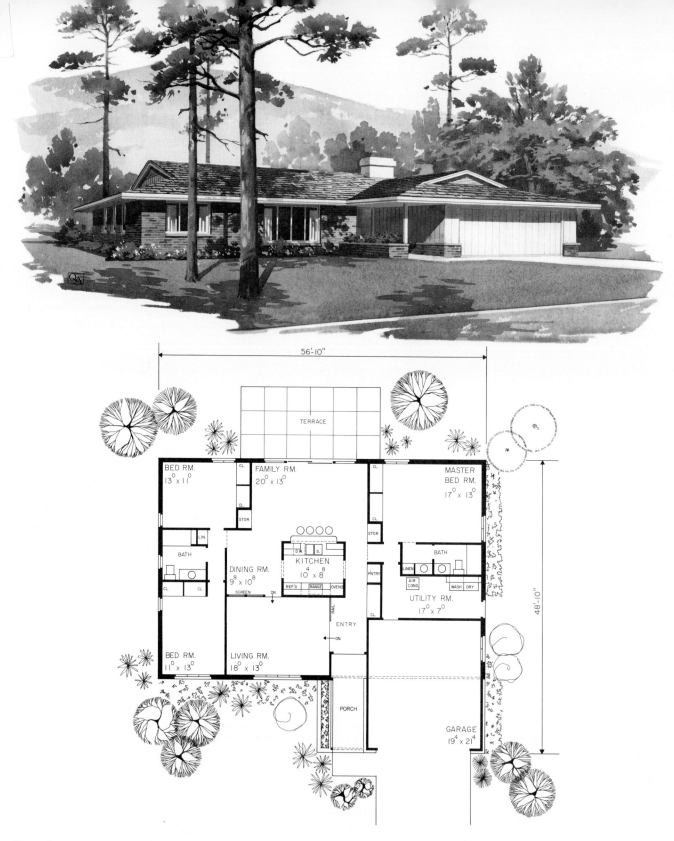

TERRACE

BED RM.
13⁰ x 11⁰

FAMILY RM.
20⁰ x 13⁰

MASTER
BED RM.
17⁰ x 13⁰

STOR

BATH

KITCHEN
10 x 8⁴ ⁸

DINING RM.
9⁸ x 10⁸

BATH

LINEN

AIR
COND.

WASH DRY

UTILITY RM.
17⁰ x 7⁰

REF'G RANGE OVENS

PNTRY

SCREEN

ENTRY

DN.

BED RM.
11⁰ x 13⁰

LIVING RM.
18⁰ x 13⁰

PORCH

GARAGE
19⁴ x 21⁴

56'-10"

48'-10"

Design T172351 1,862 Sq. Ft.; 22,200 Cu. Ft.

● The extension of the wide over-hanging roof of this distinctive home provides shelter for the walkway to the front door. A raised brick planter adds appeal to the outstanding exterior design. The living patterns offered by this plan are delightfully different, yet ex-tremely practical. Notice the separation of the master bedroom from the other two bedrooms. While assuring an extra measure of quiet privacy for the parents, this master bedroom location may be ideal for a live-in-relative. Locating the kitchen in the middle of the plan frees up valuable outside wall space and leads to interesting planning. The front living room is sunken for dramatic appeal and need not have any cross-room traffic. The utility room houses the laundry and the heating and cooling equipment.

Design T172818 1,566 Sq. Ft.; 20,030 Cu. Ft.

● This is most certainly an outstanding contemporary design. Study the exterior carefully before your journey to inspect the floor plan. The vertical lines are carried from the siding to the paned windows to the garage door. The front entry is recessed so the overhanging roof creates a covered porch.

Note the planter court with privacy wall. The floor plan is just as outstanding. The rear gathering room has a sloped ceiling, raised hearth fireplace, sliding glass doors to the terrace and a snack bar with pass-thru to the kitchen. In addition to the gathering room, there is the living room/study. This

room could be utilized in a variety of ways depending on your family's choice. The formal dining room is convenient to the U-shaped kitchen. Three bedrooms and two closely located baths are in the sleeping wing. This plan includes details for the construction of an optional basement.

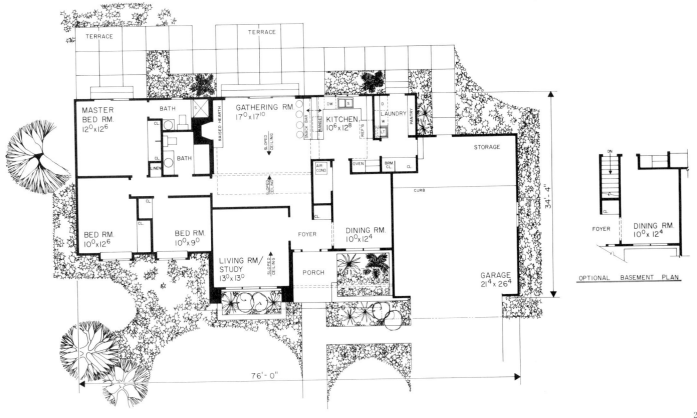

Design T172795

1,952 Sq. Ft.; 43,500 Cu. Ft.

● This three-bedroom design leaves no room for improvement. Any size family will find it difficult to surpass the fine qualities that this home offers. Begin with the exterior. This fine contemporary design has open trellis work above the front, covered private court. This area is sheltered by a privacy wall extending from the projecting garage. Inside, the floor plan will be just as breathtaking. Begin at the foyer and choose a direction. To the right is the sleeping wing equipped with three bedrooms and two baths. Straight ahead from the foyer is the gathering room with thru-fireplace to the dining room. To the right is the work center. This area includes a breakfast room, a U-shaped kitchen and laundry.

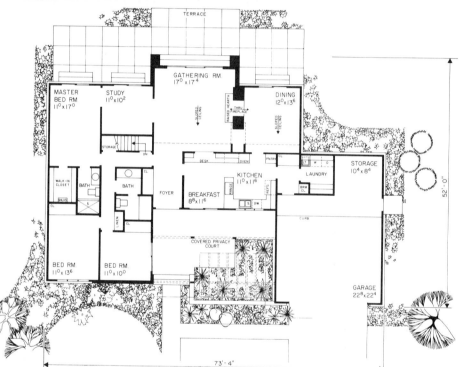

Design T172754
1,844 Sq. Ft.; 26,615 Cu. Ft.

● This really is a most dramatic and refreshing contemporary home. The slope of
its wide overhanging roofs is carried right
indoors to provide an extra measure of
spaciousness. The U-shaped privacy wall
of the front entrance area provides an appealing outdoor living spot accessible
from the front bedroom. The rectangular
floor plan will be economical to build.
Notice the efficient use of space and how
it all makes its contribution to outstanding
livability. The small family will find its
living patterns delightful, indeed. Two
bedrooms and two full baths comprise the
sleeping zone. The open planning of the
L-shaped living and dining rooms is most
desirable. The thru-fireplace is just a
great room divider. The kitchen and
breakfast nook function well together.
There is laundry and mechanical room
nearby.

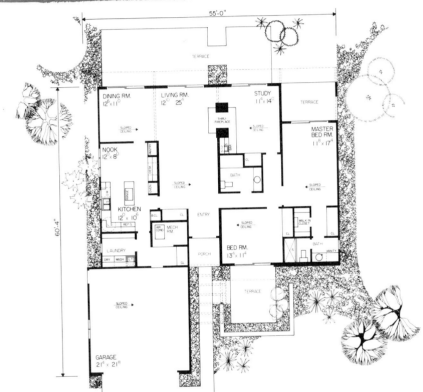

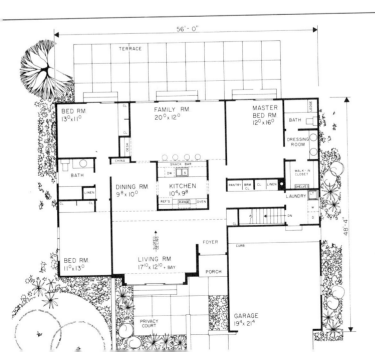

Design T172796
1,828 Sq. Ft.; 39,990 Cu. Ft.

● This home features a front living room with sloped ceiling and sliding glass doors which lead to a front private
court. What a delightful way to introduce this design. This
bi-nuclear design has a great deal to offer. First - the
children's and parent's sleeping quarters are on opposite
ends of this house to assure the utmost in privacy. Each
area has its own full bath. The interior kitchen is a great
idea. It frees up valuable wall space for the living areas ex-
clusive use. There is a snack bar in the kitchen/family
room for those very informal meals. Also, a planning desk
is in the family room. The dining room is conveniently located near the kitchen plus it has a built-in china cabinet.
The laundry area has plenty of storage closets plus the
stairs to the basement. This home will surely be a welcome
addition to any setting.

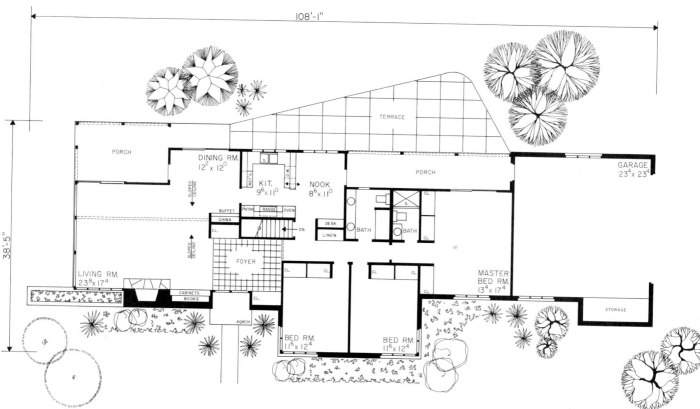

Design T172330 *1,854 Sq. Ft.; 30,001 Cu. Ft.*

● Your family will never tire of the living patterns offered by this appealing home with its low-pitched, wide overhanging roof. The masonry masses of the exterior are pleasing. While the blueprints call for the use of stone, you may wish to substitute brick veneer.

Sloping ceiling and plenty of glass will assure the living area of a fine feeling of spaciousness. The covered porches enhance the enjoyment of outdoor living. Two baths serve the three bedroom sleeping area. Not to be overlooked are such features as the fire-

place wall, the built-ins, the basement for extra recreational space, and the large garage with its storage area. The kitchen overlooking the rear yard is strategically located between dining room and nook. Here's a sound investment for your future years!

Contemporary Two-Story Houses

Here is a diverse selection of designs offering two or more levels of livability. The addition of a "second floor" of livability results in a whole new series of shapes and configurations. While some designs retain ground-hugging qualities, others highlight soaring roof lines with high, dramatic glass areas. Inside, sloping cathedral ceilings allow for upper-level balconies and lounges that overlook living areas and help create exceptional spaciousness.

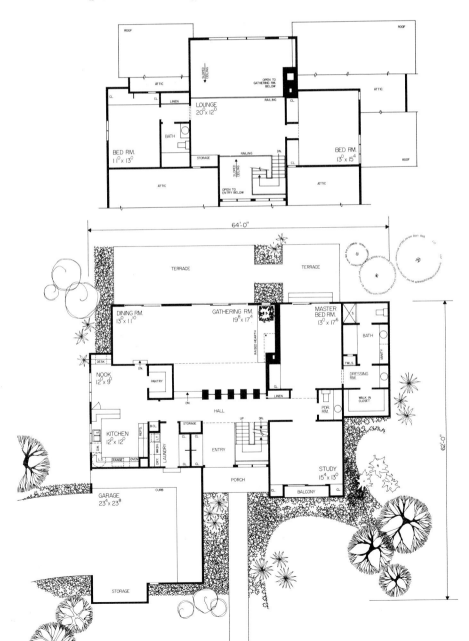

Design T172708

2,108 Sq. Ft. - First Floor
824 Sq. Ft. - Second Floor
52,170 Cu. Ft.

● Here is a one-and-a-half story home whose exterior is distinctive. It has a contemporary feeling, yet it retains some of the fine design features and proportions of traditional exteriors. Inside the appealing double front doors, there is livability galore. The sunken rear living-dining area is delightfully spacious and is looked down into from the second floor lounge. The open end fireplace with its raised hearth and planter is another focal point. The master bedroom features a fine compartmented bath with both shower and tub. The study is just a couple steps away. The U-shaped kitchen is outstanding. Notice the pantry and laundry. Upstairs provides children with their own sleeping, studying and TV quarters. Absolutely a great design! Study all of the fine details closely with your family.

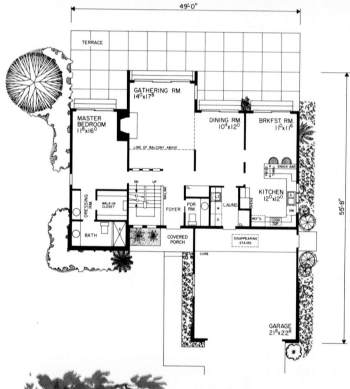

49'-0"

TERRACE

GATHERING RM.
14⁰x17⁸

MASTER
BEDROOM
11⁸x16⁰

DINING RM.
10⁴x12⁰

BRKFST. RM.
11⁰x11⁶

LINE OF BALCONY ABOVE

SNACK BAR

DRESSING RM.

WALK-IN CLOSET

DN UP

RAILING

FOYER

CL.

PDR. RM.

LAUND.

OVENS

KITCHEN
12⁰x12⁰

REF'G.

COOK TOP

BATH

COVERED PORCH

DISAPPEARING STAIRS

CURB

55'-8"

GARAGE
21⁸x22⁸

UPPER GATHERING RM.

BEDROOM
10⁴x10⁴

BEDROOM
11⁰x16⁰

CL

RAILING

LOUNGE

DN

RAILING

SKYLIGHT

LINEN

BATH

WALK-IN CLOSET

UPPER FOYER

OPEN

Design T172905

1,342 Sq. Ft. - First Floor
619 Sq. Ft. - Second Floor; 33,655 Cu. Ft.

● All of the livability in this plan is in the back! Each first floor room, except the kitchen, has access to the rear terrace via sliding glass doors. A great way to capture an excellent view. This plan is also ideal for a narrow lot seeing that its width is less than 50 feet. Two bedrooms and a lounge, overlooking the gathering room, are on the second floor.

Design T172868
1,203 Sq. Ft. - Upper Level
1,317 Sq. Ft. - Lower Level; 29,595 Cu. Ft.

Common Living Areas –
Sleeping Privacy

● Two couples sharing the expense of a house has got to be ideal and, of course, economical. The occupants of this house could do just that. The lower level, housing the kitchen, dining room, family and living rooms and the laundry facilities, is the common area to be shared by both couples. Centrally located, the kitchen and dining room act as a space divider to the living and family rooms so both couples can enjoy privacy.

Separate stairways lead to the upper level from the skylit foyer. Each private area has two bedrooms, a dressing room and a full bath. Individual entrances can be locked for additional privacy. Sliding glass doors are in each of the rear rooms on both levels so the outdoors can be enjoyed to its fullest.

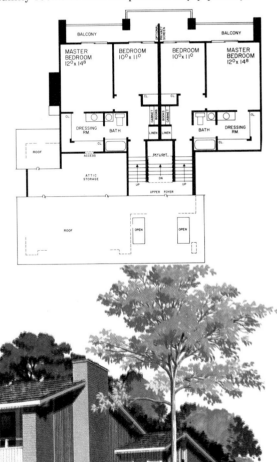

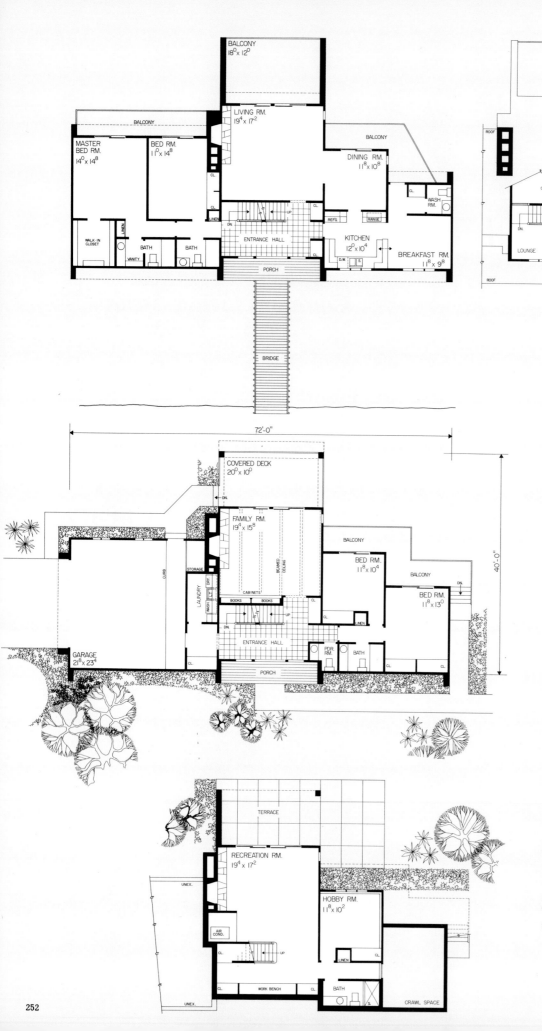

BALCONY
18⁰ x 12⁰

LIVING RM.
19⁴ x 17²

BALCONY

MASTER
BED RM.
14⁰ x 14⁸

BED RM.
11⁰ x 14⁸

BALCONY

DINING RM.
11⁸ x 10⁸

WASH
RM.

WALK-IN
CLOSET

LINEN

CL.

CL.

LINEN

DN.

UP

ENTRANCE HALL

CL.

REFG.

RANGE

BATH

BATH

VANITY

CL.

PORCH

KITCHEN
12⁰ x 10⁴

D.W. S.

BREAKFAST RM.
11⁸ x 9⁸

BRIDGE

ROOF

ROOF

STUDIO
11⁸ x 12⁸

ROOF

OPEN TO LIVING RM. BELOW

RAILING

DN.

LOUNGE

CL.

ROOF

ROOF

72'-0"

COVERED DECK
20⁰ x 10⁰

DN.

FAMILY RM.
19⁴ x 15⁸

BALCONY

BED RM.
11⁸ x 10⁴

BALCONY

BED RM.
11⁸ x 13⁰

DN.

40'-0"

CURB

STORAGE

LAUNDRY

WASH DRY

BEAMED CEILING

CABINETS

BOOKS BOOKS

LINEN

UP

DN.

ENTRANCE HALL

GARAGE
21⁸ x 23⁴

PDR.
RM.

BATH

CL.

CL.

CL.

PORCH

TERRACE

RECREATION RM.
19⁴ x 17²

UNEX.

AIR
COND.

HOBBY RM.
11⁸ x 10²

UP

CL.

CL.

LINEN

WORK BENCH

CL.

BATH

UNEX.

CRAWL SPACE

Design T172392

1,691 Sq. Ft. - Main Level
1,127 Sq. Ft. - Lower Entry Level
396 Sq. Ft. - Upper Level
844 Sq. Ft. - Lower Level
40,026 Cu. Ft.

● Try to imagine the manner in which you and your family will function in this four-level hillside design. Surely it will be an adventure in family living that will be hard to surpass. For instance, can you picture a family member painting or sewing in the upper level studio, while another is building models or developing pictures in the lower level hobby room? Or, can you visualize a group in quiet conversation in the living room, another lounging in the family room, while a third plays table tennis or pool in the recreation room? Be sure not to overlook the fireplace in each of these living areas. As for sleeping and bath facilities, your family will have plenty, four bedrooms and four baths, plus a powder room and a washroom. They also will enjoy the eating facilities with a breakfast room, a dining room and an outdoor balcony nearby. Then, too, there is the lounge of the upper level.

A Lifetime of Exciting, Contemporary Living Patterns

Here is a home for those with a bold, contemporary living bent. The exciting exteriors give notice of an admirable flair for something delightfully different. The varying roof planes and textured blank wall masses are distinctive. Two sets of panelled front doors permit access to either level. The inclined ramp to the upper main level is dramatic, indeed. The rear exterior highlights a veritable battery of projecting balconies. This affords direct access to outdoor living for each of the major rooms in the house. Certainly an invaluable feature should your view be particulary noteworthy. Notice two covered outdoor balconies plus a covered terrace. Indoor-outdoor living at its greatest.

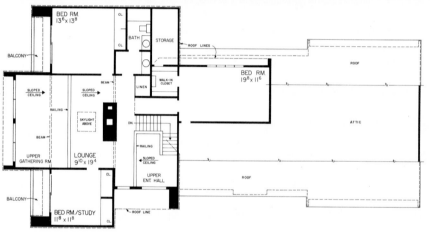

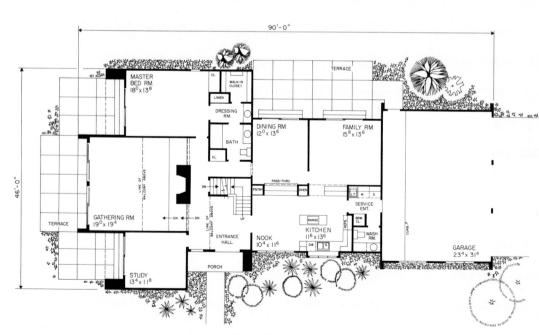

Design T172781

2,132 Sq. Ft. - First Floor
1,156 Sq. Ft. - Second Floor
47,365 Cu. Ft.

● This beautifully designed two-story could be considered a dream house of a
lifetime. The exterior is
sure to catch the eye of
anyone who takes sight of
its unique construction.
The front kitchen features
an island range, adjacent
breakfast nook and pass-
thru to formal dining room.
The master bedroom suite
with its privacy and con-
venience on the first floor
has a spacious walk-in
closet and dressing room.
The side terrace is accessible thru sliding glass doors
from the master bedroom,
gathering room and study.
The second floor has three
bedrooms and storage
space galore. Also notice
the lounge which has sloped ceilings and a skylight
above. This delightful area
looks down into the gathering room. The outdoor balconies overlook the wrap-
around terrace. Surely an
outstanding trend house for
the 90's and for decades to
come.

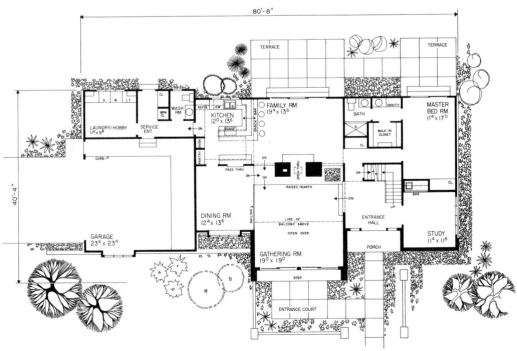

Design T172782

2,060 Sq. Ft. - First Floor
897 Sq. Ft. - Second Floor
47,750 Cu. Ft.

● What makes this such a distinctive four bedroom design? Let's list some of the features. This plan includes great formal and informal living for the family at home or when entertaining guests. The formal gathering room and informal family room share a dramatic raised-hearth fireplace. Other features of the sunken gathering room include: high, sloped ceilings, built-in planter and sliding glass doors to the front entrance court. The kitchen has a snack bar, many built-ins, a pass-thru to dining room and easy access to the large laundry/wash room. The master bedroom suite is located on the main level for added privacy and convenience. There's even a study with a built-in bar. The upper level has three more bedrooms, a bath and a lounge looking down into the gathering room.

255

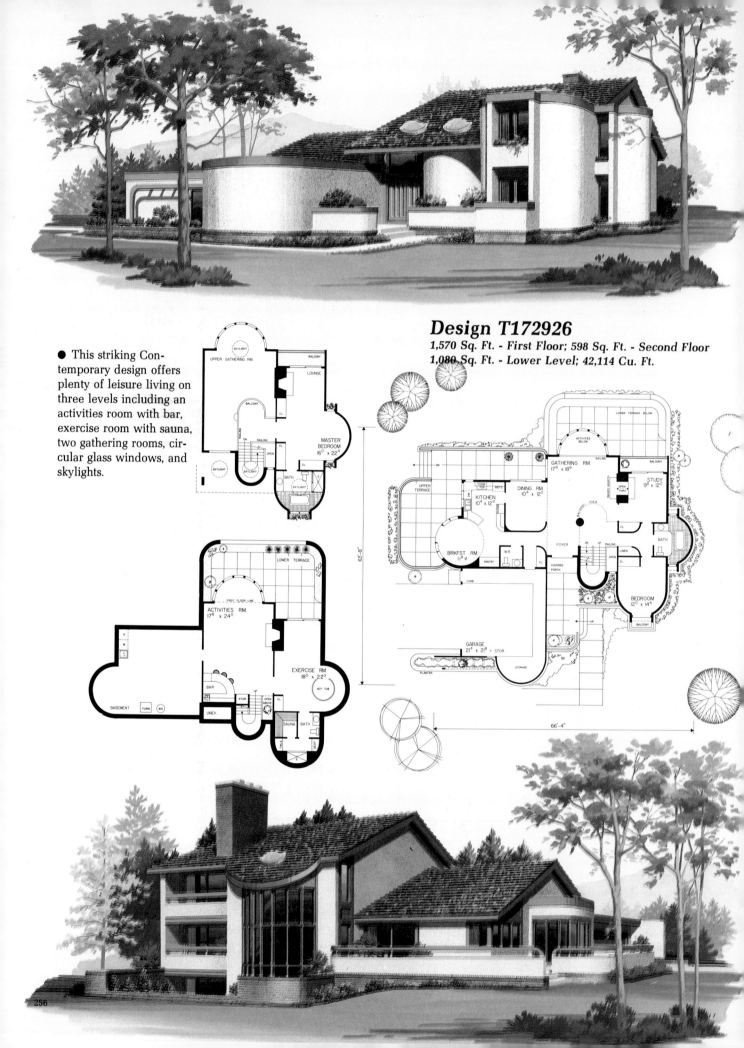

● This striking Contemporary design offers plenty of leisure living on three levels including an activities room with bar, exercise room with sauna, two gathering rooms, circular glass windows, and skylights.

Design T172926

1,570 Sq. Ft. - First Floor; 598 Sq. Ft. - Second Floor
1,080 Sq. Ft. - Lower Level; 42,114 Cu. Ft.

SKYLIGHT

UPPER GATHERING RM.

BALCONY

LOUNGE

BALCONY

CL

CL

MASTER BEDROOM
16⁰ x 22⁴

DN

RAILING

RAILING

OPEN

SKYLIGHT

SKYLIGHT

BATH

SKYLIGHT

LOWER TERRACE

FIRST FLOOR LINE

ACTIVITIES RM.
17⁸ x 24⁰

EXERCISE RM.
18⁰ x 22⁰

BAR

HOT TUB

BASEMENT

FURN.

W.H.

STOR

OPEN ABOVE

CL

UNEX.

SAUNA

BATH

63'-8"

LOWER TERRACE BELOW

ACTIVITIES BELOW

RAILING

GATHERING RM.
17⁸ x 18⁸

BALCONY

DN

UPPER TERRACE

KITCHEN
10⁴ x 12⁴

DINING RM.
10⁴ x 12⁰

OPEN THRU

STUDY
9⁸ x 12⁰

RAISED HEARTH

BRKFST. RM.
11⁸ ∅

W.R.

PANTRY

CL

FOYER

BALCONY OVER

DN UP

RAILING

OPEN

LINEN

CL

BATH

COVERED PORCH

CURB

UP

BEDROOM
12⁰ x 14⁴

BALCONY

GARAGE
21⁴ x 21⁸ + STOR.

STORAGE

PLANTER

66'-4"

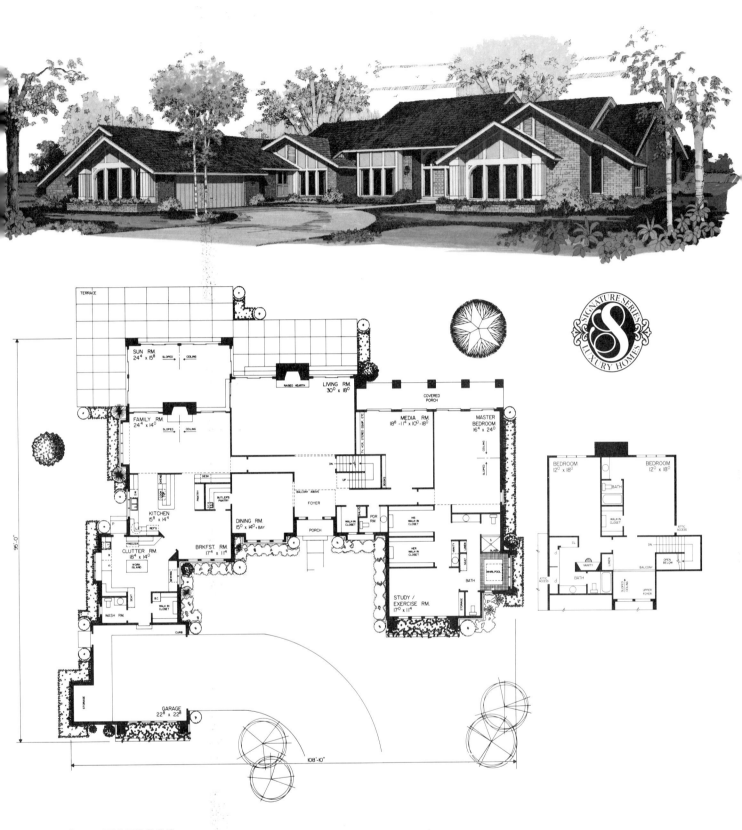

Design T172938 4,518 Sq. Ft. - First Floor
882 Sq. Ft. - Second Floor; 106,353 Cu. Ft.

● A semi-circular fanlight and side-lights grace the entrance of this striking contemporary. The lofty foyer, with balcony above, leads to an elegant, two-story living room with fireplace. The family room, housing a second fireplace, leads to a glorious sunroom; both have dramatic sloped ceilings.

The kitchen and breakfast room are conveniently located for access to the informal family room or to the formal dining room via the butler's pantry. The large adjoining clutter room with work island offers limitless possibilities for the seamstress, hobbyist, or indoor gardener. An executive-sized, first-floor master suite offers privacy and relaxation; the bath with whirlpool tub and dressing area with twin walk-in closets open to a study that could double as an exercise room. Two second-floor bedrooms with private baths and walk-in closets round out the livability in this gracious home.

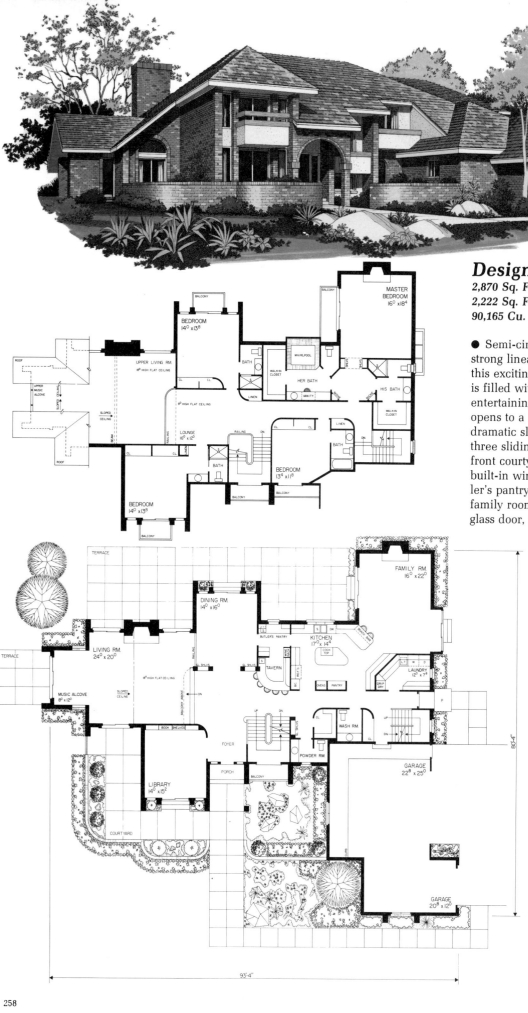

Design T172952

2,870 Sq. Ft. - First Floor
2,222 Sq. Ft. - Second Floor
90,165 Cu. Ft.

● Semi-circular arches complement the strong linear roof lines and balconies of this exciting contemporary. The first floor is filled with well-planned amenities for entertaining and relaxing. The foyer opens to a step-down living room with a dramatic sloped ceiling, fireplace, and three sliding glass doors that access the front courtyard and terrace. A tavern with built-in wine rack and an adjacent butler's pantry are ideal for entertaining. The family room features a fireplace, sliding glass door, and a handy snack bar. The kitchen allows meal preparation, cooking and storage within a step of the central work island. Three second-floor bedrooms, each with a private bath and balcony, are reached by either of two staircases. The master suite, with His and Hers baths and walk-in closets, whirlpool, and fireplace, adds the finishing touch to this memorable home.

Design T172956

4,222 Sq. Ft. - First Floor
1,762 Sq. Ft. - Second Floor
130,174 Cu. Ft.

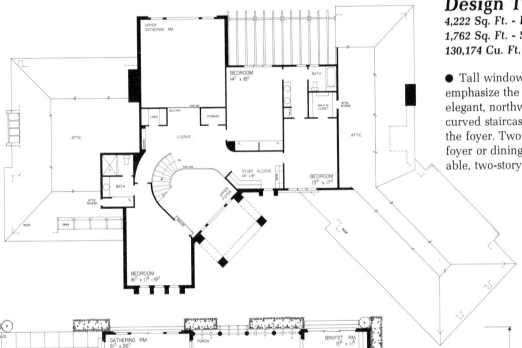

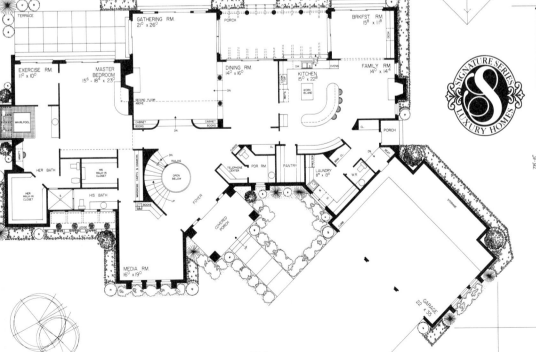

● Tall windows and two-story arches emphasize the soaring height of this elegant, northwest contemporary. A curved staircase is the focal point of the foyer. Two steps down from the foyer or dining room is the comfortable, two-story gathering room featuring a fireplace and three sliding glass doors. A large walk-in pantry, work island, snack bar, and view of the family room fireplace make the kitchen functional and comfortable. The master suite is secluded in its own wing. The bedroom, with a curved-hearth fireplace, and exercise room open to the terrace through sliding glass doors. His and Hers walk-in closets and baths (Hers with whirlpool tub) are added luxuries. A media room with wet bar, accessible from master bedroom and foyer, is the perfect place to relax. The second floor stairs open to a lounge which overlooks the gathering room. Three additional bedrooms and a quiet study alcove on the second floor round out the living area of this gracious and functional home.

● This attractive, contemporary bi-level will overwhelm you with its features: two balconies, an open staircase with planter below, two lower level bedrooms, six sets of sliding glass doors and an outstanding master suite loaded with features. The occupants of this house will love the large exercise room. After a tough workout, you can relax in the whirlpool or the sauna or simply take a shower!

Design T172856 1,801 Sq. Ft. - Upper Level
2,170 Sq. Ft. - Lower Level; 44,935 Cu. Ft.

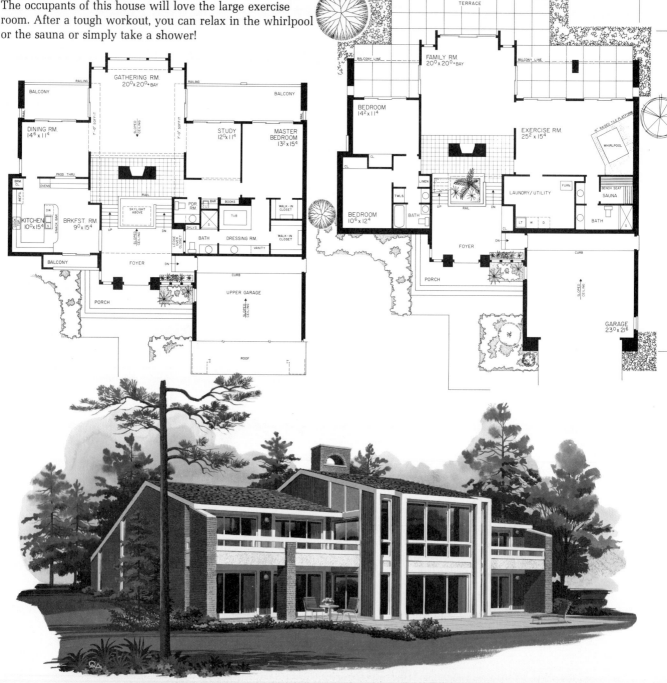

Design T172933
1,570 Sq. Ft. - Upper Level; 1,046 Sq. Ft. - Living Room Level
1,464 Sq. Ft. - Lower Level; 61,370 Cu. Ft.

● This is a masterful multi-level with all the comforts of home—and more: living room with fireplace; family room with fireplace; huge kitchen with prep island, snack bar, and breakfast room; large formal dining room; separate media room; light-filled atrium; sizable master bedroom suite; upper-level lounge; lots of storage; and three individual terraces.

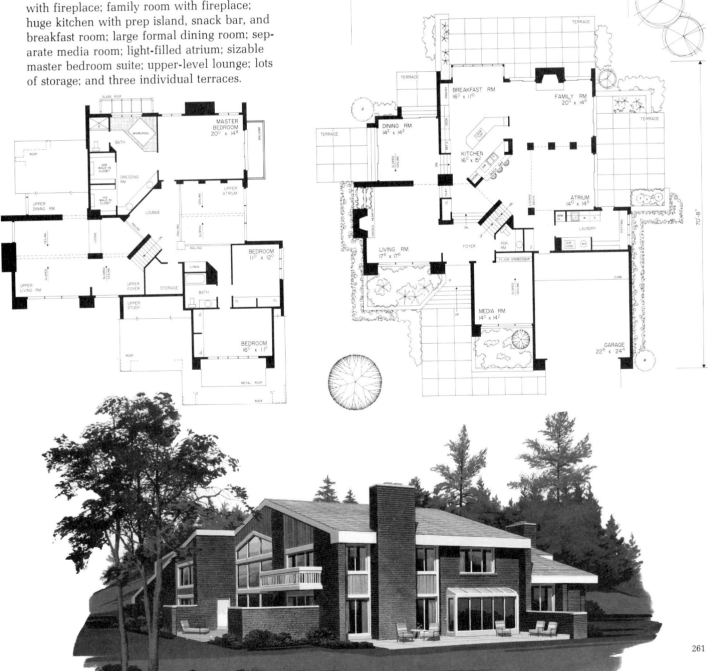

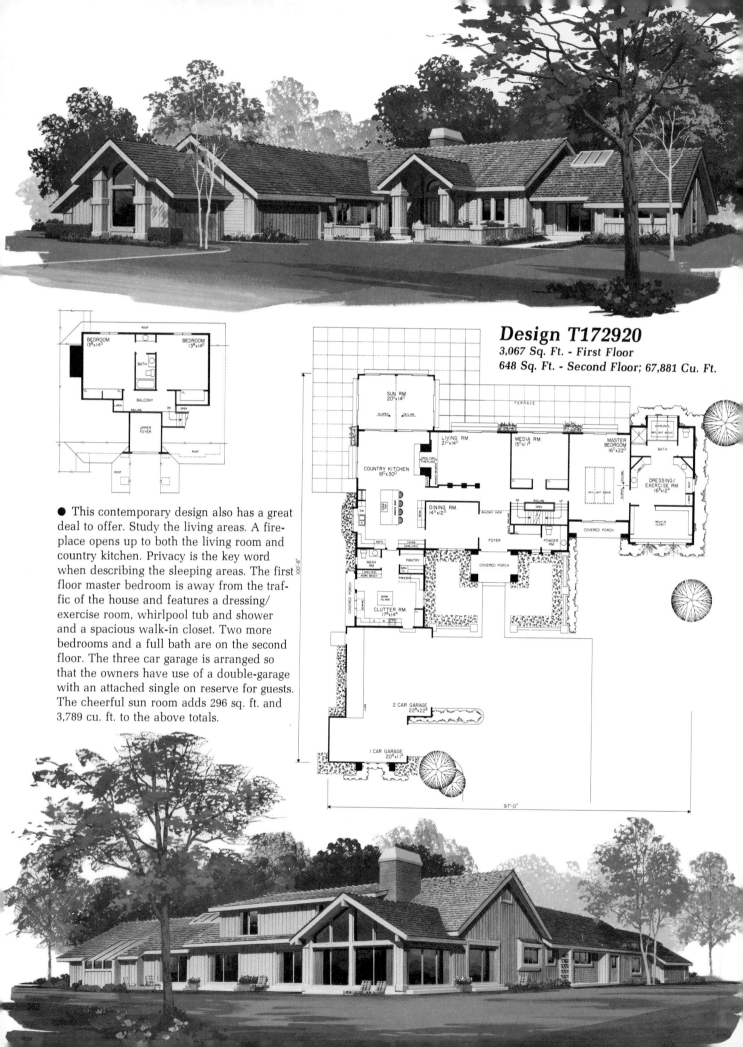

Design T172920

3,067 Sq. Ft. - First Floor
648 Sq. Ft. - Second Floor; 67,881 Cu. Ft.

Second floor plan labels: BEDROOM 13⁸x14⁰, BEDROOM 13⁸x14⁰, ROOF, BATH, CL, CL, LINEN, BALCONY, UPPER FOYER, RAILING, DN OPEN, ROOF, ROOF

First floor plan labels: SUN RM. 20⁰x14⁰, SLOPED CEILING, TERRACE, LIVING RM. 21⁵x14⁰, MEDIA RM. 15⁰x11⁸, MASTER BEDROOM 16⁰x22⁰, WHIRLPOOL SKYLIGHT ABOVE, BATH, COUNTRY KITCHEN 18⁰x30⁰, OPEN THRU FIREPLACE, RAISED HEARTH, DRESSING/EXERCISE RM. 16⁸x12⁴, WALK-IN CLOSET, DINING RM. 14⁰x12⁰, BALCONY OVER, OPEN, SKYLIGHT ABOVE, SLOPED CEILING, DW, REF'G, FOYER, POWDER RM., COVERED PORCH, CHINA SHELVES, WASH RM., PANTRY, COVERED PORCH, SHELVES WORK BENCH, FREEZER, WORK ISLAND, CLUTTER RM. 17⁸x14⁰, COVERED PORCH, CURB, 2 CAR GARAGE 22⁸x22⁰, 1 CAR GARAGE 20⁸x11⁴

100'-8"
97'-0"

● This contemporary design also has a great deal to offer. Study the living areas. A fireplace opens up to both the living room and country kitchen. Privacy is the key word when describing the sleeping areas. The first floor master bedroom is away from the traffic of the house and features a dressing/exercise room, whirlpool tub and shower and a spacious walk-in closet. Two more bedrooms and a full bath are on the second floor. The three car garage is arranged so that the owners have use of a double-garage with an attached single on reserve for guests. The cheerful sun room adds 296 sq. ft. and 3,789 cu. ft. to the above totals.

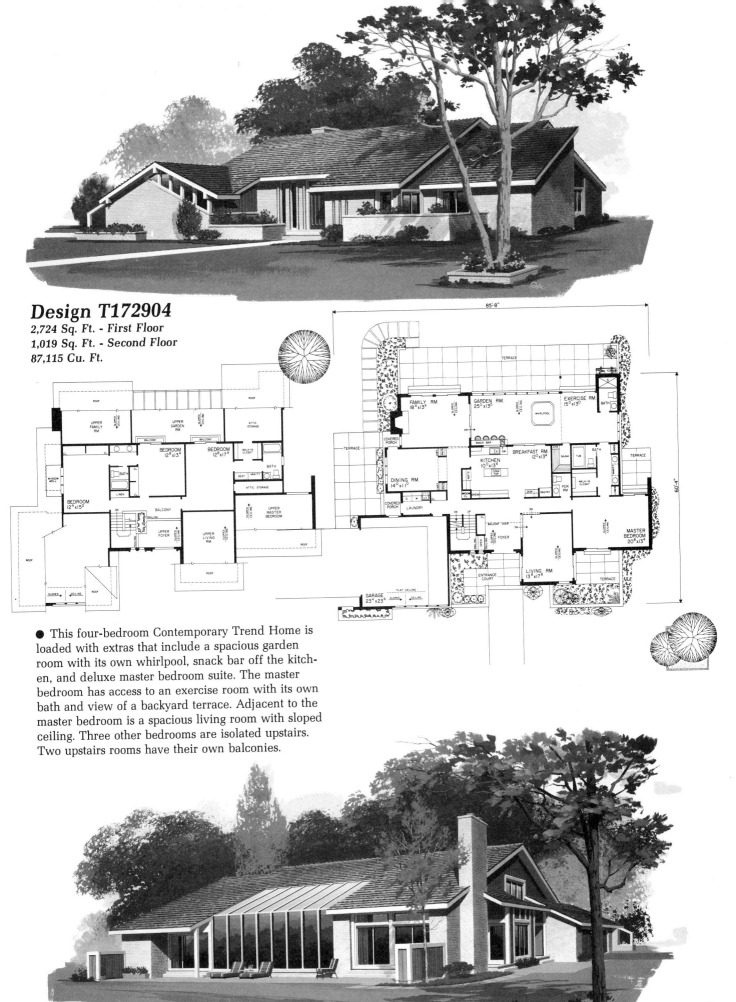

Design T172904

2,724 Sq. Ft. - First Floor
1,019 Sq. Ft. - Second Floor
87,115 Cu. Ft.

● This four-bedroom Contemporary Trend Home is loaded with extras that include a spacious garden room with its own whirlpool, snack bar off the kitchen, and deluxe master bedroom suite. The master bedroom has access to an exercise room with its own bath and view of a backyard terrace. Adjacent to the master bedroom is a spacious living room with sloped ceiling. Three other bedrooms are isolated upstairs. Two upstairs rooms have their own balconies.

Design T172823
1,370 Sq. Ft. - First Floor
927 Sq. Ft. - Second Floor
34,860 Cu. Ft.

● The street view of this contemporary design features a small courtyard entrance as well as a private terrace off the study. Inside the livability will be outstanding. This design features spacious first floor activity areas that flow smoothly into each other. In the gathering room a raised hearth fireplace creates a dramatic focal point. An adjacent covered terrace, featuring a skylight, is ideal for outdoor dining and could be screened in later for an additional room.

Design T172831
1,758 Sq. Ft. - First Floor
1,247 Sq. Ft. - Second Floor
44,265 Cu. Ft.

● You can incorporate energy-saving features into the elevation of this passive solar design to enable you to receive the most sunlight on your particular site. Multiple plot plans (included with the blueprints) illustrate which elevations should be solarized for different sites and which extra features can be incorporated. The features can include a greenhouse added to the family room, the back porch turned into a solarium or skylights installed over the entry.

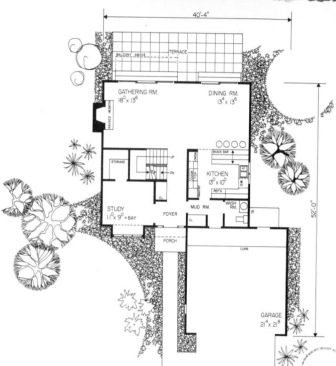

Design T172711 975 Sq. Ft. - First Floor
1,024 Sq. Ft. - Second Floor; 31,380 Cu. Ft.

● Special features! A complete master suite with a private balcony plus two more bedrooms and a bath upstairs. The first floor has a study with a storage closet. A convenient snack bar between kitchen and dining room. The kitchen offers many built-in appliances. Plus a gathering room and dining room that measures 31 feet wide. Note the curb area in the garage and fireplace in gathering room.

Design T172748
1,232 Sq. Ft. - First Floor
720 Sq. Ft. - Second Floor
27,550 Cu. Ft.

● This four bedroom contemporary will definitely have appeal for the entire family. The U-shaped kitchen-nook area with its built-in desk, adjacent laundry/wash room and service entrance will be very efficient for the busy kitchen activities. The living and family rooms are both sunken one step.

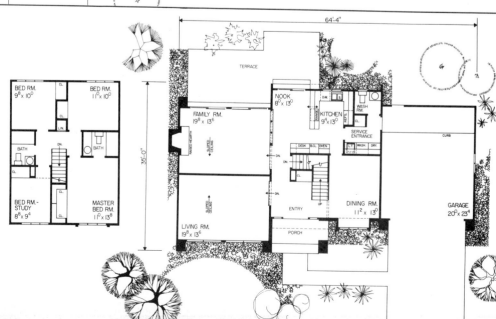

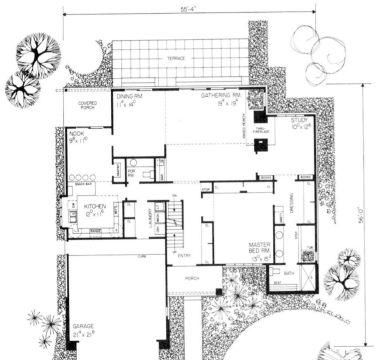

Design T172701 1,909 Sq. Ft. - First Floor
891 Sq. Ft. - Second Floor; 50,830 Cu. Ft.

● A snack bar in the kitchen! Plus a breakfast nook and formal dining room. Whether it's an elegant dinner party or a quick lunch, this home provides the right spot. There's a wet bar in the gathering room. Built-in bookcases in the study. And between these two rooms, a gracious fireplace. Three large bedrooms. Including a luxury master suite. Plus a balcony lounge overlooking gathering room below.

Design T172896
1,856 Sq. Ft. - Main Level; 1,454 Sq. Ft. - Lower Level; 43,390 Cu. Ft.

● This design is very inviting with its contemporary appeal. A large kitchen with an adjacent snack bar makes light meals a breeze. The adjoining breakfast room offers a scenic view through sliding glass doors. Notice the sloped ceiling in the dining and gathering rooms. A fireplace in the gathering room adds a cozy air. An interesting feature is the master bedroom's easy access to the study. Also, take note of the sliding doors in the master bedroom which lead to a private balcony. On the lower level, a large activities room will be a frequently used spot by family members. The fireplace and wet bar add a nice touch for entertaining friends. Also, notice the sliding glass doors which lead to the terrace. Take note of the two or optional three bedrooms - the choice is yours.

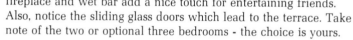

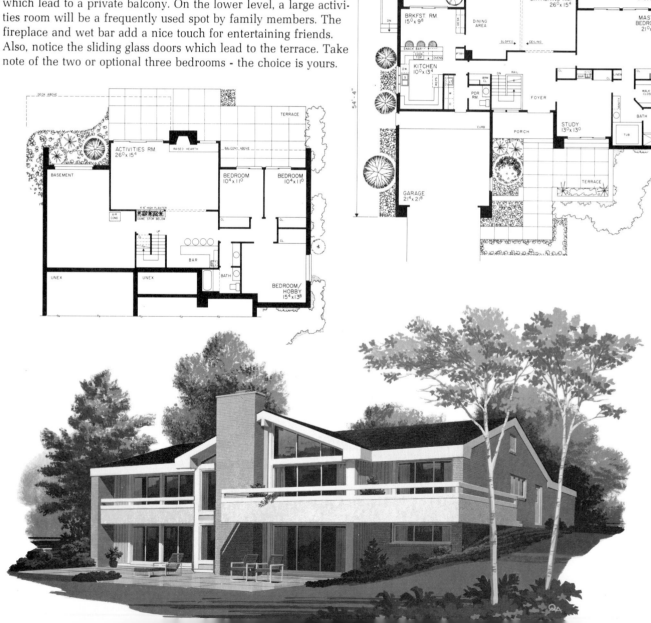

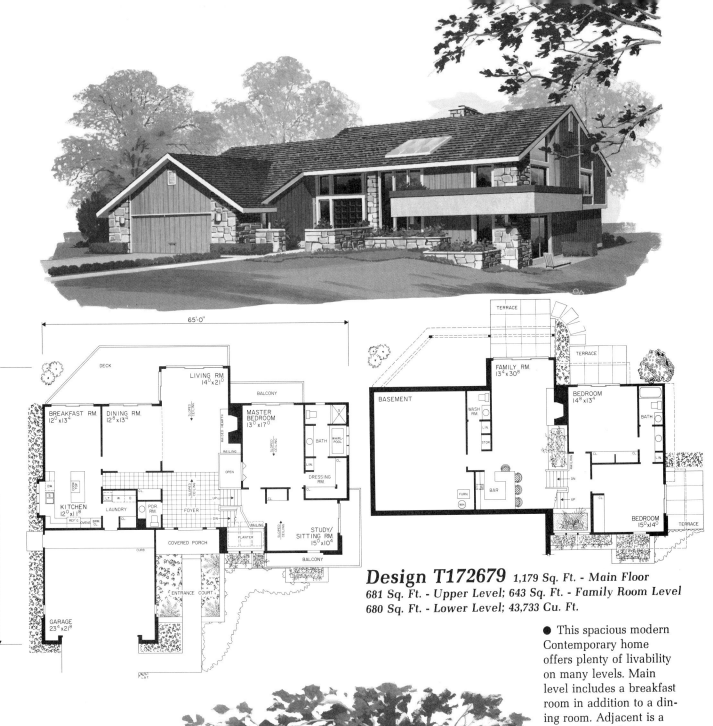

65'-0"

DECK

LIVING RM.
14⁰x21⁰

BALCONY

BREAKFAST RM.
12⁰x13⁴

DINING RM.
12⁸x13⁴

MASTER
BEDROOM
13⁰x17⁰

BATH

WHIRL-
POOL

RAISED HEARTH

SLOPED CEILING

RAILING

OPEN

KITCHEN
12⁰x11⁸

LT W D

LAUNDRY

PDR.
RM.

FOYER

UP

LIN.

DRESSING
RM.

CL

DW

COOK TOP

S

REF'G

OVENS

BRM
CL

SLOPED CEILING

DN

RAILING

SLOPED CEILING

STUDY/
SITTING RM.
15⁰x10⁴

CURB

COVERED PORCH

PLANTER

BALCONY

ENTRANCE COURT

GARAGE
23⁴x21⁸

TERRACE

TERRACE

FAMILY RM.
13⁴x30⁸

BASEMENT

BEDROOM
14⁸x13⁴

BATH

WASH
RM.

LIN

STOR

LIN

CL

FURN

WH

BAR

UP

CL

LIN

BEDROOM
15⁰x14⁰

TERRACE

Design T172679 1,179 Sq. Ft. - Main Floor
681 Sq. Ft. - Upper Level; 643 Sq. Ft. - Family Room Level
680 Sq. Ft. - Lower Level; 43,733 Cu. Ft.

● This spacious modern Contemporary home offers plenty of livability on many levels. Main level includes a breakfast room in addition to a dining room. Adjacent is a sloped-ceiling living room with raised hearth. The upper level features isolated master bedroom suite with adjoining study or sitting room and balcony. Family room level includes a long rectangular family room with adjoining terrace on one end and adjoining bar with washroom at the other end. A spacious basement is included. Two other bedrooms are positioned in the lower level with their own view of the terrace and quiet privacy. Note the rear deck.

269

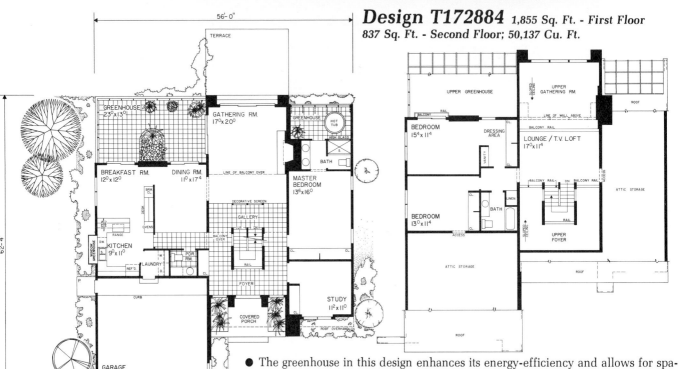

Design T172884 1,855 Sq. Ft. - First Floor
837 Sq. Ft. - Second Floor; 50,137 Cu. Ft.

● The greenhouse in this design enhances its energy-efficiency and allows for spacious and interesting living patterns. Being a one-and-a-half story design, the second floor could be developed at a later date when the space is needed. The greenhouses add an additional 418 sq. ft. and 8,793 cu. ft. to the above quoted figures.

Design T172827 1,618 Sq. Ft. - Upper Level
1,458 Sq. Ft. - Lower Level; 41,370 Cu. Ft.

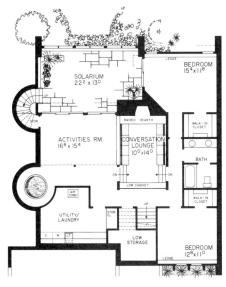

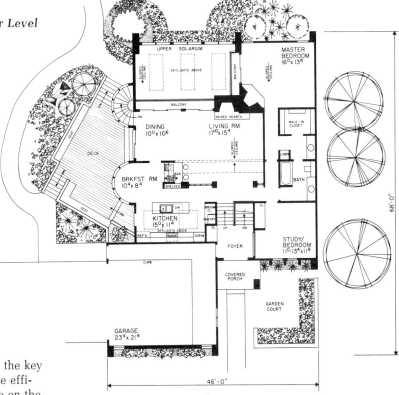

● The two-story solarium with skylights above is the key to energy savings to this bi-level design. Study the efficiency of this floor plan. The conversation lounge on the lower level is a unique focal point.

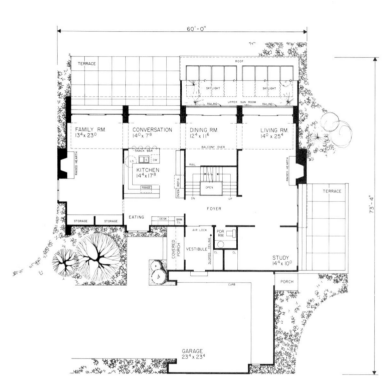

Design T172834
1,775 Sq. Ft. - First Floor; 1,041 Sq. Ft. - Second Floor
1,128 Sq. Ft. - Lower Level; 55,690 Cu. Ft.

● This passive solar design offers 4,200 square feet of livability situated on three levels. The primary passive element will be the lower level sun room which admits sunlight for direct-gain heating. The solar warmth collected in the sun room will radiate into the rest of the house after it passes the sliding glass doors. During the warm summer months, shades are put over the skylight to protect it from direct sunlight. This design has the option of incorporating active solar heating panels to the roof. The collectors would be installed on the south-facing portion of the roof. They would absorb the sun's warmth for both domestic water and supplementary space heating. An attic fan exhausts any hot air out of the house in the summer and circulates air in the winter. With or without the active solar panels, this is a marvelous two-story contemporary.

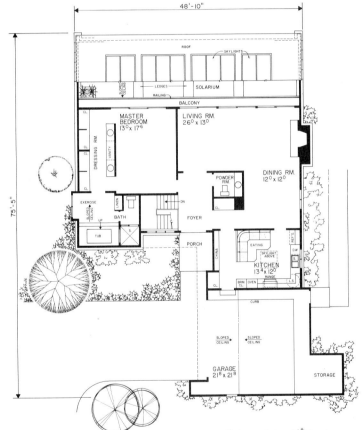

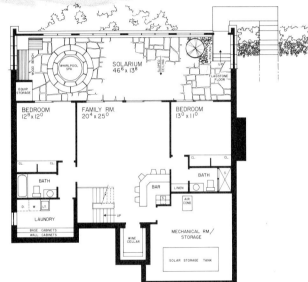

Design T172835 1,626 Sq. Ft. - Main Level
2,038 Sq. Ft. - Lower Level; 50,926 Cu. Ft.

● Passive solar techniques with the help of an active solar component - they can work together or the active solar component can act as a back-up system - heat and cool this striking contemporary design. The lower level solarium is the primary passive element. It admits sunlight during the day for direct-gain heating. The warmth, which was absorbed into the thermal floor, is then radiated into the structure at night. The earth berms on the three sides of the lower level help keep out the winter cold and summer heat. The active system uses collector panels to gather the sun's heat. The heat is transferred via a water pipe system to the lower level storage tank where it is circulated throughout the house by a heat exchanger. Note that where active solar collectors are a design OPTION, which they are in all of our active/passive designs, they must be contracted locally. The collector area must be tailored to the climate and sun angles that characterize your building location.

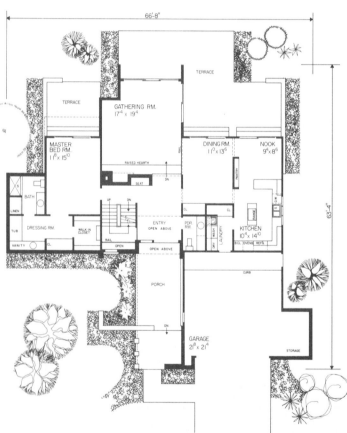

Design T172729

1,590 Sq. Ft. - First Floor
756 Sq. Ft. - Second Floor
39,310 Cu. Ft.

● Entering this home will surely be a pleasure through the sheltered walk-way to the double front doors. And the pleasure and beauty does not stop there. The entry hall and sunken gathering room are open to the upstairs for added dimension.

There's even a built-in seat in the entry area. The kitchen-nook area is very efficient with its many built-ins and the adjacent laundry room. There is a fine indoor-outdoor living relationship in this design. Note the private terrace off the luxurious

master bedroom suite, a living terrace accessible from the gathering room, dining room and nook plus the balcony off the upstairs bedroom. Upstairs there is a total of two bedrooms, each having its own private bath and plenty of closets.

Design T172379 *1,525 Sq. Ft. - First Floor; 748 Sq. Ft. - Second Floor; 26,000 Cu. Ft.*

● A house that has "everything" may very well look just like this design. Its exterior is well-proportioned and impressive. Inside the inviting double front doors there are features galore. The living room and family room level are sunken. Separating these two rooms is a dramatic thru fireplace. A built-in bar, planter and beamed ceiling highlight the family room. Nearby is a full bath and a study which could be utilized as a fourth bedroom. The fine functioning kitchen has a pass-thru to the snack bar in the breakfast nook. The adjacent dining room overlooks the living room and has sliding doors to the covered porch. Upstairs three bedrooms, two baths and an outdoor balcony. Blueprints for this design include optional basement details.

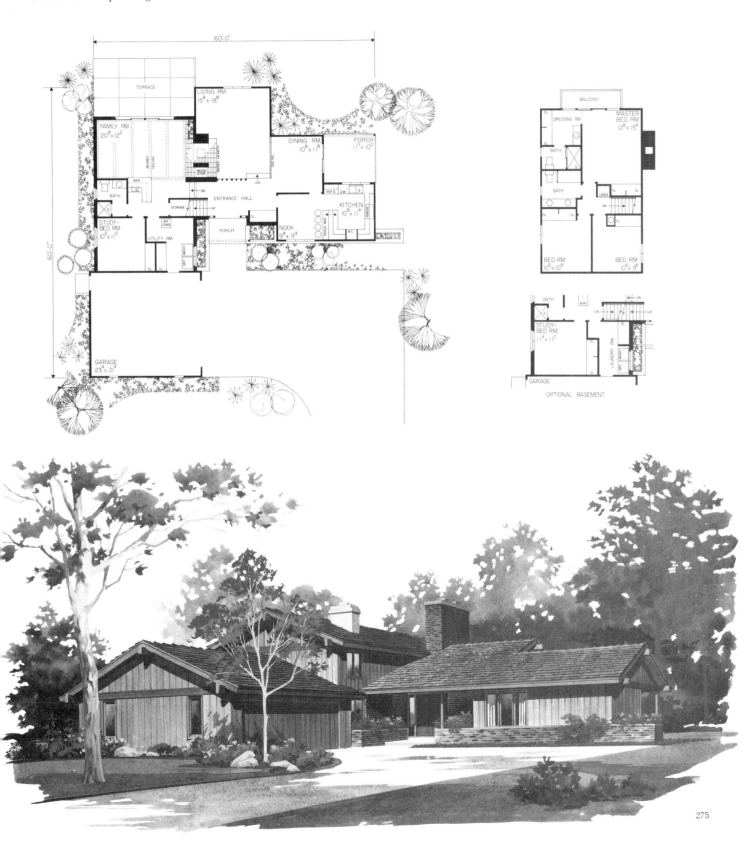

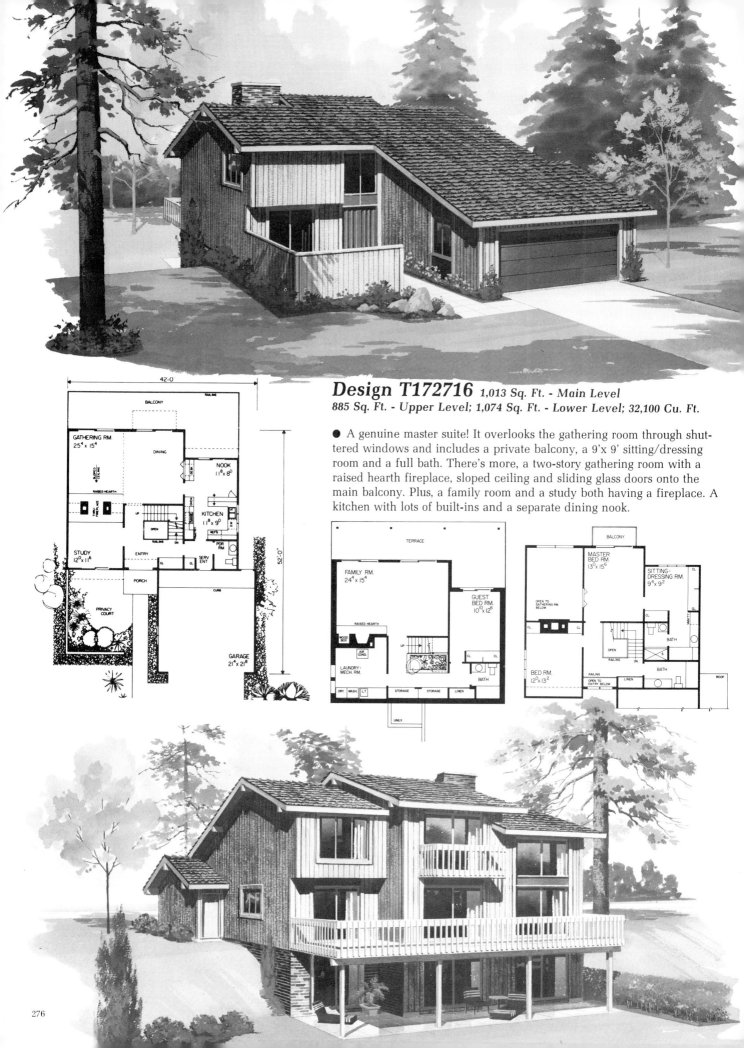

Design T172716 1,013 Sq. Ft. - Main Level
885 Sq. Ft. - Upper Level; 1,074 Sq. Ft. - Lower Level; 32,100 Cu. Ft.

● A genuine master suite! It overlooks the gathering room through shuttered windows and includes a private balcony, a 9'x 9' sitting/dressing room and a full bath. There's more, a two-story gathering room with a raised hearth fireplace, sloped ceiling and sliding glass doors onto the main balcony. Plus, a family room and a study both having a fireplace. A kitchen with lots of built-ins and a separate dining nook.

Design T172511
1,043 Sq. Ft. - Main Level
703 Sq. Ft. - Upper Level
794 Sq. Ft. - Lower Level
30,528 Cu. Ft.

Upper Level Plan

UPPER GATHERING RM.

BALCONY

BALCONY

BED RM.
11⁸ x 13⁸

BUNK RM.
11⁸ x 19⁰

BALCONY · RAILING

CL · CL

BATH · RAILING · DN · CL · CL

UPPER FOYER

Lower Level Plan

TERRACE

ACTIVITIES RM.
15⁴ x 18⁴

BASEMENT

BUNK RM. OPTIONAL
11⁴ x 15⁸

RAISED HEARTH · AIR COND

BATH

STORAGE · UP · CL

CABINETS · LT. · WASH. · DRY

Main Level Plan

40'-4"

52'-0"

GATHERING RM.
15⁴ x 18⁴

DECK

BALCONY

STUDY-BED RM.
11⁸ x 13⁸

DINING RM.
11⁸ x 11⁸

SNACK BAR

KITCHEN
11⁸ x 9⁸

LINEN · CL

BATH

DN · UP

FOYER · PANTRY · REF · G · RANGE

PORCH

ENTRANCE COURT · OPEN TRELLIS

STORAGE

CARPORT
11⁸ x 20⁰

● Study this outstanding multi-level with its dramatic outdoor deck and balconies. This home is ideal if you are looking for a home that is new and exciting. The livability that it offers will efficiently serve your family.

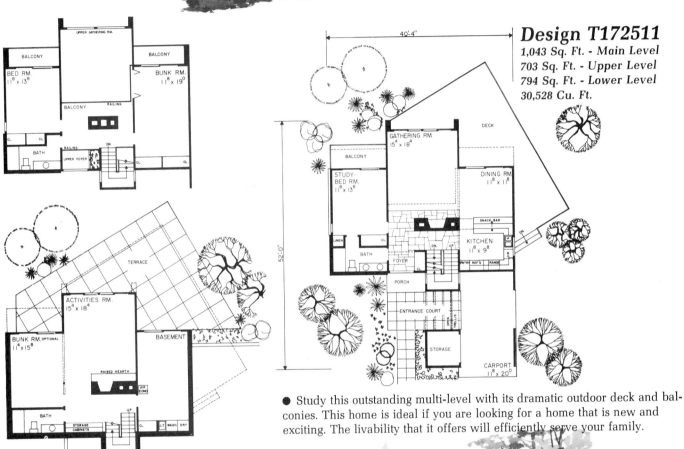

Design T172780

2,006 Sq. Ft. - First Floor
718 Sq. Ft. - Second Floor; 42,110 Cu. Ft.

● This 1½-story contemporary has more fine features than one can imagine. The livability is outstanding and can be appreciated by the whole family. Note the fine indoor-outdoor living relationships.

Design T172772

1,579 Sq. Ft. - First Floor
1,240 Sq. Ft. - Second Floor; 39,460 Cu. Ft.

● This four-bedroom two-story contemporary design is sure to suit your growing family needs. The rear U-shaped kitchen, flanked by the family and dining rooms, will be very efficient to the busy homemaker. Parents will enjoy all the convenience of the master bedroom suite.

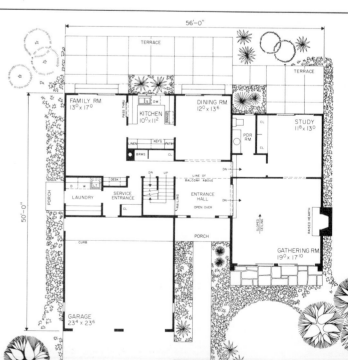

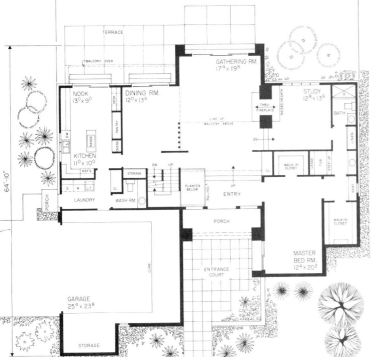

Floor plan labels:

TERRACE

BALCONY OVER

GATHERING RM.
17⁴ x 19⁸

NOOK
13⁰ x 9⁰

DINING RM.
12⁰ x 13⁶

STUDY
12⁸ x 13⁶

BATH

THRU-FIREPLACE
RAISED HEARTH

LINE OF BALCONY ABOVE

LINEN

KITCHEN
11⁰ x 10⁰

STORAGE

DN UP

PLANTER BELOW

UP

ENTRY

WALK-IN CLOSET

LEDGE

STEP-UP

SEAT

LAUNDRY

WASH RM.

CL

PORCH

WALK-IN CLOSET

TUB

PORCH

ENTRANCE COURT

MASTER BED RM.
12⁴ x 20²

GARAGE
25⁴ x 23⁸

STORAGE

64'-10"

64'-10"

Design T172771

2,087 Sq. Ft. - First Floor
816 Sq. Ft. - Second Floor; 53,285 Cu. Ft.

● This design will provide an abundance of livability for your family. The second floor is highlighted by an open lounge which overlooks both the entry and the gathering room below.

Second floor labels:

BALCONY

BED RM.
11⁰ x 17⁰

BED RM.
11⁸ x 13⁶

UPPER GATHERING RM.

SLOPED CEILING

RAILING

LOUNGE
17⁴ x 10⁰

RAILING

UPPER ENTRANCE

SLOPED CEILING

WALK-IN CLOSET

BATH

VANITY

DN

DESK

CL

LIN

Design T172887 1,338 Sq. Ft. - First Floor; 661 Sq. Ft. - Second Floor; 36,307 Cu. Ft.

● This attractive, contemporary one-and-a-half story will be the envy of many. First, examine the efficient kitchen. Not only does it offer a snack bar for those quick meals but also a large dining room. Notice the adjacent dining porch. The laundry and garage access are also adjacent to the kitchen.

An exciting feature is the gathering room with fireplace. The first floor also offers a study with a wet bar and sliding glass doors that open to a private porch. This will make those quiet times cherishable. Adjacent to the study is a full bath followed by a bedroom. Upstairs a large master bedroom suite oc-

cupies the entire floor. It features a bath with an oversized tub and shower, a large walk-in closet with built-ins and an open lounge with fireplace. Both the lounge and master bedroom, along with the gathering room, have sloped ceilings. Develop the lower level for additional space.

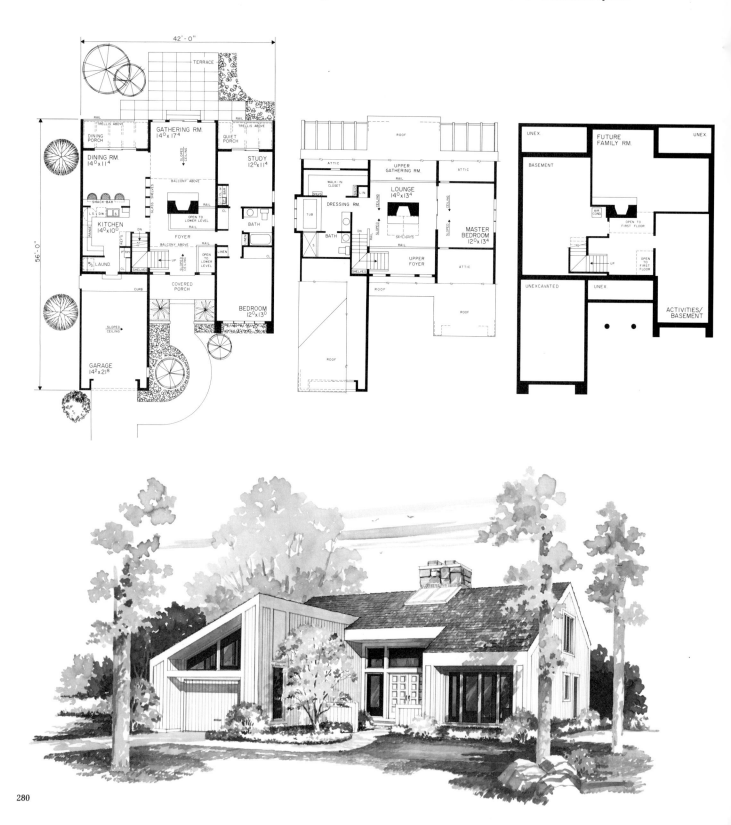

French Houses

French facades, with their formal ambience, are an architectural favorite of many people. Like other styles they, too, have numerous faces. As this group of designs shows, French detailing can be adapted in a pleasing fashion to one-, 1½- and two-story houses. Of interest is the contrast between the rambling hip-roof 1½-story designs, the two-story mansard roof designs, the stately French provincial designs and the impressive Norman manor houses.

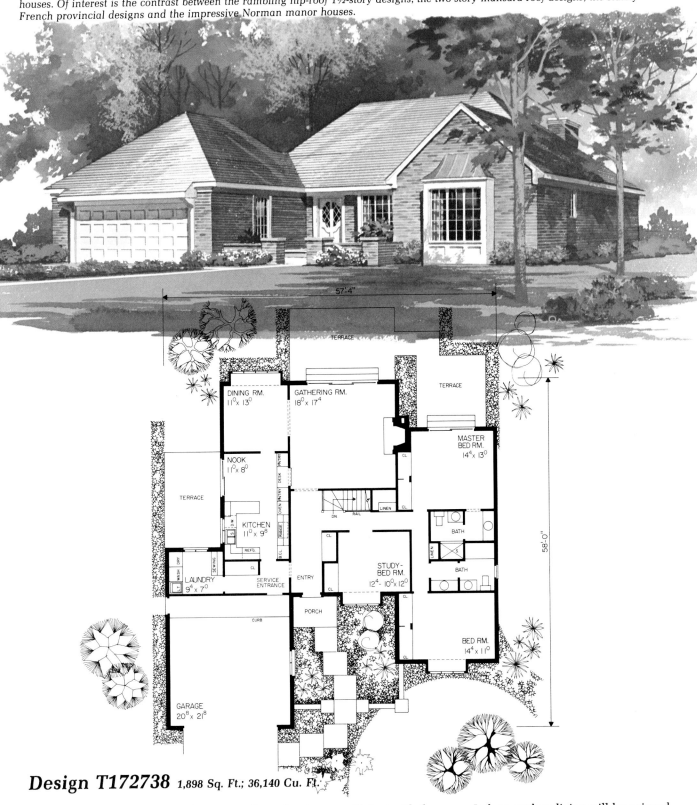

Design T172738 1,898 Sq. Ft.; 36,140 Cu. Ft.

● Impressive architectural work is indeed apparent in this three bedroom home. The three foot high entrance court wall, the high pitched roof and the paned glass windows all add to this home's appeal. It is apparent that the

floor plan is very efficient with the side U-shaped kitchen and nook with two pantry closets, the rear dining and gathering rooms and the three (or make it two with a study) bedrooms and two baths of the sleeping wing.

Indoor-outdoor living will be enjoyed in this home with a dining terrace off the nook and a living terrace off the gathering room and master bedroom. Note the fireplace in the gathering room and bay window in dining room.

Design T171228 2,583 Sq. Ft. - First Floor; 697 Sq. Ft. - Second Floor; 51,429 Cu. Ft.

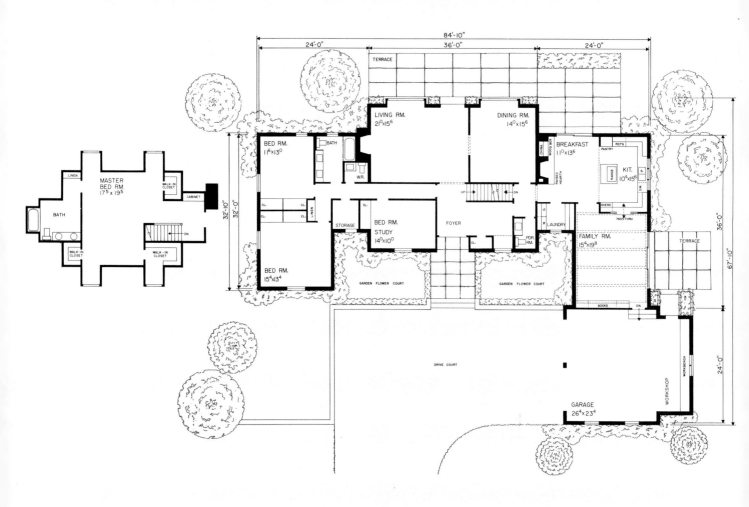

● This beautiful house has a wealth of detail taken from the rich traditions of French Regency design. The roof itself is a study in pleasant dormers and the hips and valleys of a big flowing area. A close examination of the plan shows the careful arrangement of space for privacy as well as good circulation of traffic. The spacious formal entrance hall sets the stage for good zoning. The informal living area is highlighted by the updated version of the old country kitchen. Its features include a fireplace with built-in wood box and china stor-age, an island cooking surface, adjacent laundry and pass-thru to the family room. While there is a half-story devoted to the master bedroom suite, this home functions more as a one-story country estate design than as a 1½-story home.

UPPER LOUNGE
10¹⁰ x 10²

BED RM.
13² x 16⁸

BED RM.
12⁸ x 16⁸

Design T172342

2,824 Sq. Ft. - First Floor
1,013 Sq. Ft. - Second Floor
59,882 Cu. Ft.

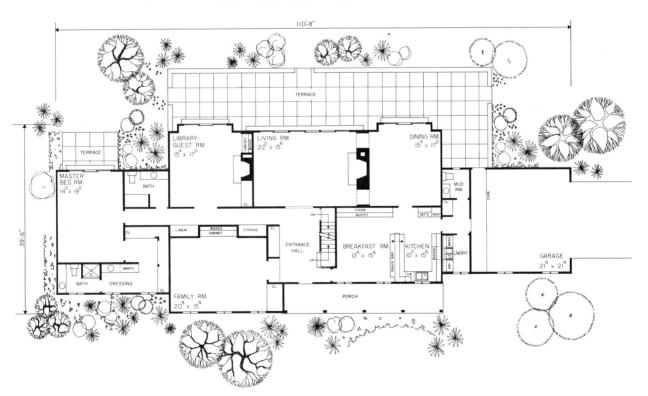

110'-8"

39'-6"

TERRACE

TERRACE

LIBRARY-
GUEST RM.
15⁴ x 17⁰

LIVING RM.
22⁰ x 15⁶

DINING RM.
15⁴ x 17⁰

MASTER
BED RM.
14⁰ x 19⁰

BATH

MUD
RM.

CHINA
BUFFET

REFG PANT

LINEN   BOOKS
CABINET   STORAGE

ENTRANCE
HALL

BREAKFAST RM.
12⁴ x 15⁶

KITCHEN
10⁰ x 15

GARAGE
21⁴ x 21

BATH   DRESSING   VANITY

FAMILY RM.
20⁸ x 24⁴

PORCH

● A distinctive exterior characterized by varying roof planes, appealing window treatment, attractive chimneys and a covered front porch with prominent vertical columns. The main portion of the house is effectively balanced by the master bedroom wing on the one side and the garage wing on the other. As a buffer between house and garage is the mud room and the laundry. The kitchen is U-shaped, efficient, and strategically located to serve the breakfast and dining rooms. Notice how the rooms at the rear function through sliding glass doors with the outdoor terrace areas. Fireplaces highlight both the spacious living room and the large library. The big family room features built-in book shelve and cabinet. Upstairs, two bedrooms and a study alcove.

Design T172376

1,422 Sq. Ft. - First Floor
1,020 Sq. Ft. - Second Floor; 38,134 Cu. Ft.

● Make your next home one that will be truly distinctive and a reflection of your good taste. This high styled design will surely catch the eye of even the most casual of passers-by. The appealing roof lines, the window treatment, the arched openings and the stucco exterior set the charming character of this two-story. The covered front porch provides sheltered entry to the spacious foyer. From this point traffic patterns flow efficiently to all areas. Notice how the family room/ laundry zone is sunken one step. The kitchen is flanked by the two eating areas and they overlook the rear yard. Each of the two large living areas feature a fireplace and functions directly through sliding glass doors with a covered porch. Upstairs there are four bedrooms, two baths and plenty of closets to serve the entire family adequately.

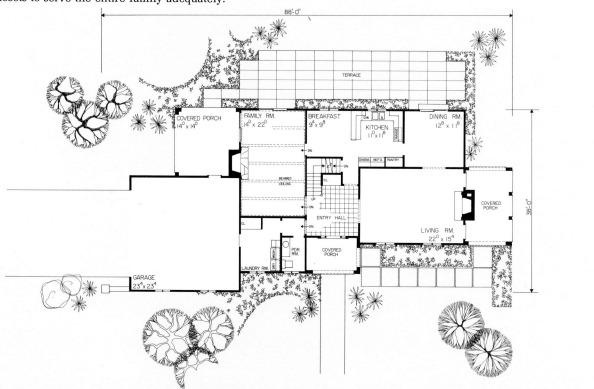

Design T172543

2,345 Sq. Ft. - First Floor
1,687 Sq. Ft. - Second Floor; 76,000 Cu. Ft.

● Certainly a dramatic French adaptation highlighted by effective window treatment, delicate cornice detailing, appealing brick quoins and excellent proportion. Stepping through the double front doors the drama is heightened by the spacious entry hall with its two curving staircases to the second floor. The upper hall is open and looks down to the hall below. There is a study and a big gathering room which look out on the raised terrace. The work center is outstanding. The garage will accommodate three cars.

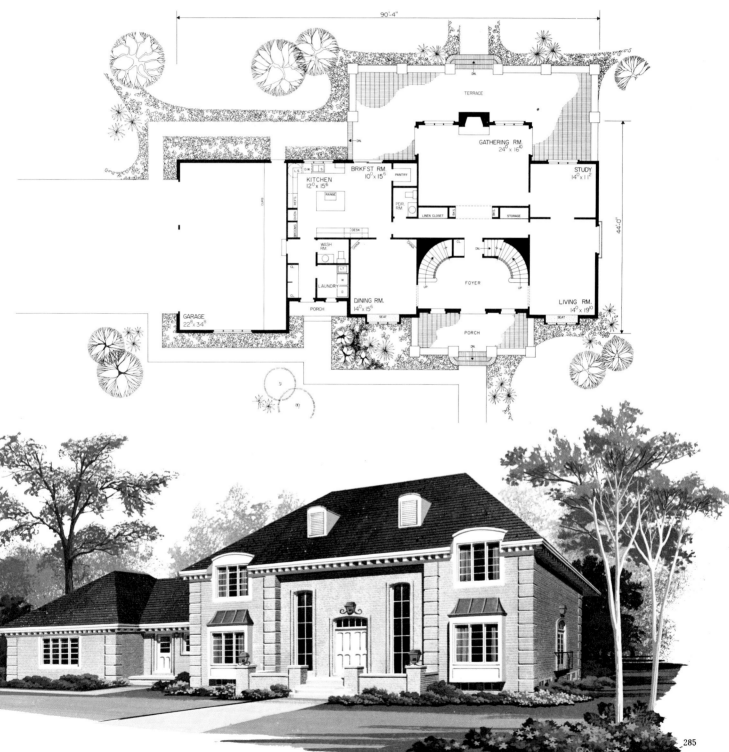

Design T172779 3,225 Sq. Ft.; 70,715 Cu. Ft.

● This French design is surely impressive. The exterior appearance will brighten any area with its French roof, paned-glass windows, masonry brick privacy wall and double front doors. The inside is just as appealing. Note the unique placement of rooms and features. Enter this home into the entry hall. It is large and leads to each of the areas in this plan. To the left, the formal dining room is outstanding. While serving a formal dinner one can enter by way of the butler's pantry (notice it's size and that it has a sink). To the right of the entry is a sizable parlor and beyond that is the three bedroom sleeping area. The gathering room with fireplace, sliding glass doors and adjacent study is in the back of the plan. The work center is also outstanding. There is the U-shaped kitchen, island range, snack bar, breakfast nook, pantry plus wash room and large laundry near service entrance.

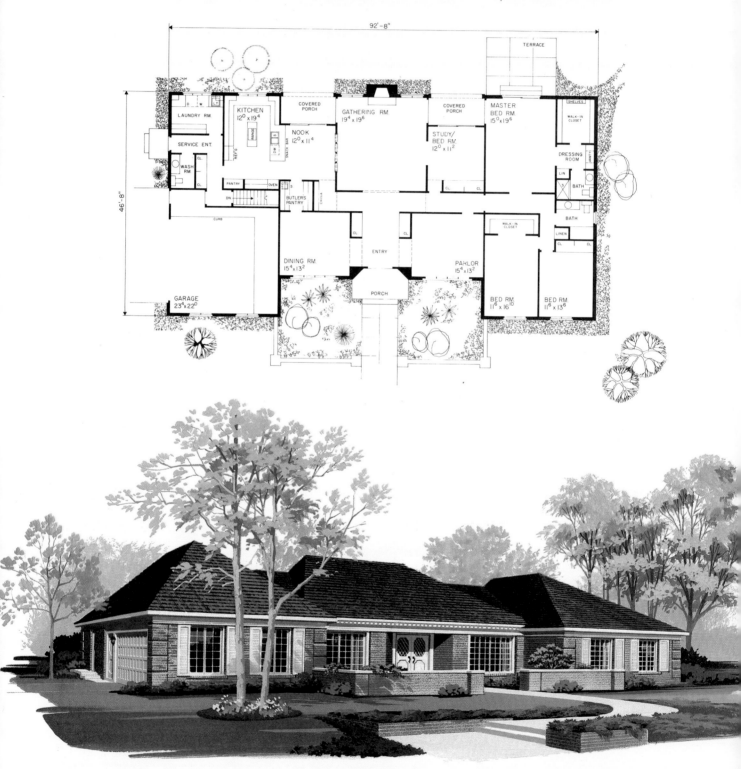

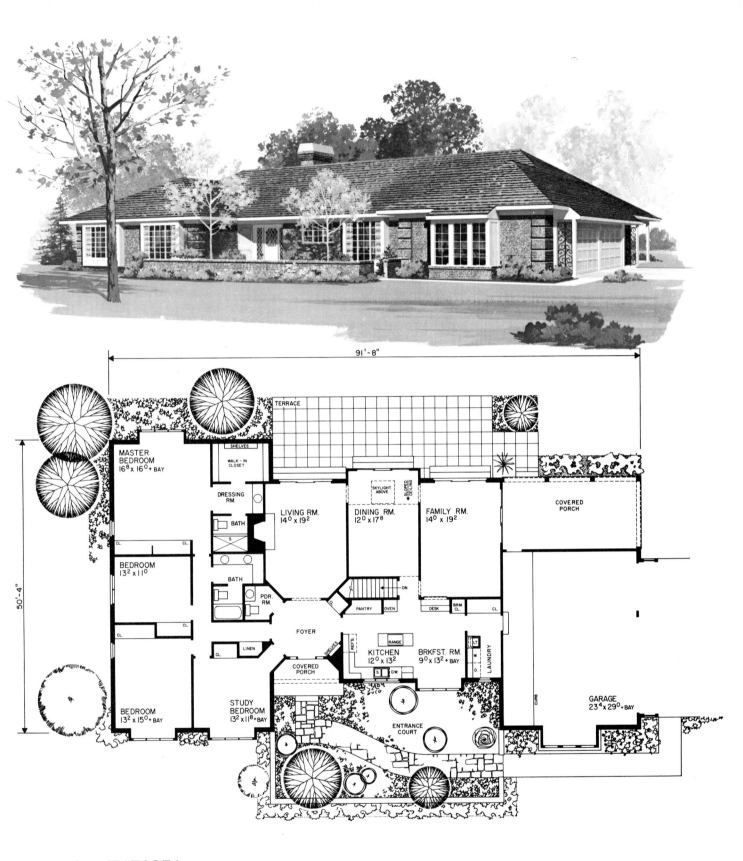

TERRACE

MASTER
BEDROOM
16⁸ x 16⁰ + BAY

SHELVES

WALK - IN
CLOSET

DRESSING
RM.

SKYLIGHT
ABOVE

SLOPED
CEILING

LIVING RM.
14⁰ x 19²

DINING RM.
12⁰ x 17⁸

FAMILY RM.
14⁰ x 19²

COVERED
PORCH

BATH

BEDROOM
13² x 11⁰

CL

CL

BATH

PDR.
RM.

PANTRY

OVEN

DESK

BRM.
CL.

CL.

91'-8"

50'-4"

CL

CL

LINEN

CL

FOYER

SHELVES

REF'G.

RANGE

KITCHEN
12⁰ x 13²

D.W.

BRKFST. RM.
9⁰ x 13² + BAY

W

D

LAUNDRY

COVERED
PORCH

BEDROOM
13² x 15⁰ + BAY

STUDY
BEDROOM
13² x 11⁸ + BAY

ENTRANCE
COURT

CURB

GARAGE
23⁴ x 29⁰ + BAY

Design T172851 *2,739 Sq. Ft.; 55,810 Cu. Ft.*

● This spacious one-story has a classic Country French hip roof. The front entrance creates a charming entry. Beyond the covered porch is an octagonal foyer. A closet, shelves and powder room are contained in the foyer. All of the living areas overlook the rear yard.

Sliding glass doors open each of these areas to the rear terrace. Their features include a fireplace in the living room, skylight in the dining room and a second set of sliding glass doors in the family room leading to a side covered porch. An island range and other built-

ins are featured in the spacious, front kitchen. Adjacent is the breakfast room which will be used for informal dining. The four bedrooms and bath facilities are all clustered in one wing. Note the bay windows in the master bedroom, breakfast room and the three-car garage.

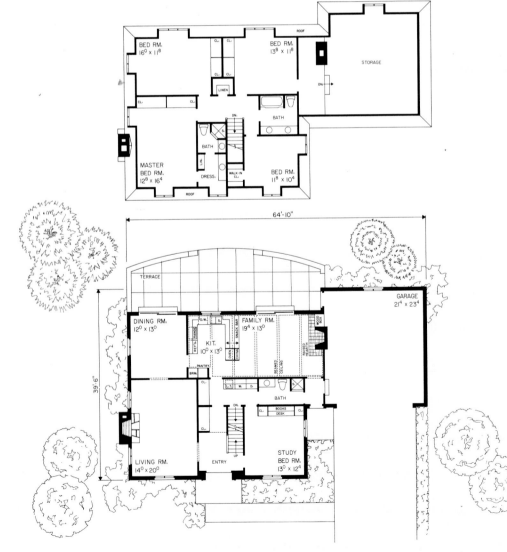

BED RM.
16⁰ x 11⁸

BED RM.
13⁸ x 11⁸

STORAGE

LINEN

BATH

BATH

MASTER
BED RM.
12⁸ x 16⁴

BED RM.
11⁸ x 10⁴

DRESS.

WALK-IN CL.

64'-10"

TERRACE

GARAGE
21⁴ x 23⁴

DINING RM.
12⁰ x 13⁰

FAMILY RM.
19⁴ x 13⁰

KIT.
10⁰ x 13⁰

39'-6"

PANTRY

BATH

LIVING RM.
14⁰ x 20⁰

ENTRY

STUDY
BED RM.
13⁰ x 12⁴

BOOKS
DESK

Design T172249
1,417 Sq. Ft. - First Floor
1,171 Sq Ft. - Second Floor
39,714 Cu. Ft.

● The formality of French design is certainly impressive. This Mansard version has a noticeably hipped roof. The delicate nature of the exterior's architectural detailing is pleasing to behold. The recessed front entrance features patterned double doors. Radial topped window openings add that extra measure of distinction. The dentil work, the brick quoins at the corners, the carriage lamps, the chimney caps, and the contrasting exterior materials (wood shingles and brick veneer) are among the additional exterior features. The interior layout is practical and, indeed, efficient. The end-living and dining rooms will foster formal living patterns, while the outstanding kitchen and family room will function together in a delightfully informal fashion.

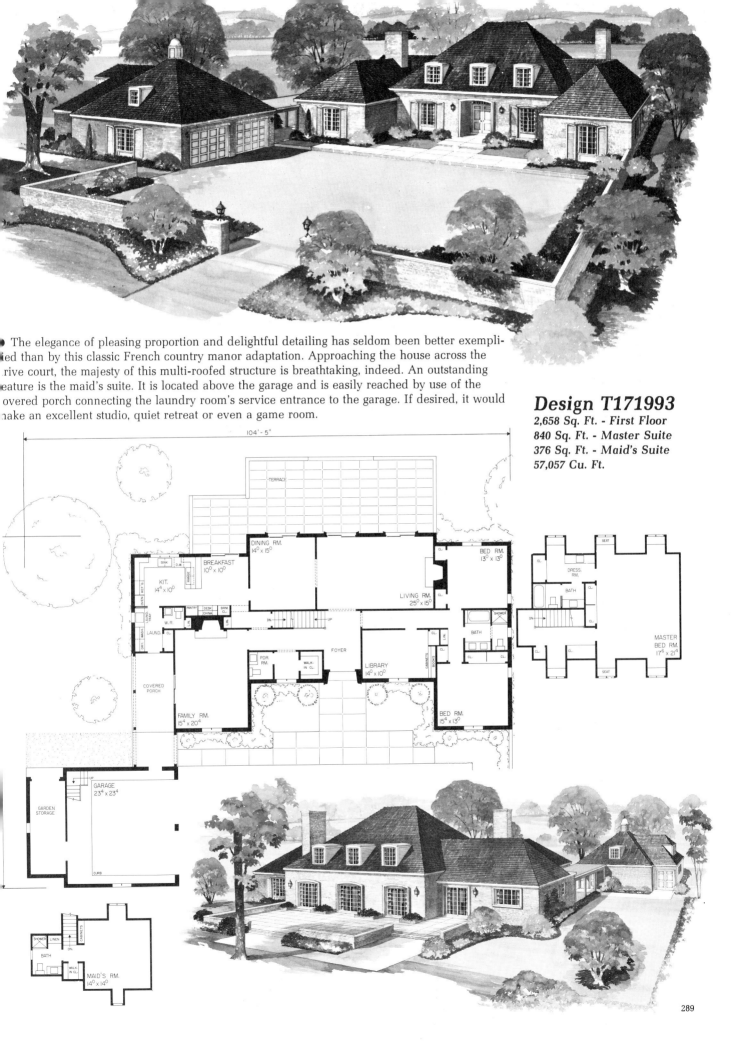

The elegance of pleasing proportion and delightful detailing has seldom been better exemplified than by this classic French country manor adaptation. Approaching the house across the drive court, the majesty of this multi-roofed structure is breathtaking, indeed. An outstanding feature is the maid's suite. It is located above the garage and is easily reached by use of the covered porch connecting the laundry room's service entrance to the garage. If desired, it would make an excellent studio, quiet retreat or even a game room.

Design T171993
2,658 Sq. Ft. - First Floor
840 Sq. Ft. - Master Suite
376 Sq. Ft. - Maid's Suite
57,057 Cu. Ft.

Design T172940   4,786 Sq. Ft. - First Floor; 1,842 Sq. Ft. - Second Floor; 144,048 Cu.

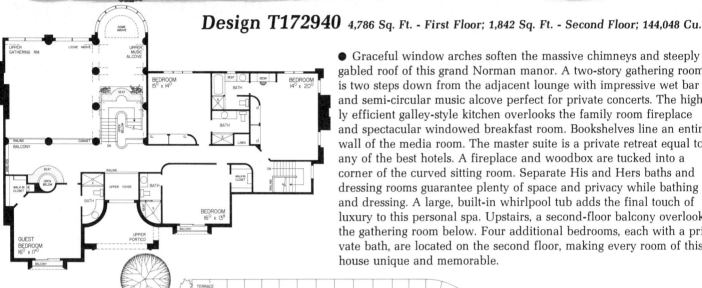

● Graceful window arches soften the massive chimneys and steeply gabled roof of this grand Norman manor. A two-story gathering room is two steps down from the adjacent lounge with impressive wet bar and semi-circular music alcove perfect for private concerts. The highly efficient galley-style kitchen overlooks the family room fireplace and spectacular windowed breakfast room. Bookshelves line an entire wall of the media room. The master suite is a private retreat equal to any of the best hotels. A fireplace and woodbox are tucked into a corner of the curved sitting room. Separate His and Hers baths and dressing rooms guarantee plenty of space and privacy while bathing and dressing. A large, built-in whirlpool tub adds the final touch of luxury to this personal spa. Upstairs, a second-floor balcony overlooks the gathering room below. Four additional bedrooms, each with a private bath, are located on the second floor, making every room of this house unique and memorable.

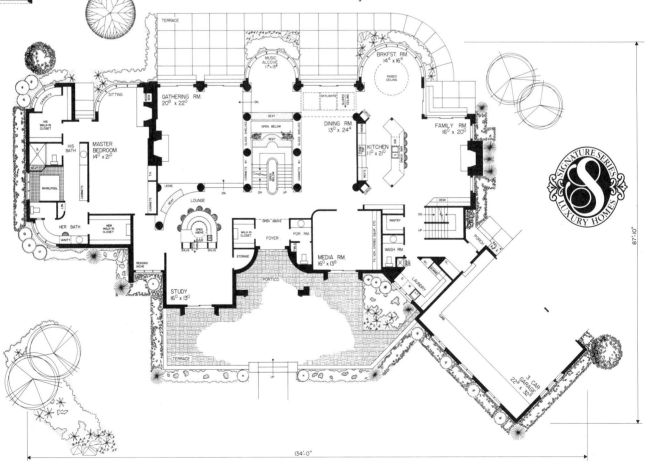

Design T172968 *3,736 Sq. Ft. - First Floor; 2,264 Sq. Ft. - Second Floor; 92,050 Cu. Ft.*

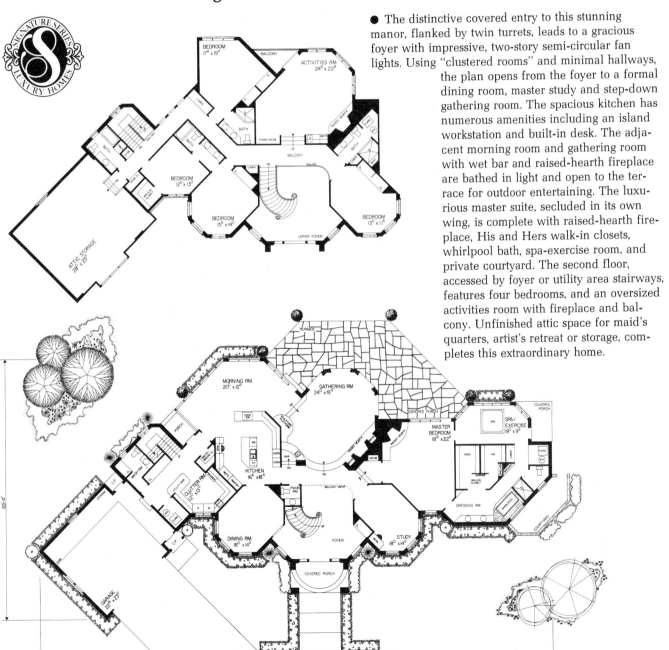

● The distinctive covered entry to this stunning manor, flanked by twin turrets, leads to a gracious foyer with impressive, two-story semi-circular fan lights. Using "clustered rooms" and minimal hallways, the plan opens from the foyer to a formal dining room, master study and step-down gathering room. The spacious kitchen has numerous amenities including an island workstation and built-in desk. The adjacent morning room and gathering room with wet bar and raised-hearth fireplace are bathed in light and open to the terrace for outdoor entertaining. The luxurious master suite, secluded in its own wing, is complete with raised-hearth fireplace, His and Hers walk-in closets, whirlpool bath, spa-exercise room, and private courtyard. The second floor, accessed by foyer or utility area stairways, features four bedrooms, and an oversized activities room with fireplace and balcony. Unfinished attic space for maid's quarters, artist's retreat or storage, completes this extraordinary home.

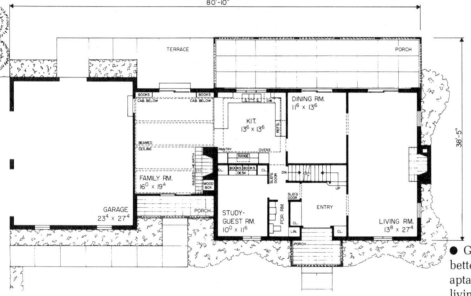

80'-10"

TERRACE · PORCH

DINING RM. 11⁶ x 13⁶

KIT. 13⁶ x 13⁶

BOOKS CAB BELOW · BOOKS CAB BELOW

BEAMED CEILING

PANTRY · RANGE · OVENS

FAMILY RM. 16⁰ x 19⁴

RAISED HEARTH

BOOKS BOOKS DESK

WOOD BOX

SLID'G DOOR

DN UP

ENTRY

38'-5"

GARAGE 23⁴ x 27⁴

PORCH

STUDY-GUEST RM. 10⁰ x 11⁶

PDR. RM.

SLID'G DOOR

CL. LIN

LIVING RM. 13⁸ x 27⁴

CL.

PORCH

BED RM. 13⁶ x 13⁶ · DRESS. RM. · MASTER BED RM. 17⁰ x 13⁶

CL.

BATH

CL. CL.

DN

HALL

BED RM. 10⁰ x 11² · LINEN · LIN. · BATH · PDR. RM. · BED RM. 13⁰ x 13⁶

Design T172222

1,485 Sq. Ft. - First Floor
1,175 Sq. Ft. - Second Floor
45,500 Cu. Ft.

● Gracious, formal living could hardly find a better backdrop than this two-story French adaptation. The exterior is truly exquisite. Inside, living patterns will be most enjoyable.

Design T172281

1,961 Sq. Ft. - First Floor
1,472 Sq. Ft. - Second Floor; 49,974 Cu. Ft.

● Regal in character, this French design is a fine example of excellent proportion and perfect symmetry. The distinctiveness of this home continues right through the front doors into the spacious entrance hall with its curving staircase.

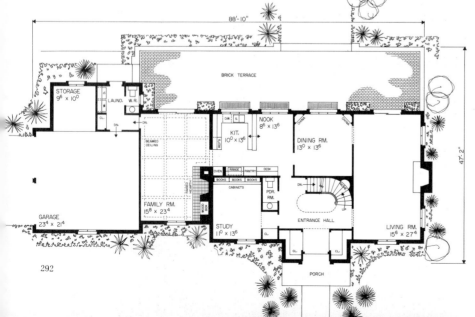

88'-10"

BRICK TERRACE

STORAGE 9⁶ x 10⁰

LAUND. · W.R.

DN

NOOK 8⁶ x 13⁶

KIT. 10⁰ x 13⁶

DINING RM. 13⁰ x 13⁶

BEAMED CEILING

OVEN RANGE PANTRY DESK

BOOKS BOOKS BOOKS

CABINETS

PDR. RM.

DN

UP

47'-2"

GARAGE 23⁴ x 21⁴

FAMILY RM. 15⁸ x 23⁴

STUDY 11⁰ x 13⁶

ENTRANCE HALL

LIVING RM. 15⁶ x 27⁴

PORCH

BED RM. 10⁴ x 13⁶ · BATH · BED RM. 13⁰ x 11⁰ · BATH · VANITY · DRESSING RM.

CL.

LINEN CL. CL. CL. CL.

DN

OPEN STAIR WELL RAILING

BED RM. 15⁰ x 11⁰ · STAIR HALL · MASTER BED RM. 15⁴ x 17⁸

292

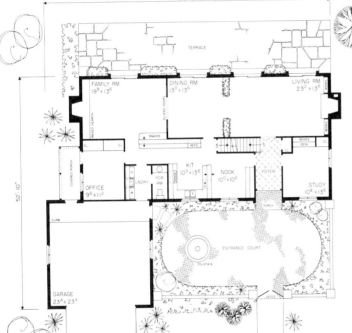

Design T172326
1,674 Sq. Ft. - First Floor
1,107 Sq. Ft. - Second Floor
53,250 Cu. Ft.

● If your family enjoys the view of the backyard, then this is the design for you. The main rooms, family, dining and living, are all in the back of the plan, each having sliding glass doors to the terrace. They are away from the confusion of the work center, yet easily accessible. A study and separate office are also available. Four bedrooms are on the second floor. Be sure to note all of the features in the master bedroom suite.

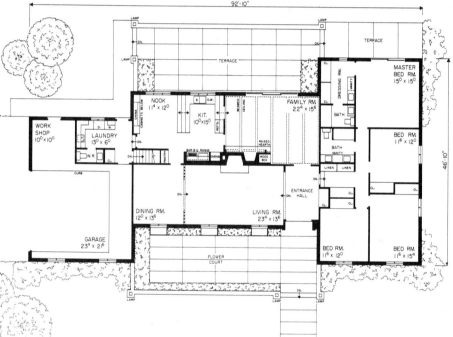

Design T172220
2,646 Sq. Ft.; 46,880 Cu. Ft.

● The gracious formality of this home is reminiscent of a popularly accepted French styling. The hip-roof, the brick quoins, the cornice details, the arched window heads, the distinctive shutters, the recessed double front doors, the massive center chimney, and the delightful flower court are all features which set the dramatic appeal of this home. This floor plan is a favorite of many. The four bedroom, two bath sleeping wing is a zone by itself. Further, the formal living and dining rooms are ideally located. For entertaining they function well together and look out upon the pleasant flower court. Overlooking the raised living terrace at the rear are the family and breakfast rooms and work center. Don't miss the laundry, extra washroom and workshop in garage.

Design T171892
2,036 Sq. Ft.; 26,575 Cu. Ft.

● The romance of French Provincial is
captured here by the hip-roof masses,
the charm of the window detailing, the
brick quoins at the corners, the delicate
dentil work at the cornices, the massive
centered chimney, and the recessed
double front doors. The slightly raised
entry court completes the picture. The
basic floor plan is a favorite of many.
And little wonder, for all areas work
well together, while still maintaining a
fine degree of separation of functions.
The highlight of the interior, perhaps,
will be the sunken living room. The
family room, with its beamed ceiling,
will not be far behind in its popularity.
The separate dining room, mud room,
efficient kitchen, complete the livability.

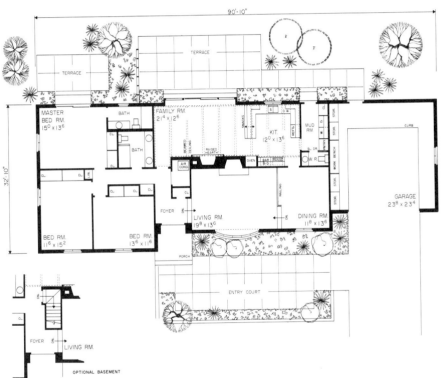

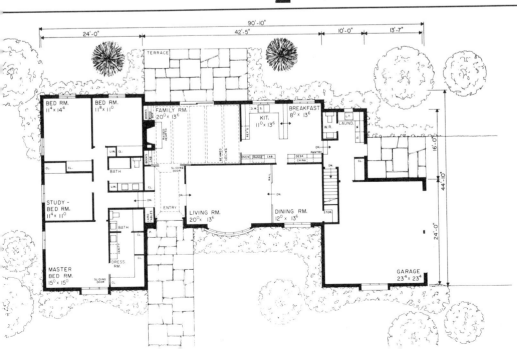

Design T172134
2,530 Sq. Ft.; 44,458 Cu. Ft.

● This delightfully symmetrical
French adaptation features two
projecting wings with hip-roofs,
brick quoins, and effective window treatment. Contrast this
popular basic floor plan with
others on these two pages. Observe the different location of
the master bedroom, the differing laundry layout and the
family room fireplace. The U-
shaped kitchen has an abundance of cupboard and counter
space and features a pass-thru
to the breakfast room. Don't
miss the planning desk, china
cabinet and pantry storage.

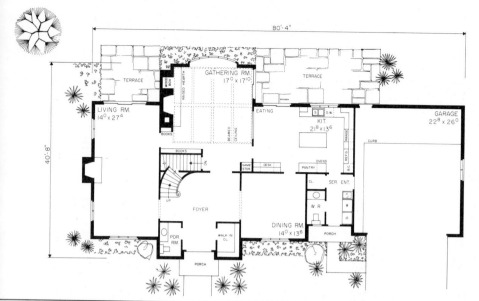

Design T172503
1,847 Sq. Ft. - First Floor
1,423 Sq. Ft. - Second Floor
50,671 Cu. Ft.

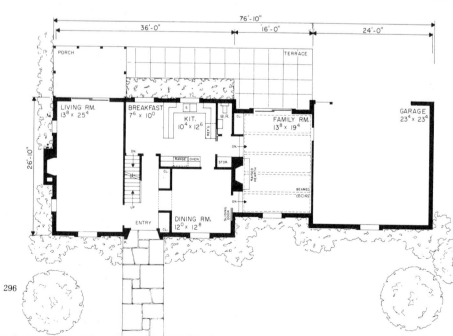

Design T171260
1,318 Sq. Ft. - First Floor
989 Sq. Ft. - Second Floor
31,787 Cu. Ft.

296

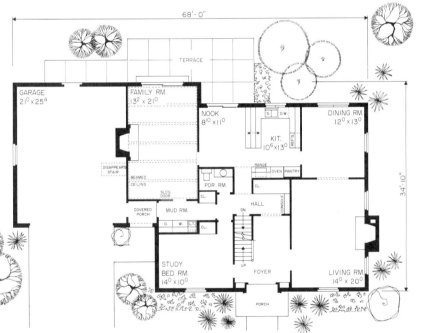

GARAGE
21⁰ x 25⁴

TERRACE

FAMILY RM.
13² x 21⁰

NOOK
8¹⁰ x 11⁰

DINING RM.
12⁰ x 13⁰

KIT.
10⁶ x 13⁰

DISAPPEARING STAIR

BEAMED CEILING

SLD'G DOOR

PDR. RM.

RANGE OVEN PANTRY

COVERED PORCH

MUD RM.

HALL

STUDY
BED RM.
14⁰ x 10⁰

DN

UP

FOYER

LIVING RM.
14⁰ x 20⁰

PORCH

68'-0"

34'-10"

BED RM.
15⁴ x 11⁴

BED RM.
15⁸ x 11⁴

BATH

BATH

BED RM.
12⁴ x 10⁰

MASTER
BED RM.
17⁰ x 13⁰

STORAGE

DN

LIN.

Design T171774
1,574 Sq. Ft. - First Floor
1,124 Sq. Ft. - Second Floor
37,616 Cu. Ft.

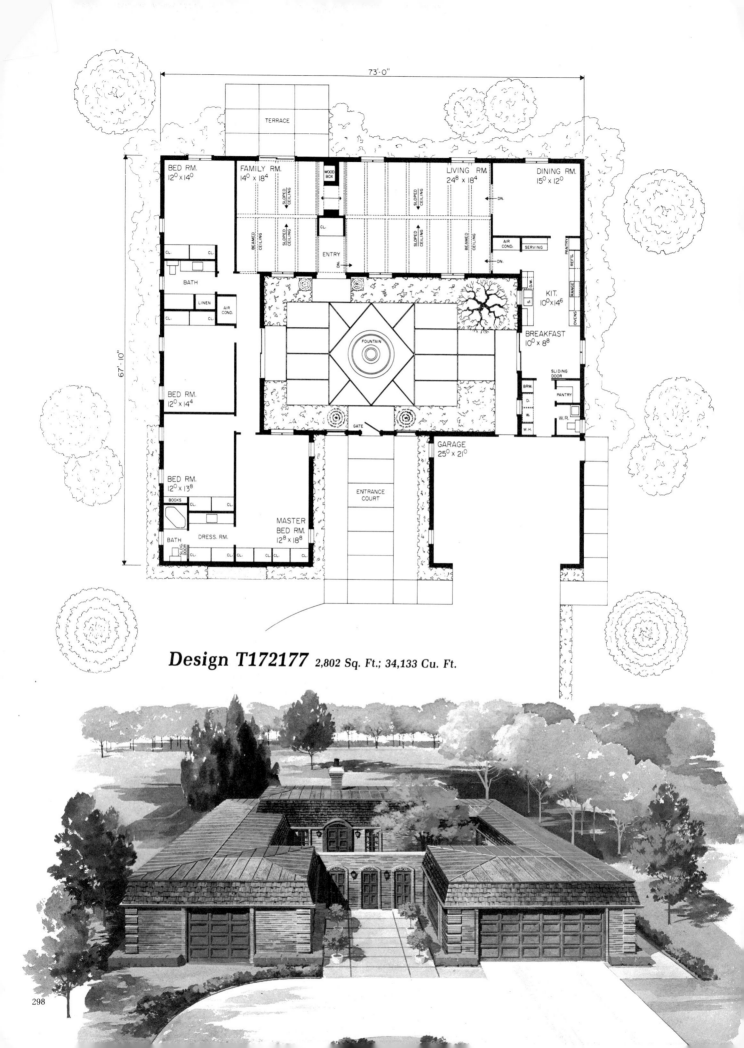

73'-0"

67'-10"

TERRACE

BED RM.
12⁰ x 14⁰

FAMILY RM.
14⁰ x 18⁴

WOOD BOX

LIVING RM.
24⁸ x 18⁴

DINING RM.
15⁰ x 12⁰

SLOPED CEILING

BEAMED CEILING

SLOPED CEILING

CL.

ENTRY

DN.

DN.

AIR COND.

SERVING

PANTRY

REF'L.

RANGE

OVENS

CL.

CL.

BATH

LINEN

AIR COND.

CL.

CL.

KIT.
10⁰ x 14⁶

LOW

BREAKFAST
10⁰ x 8⁸

FOUNTAIN

BED RM.
12⁰ x 14⁴

BRM.

D.

W.

W.H.

SLIDING DOOR

PANTRY

W.R.

GATE

BED RM.
12⁰ x 13⁸

BOOKS

CL.

CL.

GARAGE
25⁰ x 21⁰

BATH

SLIDING DOOR

DRESS. RM.

CL.

CL.

CL.

CL.

CL.

MASTER BED RM.
12⁸ x 18⁸

ENTRANCE COURT

Design T172177 2,802 Sq. Ft.; 34,133 Cu. Ft.

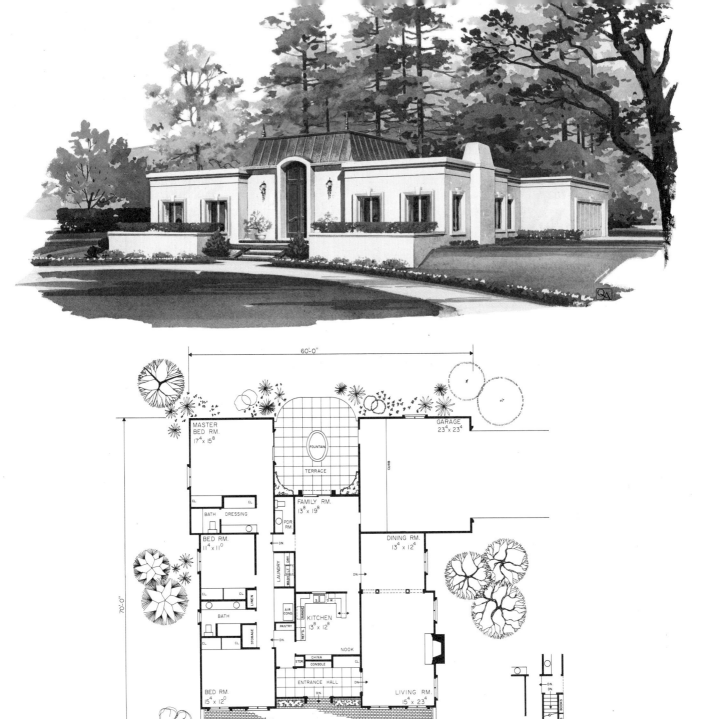

MASTER BED RM. 17⁴ x 15⁸

GARAGE 23⁴ x 23⁴

60'-0"

FOUNTAIN

TERRACE

BATH   DRESSING

CL   CL

FAMILY RM. 13⁸ x 19⁸

POR. RM.

DN.

BED RM. 11⁴ x 11⁰

DINING RM. 13⁴ x 12⁴

70'-0"

CL

LAUNDRY   WASH   DRY

DN.

CL   CL   LINEN

BATH

AIR COND.

PANTRY

RANGE   S   D.W.

KITCHEN 13⁸ x 12⁸

REF'S.

CL

STORAGE

DN.

NOOK

STOR.   CHINA   CONSOLE   CL

BED RM. 15⁴ x 12⁰

ENTRANCE HALL

DN.

DN.

DN.

LIVING RM. 15⁴ x 23⁴

TERRACE

DN.

DN.

BOOKS   BOOKS

LINEN   LAUNDRY   WASH   DRY   RANGE

STORAGE   PANTRY   REF'S.   DN.

OPTIONAL BASEMENT

Design T172347 2,322 Sq. Ft.; 26,572 Cu. Ft.

● The regal character of this distinctive home is most inviting. The symmetry of the front exterior is enhanced by the raised terrace. The recessed front entrance shelters panelled double doors which open to the formal hall. Traffic may pass to the right directly into the sunken living room. To the left is the sunken three bedroom, two-bath sleeping area. The center of the plan features the efficient kitchen with nook space and the family room. The rear terrace, enclosed on three sides to assure privacy, is accessible from master bedroom, as well as family room, through sliding glass doors. Separating the formal living and dining rooms are finely proportioned, round wood columns. Don't overlook the first floor laundry. Blueprints include details for optional partial basement.

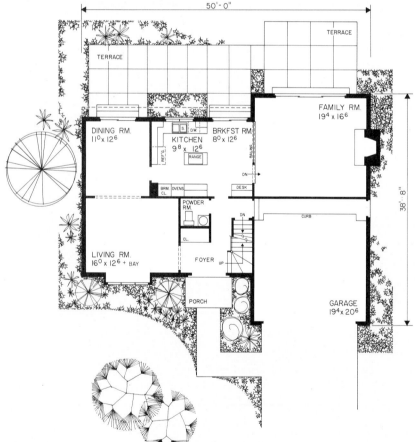

Design T172798
1,149 Sq. Ft. - First Floor
850 Sq. Ft. - Second Floor
28,450 Cu. Ft.

● An island range in the kitchen is a great feature of the work center in this two-story French designed home. The breakfast room has an open railing to the sunken family room so it can enjoy the view of the family room's fireplace.

Sliding glass doors in each of the major rear rooms, dining, breakfast and family rooms, lead to the terrace for outdoor enjoyment. The front, formal living room is highlighted by a bay window. A powder room is conven-

iently located on the first floor near all of the major areas. All of the sleeping facilities are housed on the second floor. Each of the four bedrooms will serve its occupants ideally. A relatively narrow lot can house this design.

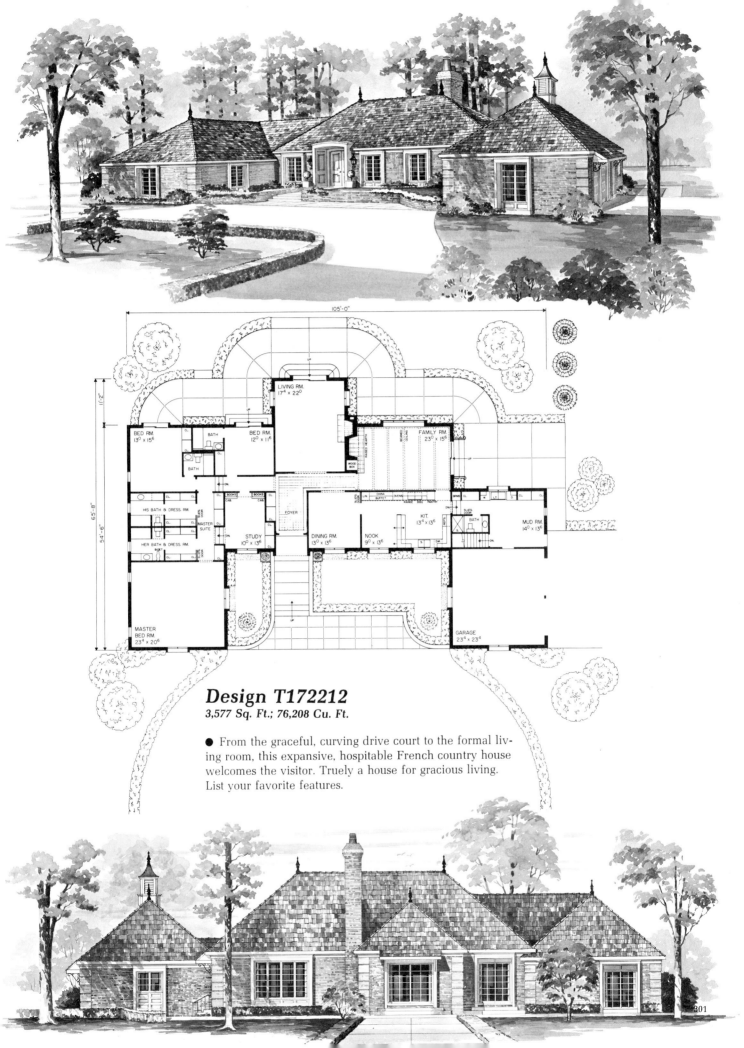

Design T172212

3,577 Sq. Ft.; 76,208 Cu. Ft.

● From the graceful, curving drive court to the formal living room, this expansive, hospitable French country house welcomes the visitor. Truely a house for gracious living. List your favorite features.

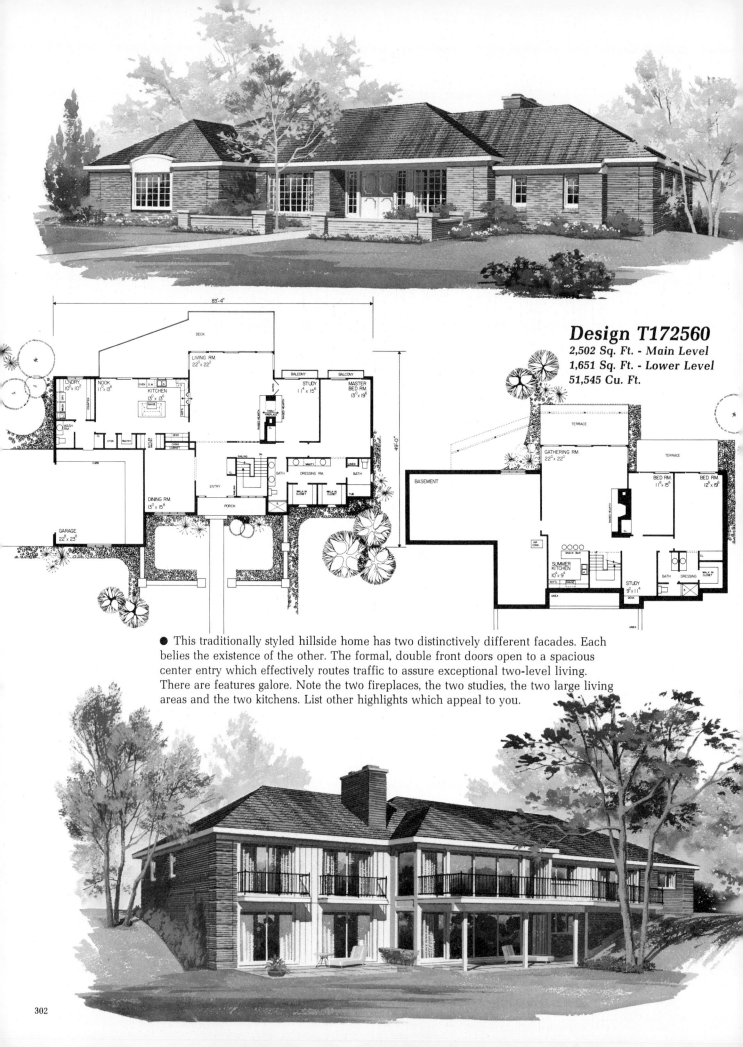

Design T172560
2,502 Sq. Ft. - Main Level
1,651 Sq. Ft. - Lower Level
51,545 Cu. Ft.

83'-4"

49'-0"

DECK

LIVING RM.
22⁰ x 22²

BALCONY | BALCONY

STUDY
11⁴ x 15⁶

MASTER
BED RM.
13⁰ x 19⁶

LNDRY.
10⁰ x 10²

NOOK
11⁰ x 13⁶

OVEN D.W.

KITCHEN
13⁰ x 13⁶

RANGE

THRU
FIREPLACE

CL.

WASH.
RM.

STOR. PANTRY

BUTLER'S
PANTRY

DESK

CHINA
CABINET

RAILING DN

BATH

VANITY

DRESSING RM.

LINEN

BATH

CURB

CL.

ENTRY

WALK IN
CLOSET

WALK IN
CLOSET

TUB

DINING RM.
13⁰ x 15⁶

PORCH

GARAGE
22⁸ x 23⁰

TERRACE

GATHERING RM.
22⁰ x 22⁰

TERRACE

BASEMENT

BED RM.
11⁸ x 15⁶

BED RM.
12⁸ x 19⁸

CL.

AIR
COND

SNACK BAR

SUMMER
KITCHEN
10⁰ x 9⁰

REF. RANGE

STUDY
9⁰ x 11⁴

DESK

BATH

DRESSING

WALK IN
CLOSET

UNEX.

UNEX.

● This traditionally styled hillside home has two distinctively different facades. Each belies the existence of the other. The formal, double front doors open to a spacious center entry which effectively routes traffic to assure exceptional two-level living. There are features galore. Note the two fireplaces, the two studies, the two large living areas and the two kitchens. List other highlights which appeal to you.

How To Read Floor Plans and Blueprints

Selecting the most suitable house plan for your family is a matter of matching your needs, tastes, and life-style against the many designs we offer. When you study the floor plans in this issue, and the blueprints that you may subsequently order, remember that they are simply a two-dimensional representation of what will eventually be a three-dimensional reality.

Floor plans are easy to read. Rooms are clearly labeled, with dimensions given in feet and inches. Most symbols are logical and self-explanatory: The location of bathroom fixtures, planters, fireplaces, tile floors, cabinets and counters, sinks, appliances, closets, and sloped or beamed ceilings will be obvious.

A blueprint, although much more detailed, is also easy to read; all it demands is concentration. The blueprints that we offer come in many large sheets, each one of which contains a different kind of information. One sheet contains foundation and excavation drawings, another has a precise plot plan. An elevations sheet deals with the exterior walls of the house; section drawings show precise dimensions, fittings, doors, windows, and roof structures. This provides all the construction information needed by your contractor. And each set of blueprints contains a lengthy materials list with size and quantities of all necessary components. Using this list, your contractor and suppliers can make a start at calculating costs for you.

When you first study a floor plan or blueprint, imagine that you are walking through the house. By mentally visualizing each room in three dimensions, you can transform the technical data and symbols into something more real. Interior space should be organized in a logical way, based on the intended use of such space. Usually the space is divided into rooms which fall into one of three categories. The sleeping area includes bedrooms and bathrooms; the work area includes the kitchen, laundry, utility room, garage and other functional rooms; the living area includes the living and dining rooms, family room, and other gathering areas as well as entrance ways.

To begin a mental tour of the home, start at the front door. It's preferable to have a foyer or entrance hall in which to receive guests. A closet here is desirable; a powder room is a plus.

Look for good traffic circulation as you study the floor plan. You should not have to pass all the way through one main room to reach another. From the entrance area you should have direct access to the three principal areas of a house—the living, work, and sleeping zones. For example, a foyer might provide separate entrances to the living room, kitchen, patio, and a hallway or staircase leading to the bedrooms.

Study the layout of each zone. Most people expect the living room to be protected from cross traffic. The kitchen, on the other hand, should connect with the dining room—and perhaps also the utility room, basement, garage, patio or deck, or a secondary entrance. A homemaker whose workday centers in the kitchen may have special requirements: a window that faces the backyard; a clear view of the family room where children play; a garage or driveway entrance that allows for a short trip with groceries; laundry facilities close at hand. Check for efficient placement of kitchen cabinets, counters, and appliances. Is there enough room in the kitchen for additional appliances, for eating in? Is there a dining nook?

Perhaps this part of the house contains a family room or a den/bedroom/office. It's advantageous to have a bathroom or powder room in this section.

As you study the plan, you may encounter a staircase, indicated by a group of parallel lines, the number of lines equaling the number of steps. Arrows labeled "up" mean that the staircase leads to a higher level, and those pointing down mean it leads to a lower one. Staircases in a split-level will have both up and down arrows on one staircase because two levels are depicted in one drawing and an extra level in another.

Notice the location of the stairways. Is too much floor space lost to them? Will you find yourself making too many trips?

Study the sleeping quarters. Are the bedrooms situated as you like? You may want the master bedroom near the kids, or you may want it as far away as possible. Is there at least one closet per person in each bedroom or a double one for a couple? Bathrooms should be convenient to each bedroom—if not adjoining, then with hallway access and on the same floor.

Once you are familiar with the relative positions of the rooms, look for such structural details as:

- Sufficient uninterrupted wall space for furniture arrangement.

- Adequate room dimensions.

- Potential heating or cooling problems—such as a room over a garage or next to the laundry.

- Window and door placement for good ventilation and natural light.

- Location of doorways— avoid having a basement staircase or a bathroom in view of the dining room.

- Adequate auxiliary space— closets, storage, bathrooms, countertops.

- Separation of activity areas. (Will noise from the recreation room disturb sleeping children or a parent at work?)

As you complete your mental walk through the house, bear in mind your family's long-range needs. A good house plan will allow for some adjustments now and additions in the future.

Take time to notice special amenities about the house. Look for through-fireplaces and raised hearths, work islands in the kitchen, pass-through countertops between kitchen and breakfast nook, whirlpool baths, and convenient built-ins such as bookcases and wet bars. Note the placement of decks and balconies. Each member of your family may find the listing of favorite features a most helpful exercise. Why not try it?

Ordering Your Plans

The Basic Blueprint Package

Each set of blueprints is an interrelated collection of plans, measurements, drawings, and diagrams showing precisely how your house comes together. Here's what it includes.

Building a home? Planning a home? The Basic Blueprint Package from Home Planners, Inc., contains nearly everything you need to get the job done right, whether you're working on your own or with help from an architect, designer, builder, or subcontractors. Each Basic Blueprint Package includes detailed architect's blueprints and a specification outline.

Foundation plan. A complete basement and foundation plan in ¼-inch scale, plus a sample plot plan for locating your house on a building site.

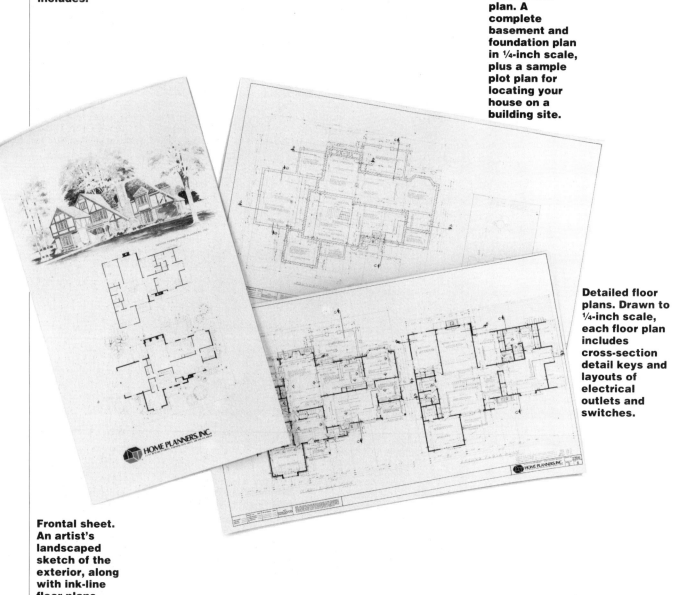

Detailed floor plans. Drawn to ¼-inch scale, each floor plan includes cross-section detail keys and layouts of electrical outlets and switches.

Frontal sheet. An artist's landscaped sketch of the exterior, along with ink-line floor plans.

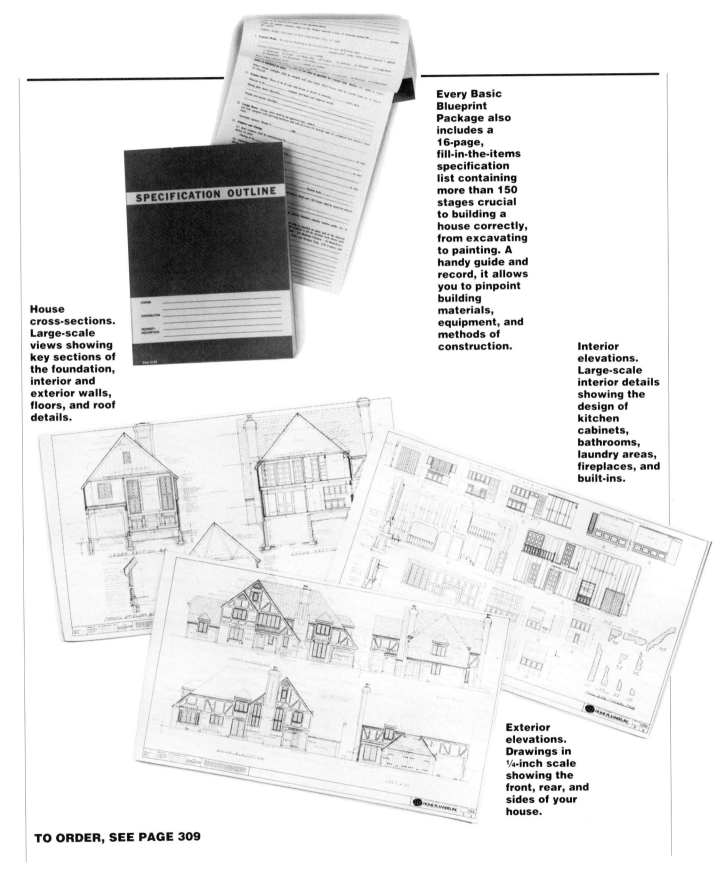

House cross-sections. Large-scale views showing key sections of the foundation, interior and exterior walls, floors, and roof details.

Every Basic Blueprint Package also includes a 16-page, fill-in-the-items specification list containing more than 150 stages crucial to building a house correctly, from excavating to painting. A handy guide and record, it allows you to pinpoint building materials, equipment, and methods of construction.

Interior elevations. Large-scale interior details showing the design of kitchen cabinets, bathrooms, laundry areas, fireplaces, and built-ins.

Exterior elevations. Drawings in ¼-inch scale showing the front, rear, and sides of your house.

TO ORDER, SEE PAGE 309

Important Extras

MATERIALS LIST

If you choose, we can provide a materials take-off for your plan. An important part of the building package, this list outlines the quantity, type, and size of everything needed to build your house (with the exception of mechanical materials). Included are:
- masonry, veneer, and fireplace;
- framing lumber;
- roofing and sheet metal;
- windows and door frames;
- exterior trim and insulation;
- tile and flooring;
- interior trim;
- kitchen cabinets;
- rough and finish hardware.

The list, which you pay for only once no matter how many blueprints you order, is not only a directory of the products destined for your house, it's a useful tool, as well. It can help you cost out materials and serve as a handy reference sheet when you're compiling bids. And it can help coordinate the substitution of building materials when you need to meet local codes, use available supplies, satisfy personal preferences, and the like.

(Because of differing codes and methods of installation, our lists don't include mechanical materials and specifications. To get the necessary take-offs, consult local heating, plumbing, and electrical contractors or a local lumberyard or building supply center. Materials lists are not sold separately from the Blueprint Package.)

PLUMBING DETAILS

The Basic Blueprint Package includes locations for all the plumbing fixtures in your house, including sinks, lavatories, tubs, showers, toilets, laundry trays and water heaters. If you want to find out more about the intricacies of household plumbing, these 24 x 36-inch drawings—six individual, fact-packed sheets—will prove to be remarkably useful tools. Prepared to meet requirements of the National Plumbing Code, these valuable Plumbing Details show pipe schedules, fittings, sump-pump details, water-softener hookups, septic system details and many more. Sheets are bound together and color coded for easy reference. A glossary of terms is included.

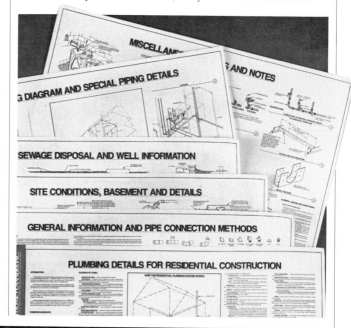

CONSTRUCTION DETAILS

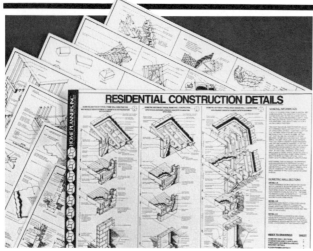

The Basic Blueprint Package contains everything an experienced builder needs to construct a particular plan. However, it doesn't show all the different ways building materials come together to form a house, or all construction techniques used by skilled artisans. To show you a variety of additional techniques and materials, we also offer a complete set of detail drawings that depict—in an exquisitely precise way—the materials and methods used to build foundations, fireplaces, walls, floors, and roofs. What's more, where appropriate, the drawings depict acceptable alternatives. For the advanced do-it-yourselfer, owner-builder-to-be, or the inquisitive home planner, these construction details are the perfect complement to the basic package.

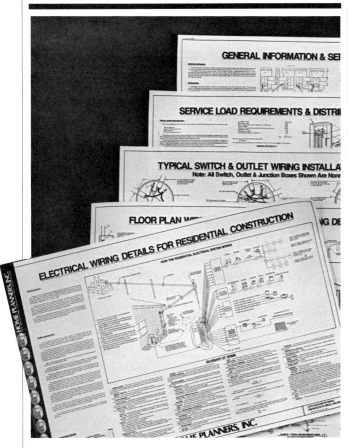

ELECTRICAL DETAILS

The Basic Blueprint Package shows positions for every electrical switch, plug, and outlet. However, our Electrical Details go further to take the mystery out of household electrical systems. These comprehensive 24 x 36-inch drawings come packed with helpful details. Prepared to meet requirements of the National Electrical Code, the six fact-filled sheets cover a variety of topics including appliance wattage, wire sizing, switch-installation schematics, cable-routing details, doorbell hookups, and many others. Sheets are bound together and color coded for easy reference. A glossy of terms is also included.

Our plumbing, electrical and construction details can be remarkably useful tools. Although we don't recommend that you attempt intricate plumbing or electrical installations, or complicated building projects, these drawings will help you accomplish certain tasks and will give you and your family a thorough working knowledge with which to deal confidently with subcontractors.

PLAN-A-HOME™

Plan-A-Home™ is a very useful tool. It's an easy-to-use product that will help you design a new home, arrange furniture in a new or existing home or plan a remodeling project. Each package contains:

● more than **700 planning symbols** on a self-stick vinyl sheet, including walls, windows, doors, furniture, kitchen components, bath fixtures, and many more. All are made of a durable, peel-and-stick vinyl you can use over and over;

● a reusable, transparent, **¼-inch-scale planning grid** that can help you create house layouts up to 140x92 feet;

● **tracing paper** and a protective separating sheet;

● a **felt-tip pen**, with water-soluble ink that wipes away quickly. The transparent planning grid matches the scale of actual working blueprints (¼ inch equals 1 foot). You can lay it over existing drawings and modify them as necessary or plan furniture arrangements before you build. Every Plan-A-Home™ package lets you lay out areas as large as a 7,500-square-foot, six-bedroom, seven-bath home. Note, however, that Plan-A-Home™ isn't meant to replace construction drawings. When you've planned a building project, consult an architect, designer, or contractor for help in developing or revising your drawings.

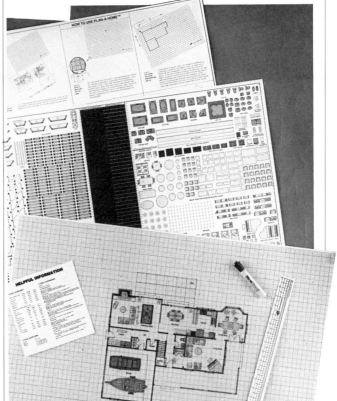

TO ORDER, SEE PAGE 309

Price Schedule & Design Index

The blueprints you order are a master plan for building your new home (as well as an entertaining introduction to the shape of things to come). Even the smallest house featured in this plan book is a complicated combination of construction data and architectural detailing. Bigger houses, irregularly shaped houses, and houses with an abundance of design features are even more complex and require proportionately greater resources to plan and develop. The schedule below takes these factors into account when pricing each of the plans. When you're ready to fill out an order, note the index letter (A,B,C,D or E) opposite the design number of your choice below. Then refer to the appropriate prices to the right.

NUMBER OF SETS	PRICE GROUP				
	A	B	C	D	E
1	$125	$150	$175	$200	$300
4	$175	$200	$225	$250	$350
8	$225	$250	$275	$300	$400
Sepia	$250	$300	$350	$400	$500

Additional identical sets in same order $30 each.

Reverse sets (mirror image) $30 each.

Materials List just $25 for Price Group A-D, $35 for Price Group E. (One list supplied with each set.)

Before You Order

1. STUDY THE DESIGNS . . . found in Home Planners and Heritage Homes plan books. As you review these delightful custom homes, you should keep in mind the total living requirements of your family — both indoors and outdoors. Although we do not make changes in plans, many minor changes can be made prior to construction. If major changes are involved to satisfy your personal requirements, you should consider ordering one set of sepias and having them modified. Consultation with your architect is strongly advised when contemplating major changes.

2. HOW TO ORDER BLUEPRINTS . . . After you have chosen the design that satisfies your requirements, or if you have selected one that you wish to study in more detail, simply clip the accompanying order blank and mail with your remittance. However, if it is not convenient for you to send a check or money order, you can use your credit card, or merely indicate C.O.D. shipment. Postman will collect all charges, including postage and C.O.D. fee. C.O.D. shipments are not permitted to Canada or foreign countries. Should time be of essence, as it sometimes is with many of our customers, your telephone order usually can be processed and shipped in the next day's mail. Simply call toll free 1-800-521-6797.

3. OUR SERVICE . . . Home Planners makes every effort to process and ship each order for blueprints and books within 48 hours. Because of this, we have deemed it unnecessary to acknowledge receipt

How Many Blueprints Do You Need?

Because additional sets of the same design in each order are only $30.00 each, you save considerably by ordering your total requirements now. To help you determine the exact number of sets, please refer to the handy checklist below.

Blueprint Checklist

___**OWNER'S SET(S)**

___**BUILDER** (Usually requires at least three sets: one as legal document; one for inspection; and at least one for tradesmen — usually more.)

___**BUILDING PERMIT** (Sometimes two sets are required.)

___**MORTGAGE SOURCE** (Usually one set for a conventional mortgage; three sets for F.H.A. or V.A. type mortgages.)

___**SUBDIVISION COMMITTEE** (If any.)

___**TOTAL NUMBER SETS REQUIRED**

BLUEPRINT HOTLINE

PHONE TOLL FREE: 1-800-521-6797.
Orders received by 6 p.m. (Eastern time) will be processed the same day and shipped to you the following day. Use of this line is restricted to blueprint and book ordering only.

KINDLY NOTE: When ordering by phone, please state Order Form Key Number located in box at lower left corner of the blueprint order form.

IN CANADA: Add 20% to prices listed on this order form and mail in Canadian funds to:
HOME PLANNERS, INC.
20 Cedar St. North
Kitchener, Ontario N2H 2W8
Phone: (519) 743-4169

of our customers orders. See order coupon for the postage and handling charges for surface mail, air mail or foreign mail.

4. MODIFYING OUR PLANS . . . Slight revisions are easy to do before you start building. (We don't alter plans, by the way.) If you're thinking about major changes, consider ordering a set of sepias. After changes have been made on the sepia, additional sets of plans may be reproduced from the sepia master. Should you decide to revise the plan significantly, we strongly suggest that you consult an experienced architect or designer.

5. A NOTE REGARDING REVERSE BLUE-PRINTS . . . As a special service to those wishing to build in reverse of the plan as shown, we do include an extra set of reversed blueprints for only $30.00 additional with each order. Even though the lettering and dimensions appear backward on reversed blueprints, they make a handy reference because they show the house just as it's being built in reverse from the standard blueprints — thereby helping you visualize the home better.

6. OUR EXCHANGE POLICY . . . Since blueprints are printed in response to your order, we cannot honor requests for refunds. However, we will exchange your entire first order for an equal number of blueprints at a price of $20.00 for the first set and $10.00 for each additional set. All sets from the previous order must be returned before the exchange can take place. Please add $3.00 for postage and handling via surface mail; $4.00 via air mail.

TO: ⬡ **HOME PLANNERS, INC., 3275 WEST INA ROAD, SUITE 110 TUCSON, ARIZONA 85741**

Please rush me the following:

___ SET(S) BLUEPRINTS FOR DESIGN NO(S). . . . . Kindly refer to Blueprint Price Schedule on opposite page.	$___
___ SEPIA FOR DESIGN NO(S).	$___
___ MATERIALS LIST @ $25.00.	$___
___ ADDITIONAL SPECIFICATION OUTLINES @ $5.00 each	$___
___ DETAIL SETS @ $14.95 ea.; any two for $22.95; all three for $29.95 . . . . . ☐ PLUMBING ☐ ELECTRICAL ☐ CONSTRUCTION	$___
___ PLAN-A-HOME™ Design Kit @ $24.95 ea. (plus $3.00 postage)	$___
Arizona Residents add 5% sales tax; Michigan residents add 4% sales tax	$___

FOR POSTAGE AND HANDLING PLEASE CHECK ✔ & REMIT
- ☐ $4.00 Added to Order for Surface Mail (UPS) – Any Mdse.
- ☐ $5.00 Added for Priority Mail of One-Three Sets of Blueprints.
- ☐ $8.00 Added for Priority Mail of Four or more Sets of Blueprints.
- ☐ For Canadian orders add $2.00 to above applicable rates.

$___

☐ C.O.D. PAY POSTMAN (U.S. ONLY)   TOTAL in U.S. funds $___

PLEASE PRINT
Name ___
Street ___
City ___ State ___ Zip ___

CREDIT CARD ORDERS ONLY: Fill in the boxes below   Prices subject to change without notice
Credit Card No. [ ][ ][ ][ ][ ][ ][ ][ ][ ][ ][ ][ ][ ][ ]   Expiration Date Month/Year [ ][ ][ ][ ]

CHECK ONE: ☐ *VISA* ☐ MasterCard

Order Form Key TB17   Your Signature ___

BLUEPRINT ORDERS SHIPPED WITHIN 48 HOURS OF RECEIPT!

TO: ⬡ **HOME PLANNERS, INC., 3275 WEST INA ROAD, SUITE 110 TUCSON, ARIZONA 85741**

Please rush me the following:

___ SET(S) BLUEPRINTS FOR DESIGN NO(S). . . . . Kindly refer to Blueprint Price Schedule on opposite page.	$___
___ SEPIA FOR DESIGN NO(S).	$___
___ MATERIALS LIST @ $25.00.	$___
___ ADDITIONAL SPECIFICATION OUTLINES @ $5.00 each	$___
___ DETAIL SETS @ $14.95 ea.; any two for $22.95; all three for $29.95 . . . . . ☐ PLUMBING ☐ ELECTRICAL ☐ CONSTRUCTION	$___
___ PLAN-A-HOME™ Design Kit @ $24.95 ea. (plus $3.00 postage)	$___
Arizona Residents add 5% sales tax; Michigan residents add 4% sales tax	$___

FOR POSTAGE AND HANDLING PLEASE CHECK ✔ & REMIT
- ☐ $4.00 Added to Order for Surface Mail (UPS) – Any Mdse.
- ☐ $5.00 Added for Priority Mail of One-Three Sets of Blueprints.
- ☐ $8.00 Added for Priority Mail of Four or more Sets of Blueprints.
- ☐ For Canadian orders add $2.00 to above applicable rates.

$___

☐ C.O.D. PAY POSTMAN (U.S. ONLY)   TOTAL in U.S. funds $___

PLEASE PRINT
Name ___
Street ___
City ___ State ___ Zip ___

CREDIT CARD ORDERS ONLY: Fill in the boxes below   Prices subject to change without notice
Credit Card No. [ ][ ][ ][ ][ ][ ][ ][ ][ ][ ][ ][ ][ ][ ]   Expiration Date Month/Year [ ][ ][ ][ ]

CHECK ONE: ☐ *VISA* ☐ MasterCard

Order Form Key TB17   Your Signature ___

THE DESIGN CATEGORY SERIES

210 ONE STORY HOMES OVER 2,000 SQUARE FEET
Spacious homes for gracious living. Includes all popular styles—Spanish, Western, Tudor, French, Contemporary, and others. Amenity-filled plans feature master bedroom suites, atriums, courtyards, and pools.

1. 192 pages. $4.95 ($5.95 Canada)

315 ONE STORY HOMES UNDER 2,000 SQUARE FEET
Economical homes in a variety of styles. Efficient floor plans contain plenty of attractive features—gathering rooms, formal and informal living and dining rooms, mudrooms, outdoor living spaces, and more. Many plans are expandable.

2. 192 pages. $4.95 ($5.95 Canada)

150 1½ STORY HOMES
From starter homes to country estates. Includes classic story-and-a-half styles: Contemporary, Williamsburg, Georgian, Tudor, and Cape Cod. Outstanding outdoor livability. Many expandable plans.

3. 128 pages. $3.95 ($4.95 Canada)

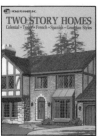

360 TWO STORY HOMES
Plans for all budgets and all families—in a wide range of styles: Tudors, Saltboxes, Farmhouses, Southern Colonials, Georgians, Contemporaries, and more. Many plans have extra-large kitchens, extra bedrooms, and extra baths.

4. 288 pages. $6.95 ($8.95 Canada)

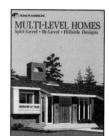

215 MULTI-LEVEL HOMES
Distinctive styles for both flat and sloping sites. Tailor-made for great outdoor living. Features include exposed lower levels, upper-level lounges, balconies, decks, and terraces. Includes plans for all building budgets.

5. 192 pages. $4.95 ($5.95 Canada)

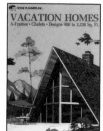

223 VACATION HOMES
Full-color volume features A-frames, chalets, lodges, hexagons, cottages, and other attractive styles in one-story, two-story, and multi-level plans ranging from 480 to 3,238 square feet. Perfect for woodland, lakeside, or seashore.

6. 176 pages. $4.95 ($5.95 Canada)

THE EXTERIOR STYLE SERIES

7.

330 EARLY AMERICAN HOME PLANS
A heart-warming collection of the best in Early American architecture. Traces the style from colonial structures to popular Traditional versions. Includes a history of different styles.
304 pages. $9.95 ($11.95 Canada)

8.

335 CONTEMPORARY HOME PLANS
Required reading for anyone interested in the clean-lined elegance of Contemporary design. Features plans of all sizes and types, as well as a fascinating look at the history of this style.
304 pages. $9.95 ($11.95 Canada)

9.

TUDOR HOUSES Here is the stuff that dream houses are made of! A superb portfolio of 80 enchanting Tudor-style homes, from cozy Cotswold cottages to impressive Baronial manors. Includes a decorating section filled with colorful photographs and illustrations showing 24 different furniture arrangements.
208 pages. $10.95 ($12.95 Canada)

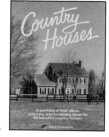

10.

COUNTRY HOUSES Shows off 80 gorgeous country homes in three eye-catching styles: Cape Cods, Farmhouses, and Center-Hall Colonials. Each features an architect's exterior rendering, artist's depiction of a furnished interior room, large floor plans, and planning tips. Full-color section presents decorating schemes for nine different rooms.
208 pages. $10.95 ($12.95 Canada)

PLAN PORTFOLIOS

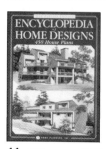

ENCYCLOPEDIA OF HOME DESIGNS (450 PLANS) The largest book of its kind—450 plans in a complete range of housing types, styles, and sizes. Includes plans for all building budgets, families, and styles of living.

11. 320 pages. $9.95 ($11.95 Canada)

MOST POPULAR HOME DESIGNS (360 PLANS) Our customers' favorite plans, including one-story, 1½-story, two-story, and multi-level homes in a variety of styles. For families large and small. Designs feature many of today's most popular amenities: lounges, clutter rooms, sunspaces, media rooms, and more.

12. 272 pages. $8.95 ($10.95 Canada)

COLOR PORTFOLIO OF HOUSES & PLANS (310 PLANS) A beautiful full-color guide to Home Planners' best plans, including Early American, Spanish, French, Tudor, Contemporary, and our own Trend Home styles. One-story, 1½-story, two-story, and multi-level designs for all budgets.

13. 288 pages. $12.95 ($14.95 Canada)

Landscaping That's Yards Ahead

Landscape Plan L220
Home Plan 2802

This revolutionary guide contains 55 gorgeous landscapes for front and back yards that you can do yourself or hire done. Designed and drawn by an award-winning landscape firm, the plans fit virtually any style house.

THE HOME LANDSCAPER
55 PROFESSIONAL LANDSCAPES YOU CAN DO
IRELAND-GANNON ASSOCIATES
AWARD-WINNING LANDSCAPE DESIGNERS

Paperback, 208 pages,
$10.95 ($12.95 Canada)

Features:
- **Colorful renderings of landscaping at full maturity**
- **Plot plans that give scale, contour, and plants**
- **Methods for adapting plans to your specific site**
- **A wealth of ideas, advice, and design tips**

PLUS a comprehensive **Blueprint Package** (available separately) that includes:
- **Regionalized plant lists**
- **Materials schedules**
- **Charts for substituting plants**
- **Installation and maintenance instructions**

Includes 40 different plans to fit these architectural styles:

- Cape Cod Traditional
- Williamsburg Cape
- Cape Cod Cottage
- Gambrel-Roof Colonial
- Center-Hall Colonial
- Classic New England Colonial
- Southern Colonial
- Country-Style Farmhouse
- Pennsylvania Stone Farmhouse
- Raised-Porch Farmhouse
- New England Barn-Style House
- New England Country House

- Traditional Country Estate
- French Provincial Estate
- Georgian Manor
- Grand-Portico Georgian
- Brick Federal
- Country French Rambler
- French Manor House
- Elizabethan Tudor
- Tudor One-Story
- English-Style Cottage
- Medieval Garrison
- Queen Anne Victorian
- Gothic Victorian
- Basic Ranch

- L-Shaped Ranch
- Sprawling Ranch
- Traditional Split-Level
- Shed-Roof Contemporary
- Wood-Sided Contemporary
- Hillside Contemporary
- Florida Rambler
- California Stucco
- Low-Gable Contemporary
- Northern Brick Chateau
- Mission-Tile Ranch
- Adobe-Block Hacienda
- Courtyard Patio Home
- Center-Court Contemporary

Plus, 15 back yard plans suited to virtually any lifestyle or activity:
- Deck and Terrace for Entertaining
- Japanese-Style Garden
- Shade Garden
- Formal Garden for Entertaining
- Children's Play Yard
- Garden to Attract Birds
- Naturalistic Grass Garden
- Pool and Deck Garden
- Naturalistic Swimming Pool
- Second-Story Deck
- Cottage Garden
- Raised Perennial Border
- Edible Landscape
- Water Garden
- Formal Rose Garden

Turn to page 311 to order.

Victorian Houses

The recent rebirth in popularity of Victorian styling is surely a welcomed development. It reintroduces to the American housing scene a unique, pleasing, and nostalgic exterior style. As this presentation illustrates, Victorian houses can come in a variety of sizes and shapes. It will be fun to compare the livability of the 1,722-square-foot design with that of the 4,540-square-foot design. As you can see, porches and verandas have returned.

Design T172971 1,766 Sq. Ft. - First Floor
1,519 Sq. Ft. - Second Floor; 55,980 Cu. Ft.

● The stately proportions and the exquisite detailing of Victorian styling are exciting, indeed. Like so many Victorian houses interesting roof lines set the character with this design. Observe the delightful mixture of gable roof, hip roof and the dramatic turret. Horizontal siding, wood shingling, wide fascia, rake and corner boards make a strong statement. Of course, the delicate detailing of the windows, railings, cornices and front entry is most appealing to the eye. Inside, a great four bedroom family living plan.

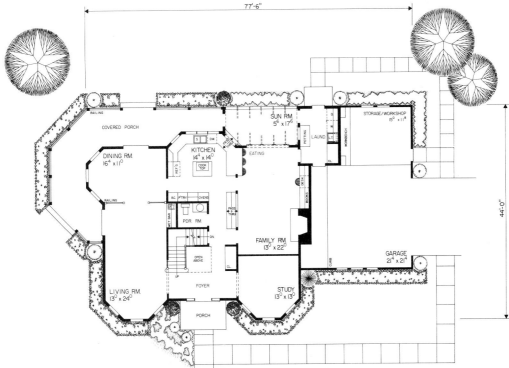

Design T172954

3,079 Sq. Ft. - First Floor
1,461 Sq. Ft. - Second Floor
112,790 Cu. Ft.

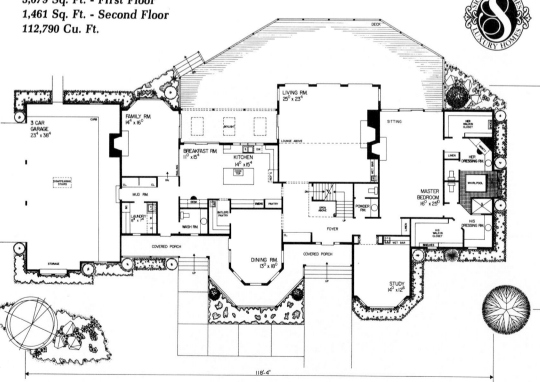

● This enchanting manor displays architectural elements typical of the Victorian style: asymmetrical facade, decorative shingles and gables, and a covered porch. The two-story living room with fireplace and wet bar is located at the rear of this home where it opens to the glass-enclosed porch with skylights. A spacious kitchen is filled with amenities including an island cooktop, built-in desk, and butler's pantry connecting to the dining room. The master suite, adjacent to the study, opens to a rear deck, perfect for taking in the night air before retiring. A cozy fireplace keeps the room warm on chilly evenings. Separate His and Hers dressing rooms are outfitted with vanities and walk-in closets, and a luxurious whirlpool tub connects the baths. The second floor opens to a large lounge with built-in cabinets and bookshelves ideal for study or peaceful relaxation. Three bedrooms and two full baths complete the second-floor livability. A three-car garage with disappearing stairs to a huge attic storage area makes this home as practical as it is charming.

● A magnificent, finely wrought covered porch wraps around this impressive Victorian estate home. The gracious two-story foyer provides a direct view past the stylish bannister and into the great room with large central fireplace. To the left of the foyer is a bookshelf-lined library and to the right is a dramatic, octagonal-shaped dining room. The island cooktop completes a convenient work triangle in the kitchen, and a pass-through connects this room with the Victorian-style morning room. A butler's pantry, walk-in closet, and broom closet offer plenty of storage space. A luxurious master suite is located on the first floor and opens to the rear covered porch. A through-fireplace warms the bedroom, sitting room, and dressing room, which includes His and Hers walk-in closets. The step-up whirlpool tub is an elegant focal point to the master bath. Four uniquely designed bedrooms, three full baths, and a restful lounge with fireplace are located on the second floor. Who says you can't combine the absolute best of today's amenities with the quaint styling and comfortable warmth of the Victorian past!

Design T172953
2,991 Sq. Ft. - First Floor
1,802 Sq. Ft. - Second Floor
132,887 Cu. Ft.

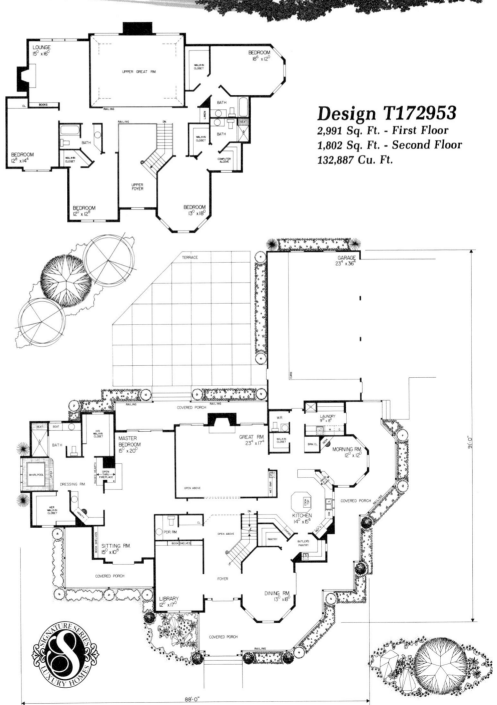

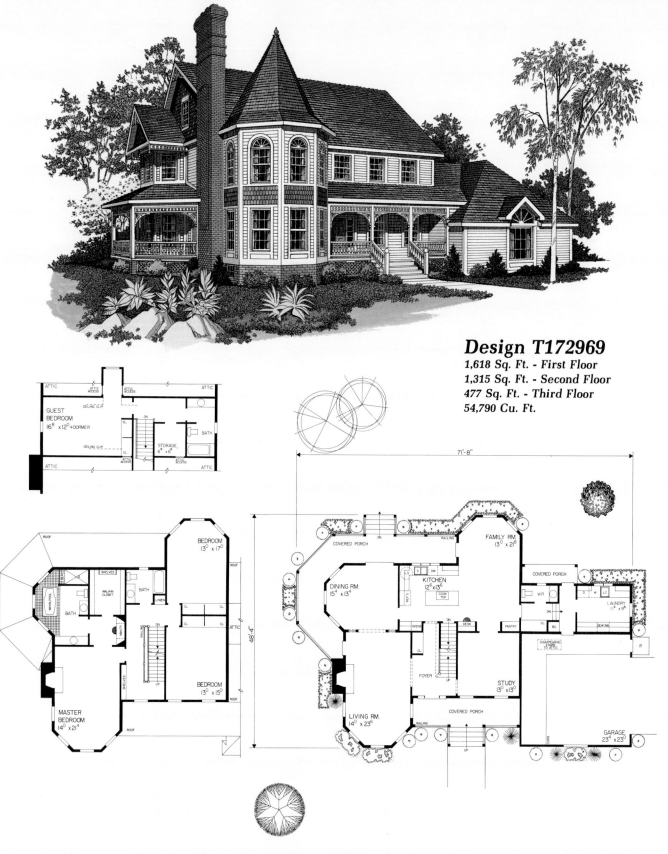

Design T172969
1,618 Sq. Ft. - First Floor
1,315 Sq. Ft. - Second Floor
477 Sq. Ft. - Third Floor
54,790 Cu. Ft.

● What could beat the charm of a turreted Victorian with covered porches to the front, side and rear? This delicately detailed exterior houses an outstanding family oriented floor plan. Projecting bays make their contribution to the exterior styling. In addition, they provide an extra measure of livability to the living, dining and family rooms, plus two of the bedrooms. The efficient kitchen, with its island cooking station, functions well with the dining and family rooms. A study provides a quiet first floor haven for the family's less active pursuits. Upstairs there are three big bedrooms and a fine master bath. The third floor provides a guest suite and huge bulk storage area (make it a cedar closet if you wish). This house has a basement for the development of further recreational and storage facilities. Don't miss the two fireplaces, large laundry and attached two-car garage. A great investment.

Design T172973

1,269 Sq. Ft. - First Floor
1,227 Sq. Ft. - Second Floor; 48,540 Cu. Ft.

● A most popular feature of the Victorian house has always been its covered porches. These finely detailed outdoor living spaces may be found on the front, the side, the rear or even in all three locations at once. The two designs on these two pages show just that. In addition to being an appealing exterior design feature, covered porches have their practical side, too. They provide wonderful indoor-outdoor living relationships. Imagine, sheltered outdoor living facilities for the various formal and informal living and dining areas of the plan. This home has a myriad of features to cater to the living requirements of the growing, active family.

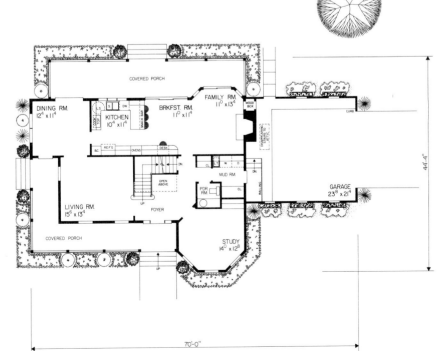

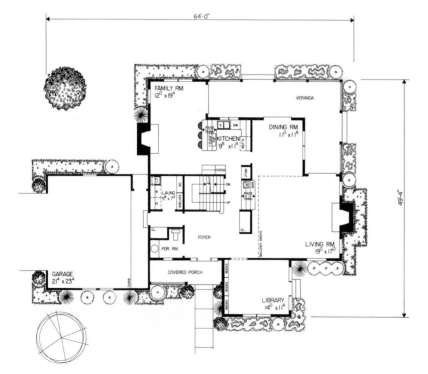

Design T172972

1,526 Sq. Ft. - First Floor
1,091 Sq. Ft. - Second Floor
53,930 Cu. Ft.

● The spacious foyer of this Victorian welcomes one to a practical and efficient interior. While the exterior captures all of the nostaglia of yesteryears, the interior reflects what is new in contemporary floor planning. Traffic patterns are orderly and flexible. Zoning is outstanding. The formal living and dining area is located to one side of the plan. Both rooms function well together and have access to the covered veranda. Spaciousness is the byword with that glorious two-story sloping ceiling and the open planning between the two rooms. The more active informal area of the plan includes the fine U-shaped kitchen which opens to the big family room. Here, again, the veranda plays a part. Double French doors access it from the family room while the kitchen looks out upon it. Just inside the entrance from the garage is the laundry, a coat closet with the powder room a few steps away. The library will enjoy its full measure of privacy. Note its access to the front yard. Upstairs, the three bedroom sleeping zone with a fireplace.

Design T172970 1,538 Sq. Ft. - First Floor
1,526 Sq. Ft. - Second Floor; 658 Sq. Ft. - Third Floor
64,050 Cu. Ft.

● A porch, is a porch, is a porch. But, when it wraps around to a side, or even two sides, of the house, we have called it a veranda. This charming Victorian features a covered outdoor living area on all four sides! It even ends at a screened porch which features a sun deck above. This interesting plan offers three floors of livability. And what livability it is! Plenty of formal and informal living facilities to go along with the potential of five bedrooms. The master suite is just that. It is adjacent to an interesting sitting room. It has a sun deck and excellent bath/personal care facilities. The third floor will make a wonderful haven for the family's student members.

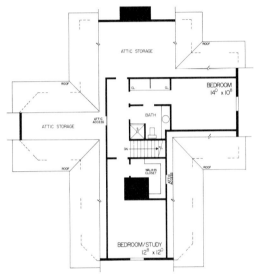

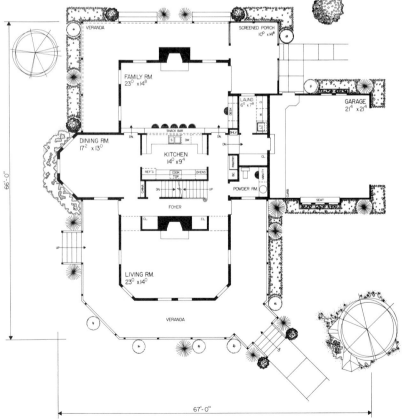

Design T172974

911 Sq. Ft. - First Floor; 861 Sq. Ft. - Second Floor
33,160 Cu. Ft.

● Victorian houses are well known for their orientation on narrow building sites. And when this occurs nothing is lost to captivating exterior styling. This house is but 38 feet wide. Its narrow width belies the tremendous amount of livability found inside. And, of course, the ubiquitous porch/veranda contributes mightily to style as well as livability. The efficient, U-shape kitchen is flanked by the informal breakfast room and formal dining room. The rear living area is spacious and functions in an exciting manner with the outdoor areas. Bonus recreational, hobby and storage space is offered by the basement and the attic.

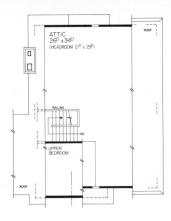

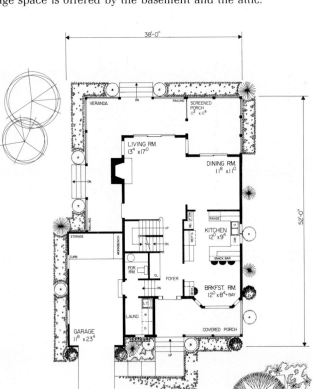